CST-22   NEW YORK STATE TEACHER CERTIFICATION SERIES

This is your
PASSBOOK for...

Mathematics

Test Preparation Study Guide
Questions & Answers

COPYRIGHT NOTICE

This book is SOLELY intended for, is sold ONLY to, and its use is RESTRICTED to individual, bona fide applicants or candidates who qualify by virtue of having seriously filed applications for appropriate license, certificate, professional and/or promotional advancement, higher school matriculation, scholarship, or other legitimate requirements of education and/or governmental authorities.

This book is NOT intended for use, class instruction, tutoring, training, duplication, copying, reprinting, excerption, or adaptation, etc., by:

1) Other publishers
2) Proprietors and/or Instructors of "Coaching" and/or Preparatory Courses
3) Personnel and/or Training Divisions of commercial, industrial, and governmental organizations
4) Schools, colleges, or universities and/or their departments and staffs, including teachers and other personnel
5) Testing Agencies or Bureaus
6) Study groups which seek by the purchase of a single volume to copy and/or duplicate and/or adapt this material for use by the group as a whole without having purchased individual volumes for each of the members of the group
7) Et al.

Such persons would be in violation of appropriate Federal and State statutes.

PROVISION OF LICENSING AGREEMENTS – Recognized educational, commercial, industrial, and governmental institutions and organizations, and others legitimately engaged in educational pursuits, including training, testing, and measurement activities, may address request for a licensing agreement to the copyright owners, who will determine whether, and under what conditions, including fees and charges, the materials in this book may be used them. In other words, a licensing facility exists for the legitimate use of the material in this book on other than an individual basis. However, it is asseverated and affirmed here that the material in this book CANNOT be used without the receipt of the express permission of such a licensing agreement from the Publishers. Inquiries re licensing should be addressed to the company, attention rights and permissions department.

All rights reserved, including the right of reproduction in whole or in part, in any form or by any means, electronic or mechanical, including photocopying, recording, or by any information storage and retrieval system, without permission in writing from the Publisher.

Copyright © 2025 by
National Learning Corporation

212 Michael Drive, Syosset, NY 11791
(516) 921-8888 • www.passbooks.com
E-mail: info@passbooks.com

PASSBOOK® SERIES

THE *PASSBOOK® SERIES* has been created to prepare applicants and candidates for the ultimate academic battlefield – the examination room.

At some time in our lives, each and every one of us may be required to take an examination – for validation, matriculation, admission, qualification, registration, certification, or licensure.

Based on the assumption that every applicant or candidate has met the basic formal educational standards, has taken the required number of courses, and read the necessary texts, the *PASSBOOK® SERIES* furnishes the one special preparation which may assure passing with confidence, instead of failing with insecurity. Examination questions – together with answers – are furnished as the basic vehicle for study so that the mysteries of the examination and its compounding difficulties may be eliminated or diminished by a sure method.

This book is meant to help you pass your examination provided that you qualify and are serious in your objective.

The entire field is reviewed through the huge store of content information which is succinctly presented through a provocative and challenging approach – the question-and-answer method.

A climate of success is established by furnishing the correct answers at the end of each test.

You soon learn to recognize types of questions, forms of questions, and patterns of questioning. You may even begin to anticipate expected outcomes.

You perceive that many questions are repeated or adapted so that you can gain acute insights, which may enable you to score many sure points.

You learn how to confront new questions, or types of questions, and to attack them confidently and work out the correct answers.

You note objectives and emphases, and recognize pitfalls and dangers, so that you may make positive educational adjustments.

Moreover, you are kept fully informed in relation to new concepts, methods, practices, and directions in the field.

You discover that you are actually taking the examination all the time: you are preparing for the examination by "taking" an examination, not by reading extraneous and/or supererogatory textbooks.

In short, this PASSBOOK®, used directedly, should be an important factor in helping you to pass your test.

NEW YORK STATE TEACHER CERTIFICATION EXAMINATIONS™
INTRODUCTION

GENERAL INFORMATION

About the Testing Program

Those seeking a New York State teaching certificate for the common branch subjects in prekindergarten through grade 6 or for academic subjects in the secondary grades 7 through 12, i.e., English, a language other than English, mathematics, a science (biology, chemistry, earth science, physics), or social studies, must pass the New York State Teacher Certification Examinations (NYSTCE®) as part of the requirements for certification.

Those seeking a New York State teaching certificate in other areas may need to achieve qualifying scores on the NYSTCE® as indicated in the table which follows.

The New York State Teacher Certification Examinations™ program consists of the

- Liberal Arts and Sciences Test (LAST)
- Elementary and Secondary Assessment of Teaching Skills Written (ATS-W)
- Content Specialty Tests (CSTs)
- Language Proficiency Assessments (LPAs)
- Assessment of Teaching Skills - Performance (ATS-P) (Video)

These exams provide an objective basis of competency and skill for teaching in New York State.

For the requirements, check the summary table of testing requirements which follows.

Test Development

The New York State Teacher Certification Examinations™ are criterion referenced and objective based. A criterion-referenced test is designed to measure a candidate's knowledge and skills in relation to an established standard rather than in relation to the performance of other candidates. The purpose of these exams is to certify candidates who have demonstrated requisite knowledge and skills necessary for a public school teacher.

> The New York State Teacher Certification Examination C"NYSTCE.") program was developed and is administered by the New York State Education Department ("NYSED® ") and National Evaluation Systems, Inc. ("NES"), and this test preparation guide was neither developed in connection with these organizations, nor is it endorsed by them. The NES® and NYSTCE®names and logos are registered service marks of. National Evaluation Systems, Inc. for use with testing services and related products.

An individual's performance on a test is evaluated against an established standard. The passing score for each test is established by the New York State Commissioner of Education based on the professional judgments and recommendations of New York State educators. Examinees who do not pass a test may retake it at any of the subsequent scheduled test administrations.

Description of the Tests

The following is a description of the tests within the NYSTCE® program.

Liberal Arts and Sciences Test (LAST). The Liberal Arts and Sciences Test consists of multiple-choice test questions and a written assignment. Candidates are asked to demonstrate conceptual and analytical skills, critical-thinking and communication skills, and multicultural awareness. The test covers scientific and mathematical processes, historical and social scientific awareness, artistic expression and the humanities, communication skills, and written n analysis and expression. The Liberal Arts and Sciences Test is required for a provisional certificate.

Elementary and Secondary Versions of the Assessment of Teaching Skills - Written (ATS-W). There are two versions of the Assessment of Teaching Skills - Written (ATS-W). The elementary ATS-W should be taken by individuals seeking a PreK-6, common branch subject teaching certificate. The secondary ATS-W should be taken by individuals seeking a certificate for a secondary academic subject. Individuals seeking a certificate in other titles may take either the elementary or the secondary ATS-W. The ATS-W is required for a provisional certificate.

The elementary and secondary versions of the Assessment of Teaching Skills - Written consists of multiple-choice test questions and a written assignment. These tests address knowledge of the learner, instructional planning and assessment, instructional delivery, and the professional environment.

Content Specialty Tests (CSTs). There are currently 21 Content Specialty Tests. For a complete list of test titles, see the list that follows.

The Content Specialty Tests (except Japanese, Russian, Mandarin, Cantonese, Hebrew, and Greek) contain multiple-choice test questions. The CSTs for languages other than English also include audiotaped listening and speaking components and writing components. The CSTs are required for a permanent certificate.

Language Proficiency Assessments (ELPA-C, ELPA-N, TLPAs). The Language Proficiency Assessments are required for ESOL certificates and for bilingual education extension certificates in New York State.

Assessment of Teaching Skills - Performance (ATS-P) (video). The Assessment of Teaching Skills - Performance (ATS-P) (video) is one requirement for individuals seeking a permanent New York State teaching certificate in specified areas. For this assessment, candidates are required to prepare a videotape of their instruction with students who are part of their regular teaching assignments in grades PreK through 12. The teaching skills assessed by the ATS-P (video) are defined by the five objectives in the Instructional Delivery subarea of the Assessment of Teaching Skills test framework.

From the official announcement for instructional purposes

TESTS

Test (Test Code)

Liberal Arts and Sciences Test (LAST) (01)
Elementary Assessment of Teaching Skills - Written (ATS-W) (90)
Secondary Assessment of Teaching Skills - Written (ATS-W) (91)
Elementary Education (02)
English (03)
Mathematics (04)
Social Studies (05)
Biology (06)
Chemistry (07)
Earth Science (08)
Physics (09)
Early Childhood (21)
Latin (10)
Cantonese (11)
French (12)
German (13)
Greek (14)
Hebrew (15)
Italian (16)
Japanese (17)
Mandarin (18)
Russian (19)
Spanish (20)
English to Speakers of Other Languages (ESOL) (22)
English Language Proficiency Assessment for Classroom Personnel (ELPA-C) (23)
English Language Proficiency Assessment for Nonclassroom Personnel (ELPA-N) (25)
Target Language Proficiency Assessment - Spanish (24)
Target Language Proficiency Assessment other than Spanish

NEW YORK STATE TEACHER CERTIFICATION TESTING REQUIREMENTS

(Commissioner's Regulation) Teaching Certificates	Current Requirements		Projected Requirements
(8 NYCRR 80.15) PreK-6, Common Branch Subjects	LAST ATS-W CST (Elementary Education) ATS-P	Provisional Provisional Permanent Permanent	Same as current requirements
7-9 Extension	Same as base certificate, PLUS: CST in academic subject	Permanent	
Early Childhood Annotation (PreK-3)	CST in annotation	Permanent	
(8 NYCRR 80.16) 7-12 Academic Subjects, e.g., English, Language other than English, Mathematics, Science (Biology, Chemistry, Earth Science, Physics), Social Studies	LAST ATS-W CST (in academic subject) ATS-P	Provisional Provisional Permanent Permanent	Same as current requirements
5-6 Extension	Same as base certificate		
(8 NYCRR 80.9) Bilingual Education [Extension]	Same as base certificate, PLUS: LPA in English (oral)* LPA in Target Language (oral & written)*	Prov./Perm. Prov./Perm.	Same as current requirements
(8 NYCRR 80.10) English to speakers of other languages (ESOL)	LAST* ATS-W* LPA in English (oral)* CST* (ESOL) ATS-P*	Provisional Provisional Provisional Permanent Permanent	Same as current requirements
(8 NYCRR 80.5) Occupational Subjects, e.g. Agricultural Subjects, Business/Distributive Education, Health Occupations, Trade Subjects, Technical Subjects, Home Economics Subjects	Baccalaureate-based certificates: LAST + ATS-W or NTE Core Battery Associate & non-degree-based certificate titles: ATS-W or NTE Core Battery	Provisional Permanent	Baccalaureate-based certificates: LAST Provisional ATS-W Provisional CST Permanent ATS-P Permanent Associate & non-degree-based certificate titles: ATS-W Provisional ATS-P Permanent

NEW YORK STATE TEACHER CERTIFICATION TESTING REQUIREMENTS

(Commissioner's Regulation) Teaching Certificates	Current Requirements		Projected Requirements	
(8 NYCRR 80.6) **Special Education**, e.g. Special Education, Blind/ Partially Sighted, Deaf/ Hearing Impaired Speech/Hearing Handicapped	LAST & ATS-W or NTE Core Battery	Provisional	Same as for PreK-6 or 7-12 certificate, PLUS: Special Education Supplement to ATS-W Special Education supplement to ATS-P	Provisional Permanent
(8 NYCRR 80.7) Reading	LAST & ATS-W or NTE Core Battery	Provisional	Same as for PreK-6 or 7-12 certificate, PLUS: CST in Reading	Permanent
(8 NYCRR 80.8) School Media Specialist	LAST + ATS-W or NTE Core Battery	Provisional	LAST ATS-W CST ATS-P	Provisional Provisional Permanent Permanent
(8 NYCRR 80.17) **Special Subjects**, e.g. Art, Business/Distributive Education, Dance, Health, Home Economics, Music, Physical Education, Recreation, Speech, Technology Education	LAST + ATS-W or NTE Core Battery	Provisional	LAST ATS-W CST ATS-P	Provisional Provisional Permanent Permanent

LAST = Liberal Arts & Sciences Test
ATS-W = Assessment of Teaching Skills - Written
CST   = Content Specialty Test
ATS-P = Assessment of Teaching Skills - Performance (video)
LPA   = Language Proficiency Assessment

FOR FURTHER INFORMATION

If you have questions regarding which test(s) you must take, contact the teacher certification contact person at your college or:

**NEW YORK STATE EDUCATION DEPARTMENT
OFFICE OF TEACHING
CULTURAL EDUCATION CENTER
ALBANY, N.Y. 12230**

TELEPHONE: (518) 474-3901
9:00-11:45 A.M., 12:45-4:30 P.M. Eastern Time

Relay center telephone number for the deaf within New York State: 1-800-622-1220

Nationwide AT&T Relay Operator for the Deaf: 1-800-855-2880 (TTY)

If you have questions regarding the Test Registration, Administration Procedures, Admission Ticket, or Score Report, contact:

**NYSTCE
NATIONAL EVALUATION SYSTEMS, INC.
30 GATEHOUSE ROAD
P.O. BOX 660
AMHERST, MA 01004-9008**

TELEPHONE: (413) 256-2882
9:00 A.M. - 5:00 P.M. Eastern Time

Telephone number for the deaf: (413) 256-8032 (TTY)

NEW YORK STATE TEACHER CERTIFICATION EXAMINATIONS™

FIELD 04: MATHEMATICS
TEST FRAMEWORK

Mathematical Reasoning and Communication
Algebra
Trigonometry and Calculus
Measurement and Geometry
Data Analysis, Probability, Statistics, and Discrete Mathematics
Algebra: Constructed-Response Assignment

The New York State mathematics educator has the knowledge and skills necessary to teach effectively in New York State public schools. The mathematics teacher is adept at utilizing the mathematical systems of algebra, geometry, trigonometry, and calculus and can address and solve problems involving data analysis, probability, statistics, and discrete mathematics. The mathematics teacher is able to reason logically and understands the connections between mathematics and other disciplines. Most importantly, the mathematics teacher is able to communicate mathematically and use language skills to explain mathematical concepts and processes, is able to apply mathematics in real-world settings, and is able to solve problems through the integrated use of multiple mathematical skills and concepts.

SUBAREA I—MATHEMATICAL REASONING AND COMMUNICATION

0001 Understand reasoning processes, including inductive and deductive logic and symbolic logic.

For example:

- analyzing mathematical situations by gathering evidence, making conjectures, formulating counterexamples, and constructing and evaluating arguments

- analyzing the nature and purpose of axiomatic systems (including those of the various geometries)

- analyzing and interpreting the truth value of simple and compound statements (e.g., negations, disjunctions, conditionals) in truth tables and Venn diagrams

- using laws of inference to draw conclusions and to test the validity of conclusions

- applying the principle of mathematical induction to prove theorems

Authorized for Distribution by the New York State Education Department

FIELD 04: MATHEMATICS
TEST FRAMEWORK

SUBAREA II—ALGEBRA

0004 **Understand principles and properties of the set of complex numbers and its subsets.**

For example:

- applying principles of number theory (e.g., prime numbers, divisibility) to solve problems
- applying number concepts (e.g., fractions, percents, exponents) to solve problems
- applying knowledge of real numbers to arithmetic and algebraic operations
- justifying the need for the extension of a given number system
- using multiple representations of the complex numbers and their operations (e.g., polar form; algebraic and geometric interpretations of the sum, difference, and product of complex numbers)
- analyzing and applying the properties of vectors, groups, and fields to the complex numbers and its subsets

0005 **Understand the principles and properties of patterns and algebraic operations and relations.**

For example:

- determining algebraic expressions that best represent patterns among data presented in tables, graphs, and diagrams
- generalizing patterns using explicitly defined and recursively defined functions
- performing and analyzing basic operations on numbers and algebraic expressions
- deriving an algebraic model that best represents a given situation and evaluating the strengths and weaknesses of that model
- applying algebraic concepts of relation and function (e.g., range, domain, inverse) to analyze mathematical relationships
- analyzing the results of transformations (e.g., translations, dilations, reflections, rotations) on the graphs of functions

FIELD 04: MATHEMATICS
TEST FRAMEWORK

0008 **Understand the properties of rational, radical, and absolute value functions and relations.**

For example:

- analyzing the properties of a given function (e.g., range, domain, asymptotes)
- solving problems involving rational, radical, and absolute value functions using various algebraic techniques
- modeling and solving problems graphically using systems of equations and inequalities involving rational, radical, and absolute value relations (including the use of graphing calculators)
- interpreting and analyzing the effects of transformations on the graph of a function
- applying the properties of rational, radical, and absolute value functions and relations to model and solve problems

0009 **Understand the properties of exponential and logarithmic functions.**

For example:

- analyzing the relationship between logarithmic and exponential functions
- applying the laws of logarithms to manipulate and simplify expressions
- analyzing the graph of a logarithmic or exponential function or relation
- solving problems involving exponential growth and decay
- modeling and solving problems analytically or graphically using exponential and logarithmic relations

FIELD 04: MATHEMATICS
TEST FRAMEWORK

0012 Demonstrate an understanding of the fundamental concepts of calculus.

For example:

- analyzing the concept of limit numerically, algebraically, graphically, and in writing
- interpreting the derivative as the limit of the difference quotient
- interpreting the definite integral as the limit of a Riemann sum
- applying the fundamental theorem of calculus
- applying concepts of derivatives to interpret gradients, tangents, and slopes
- applying the concept of limit to analyze and interpret the properties of functions (e.g., continuity, asymptotes)
- applying the concept of rate of change to interpret statements from science, technology, economics, and other disciplines

0013 Apply the principles and techniques of calculus to model and solve problems.

For example:

- using derivatives to model and solve real-world problems (e.g., rates of change, related rates, optimization)
- applying properties of derivatives to analyze the graphs of functions
- using integration to model and solve problems (e.g., the area under a curve, work, applications of antiderivatives)
- modeling and solving problems involving first order differential equations (e.g., separation of variables, initial value problems)

FIELD 04: MATHEMATICS
TEST FRAMEWORK

0016 Understand the principles and properties of coordinate geometry.

For example:

- applying the principles of distance, midpoint, slope, parallelism, and perpendicularity to characterize coordinate geometric relationships
- using coordinate geometry to prove theorems about geometric figures (e.g., triangle, parallelogram, circle, parabola, hyperbola)
- representing two- and three-dimensional geometric figures in various coordinate systems (e.g., Cartesian, polar)
- analyzing and applying transformations in the coordinate plane
- applying the distance formula to derive the equation of a conic section
- modeling and solving problems using conic sections

0017 Apply mathematical principles and techniques to model and solve problems involving vector and transformational geometries.

For example:

- modeling and solving problems involving vector addition and scalar multiplication (e.g., force)
- applying principles of geometry to model and solve problems involving the composition of transformations (e.g., translations, reflections, dilations, rotations)
- analyzing how transformational geometry and symmetry are used in art and architecture (e.g., tessellations, tilings, frieze patterns, fractals)
- using multiple representations of geometric transformations (e.g., coordinate, matrix, diagrams)
- proving theorems using vector and transformational methods

FIELD 04: MATHEMATICS
TEST FRAMEWORK

0020 Understand the principles, properties, and techniques of data analysis and statistics.

    For example:

- applying measures of central tendency, dispersion, and skewness to summarize and interpret data presented in graphic, tabular, or pictorial form
- evaluating the statistical claims made for a given set of data (e.g., analyzing assumptions made in the sampling, analysis, and testing of statistical hypotheses) and how measures of reliability vary by discipline
- interpreting the outcomes of a given statistical test (e.g., t-test, chi-square analysis, correlation, linear regression)
- using graphing calculators to analyze and interpret data from a variety of disciplines (e.g., sciences, social sciences, technology)
- analyzing data using linear, logarithmic, exponential, and power regression models

0021 Understand how techniques of discrete mathematics (e.g., diagrams, graphs, matrices, propositional statements) are applied in the analysis, interpretation, communication, and solution of problems.

    For example:

- representing finite data using a variety of techniques
- representing real-world situations and relationships using sequences and recurrence relations
- modeling and solving problems using graphs and matrices
- evaluating the use of computers and calculators to solve problems (e.g., developing and analyzing algorithms)

SUBAREA VI—ALGEBRA: CONSTRUCTED-RESPONSE ASSIGNMENT

    The content to be addressed by the constructed-response assignment is described in Subarea II, Objectives 04–09.

HOW TO TAKE A TEST

You have studied long, hard and conscientiously.

With your official admission card in hand, and your heart pounding, you have been admitted to the examination room.

You note that there are several hundred other applicants in the examination room waiting to take the same test.

They all appear to be equally well prepared.

You know that nothing but your best effort will suffice. The "moment of truth" is at hand: you now have to demonstrate objectively, in writing, your knowledge of content and your understanding of subject matter.

You are fighting the most important battle of your life—to pass and/or score high on an examination which will determine your career and provide the economic basis for your livelihood.

What extra, special things should you know and should you do in taking the examination?

I. YOU MUST PASS AN EXAMINATION

A. WHAT EVERY CANDIDATE SHOULD KNOW
Examination applicants often ask us for help in preparing for the written test. What can I study in advance? What kinds of questions will be asked? How will the test be given? How will the papers be graded?

B. HOW ARE EXAMS DEVELOPED?
Examinations are carefully written by trained technicians who are specialists in the field known as "psychological measurement," in consultation with recognized authorities in the field of work that the test will cover. These experts recommend the subject matter areas or skills to be tested; only those knowledges or skills important to your success on the job are included. The most reliable books and source materials available are used as references. Together, the experts and technicians judge the difficulty level of the questions.
Test technicians know how to phrase questions so that the problem is clearly stated. Their ethics do not permit "trick" or "catch" questions. Questions may have been tried out on sample groups, or subjected to statistical analysis, to determine their usefulness.
Written tests are often used in combination with performance tests, ratings of training and experience, and oral interviews. All of these measures combine to form the best-known means of finding the right person for the right job.

II. HOW TO PASS THE WRITTEN TEST

A. BASIC STEPS

1) Study the announcement

How, then, can you know what subjects to study? Our best answer is: "Learn as much as possible about the class of positions for which you've applied." The exam will test the knowledge, skills and abilities needed to do the work.

Your most valuable source of information about the position you want is the official exam announcement. This announcement lists the training and experience qualifications. Check these standards and apply only if you come reasonably close to meeting them. Many jurisdictions preview the written test in the exam announcement by including a section called "Knowledge and Abilities Required," "Scope of the Examination," or some similar heading. Here you will find out specifically what fields will be tested.

2) Choose appropriate study materials

If the position for which you are applying is technical or advanced, you will read more advanced, specialized material. If you are already familiar with the basic principles of your field, elementary textbooks would waste your time. Concentrate on advanced textbooks and technical periodicals. Think through the concepts and review difficult problems in your field.

These are all general sources. You can get more ideas on your own initiative, following these leads. For example, training manuals and publications of the government agency which employs workers in your field can be useful, particularly for technical and professional positions. A letter or visit to the government department involved may result in more specific study suggestions, and certainly will provide you with a more definite idea of the exact nature of the position you are seeking.

3) Study this book!

III. KINDS OF TESTS

Tests are used for purposes other than measuring knowledge and ability to perform specified duties. For some positions, it is equally important to test ability to make adjustments to new situations or to profit from training. In others, basic mental abilities not dependent on information are essential. Questions which test these things may not appear as pertinent to the duties of the position as those which test for knowledge and information. Yet they are often highly important parts of a fair examination. For very general questions, it is almost impossible to help you direct your study efforts. What we can do is to point out some of the more common of these general abilities needed in public service positions and describe some typical questions.

1) General information

Broad, general information has been found useful for predicting job success in some kinds of work. This is tested in a variety of ways, from vocabulary lists to questions about current events. Basic background in some field of work, such as sociology or economics, may be sampled in a group of questions. Often these are principles which have become familiar to most persons through exposure rather than through formal training. It is difficult to advise you how to study for these questions; being alert to the world around you is our best suggestion.

2) Verbal ability

An example of an ability needed in many positions is verbal or language ability. Verbal ability is, in brief, the ability to use and understand words. Vocabulary and grammar tests are typical measures of this ability. Reading comprehension or paragraph interpretation questions are common in many kinds of civil service tests. You are given a paragraph of written material and asked to find its central meaning.

IV. KINDS OF QUESTIONS

1. Multiple-choice Questions

Most popular of the short-answer questions is the "multiple choice" or "best answer" question. It can be used, for example, to test for factual knowledge, ability to solve problems or judgment in meeting situations found at work.

A multiple-choice question is normally one of three types:
- It can begin with an incomplete statement followed by several possible endings. You are to find the one ending which best completes the statement, although some of the others may not be entirely wrong.
- It can also be a complete statement in the form of a question which is answered by choosing one of the statements listed.
- It can be in the form of a problem – again you select the best answer.

Here is an example of a multiple-choice question with a discussion which should give you some clues as to the method for choosing the right answer:

When an employee has a complaint about his assignment, the action which will best help him overcome his difficulty is to
- A. discuss his difficulty with his coworkers
- B. take the problem to the head of the organization
- C. take the problem to the person who gave him the assignment
- D. say nothing to anyone about his complaint

In answering this question, you should study each of the choices to find which is best. Consider choice "A" – Certainly an employee may discuss his complaint with fellow employees, but no change or improvement can result, and the complaint remains unresolved. Choice "B" is a poor choice since the head of the organization probably does not know what assignment you have been given, and taking your problem to him is known as "going over the head" of the supervisor. The supervisor, or person who made the assignment, is the person who can clarify it or correct any injustice. Choice "C" is, therefore, correct. To say nothing, as in choice "D," is unwise. Supervisors have and interest in knowing the problems employees are facing, and the employee is seeking a solution to his problem.

2. True/False

3. Matching Questions

Matching an answer from a column of choices within another column.

V. RECORDING YOUR ANSWERS

Computer terminals are used more and more today for many different kinds of exams.

For an examination with very few applicants, you may be told to record your answers in the test booklet itself. Separate answer sheets are much more common. If this separate answer sheet is to be scored by machine – and this is often the case – it is highly important that you mark your answers correctly in order to get credit.

VI. BEFORE THE TEST

YOUR PHYSICAL CONDITION IS IMPORTANT

If you are not well, you can't do your best work on tests. If you are half asleep, you can't do your best either. Here are some tips:

1) Get about the same amount of sleep you usually get. Don't stay up all night before the test, either partying or worrying—DON'T DO IT!
2) If you wear glasses, be sure to wear them when you go to take the test. This goes for hearing aids, too.
3) If you have any physical problems that may keep you from doing your best, be sure to tell the person giving the test. If you are sick or in poor health, you relay cannot do your best on any test. You can always come back and take the test some other time.

Common sense will help you find procedures to follow to get ready for an examination. Too many of us, however, overlook these sensible measures. Indeed, nervousness and fatigue have been found to be the most serious reasons why applicants fail to do their best on civil service tests. Here is a list of reminders:

- Begin your preparation early – Don't wait until the last minute to go scurrying around for books and materials or to find out what the position is all about.
- Prepare continuously – An hour a night for a week is better than an all-night cram session. This has been definitely established. What is more, a night a week for a month will return better dividends than crowding your study into a shorter period of time.
- Locate the place of the exam – You have been sent a notice telling you when and where to report for the examination. If the location is in a different town or otherwise unfamiliar to you, it would be well to inquire the best route and learn something about the building.
- Relax the night before the test – Allow your mind to rest. Do not study at all that night. Plan some mild recreation or diversion; then go to bed early and get a good night's sleep.
- Get up early enough to make a leisurely trip to the place for the test – This way unforeseen events, traffic snarls, unfamiliar buildings, etc. will not upset you.
- Dress comfortably – A written test is not a fashion show. You will be known by number and not by name, so wear something comfortable.
- Leave excess paraphernalia at home – Shopping bags and odd bundles will get in your way. You need bring only the items mentioned in the official notice you received; usually everything you need is provided. Do not bring reference books to the exam. They will only confuse those last minutes and be taken away from you when in the test room.

- Arrive somewhat ahead of time – If because of transportation schedules you must get there very early, bring a newspaper or magazine to take your mind off yourself while waiting.
- Locate the examination room – When you have found the proper room, you will be directed to the seat or part of the room where you will sit. Sometimes you are given a sheet of instructions to read while you are waiting. Do not fill out any forms until you are told to do so; just read them and be prepared.
- Relax and prepare to listen to the instructions
- If you have any physical problem that may keep you from doing your best, be sure to tell the test administrator. If you are sick or in poor health, you really cannot do your best on the exam. You can come back and take the test some other time.

VII. AT THE TEST

The day of the test is here and you have the test booklet in your hand. The temptation to get going is very strong. Caution! There is more to success than knowing the right answers. You must know how to identify your papers and understand variations in the type of short-answer question used in this particular examination. Follow these suggestions for maximum results from your efforts:

1) Cooperate with the monitor

The test administrator has a duty to create a situation in which you can be as much at ease as possible. He will give instructions, tell you when to begin, check to see that you are marking your answer sheet correctly, and so on. He is not there to guard you, although he will see that your competitors do not take unfair advantage. He wants to help you do your best.

2) Listen to all instructions

Don't jump the gun! Wait until you understand all directions. In most civil service tests you get more time than you need to answer the questions. So don't be in a hurry. Read each word of instructions until you clearly understand the meaning. Study the examples, listen to all announcements and follow directions. Ask questions if you do not understand what to do.

3) Identify your papers

Civil service exams are usually identified by number only. You will be assigned a number; you must not put your name on your test papers. Be sure to copy your number correctly. Since more than one exam may be given, copy your exact examination title.

4) Plan your time

Unless you are told that a test is a "speed" or "rate of work" test, speed itself is usually not important. Time enough to answer all the questions will be provided, but this does not mean that you have all day. An overall time limit has been set. Divide the total time (in minutes) by the number of questions to determine the approximate time you have for each question.

5) Do not linger over difficult questions

If you come across a difficult question, mark it with a paper clip (useful to have along) and come back to it when you have been through the booklet. One caution if you do this – be sure to skip a number on your answer sheet as well. Check often to be sure that you have not lost your place and that you are marking in the row numbered the same as the question you are answering.

6) Read the questions

Be sure you know what the question asks! Many capable people are unsuccessful because they failed to read the questions correctly.

7) Answer all questions

Unless you have been instructed that a penalty will be deducted for incorrect answers, it is better to guess than to omit a question.

8) Speed tests

It is often better NOT to guess on speed tests. It has been found that on timed tests people are tempted to spend the last few seconds before time is called in marking answers at random – without even reading them – in the hope of picking up a few extra points. To discourage this practice, the instructions may warn you that your score will be "corrected" for guessing. That is, a penalty will be applied. The incorrect answers will be deducted from the correct ones, or some other penalty formula will be used.

9) Review your answers

If you finish before time is called, go back to the questions you guessed or omitted to give them further thought. Review other answers if you have time.

10) Return your test materials

If you are ready to leave before others have finished or time is called, take ALL your materials to the monitor and leave quietly. Never take any test material with you. The monitor can discover whose papers are not complete, and taking a test booklet may be grounds for disqualification.

VIII. EXAMINATION TECHNIQUES

1) Read the general instructions carefully. These are usually printed on the first page of the exam booklet. As a rule, these instructions refer to the timing of the examination; the fact that you should not start work until the signal and must stop work at a signal, etc. If there are any special instructions, such as a choice of questions to be answered, make sure that you note this instruction carefully.

2) When you are ready to start work on the examination, that is as soon as the signal has been given, read the instructions to each question booklet, underline any key words or phrases, such as least, best, outline, describe and the like. In this way you will tend to answer as requested rather than discover on reviewing your paper that you listed without describing, that you selected the worst choice rather than the best choice, etc.

3) If the examination is of the objective or multiple-choice type – that is, each question will also give a series of possible answers: A, B, C or D, and you are called upon to select the best answer and write the letter next to that answer on your answer paper – it is advisable to start answering each question in turn. There may be anywhere from 50 to 100 such questions in the three or four hours allotted and you can see how much time would be taken if you read through all the questions before beginning to answer any. Furthermore, if you

come across a question or group of questions which you know would be difficult to answer, it would undoubtedly affect your handling of all the other questions.

4) If the examination is of the essay type and contains but a few questions, it is a moot point as to whether you should read all the questions before starting to answer any one. Of course, if you are given a choice – say five out of seven and the like – then it is essential to read all the questions so you can eliminate the two that are most difficult. If, however, you are asked to answer all the questions, there may be danger in trying to answer the easiest one first because you may find that you will spend too much time on it. The best technique is to answer the first question, then proceed to the second, etc.

5) Time your answers. Before the exam begins, write down the time it started, then add the time allowed for the examination and write down the time it must be completed, then divide the time available somewhat as follows:
    - If 3-1/2 hours are allowed, that would be 210 minutes. If you have 80 objective-type questions, that would be an average of 2-1/2 minutes per question. Allow yourself no more than 2 minutes per question, or a total of 160 minutes, which will permit about 50 minutes to review.
    - If for the time allotment of 210 minutes there are 7 essay questions to answer, that would average about 30 minutes a question. Give yourself only 25 minutes per question so that you have about 35 minutes to review.

6) The most important instruction is to read each question and make sure you know what is wanted. The second most important instruction is to time yourself properly so that you answer every question. The third most important instruction is to answer every question. Guess if you have to but include something for each question. Remember that you will receive no credit for a blank and will probably receive some credit if you write something in answer to an essay question. If you guess a letter – say "B" for a multiple-choice question – you may have guessed right. If you leave a blank as an answer to a multiple-choice question, the examiners may respect your feelings but it will not add a point to your score. Some exams may penalize you for wrong answers, so in such cases only, you may not want to guess unless you have some basis for your answer.

7) Suggestions
    a. Objective-type questions
        1. Examine the question booklet for proper sequence of pages and questions
        2. Read all instructions carefully
        3. Skip any question which seems too difficult; return to it after all other questions have been answered
        4. Apportion your time properly; do not spend too much time on any single question or group of questions
        5. Note and underline key words – all, most, fewest, least, best, worst, same, opposite, etc.
        6. Pay particular attention to negatives
        7. Note unusual option, e.g., unduly long, short, complex, different or similar in content to the body of the question
        8. Observe the use of "hedging" words – probably, may, most likely, etc.

9. Make sure that your answer is put next to the same number as the question
10. Do not second-guess unless you have good reason to believe the second answer is definitely more correct
11. Cross out original answer if you decide another answer is more accurate; do not erase until you are ready to hand your paper in
12. Answer all questions; guess unless instructed otherwise
13. Leave time for review

b. Essay questions
1. Read each question carefully
2. Determine exactly what is wanted. Underline key words or phrases.
3. Decide on outline or paragraph answer
4. Include many different points and elements unless asked to develop any one or two points or elements
5. Show impartiality by giving pros and cons unless directed to select one side only
6. Make and write down any assumptions you find necessary to answer the questions
7. Watch your English, grammar, punctuation and choice of words
8. Time your answers; don't crowd material

8) Answering the essay question

Most essay questions can be answered by framing the specific response around several key words or ideas. Here are a few such key words or ideas:

M's: manpower, materials, methods, money, management
P's: purpose, program, policy, plan, procedure, practice, problems, pitfalls, personnel, public relations

a. Six basic steps in handling problems:
1. Preliminary plan and background development
2. Collect information, data and facts
3. Analyze and interpret information, data and facts
4. Analyze and develop solutions as well as make recommendations
5. Prepare report and sell recommendations
6. Install recommendations and follow up effectiveness

b. Pitfalls to avoid
1. Taking things for granted – A statement of the situation does not necessarily imply that each of the elements is necessarily true; for example, a complaint may be invalid and biased so that all that can be taken for granted is that a complaint has been registered
2. Considering only one side of a situation – Wherever possible, indicate several alternatives and then point out the reasons you selected the best one
3. Failing to indicate follow up – Whenever your answer indicates action on your part, make certain that you will take proper follow-up action to see how successful your recommendations, procedures or actions turn out to be
4. Taking too long in answering any single question – Remember to time your answers properly

EXAMINATION SECTION

EXAMINATION SECTION
TEST 1

DIRECTIONS: Each question or incomplete statement is followed by several suggested answers or completions. Select the one that BEST answers the question or completes the Statement. *PRINT THE LETTER OF THE CORRECT ANSWER IN THE SPACE AT THE RIGHT.*

1. In a ninth year mathematics class studying irrational numbers, several students added $3\sqrt{2} + 5\sqrt{2}$ and obtained $8\sqrt{4} = 8(2) = 16$.
   The BEST procedure for the teacher to follow is to

   1. explain that unlike radicals can be added and combined into a single term
   2. review the distributive postulate of multiplication over addition
   3. explain that rational and irrational terms cannot be added and combined into a single term
   4. point out that answers to exercises involving radicals should be left in radical form

1.____

2. In teaching a unit on the addition of arithmetic fractions, a teacher of a junior high school class planned to present the following exercises to the students:

   a. $\frac{3}{16} + \frac{5}{16}$

   b. $\frac{3}{8} + \frac{1}{4}$

   c. $\frac{2}{7} + \frac{3}{7}$

   d. $\frac{1}{6} + \frac{1}{5}$

   The BEST order for presenting these exercises is

   1. c, a, b, d   2. c, a, d, b   3. a, c, d, b   4. a, c, b, d

2.____

3. A teacher gave his class the problem of writing five numbers whose mean, median and mode are the same. Pupils A, B, C and D obtained answers of, respectively, 20, 10, 20, 10, 20; 10, 2, 16, 12, 10; 5, .05, 5, 50, 5; and 1/2, 5 x 10^{-1}, 3/4, .75, .5.
   The CORRECT answer was that of pupil

   1. A   2. B   3. C   4. D

3.____

4. A junior high school class is studying conversion of fractions to equivalent fractions. Which of the following is MOST relevant to this topic?

   1. Commutativity of multiplication   2. Associativity of multiplication
   3. Existence of multiplicative inverse   4. Existence of multiplicative identity

4.____

5. In teaching conversion of fractions to decimals, a teacher of a junior high school class was planning to present the following fractions to the students:
   a. 1/4   b. 2/3   c. 7/10   d. 5/8
   The BEST sequence in which to consider these fractions is

   1. c, a, d, b   2. a, c, d, b   3. c, a, b, d   4. a, c, b, d

5.____

6. Which of the following procedures would be BEST for motivating a lesson on rationalization of monomial denominators in a ninth year mathematics class?

   1. Ask the students to multiply the fraction $\dfrac{\sqrt{2}}{\sqrt{3}}$ by $\dfrac{\sqrt{3}}{\sqrt{3}}$ to eliminate the irrational denominator.
   2. Ask the students to simplify the fraction $\dfrac{\sqrt{125}}{\sqrt{5}}$ by division to eliminate the irrational denominator.
   3. Ask the students to find the value of the reciprocal of $\sqrt{2}$, correct to four decimal places.
   4. Explain to the class that an irrational square root in the denominator of a fraction can be rationalized by multiplying it by itself.

7. A junior high school class studying the metric system came to the following conclusions. Of these, it is INCORRECT to conclude that a(n)

   1. basketball player can be 2 meters tall
   2. football player can weigh 100 kilograms
   3. track star can run 2 kilometers in 1 minute
   4. automobile gasoline tank can hold 80 liters of gasoline

8. A class studying order of operations was considering the following exercise:

   $2 + 4 \times 2 + 9 - 6 \div 3$. Several students arrived at the answer 5.
   This answer is

   1. *correct*; the students proceeded carefully from left to right in doing their calculations
   2. *incorrect*; the students failed to distribute multiplication and division over addition and subtraction
   3. *incorrect*; the students failed to recall that addition and subtraction precede multiplication and division
   4. *incorrect*; the students failed to recall that multiplication and division precede addition and subtraction

9. Following are four statements often made by junior high school pupils:
   a. When dividing numbers, subtract the exponents.
   b. Any number divided by itself is 1
   c. When multiplying a number by 100, add 2 zeroes to the number
   d. Parallel lines are lines which never meet

   Which of these statements is mathematically CORRECT?

   1. All of the above
   2. a and b
   3. c and d
   4. None of the above

10. A pupil shows his teacher the following "proof" that 1=2.
    Let a=b
    $a^2=ab$
    $a^2-b^2=ab-b^2$
    $(a+b)(a-b)=b(a-b)$
    $a+b=b$
    $2b=b$
    $2=1$

    The teacher should explain that the reason this "proof" is INCORRECT is that
    1. it involves division by zero
    2. it is factored incorrectly
    3. a does not equal b
    4. it leads to a wrong result

11. Two successive discounts of 10% and 15% are equivalent to a SINGLE discount of
    1. 23.5%   2. 24%   3. 25%   4. 26.5%

12. The product of 32,000,000 and .000028 is
    1. 8.96×10^{-2} 2. 896×10^{-2}
    3. 8.96×10^{2} 4. 896×10^{2}

13. Which of the following is its own multiplicative inverse?
    a. -1   b. 0   c. +.1   d. +1
    The CORRECT answer is:
    1. a, d   2. b, d
    3. c, d   4. d *only*

14. A school basketball team volleyball team and baseball team are going on a school trip. There are 17 on the basketball team, 10 on the volleyball team and 21 on the baseball team. Of these, there are 12 students on both the basketball and baseball teams, 6 students on both volleyball and baseball teams and 5 students on both volleyball and basketball teams. These figures include 2 students who are on all three teams.
    For how many different students should provisions be made?
    1. 27   2. 48   3. 71   4. 73

15. Mr. P.Q. Simpson is a football fan and says that there is a 70% probability that he will attend next Sunday's local football game if it does NOT snow, but only a 30% probability if it DOES snow. The weather bureau forecast is that there is a 60% chance that it will snow on Sunday.
    The probability that Mr. Simpson will attend the game on Sunday is
    1. 28%   2. 40%   3. 46%   4. 54%

16. $\log 4 \div \log 1/4$ is equal to
    1. -1   2. 0   3. 2 log 2   4. log 2

17. $(16)^{(-2)^2}$ has the SAME value as

    1. $1/16^4$ 2. $1/2$ 3. 2 4. 16^4

18. A cylinder, sphere and cone have the same diameter and the same height as illustrated

    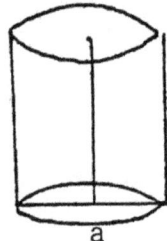 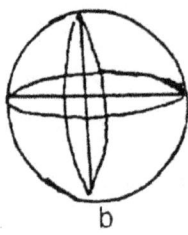 
       a   b   c

    The ratio of the volume of figures a: b: c is

    1. 1:1:1   2. π:2:1   3. 4:3:2   4. 3:2:1

19. Some properties that hold for the relation "is equal to" for real numbers are
    a. reflexive   b. symmetric   c. transitive
    Which of these properties hold true for the relation "is parallel to"?

    1. a only   2. a, b   3. a, c   4. b, c

20. The solution set of the equation $x^3-5x+6=2x^2$ is

    1. {-1, 2, -3}   2. {1,-2, -3}
    3. {-1, 1, -6}   4. {1,-2, 3}

21. The measure, in degrees, of the LARGEST angle of a triangle whose sides have lengths 3, 5 and 7 is

    1. 60   2. 90   3. 120   4. 150

22. In evaluating $\lim_{x \to \infty} \frac{(3x-2)}{(5x+4)}$, we find that the limit

    1. is 1   2. is -1/2
    3. is 3/5   4. does not exist

23. $\overline{AB}$ and $\overline{CD}$ represent exterior walls of two buildings. $\overline{AB}$ is 80 meters. $\overline{AC}$ is 50 meters. If the angle of depression from point D to point B is 60°, the height of $\overline{DC}$ in meters is

    1. $50+50\sqrt{3}$
    2. 105
    3. $80+\dfrac{100\sqrt{3}}{3}$
    4. $80+50\sqrt{3}$

    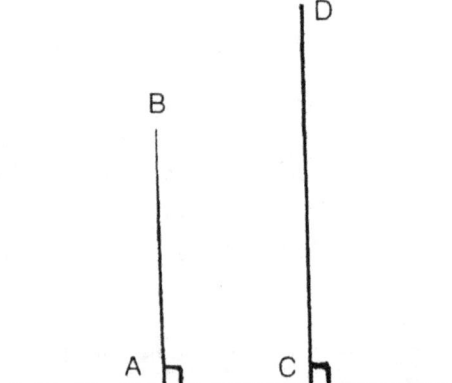

24. The measures of the angles of a pentagon are in arithmetic progression with a common difference of 10 units. The measure, in degrees, of the SMALLEST angle of the polygon is

   1. 72   2. 88   3. 108   4. 128

24._____

25. The measure of one side of a triangle is 12. Points R and S are on the other two sides of the △, and $\overline{RS}$ is parallel to the third side. The area of the trapezoid formed is one-third the area of the given triangle. The measure of $\overline{RS}$ is

   1. $4\sqrt{3}$ 2. 8   3. $6\sqrt{2}$ 4. $4\sqrt{6}$

25._____

26. The area, in the square units, of the triangle below is

   1. $24+8\sqrt{3}$
   2. $8+8\sqrt{3}$
   3. $48+16\sqrt{3}$
   4. $12+4\sqrt{3}$

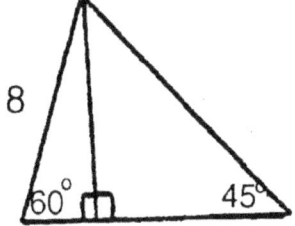

26._____

27. Chord $\overline{AB}$ and its perpendicular bisector chord $\overline{CD}$ intersect at E in circle O. Point R is on $\overline{AE}$ and $\overline{DR}$ is extended to S on the circle.
For any point R, △RED is SIMILAR to triangle

   1. DCB   2. SAE   3. CEB   4. SCD

27._____

28. The infinite repeating decimal $2.\overline{52}$ is equal to

   1. $2\frac{13}{25}$ 2. $2\frac{14}{33}$ 3. $2\frac{50}{99}$ 4. $2\frac{52}{99}$

28._____

29. The average speed of an automobile traveling from A to B is 40 mph. Returning from B to A over the same route, the average speed is 60 mph.
The average speed in mph for the ENTIRE trip is

   1. 48   2. 49   3. 50   4. 52

29._____

30. If 1 inch ≈ 2.5 centimeters, then the number of yards in a kilometer can be found by computing the fraction

   1. $\dfrac{36 \times 100{,}000}{2.5}$ 2. $\dfrac{1000}{2.5 \times 36}$
   3. $\dfrac{100{,}000}{2.5 \times 36}$ 4. $\dfrac{2.5 \times 36 \times 100}{1000}$

30._____

31. A man invested $120,000 in a new business enterprise. The first year he lost 37 1/2% of the original investment. The next year he made a profit of 40% of his net worth at the beginning of that year.
His net worth at the end of the second year was what % of his original investment?

   1. 62 1/2   2. 75   3. 87 1/2   4. 97 1/2

31._____

32. Given the equation in determinant form $\begin{vmatrix} 2x & 1 \\ x & x \end{vmatrix} = 3$, the equation is satisfied for _____ values of x.

    1. two real
    2. two imaginary
    3. no
    4. all real

33. If $0 \leq x \leq 360$, then the solution set of $2\sin^2 x = \sin x + 1$ is

    1. {0°, 150°, 210°}
    2. {30°, 150°, 180°}
    3. {90°, 150°, 330°}
    4. {90°, 210°, 330°}

34. In △ABC, m<B=30°, m<C=105°, and side a=10. The length of side b is

    1. $5\sqrt{2}$
    2. $5\sqrt{3}$
    3. $10\sqrt{2}$
    4. $10\sqrt{3}$

35. $[\sqrt{2}(\cos 45° + i\sin 45°)]^2$ in the form a+bi is

    1. $0 + \sqrt{2}i$
    2. $0 + 2i$
    3. $2 + \sqrt{2}i$
    4. $2 + 2i$

36. An equivalent expression for $\sin^4\theta - \cos^4\theta$ is

    1. $2\cos^2\theta - 1$
    2. $2\sin^2\theta - 1$
    3. $2\cos^2\theta + 1$
    4. $2\sin^2\theta + 1$

37. The arithmetic mean (average) of a set of 50 numbers is 38. If two numbers 45 and 55 are DISCARDED, the mean of the remaining set of numbers is

    1. 36.5
    2. 37.0
    3. 37.24
    4. 37.5

38. If the square of a two digit number is DECREASED by the square of the number formed by reversing the digits, then the result is NOT ALWAYS divisible by

    1. 9
    2. the product of the digits
    3. the sum of the digits
    4. the difference of the digits

39. Fifteen girls left a mixed group of boys and girls. There remained two boys for each girl. After this, 45 boys leave the group and there were 5 girls for each boy. The number of girls in the original group must have been

    1. 29
    2. 40
    3. 43
    4. 50

40. If $\log_{10}(x^2 - x - 2) = 1$, then x is equal to

    1. 4 or -3
    2. -1 or 2
    3. -4 or 3
    4. 1 or -2

41. If the discriminant of the equation $ax^2 + 2bx+c=0$ is equal to zero, then it is ALWAYS true that

    1. a, b, c form an arithmetic progression
    2. a, b, and c form a geometric progression
    3. b is always negative
    4. a and c are equal

42. The graph of $x^2 - 4y^2 = 4$ is a(n)

    1. hyperbola
    2. parabola
    3. ellipse
    4. pair of straight lines

43. The time required for one oscillation of a pendulum is given by the formula $t = 2\pi\sqrt{\dfrac{L}{G}}$ where L is the length and G is a constant. In order to DOUBLE the time for one oscillation, the length of the pendulum should be

    1. halved
    2. doubled
    3. squared
    4. quadrupled

44. The distance traveled by a falling body is given by the formula $S=16t^2$, where S is the distance in feet and t is the time in seconds. During the 5th second, a falling body will travel _____ feet.

    1. 80
    2. 144
    3. 256
    4. 400

45. If $g = \dfrac{k}{d^2}$, then d varies

    1. *directly* as the square root of g
    2. *inversely* as the square of g
    3. *inversely* as the square root of g
    4. *directly* as the square of g

46. The set of values satisfying the inequality $\left|\dfrac{5-x}{3}\right| < 2$ is

    1. 1<x<11
    2. -1<x<11
    3. x<-1 or x>11
    4. x<1 or x>11

47. When the equation $4^{\sin x} = 2$ is solved for all values of x between 0° and 360°, then x is equal to

    1. 30°
    2. 30°, 150°
    3. 45°
    4. 45°, 225°

48. A purse contains one penny, one nickel, one dime, one quarter and one half dollar. How many different sums of money can be formed using one or more of these coins?

    1. 5
    2. 16
    3. 31
    4. 32

49. The contrapositive of p → q is

   1. q → p
   2. ~q → ~p
   3. ~p → q
   4. ~p → ~q

50. The motion of a ball thrown upward from the ground with an initial velocity of 96 feet/second is described by the equation s=-16t²+96t. For how many seconds will the ball rise?

   1. 1
   2. 2
   3. 3
   4. 6

KEY (CORRECT ANSWERS)

1. 2	11. 1	21. 3	31. 3	41. 2
2. 1	12. 3	22. 3	32. 1	42. 1
3. 2	13. 1	23. 4	33. 4	43. 4
4. 4	14. 1	24. 2	34. 1	44. 2
5. 1	15. 3	25. 4	35. 2	45. 3
6. 1	16. 1	26. 1	36. 3	46. 2
7. 3	17. 3	27. 4	37. 4	47. 2
8. 4	18. 4	28. 4	38. 2	48. 3
9. 4	19. 4	29. 1	39. 2	49. 2
10. 1	20. 4	30. 3	40. 1	50. 3

SOLUTIONS TO PROBLEMS

1. By the distributive postulate, $\sqrt{2}(8)=\sqrt{2}(3+5)=(\sqrt{2})(3)+(\sqrt{2})(5)$. Thus, the correct sum is $8\sqrt{2}$. An instructor might also use substitution of the approximate value of $\sqrt{2} \approx 1.414$. Since $3\sqrt{2} \approx 3(1.414)=4.242$ and $5\sqrt{2} \approx 7.07$, then $3\sqrt{2}+5\sqrt{2} \approx 11.312$. Note that $8\sqrt{2} \approx 8(1.414)=11.312$. (Ans. #2)

2. Choice c shows how to add 2 fractions with the same denominator and no reduction of the sum is possible. Choice a is like choice c, but with the added step of reducing the answer to lowest terms. Choice b presents an example where one denominator serves as a common denominator for the fractions. Finally, choice d illustrates a problem where a common denominator does NOT appear in either of the original fractions. (Ans. #1)

3. Pupil B's example has a mean, median, and mode = 10. (Ans. #2)

4. The multiplicative identity is MOST important. For example, 3/4 can be shown equivalent to 6/8 by using the identity element 1 written as 2/2. Then (3/4)(2/2)=6/8. (Ans. #4)

5. Choice c is easiest because the denominator tells where to place the decimal point. Choice a gives an example where denominator can be divided into the numerator to obtain an answer in hundredths. Similarly, choice d illustrates an answer in thousandths. Finally, choice b illustrates a continuous (repeating) decimal. (Ans. #1)

6. An example is *almost always* BEST for motivational purposes. Students can see that, using the multiplicative identity $\frac{\sqrt{3}}{\sqrt{3}}=1$, $\frac{\sqrt{2}}{\sqrt{3}}=\frac{\sqrt{2}}{\sqrt{3}} \times \frac{\sqrt{3}}{\sqrt{3}}=\frac{\sqrt{6}}{\sqrt{9}}=\frac{\sqrt{6}}{\sqrt{3}}$ or $1/3\sqrt{6}$. (Ans. #1)

7. 2 kilometers = 1.24 miles which would require a MINIMUM of over 4 1/2 minutes for a superior athlete. (Ans. #3)

8. Multiplication and division must PRECEDE addition and subtraction (except where parentheses are involved). The CORRECT solution is 17. (Ans. #4)

9. Statement (a) should read, "When dividing numbers with the same base, subtract the exponents and retain the base." Statement(b) should read, "Any number, except 0, divided by itself is 1."
Statement(c) should read, "When multiplying a number by 100, move the decimal point 2 places to the right and add zeroes if necessary."
Statement(d) should read, "Parallel lines are lines which lie in a single plane and which never meet." (Ans. #4)

10. (a+b)(a-b)=b(a-b) is CORRECT but division by a-b is, INCORRECT since a-b=0. (Ans. #1)

11. Let x = original amount. The 10% discount gives a sale price of .90x. A subsequent discount of 15% gives a sale price of (.90x)(.85) = .765x which means a 23.5% discount from the original amount. (Ans. #1)

12. $32{,}000{,}000 = 3.2 \cdot 10^7$ and $.000028 = 2.8 \cdot 10^{-5}$. Then $(3.7 \cdot 10^7)(2.8 \cdot 10^{-5}) = 8.96 \cdot 10^2$. (Ans. #3)

13. +1 and -1 are their own multiplicative inverses. The multiplicative inverse of 0 does not exist. The multiplicative inverse of +.1 is +10. (Ans. #1)

14.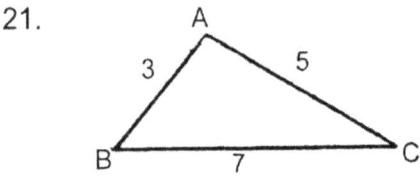

Since there are 12 students on BOTH the basketball and baseball teams, there are 10 students who play ONLY basketball and baseball. The other figures were derived similarly. The total = 27. (Ans. #1)

15. Probability = $(.70)(.40) + (.30)(.60) = .46 = 46\%$. (Ans. #3)

16. Log 4 ÷ Log 1/4 = Log 4 ÷ (Log 1 - Log 4), and since Log 1 = 0, the result is Log 4 ÷ -Log 4 = -1. (Ans. #1)

17. $(-2)^{-2} = \dfrac{1}{(-2)^2} = \dfrac{1}{4}$. Thus, $(16)^{(-2)^{-2}} = (16)^{1/4} = 2$. (Ans. #3)

18. Let height = 1 (for convenience!). The diameter of the sphere = 1 and the radius for all 3 figures = 1/2. Now, the volumes of the cylinder, sphere, and cone are

$\pi R^2 H = \dfrac{1}{4}\pi$, $\dfrac{4}{3}\pi R^3 = \dfrac{1}{6}\pi$, $\dfrac{1}{3}\pi R^2 H = \dfrac{1}{12}\pi$. The ratios reduce to 3:2:1. (Ans. #4)

19. The relation "is parallel to" is NOT *reflexive* (a line is NOT parallel to itself), but is *symmetric* (if line x is parallel to line y, then y is parallel to x) and *transitive* (if x is parallel to y and y is parallel to z, then x is parallel to z). Only choices b and c would be correct. (Ans. #4)

20. The expression $x^3 - 2x^2 - 5x + 6$ factors into $(x-1)(x+2)(x-3)$. Setting this product = to 0 gives roots of 1, -2, and 3. (Ans. #4)

21. The largest angle must be A since it lies opposite the largest side. $7^2 = 3^2 + 5^2 - (2)(3)(5)\cos\angle A$. Then $\cos\angle A = -\dfrac{1}{2}$ and $\angle A = 120°$. (Ans. #3)

22. $\lim\limits_{x \to \infty} \dfrac{3x-2}{5x+4} = \lim\limits_{x \to \infty} \dfrac{3-\frac{2}{x}}{5+\frac{4}{x}} = \dfrac{3}{5}$. (Ans. #3)

23.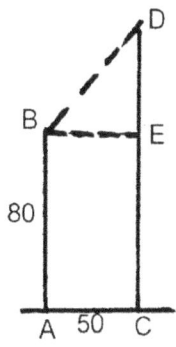

$\angle D = 90-60=30°$, $\angle DBE = 60°$.
DE=BE/tan$\angle D$=50/.577 ≈ 86.6.
DC=DE+EC ≈ 86.6+80=166.6.
Choice 4, which is $80+50\sqrt{3}$, is the correct answer. (Ans. #4)

24. Let x = smallest angle. The other angles are x+10, x+20, x+30, and x+40. The sum of the angles of a pentagon must be 540°. Then, x+(x+10)+(x+20)+(x+40) = 540°. Thus, x=88°. (Ans. #2)

25.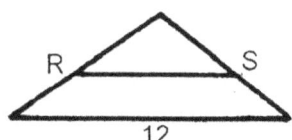

The ratio of the area of the small △ to that of the large △ is 2:3. Now, since the squares of the corresponding sides of similar triangles are in the same ratio as their corresponding areas, we get $\dfrac{(RS)^2}{(12)^2} = \dfrac{2}{3}$ and so RS=$\sqrt{96} = 4\sqrt{6}$. (Ans. #4)

26.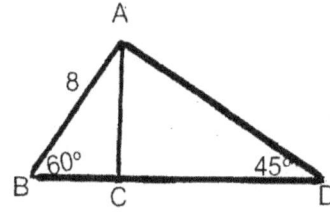

BC=1/2AB=4, AC=(BC)($\sqrt{3}$)=$4\sqrt{3}$
CD=AC=$4\sqrt{3}$. Area of △ABD = area of △ABC + area of
△ACD = $(\dfrac{1}{2})(4)(4\sqrt{3})+(\dfrac{1}{2})(4\sqrt{3})(4\sqrt{3})$ =
$8\sqrt{3}+24$. (Ans. #1)

27.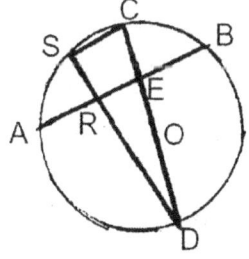

$\angle CSD=\angle RED=90$ ($\angle CSD$ is inscribed in CD, which = 180 since a perpendicular bisector of a chord must pass thru the center of the circle). $\angle D$ is the same for both △RED and △SCD. Thus, 2 angles of △RED are = to 2 angles of △SCD. Thus, these △s are *similar*. (Ans. #4)

28. Let N= $.\overline{52}$. Then $100N = 52.\overline{52}$ and by subtraction $99N = 52$. Thus, $N = \dfrac{52}{99}$, and so $2.\overline{52} = 2\dfrac{52}{99}$. (Answer #4)

29. Let x = distance from A to B or from B to A. Average speed =

    total distance ÷ total time = $(x+x)/(\frac{x}{40}+\frac{x}{60})$ = 48 mph. (Ans. #1)

30. There are 100,000 centimeters in a kilometer. Since 1 inch ≈ 2.5 centimeters, 1 yard ≈ (36)(2.5) = 90 centimeters. Thus, the number of yards in 100,000 centimeters = 100,000/90 = (100,000) [(36)(2.5)]. (Ans. #3)

31. His net worth after 1 year = ($120,000)(.625) = $75,000. His net worth after 2 years = (75,000)(1.40) = $105,000. Thus, $105,000/$120,000 = .875 = 87 1/2%. (Ans. #3)

32. The value of the determinants $\begin{vmatrix} 2x & 1 \\ x & x \end{vmatrix}$ is $2x^2-x$. Now, if $2x^2-x=3$, x can be -1 or 1 1/2, which are 2 real values. (Ans. #1)

33. $2\sin^2 x = \sin x + 1$ becomes $(2\sin x+1)(\sin x-1) = 0$.
    For $2\sin x+1=0$, x=210° and 330°. For $\sin x-1=0$, x=90°. (Ans. #4)

34. ∠A must = 180-105-30 = 45°

    Now, 10/sin 45° = b/sin 30° $b=5\sqrt{2}$. (Ans. #1)

35. $(\sqrt{2}(\cos 45° + i\sin 45°))^2 = (\sqrt{2}(\frac{1}{\sqrt{2}}+i\frac{1}{\sqrt{2}}))^2 = (1+i)^2 = 1+2i+i^2 = 2i = 0+2i$. (Ans. #2)

36. $\sin^4\theta - \cos^4\theta = (\sin^2\theta - \cos^2\theta)(\sin^2\theta + \cos^2\theta) = (2\sin^2\theta -1)(1) = 2\sin^2\theta-1$. (Ans. #3)

37. The sum of all 50 numbers = (50)(38) = 1900. By discarding the numbers 45 and 55, the new sum if 1800 for 48 numbers. The mean is then 1800/48 = 37.5. (Ans. #4)

38. Let 10t+u be the original number. Then $(10t+u)^2 - (10u+t)^2 = 99t^2 - 99u^2$ which is NOT necessarily divisible by the product of the digits, tu. Note that $99t^2-99u^2 = 99(t+u)(t-u)$ so that the quantities mentioned in selections 1, 2 and 3 are factors of (can be divided into) $99t^2-99u^2$. (Ans. #2)

39. Let x = original number of girls. When 15 girls left, x-15 was the number of girls left and 2(x-15) = the number of boys. When 45 boys then left, 2(x-15) - 45 = 2x-75 = number of boys remaining. Since there were now 5 times as many girls as boys, we have x-15 = 5(2x-75). Solving, x=40. (Ans. #2)

40. $\log_{10}(x^2-x-2) = 1$ implies $x^2-x-2=10$ or $(x-4)(x+3)=0$. Solving, x=4 or x=-3. (Ans. #1)

41. Discriminant = B^2-4AC in the equation $Ax^2+Bx+C=0$. Here, the discriminant = $4b^2-4ac$. If this expression equals 0, $b^2-ac=0$. Thus, $b^2=ac$ and so a, b, c form a geometric progression, since $\dfrac{c}{b}=\dfrac{b}{a}$.

42. Any equation which can be written as $\dfrac{x^2}{a^2}-\dfrac{y^2}{b^2}=1$ is a hyperbola (a and b are constants). Now $x^2 - 4y^2 = 4$ can be written as $\dfrac{x^2}{4}-\dfrac{y^2}{1}=1$, so that a=2 and b=1. (Ans. #1)

43. Given $t = 2\pi\dfrac{\sqrt{L}}{G}$, in order to DOUBLE the t value, the length L should be QUADRUPLED. When L is replaced by 4L, the right side of the equation becomes $2\pi\dfrac{\sqrt{4L}}{G}=4\pi\dfrac{\sqrt{L}}{G}$. This is DOUBLE the original t value. (Ans. #4)

44. The distance traveled in 5 seconds = $16(5^2)$ = 400 ft. The distance traveled in 4 seconds = $16(4^2)$ = 256 ft. Thus, the distance traveled ONLY during the 5th second = 400-256 = 144 ft. (Ans. #2)

45. From $g=\dfrac{k}{d^2}$, we can get $d=\dfrac{\sqrt{k}}{\sqrt{g}}=k'/\sqrt{g}$, where $k'=\sqrt{k}$ (k, k' are constants). This means that d varies *inversely* as the square root of g. (Ans. #3)

46. Rewrite as $-2<\dfrac{5-x}{3}<2$ and the solution becomes $-1<x<11$. (Ans. # 2)

47. $4^{\sin x}=2$ means $\sin x=1/2$. Then $x=30°$ and $150°$. (Ans. #2)

48. The number of different sums of money = $5C_1 + 5C_2 + 5C_3 + 5C_4 + 5C_5$ =5+ 10 +10 +5+1= 31. Then symbol nC_x means the number of combinations of n items taken x at a time. $nC_x = \dfrac{n!}{x!\,(n-x)!}$ (Answer #3)

49. $p \to q$ means "if p then q". The contrapositive is "if not q, then not p" which is $\sim q \to \sim p$ in symbols. (Ans. #2)

50. When the ball stops rising, v=o. Now v = ds/dt = -32t+96. Solving the equation -32t+96 = 0, t = 3. (Ans. #3)

EXAMINATION SECTION
TEST 1

DIRECTIONS: Each question or incomplete statement is followed by several suggested answers or completions. Select the one that BEST answers the question or completes the Statement. *PRINT THE LETTER OF THE CORRECT ANSWER IN THE SPACE AT THE RIGHT.*

1. In a ninth year mathematics class studying reduction of algebraic fractions, a student wrote the following:

   $\frac{10x+5}{5} = 2x$. In order to overcome this misunderstanding, this student would benefit from a review of all of the following topics EXCEPT

   1. common monomial factoring
   2. distributive postulate
   3. multiplicative inverse
   4. additive identity

   1.____

2. A mathematics class was asked to write "thirty thousand, five hundred eight" in numerals. Some students wrote "3058" and others wrote "3508".
   The BEST procedure for the teacher to follow is to

   1. discuss place value of digits in the decimal system of numeration
   2. review the history of the decimal system of numeration and the invention of the number zero
   3. contrast the Roman system of numeration with the decimal system
   4. review representation of numbers in various number bases

   2.____

3. A student who was asked to add 2/3 and 5/7 explained his solution as follows: "I multiply 2 by 7 and 3 by 5 and add them, getting a sum of 29. My answer is 29/21".
   Which of the following comments by the teacher is MOST appropriate?

   1. This procedure is incorrect since we only cross multiply when solving a proportion.
   2. This procedure is incorrect because this is an addition problem, not a multiplication.
   3. This procedure is correct because it always yields a correct answer.
   4. This procedure gives a correct answer in this case but only because the numbers used were prime. With other numbers, it would not give a correct result.

   3.____

4. In a class studying the relationship between the metric system and the English system, the following statements were made by students
   a. a meter is a little more than a yard
   b. a liter is a little more than a quart
   c. a kilometer is more than a mile
   d. a kilogram is more than a pound
   Which of these statements if FALSE?

   1. a   2. b   3. c   4. d

   4.____

15

5. In a mathematics class studying the topic of area, the formula for the area of a triangle has been taught. When asked to find the area of a right triangle whose sides measure 3, 4, 5, a student wrote the following:
A = 1/2bh = 1/2(3.4) = 1/2(3).1/2(4) = 3/2(2) = 3
Of the following, the BEST procedure for the teacher to follow is to

   1. guide the student to realize that he has incorrectly applied the associative postulate of multiplication
   2. help the student to discover that he has improperly distributed multiplication over multiplication
   3. advise the student that he has obtained an incorrect result because he used the wrong sides of the triangle in his calculation
   4. tell the student that he has arrived at the wrong answer because he has not used the correct formula for the area of a triangle

6. Students in mathematics classes often carelessly make inaccurate statements. The *only* one of the following statements which is mathematically correct is:

   1. Any number divided by itself is 1.
   2. Any angle greater than 90° is obtuse.
   3. $\sqrt{49} = 7$.
   4. The definition of parallel lines is two lines that never meet.

7. If the number of passing grades on a test given to a class is less than the teacher's expectation, which would be the MOST acceptable follow-up procedure?

   1. Regrade the test by distributing the grades on a normal curve.
   2. Repeat the test the next day as originally given.
   3. Evaluate the test, reteach selected topics in the unit, and give a new test at a later time.
   4. Move on to the next unit and make the next test easier.

8. A pupil adds his test scores and divides the sum by the number of scores. The result of this procedure would be the

   1. arithmetic mean   2. median
   3. mode   4. standard deviation

9. The students in a ninth year mathematics class ask why there is no entry in their trigonometric tables for tan 90°.
The BEST procedure for the teacher to follow is to

   1. tell the students that tan 90° is infinite
   2. tell the students that tan 90° has no value
   3. ask the students to draw an isosceles right triangle, calculate the tangent of one of the acute angles, and double the result
   4. ask the students to draw a right triangle with the base of length 1 and calculate the tangent of the acute base angle as it increases toward 90°

10. In a ninth year mathematics class studying irrational numbers, the teacher presented the students with a number of illustrations from geometry.
    Which one of the following does NOT illustrate the concept of irrational numbers? Finding the

    1. circumference of a circle whose radius is 1
    2. diagonal of a square whose side is 1
    3. hypotenuse of a right triangle whose legs are 1 and 2
    4. ratio of the shortest side to the hypotenuse in a 30° 60° - 90° triangle

11. If the product of two positive integers is divisible by 6, which of the following must be TRUE?

    1. One integer must be divisible by 2 and the other integer must be divisible by 3.
    2. At least one of the integers must be divisible by 6.
    3. At least one of the integers must be an even number.
    4. Neither of the integers can be a prime number.

12. A gas tank with a capacity of 15 gallons is 5/16 full. How many gallons of fuel must be added to the tank for it to be 5/8 full?

    1. 4 11/16   2. 5 5/8   3. 9 3/8   4. 10 5/16

13. Mr. Jones bought a house for $50,000. He sold the house at a profit of 20% of his original cost. The house was resold by the new purchaser at a profit of 20% of his cost. What percent of Mr. Jones' original purchase price is the final selling price of the house?

    A. 44%   B. 122%   C. 140%   D. 144%

14. A trip from A to B was made at a speed of 3 γ km/hr. The return trip from B to A along the same route was made at a speed of 3y km/hr.
    The average speed in km/hr for the entire trip was

    1. $\frac{5}{4}\gamma$
    2. $\frac{3}{2}\gamma$
    3. 2γ
    4. $\frac{5}{2}\gamma$

15. In calculating an average, English and Social Studies are weighted at 3 each, Mathematics is weighted at 2, and Music is weighted at 1. If a student receives a grade of 82 in English, 85 in Mathematics, and 91 in Music, what grade must he achieve in Social Studies to attain an average of 85?

    1. 82   2. 84   3. 86   4. 87

16. The roots of the quadratic equation $4 = \frac{2}{x^2} + \frac{7}{x}$ are

    1. imaginary
    2. real, unequal and rational
    3. real, unequal and irrational
    4. real, equal and rational

17. The arithmetic mean of two numbers if 17 and their geometric mean is 15. A quadratic equation of which the numbers are roots is

   1. $x^2+34x-225=0$
   2. $x^2+17x-15=0$
   3. $x^2-34x+225=0$
   4. $x^2-17x+15=0$

18. The positive value of sin (arc cos a) is

   1. $\dfrac{1}{1-a^2}$
   2. $\dfrac{1}{\sqrt{1-a^2}}$
   3. $1-a^2$
   4. $\sqrt{1-a^2}$

19. If $3x^4-3$ is factored completely, then the result is

   1. $3(x^2-1)(x^2+1)$
   2. $3(x+1)(x+1)(x-1)(x-1)$
   3. $(3x+3)(x-1)(x^2+1)$
   4. $3(x^2+1)(x+1)(x-1)$

20. If $S=\dfrac{1}{2}m(a+b)$ then a solution for b would be

   1. $b=\dfrac{2s-2a}{m}$
   2. $b=\dfrac{2m}{s-a}$
   3. $b=\dfrac{2s-am}{m}$
   4. $b=2s-am$

21. Three fair coins are tossed. What is the probability of getting exactly two heads?

   1. $\dfrac{3}{8}$
   2. $\dfrac{1}{8}$
   3. $\dfrac{2}{3}$
   4. $\dfrac{1}{2}$

22. The solution set of $x^2=2$ is NOT the empty set if the domain of x is either the

   1. real numbers or the rational numbers
   2. real numbers or the complex numbers
   3. irrational numbers or the rational numbers
   4. irrational numbers or the imaginary numbers

23. In an isosceles trapezoid, whose longer base is 12", one of the nonparallel sides is 6", and a base angle is 60. What is the *shorter* base?

   1. 6"
   2. 9"
   3. 3"
   4. (12-6/3)"

24. A man invested $1000 at 12% per year, compounded quarterly, for a period of 5 years. Which of the following represents the total of his investment at the end of that time?

   1. $1000(1.03)^{20}$
   2. $1000(1.05)^{12}$
   3. $1000(1.12)^5$
   4. $1000(1.12)^{20}$

25. H varies directly as x and inversely as d^2. If H=20 when x=2 and d=3, find H when x=4 and d=6.

   1. 10
   2. 20
   3. 40
   4. 90

26. Two of the roots of $x^3+px+q=0$ are 2 and 3. The third root is

   1. 5
   2. -5
   3. 6
   4. -6

27. If $\log_{10}12=a$ and $\log_{10}2=b$, then $\log_{10}60$ equals

   1. a-b+1   2. 5a   3. 4a+6B   4. 10a/b

28. The sum of the integers from 1 to 100 inclusive is

   1. 5049   2. 5050   3. 5051   4. 5055

29. In order to measure the height of building BC, two sightings are made from A and D with angles as shown. If the distance AD is k, then BC is

   1. $\dfrac{k}{2}$

   2. $\dfrac{k\sqrt{2}}{2}$

   3. $\dfrac{k\sqrt{3}}{2}$

   4. $\dfrac{k\sqrt{3}}{3}$

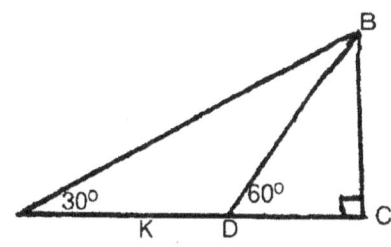

30. The area of a triangle with two adjacent sides measuring 8 inches and 10 inches and having an included angle of 45° has an area of

   1. $20\sqrt{2}$ sq. in.   2. $40\sqrt{2}$ sq. in.
   3. $20\sqrt{3}$ sq. in.   4. $40\sqrt{3}$ sq. in.

31. If $\sqrt{x+5}=3$, then $(x+5)^2$ equals

   1. 9   2. 81   3. 3   4. 4

32. The solution set of $|5-2x|<9$

   1. $\{x|x<-2\}$ 2. $\{x|x>-2\}$
   3. $\{x|-2<x<7\}$ 4. $\{x|x<-2 \text{ or } x>7\}$

33. The solution set of the equation $\log x^2 = (\log x)^2$ is

   1. $\{0, 2\}$ 2. $\{1, 100\}$
   3. {all real values of x}   4. {all real values of x>0}

34. Simplify the following expression $\dfrac{(n+k+1)!}{(n+k-1)!}$

   1. (n+k+1)(n+k)!
   2. -1
   3. (n+k+l)(n+k)
   4. The expression cannot be simplified.

35. The circle whose equation is $4x^2+4y^2-8x+24y+4=0$ has a radius whose length is

    1. 6   2. $\sqrt{6}$ 3. 3   4. 9

36. If one root of a quadratic equation is $3+i$, then which of the following is a possible equation?

    1. $x^2+6x-8=0$ 2. $x^2-6x+8=0$
    3. $x^2+6x-10=0$ 4. $x^2-6x+10=0$

37. The graph of the equation $y=\dfrac{8}{x}$

    1. two straight lines   2. an ellipse
    3. a straight line   4. a hyperbola

38. The smallest positive value of x for which $9^{\sin x}=\dfrac{1}{3}$

    1. $\dfrac{\pi}{6}$ 2. $\dfrac{\pi}{2}$ 3. $\dfrac{6\pi}{6}$ 4. $\dfrac{7\pi}{6}$

39. 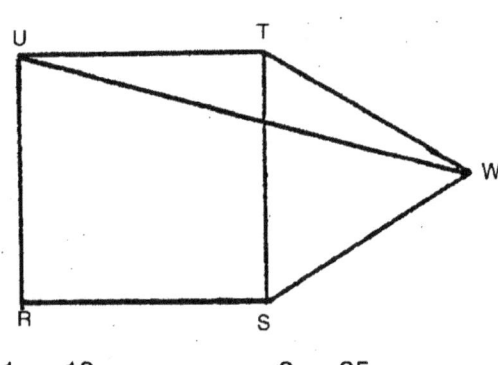 In the accompanying figure, RSTU is a square and TSW is an equilateral triangle. What is the measure of ∠TWU in degrees?

    1. 10   2. 25   3. 15   4. 12.5

40. When the base of a triangle is *increased* 10% and the altitude to this base is *decreased* 10%, the change in the area is

    1. 0%   2. 1% decrease
    3. 1% increase   4. 1/2 % decrease

41. The number of cubic FEET in the volume of a cube is the same as the number of square INCHES in its surface area.
    The length of the edge expressed in FEET is

    1. 6   2. 1728   3. 864   4. 6 x 1728

42. If an arc of 60 of circle o has the same length as an arc of 45 of circle o′, the ratio of the area of circle o to that of circle o′ is

    1. 3/4   2. 4/3   3. 16/9   4. 9/16

43. The side of an equilateral triangle is m. A circle is inscribed in the triangle and a square is inscribed in that circle.
The area of the square is

   1. $\dfrac{m^2}{6}$ 2. $\dfrac{m^2\sqrt{2}}{6}$ 3. $\dfrac{m^2\sqrt{3}}{6}$ 4. $\dfrac{m^2}{3}$

44. If the graphs of y=2 sin x and y = cos 2x are sketched on the same set of axes, at how many points will the curves intersect

   intersect where $\dfrac{\pi}{2} \le x \le \pi$

   1. 1   2. 2   3. 3   4. 0

45. How much pure hydrochloric acid should be added to 80 oz. of a 20% solution of hydrochloric acid to produce a solution which is 36% acid?

   1. 10 oz.   2. 20 oz.   3. 26.4 oz.   4. 30 oz.

46. The expression $\lim\limits_{x \to 1} \dfrac{x^2-3+2}{x^2-x}$ is equal to

   1. 1   2. -1   3. 3   4. 0

47. If f and g are functions such that f(x) = 3x+2 and f(g(x)) = x, then g(x) =

   1. $\dfrac{x-2}{3}$ 2. 2x + 3   3. -3x + 2   4. $\dfrac{x-3}{2}$

48. If V(r) represents the volume of a sphere of radius r, and S(r) represents its surface area, which one of the following statements is TRUE?

   1. $\dfrac{d^2V}{dr^2} = \dfrac{S}{r}$ 2. $\dfrac{dV}{dr} = S$ 3. $\dfrac{dS}{dr} = \dfrac{3V}{r^2}$ 4. $\dfrac{dS}{dr} = V$

49. The lines whose equations are 2x+3y = 7 and 3x-4y = -15 intersect at the point P. What is the distance from P to the origin?

   1. $\dfrac{\sqrt{34}}{3}$ 2. $\dfrac{\sqrt{85}}{4}$ 3. $\sqrt{8}$ 4. $\sqrt{10}$

50. The coefficient of the third term of the expansion of $(2x+\dfrac{1}{\sqrt{3x}})^6$ is

   1. 16/3   2. 10   3. 15   4. 80

KEY (CORRECT ANSWERS)

1. 4	11. 3	21. 1	31. 2	41. 3
2. 1	12. 1	22. 2	32. 3	42. 4
3. 3	13. 4	23. 1	33. 2	43. 1
4. 3	14. 2	24. 1	34. 3	44. 1
5. 2	15. 3	25. 1	35. 3	45. 2
6. 3	16. 2	26. 2	36. 4	46. 2
7. 3	17. 3	27. 1	37. 4	47. 1
8. 1	18. 4	28. 2	38. 4	48. 2
9. 4	19. 4	29. 3	39. 3	49. 4
10. 4	20. 3	30. 1	40. 2	50. 4

SOLUTIONS TO PROBLEMS

1. The additive identity element is 0, but this information would NOT aid the student in realizing that $\frac{10x+5}{5} \neq 2x$ The given fraction = 2x+1. (Ans. 4)

2. A clear presentation of the place value of digits in the decimal system should be shown. The correct figure is 30,508. (Ans. 1)

3. Although a correct answer will be obtained always, it should be noted that when using this technique, the answer will not always appear in reduced lowest terms. Example: 1/2 + 3/8 would equal 14/16 by this method, but the answer reduces to 7/8. (Ans. 3)

4. A kilometer is about 5/8 of a mile. (Ans. 3)

5. The student mistakenly distributed multiplication over multiplication. The correct area is 6. (Ans. 2)

6. Only $\sqrt{49} = 7$ is correct. Statement 1 should read "any number except zero divided by itself is 1". Statement 2 should read "any angle which is greater than 90° but less than 180° is obtuse". Statement 4 should mention that the 2 lines must first lie in the same plane. (Ans. 3)

7. Since most students did poorly, it would be best to reteach certain key concepts. A new test would then be given, but a teacher should still count the first test. (Ans. 3)

8. The arithmetic mean = sum of numbers divided by the number of numbers. (Ans. 1)

9. As x approaches 90°, the students will realize how tan x becomes extremely large, especially between 89° and 90°. (Ans. 4)

10. This ratio is always 1/2, which is a rational number. (Ans. 4)

11. If (A)(B)/6 is a whole number, we can conclude that either A or B or both A, B is(are) even. Furthermore, at least one of A, B must be divisible by 3. (Ans. 3)

12. The required amount of fuel = $15(\frac{5}{8} - \frac{5}{16}) = 4\frac{11}{16}$. (Ans. 1)

13. Mr. Jones sold his house for ($50,000)(1.20) = $60,000. The new buyer sold the house for ($60,000)(1.20) = $72,000. Now $72,000 is (72,000/50,000) x 100 = 144% of $50,000. (Ans. 4)

14. Average speed = total distance/total time = $(x+x)/(\frac{x}{r} + \frac{x}{3r}) = 2x/(\frac{4x}{3r}) = \frac{3}{2}r$. Here x = distance from A to B. (Ans. 2)

15. Let x = required score. Then $\dfrac{(82)(3)+(x)(3)+(85)(2)+(91)+(1)}{9} = 85$ Solving, x = 86. (Ans. 3)

16. Convert the equation to $4x^2-7x-2=0$, which becomes $(4x+1)(x-2)=0$. The answers, 2 and -1/4, are real, unequal, rational. (Ans. 2)

17. Let x = 1st number, y = 2nd number. Then $\dfrac{x+y}{2} = 17$ and xy = 225. By substitution of y=34-x from the 1st equation into the 2nd equation, x(34-x) = 225. This becomes $x^2-34x+225=0$. (Ans. 3)

18. Let arc cos a = x. Then cos x = a or $\dfrac{a}{1}$. The other leg of a right triangle where the hypotenuse is 1 and one leg is $a = \sqrt{1-a^2}$. Thus, sin(arc cos a) = sin x = $\sqrt{1-a^2}$ (Ans. 4)

19. $3x^4-3 = 3(x^4-1) = 3(x^2+1)(x+1)(x-1)$. (Ans. 4)

20. Dividing both sides by $\dfrac{1}{2}$m, $\dfrac{2S}{m} = a+b$, so $b = \dfrac{2S}{m} - a$ or equivalently $b = \dfrac{2S-am}{m}$. (Ans. 3)

21. Probability (exactly 2 heads) = (3)(Probability of getting heads on 2 specific coins) = $(3)(\dfrac{1}{8}) = \dfrac{3}{8}$ (Ans. 1)

22. $x^2 = 2$ has roots $\pm\sqrt{2}$, provided the domain of x will include irrational numbers. (Ans. 2)

23.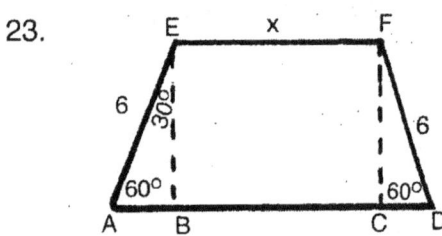
AD=12". In right $\triangle ABE = \dfrac{1}{2}\overline{AE} = 3 = \overline{AB}$ Also, CD = 1/2 FD = 3. x=BC=AD-AB-CD=6. (Ans. 1)

24. $T=P(1+\dfrac{R}{n})^{nt}$ where T=total, P=principal (investment), R=annual compounded rate, n=number of times per year being compounded, t=number of years. Thus $T=1000(1.03)^{20}$. (Ans. 1)

25. $H=\dfrac{Kx}{d^2}$ where K is a constant. When H = 20, x=2, d=3, so $K=(20)(9)/2=90$. Thus, we can write $H=90x/d^2$. Now H= (90)(4)/36=10. (Ans. 1)

26. Since 2,3 are roots, x-2, x-3 are factors. Also, by the substitution of 2,3 for x, we get 8+2p+q=0 and 27+3p+q=0.
Solving, p=-19, q=30. The equation becomes $x^3-19x+30=0$. Let R=3rd root. Then $(x-2)(x-3)(x-R) = x^3-19x+30$. Thus, R=-5. (Ans. 2)

27. $Log_{10}60 = Log_{10}((12)(10)/2) = Log_{10}12 + Log_{10}10 - Log_{10}2$ = a+1-b or a-b+1. (Ans. 1)

28. Sum = $\frac{n}{2}$ (a+L), n=# of numbers, a=1st #, L=last #, in an arithmetic progression.
Thus, Sum = $\frac{100}{2}(1+100) = 5050$. (Ans. 2)

29. Let BC=x. Since $\angle ADB = 120°$, then $\angle ABD = 30°$. Now $\triangle ADB$ is isosceles, so that DB=K. Furthermore, sin 60°=x/k. x = k sin60° = $k\sqrt{3}/2$. (Ans. 3)

30. Let x = 3rd side. Then $x^2 = 8^2+10^2-(2)(8)(10) \cdot \cos 45° \approx 7.13$. Area = $\sqrt{s(s-a)(s-b)(s-c)}$, s= semi-perimeter.
Area = $\sqrt{(12.6)(2.6)(4.6)(5.47)} \approx 28.7 \approx 20\sqrt{2}$. (Ans. 1)

31. $\sqrt{x+5} = 3$ means x=4. Then $(4+5)^2=81$. (Ans. 2)

32. $|5-2x|<9$ means -9<5-2x<9, which implies -2<x<7. (Ans. 3)

33. $Log\ x^2 = 2Log\ x$. Now $2 Log\ x = (Log\ x)^2$. Factoring, we get Log x(2-Log x)=0. If Log x=0, x=1. If 2-Log x=0, then x=100. The solution set is {1,100}. (Ans. 2)

34. $\frac{(n+k+1)!}{(n+k-1)!} = \frac{(n+k+1)(n+k)(n+k-1)(...)(1)}{(n+k-1)(n+k-2)(...)(1)} = (n+k+1)(n+k)$

35. Tranform the equation by first dividing by 4 to get $x^2-2x+y^2+6y=-1$. Then $(x^2-2x+1)+(y^2+6y+9)=-1+1+9$ or $(x-1)^2+(y+3)^2=32$. The radius=3. (Ans. 3)

36. The other root must be 3-i. The sum of the roots is 6 and the product of the roots is 10. The equation must be $x^2-6x+10=0$. (Ans. 4)

37. $y=\frac{8}{x}$ becomes xy=8. Any equation of the form xy=k, with k a constant, is a hyperbola. (Ans. 4)

38. $9^{\sin x} = \frac{1}{3}$ means $(3^2)^{\sin x} = 3^{-1}$, which implies $2\sin x = -1$. The smallest such angle for which sine value is $-.5$ is $210°$ or $7\pi/6$ radians. (Ans. 4)

39. $\angle UTS=90°$ and $\angle STW=60°$, so $\angle UTW=150°$. Now, $\angle TUW + \angle UTW = 180°$, with $\angle TUW=\angle TWU$. Since $\angle UTW=150°$, then $\angle TUW=15°$. (Ans. 3)

40. Let B=original base, H=original altitude, so that Area $=\frac{1}{2}BH$. Let $1.10B$=new base, $.90H$=new altitude so that NEW area = $(1/2)(.99)BH$. Thus, the change in area is a 1% decrease. (Ans. 2)

41. Surface area = $6e^2$, where e= number of inches in one edge. Then, since $\frac{e}{12}$ is the equivalent number of feet in one edge, $V=(e/12)^3 = e^3/1728$ in cubic feet. Now, $6e^2=e^3/1728$ and $e=10368$ inches, which converts to 864 feet. (Ans. 3)

42. Let R_1 = radius of circle O. Then the length of an arc of $60° = \frac{1}{3}\pi R_1$. Let R_2 = radius of circle O'. Then the length of an arc of $45° = \frac{1}{4}\pi R_2$. Since these lengths are equal, $\frac{1}{3}\pi R_1 = \frac{1}{4}\pi R_2$ or $R_1/R_2 = \frac{3}{4}$. Thus, the ratio of the area of circle O to that of circle $O' = (\frac{3}{4})^2 = \frac{9}{16}$. (Ans. 4)

43.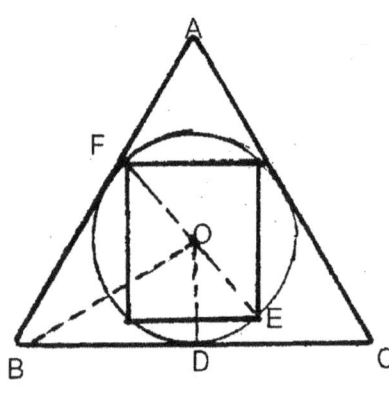

In $\triangle OBD$, $\angle OBD=30°$, $BD=\frac{m}{2}$, $OD=\frac{1}{2}OB$. Now $(OD)^2 + \frac{m^2}{4}(2.OD)^2$, from which $OD=m\sqrt{3}/6$. $OE=OD=m\sqrt{3}/6$, so $EF=m\sqrt{3}/3$
Area of square = 1/2 product of diagonals $=\frac{1}{2}(m\sqrt{3})/3 \times m\sqrt{3}/3 = m^2/6$.
(Ans. 1)

44. Points of intersection: $2\sin x = \cos 2x$, which $= 1-2\sin^2 x$. Then $2\sin^2 x + 2\sin x - 1 = 0$.

 Then $\sin x = \dfrac{-2\pm\sqrt{8}}{4} = (-1\pm\sqrt{2})/2$. When $\dfrac{\pi}{2} < x < \pi$ only the value $(-1+\sqrt{2})/2$ can be considered, since $(-1-\sqrt{2})/2$ is negative. The only admissible value of x is $\approx 168°$ or $\approx .93\pi$ radians.
 (Ans. 1)

45. Let x = amount of acid added. Originally, there was $(80)(.20) = 16$ oz. of acid. Now, $16+x=.36(80+x)$. $x=20$ oz. (Ans. 2)

46. The fraction can be written as $\dfrac{(x-2)(x-1)}{x(x-1)} = \dfrac{x-2}{x}$. Then $\lim\limits_{x \to 1} \dfrac{x-2}{x} = -1$ (Ans. 2)

47. $3(g(x)) + 2 = x$. Thus, $g(x) = \dfrac{x-2}{3}$. (Ans. 1)

48. $V = \dfrac{4}{3}\pi r^3$ and $S = 4\pi r^2$. So, $\dfrac{dV}{dr} = S$. (Ans. 2)

49. Solving $2x+3y=7$ and $3x-4y=-15$, $x=-1$, $y=3$. The point $(-1, 3)$ is $\sqrt{(-1)^2+(3)^2} = \sqrt{10}$ from the origin. (Ans. 4)

50. Third term $= \dfrac{6 \cdot 5}{1 \cdot 2}(2x)^4 \dfrac{(1)^2}{(\sqrt{3x})} = 80x^4$ so the coefficient is 80. (Ans. 4)

EXAMINATION SECTION
TEST 1

DIRECTIONS: Each question or incomplete statement is followed by several suggested answers or completions. Select the one that BEST answers the question or completes the statement. *PRINT THE LETTER OF THE CORRECT ANSWER IN THE SPACE AT THE RIGHT.*

1. A seventh grade class is learning to multiply a decimal by a decimal. In a 40 minute lesson, the MOST desirable allotment of time for a final summary is _____ minutes. 1.____

    1. 17   2. 12   3. 9   4. 5

2. Of the following, the MOST educationally valid reason for assigning a problem to a mathematics class at the beginning of a period is to 2.____

    1. furnish more material for grading students
    2. give the teacher a chance to take attendance
    3. prepare the students for the new concepts to be taught
    4. keep the class busy

3. Of the following statements about testing, the one which is most educationally valid states that 3.____

    1. each test given should be used to help ascertain what reteaching is needed
    2. frequent testing is a very effective way to motivate learning
    3. there should normally be a test given at the end of each week
    4. a standardized mathematics test is better than any teacher-made test

4. With respect to mathematics homework, the LEAST desirable policy is to 4.____

    1. assign review work as well as new work
    2. assign traditional drill to students for classroom infractions
    3. not assign homework over weekends and holidays
    4. assign it regularly regardless of weekends or holidays

5. In mathematics classes, perfect test papers and outstanding pupil projects frequently are prominently displayed. 5.____
    This practice is considered to be of

    1. positive value, because it creates a feeling of pride in work well done
    2. unknown value, because only a limited number of pupils read the material posted
    3. unknown value, because exhibited work frequently contains mistakes and errors both of fact and of expression
    4. poor educational value, because it creates resentment on the part of pupils whose work is not so posted

6. Of the following, the BEST reason for a study of the Roman system of numeration is that such study 6.____

    1. correlates with work in history
    2. reinforces an understanding of the decimal system of numeration by providing a contrast

3. enables students to read the dates on cornerstones of buildings
4. provides good material for mathematical problems and recreations

7. A pupil in your ninth year mathematics class insists that x+1/ x+2 equals 1/2. Of the following, the BEST procedure to follow is to tell the pupil

   1. that he did not use the distributive law correctly
   2. to substitute a positive integer for x
   3. x+1/x+2 is not equal to 1/2
   4. that it is incorrect to cancel the x's

8. With reference to the meaning of 4+6x3, Dan says it equals 30, while Paul says it equals The MOST desirable action to take would be to

   1. tell Dan he should be sure of his facts before he reaches a conclusion
   2. tell the class that Paul is correct and to give him extra credit
   3. involve the entire class in a review of the order of operations
   4. postpone discussion of this topic until another time

9. A teacher presents the following problem to his mathematics class, "The length of one leg of a right triangle is half the length of the hypotenuse. Express the value of the tangent of the smallest angle of that triangle."

   Alan writes $\dfrac{1}{\sqrt{3}}$ Jean writes $\dfrac{\sqrt{3}}{3}$

   1. Both Alan and Jean are wrong.
   2. Alan is right and Jean is wrong.
   3. Alan is wrong and Jean is right.
   4. Both Alan and Jean are right.

10. In eighth grade mathematics, a teacher plans to present the following topics:
    a. Development of the formula for the area of a circle
    b. Development of the formula for the area of a triangle
    c. Circle terminology
    d. Development of the formula for the circumference of a circle
    The BEST of the following teaching sequences is

    1. c, b, a, d   2. c, d, a, b
    3. b, c, d, a   4. c, a, b, d

11. The maximum area that a rectangle whose perimeter is 18 can enclose is

    1. 324   2. 20 1/4   3. 20   4. 81

12. As part of its aircraft officer training program, the Navy sends sailors to radio school. Of those who are sent to radio school,1/3 drop out during the course. Of those who graduate, 4/5 are assigned to aircraft carriers.
    If 3/4 of these become officers, how many sailors should the Navy send to radio school if it needs 60 aircraft officers?

    1. 120   2. 150   3. 180   4. 300

13. Mr. Grey sold two pipes at $1.20 each. Based on the cost of the first, his profit was 20%. Based on the cost of the second, his loss was 20%.
    What was the *combined* effect of the two transactions?

    1. Gain of 10¢
    2. Loss of 4¢
    3. Gain of 4¢
    4. Loss of 10¢

14. Two junior high school classes took the same test. The first class of 20 students attained an average grade of 80%. The second class of 30 students attained an average grade of 70%.
    The average grade for all students in both classes is _____ %.

    1. 72
    2. 73
    3. 74
    4. 75

15. The infinite repeating decimal $0.0\overline{4}$ (where 4 is repeated) is equal to

    1. 2/45
    2. 1/25
    3. 11/225
    4. 11/250

16. What is the ratio between the radii of the inscribed and circumscribed circles of an equilateral triangle?

    1. 1:2
    2. 1:3
    3. $1:\sqrt{2}$
    4. $1:\sqrt{3}$

17. A square 4 centimeters on a side is cut from each corner of a rectangular piece of cardboard 38 centimeters by 48 centimeters and the remaining piece is folded into a box. The number of cubic centimeters in the volume of the box is

    1. 4800
    2. 5984
    3. 344
    4. 1200

18. In the figure shown in the accompanying sketch, angle A and angle CBD are right angles. If AB = 9, AC = 12, and BD = 8, then the length of CD is
    1. 25
    2. 22
    3. 18
    4. 17

19. The number of revolutions of a wheel, with fixed center and with an outside diameter of 6 feet, required to cause a point on the rim to go one mile is

    1. 880
    2. $\dfrac{440}{\pi}$
    3. $\dfrac{880}{\pi}$
    4. 440π

20. Two points A and B are on the same side of a tower and in line with the center of the base of the tower. The angles of elevation of the top of the tower from A and B are equal to 60° and 30°, respectively.
    If AB = 8, then the height of the tower is

    1. $8\sqrt{3}$
    2. 8
    3. $4\sqrt{3}$
    4. 4

21. Some properties that hold for equalities of real numbers are
    a. reflexive property
    b. symmetric property
    c. transitive property
    Which of these properties hold true for the relation "greater than" applied to real numbers?

    1. c only
    2. a, b, c
    3. b, c
    4. a, c

22. In one dimension, the set of points at a given distance greater than zero from a fixed point

    1. contains one point
    2. contains two points
    3. is a circle
    4. is a line segment

23. Find the number of cubic inches in the volume of a pyramid whose base is a square 6 inches on a side and whose altitude is 14 inches.

    1. 504
    2. 336
    3. 252
    4. 168

24. The number designated by 2021_{three} can be denoted in the binary system by

    1. 111101_{two}
    2. 101011_{two}
    3. 110111_{two}
    4. 101111_{two}

25. A representation for the number .00792 in scientific notation is

    1. 7.92×10^{-3}
    2. 7.92×10^{-4}
    3. 7.92×10^{2}
    4. 7.92×10^{3}

26. The fraction $\dfrac{2}{1+2\sqrt{3}}$ is equivalent to

    1. $\dfrac{4\sqrt{3}+2}{13}$
    2. $\dfrac{4\sqrt{3}-2}{11}$
    3. $\dfrac{4\sqrt{3}+1}{13}$
    4. $\dfrac{4\sqrt{3}-1}{11}$

27. If c represents a real number and $c \neq 0$, then the sum of the additive and multiplicative inverses of c is

    1. -1
    2. 1 - c
    3. $\dfrac{(1+c)(1-c)}{c}$
    4. $\dfrac{1+c^2}{c}$

28. If A is the set of odd integers between 0 and 10 and B is a subset of the set of integers such that B={x|1<x<6}, then the set A B is:

    1. {3, 5}
    2. {1, 3, 5}
    3. {1, 3, 5, 7, 9}
    4. {1, 2, 3, 4, 5, 7, 9}

29. The sum of two numbers a and b is equal to their product. An equation which expresses this fact is:

    1. $b=\dfrac{a-1}{a}$
    2. $b=\dfrac{a}{a-1}$
    3. $b=\dfrac{a+1}{2}$
    4. $b=\dfrac{a}{a+1}$

30. When $x^3 + 4x^2 + 3x - 10$ is divided by $x-1$, the remainder is   30._____

    1. -18   2. -9   3. -10   4. -2

31. Two "fair" coins are tossed. The probability that both coins show heads is   31._____

    1. 1   2. 3/4   3. 1/2   4. 1/4

32. If the roots of $x^2 + bx + c = 0$ are the negatives of the roots of $x^2 + 3x + 2 = 0$, then   32._____

    1. b = 3 and c = 2
    2. b = 3 and c = -2
    3. b = -3 and c = 2
    4. b = -3 and c = -2

33. Let $b \in R$, the set of real numbers. The solution set of $b^2 > b$ is   33._____

    1. $\{b \mid b>1\}$
    2. $\{b \mid b<0 \text{ or } b>1\}$
    3. $\{b \mid b<-1 \text{ or } b>1\}$
    4. R

34. If k represents a positive integer, $2^{k+1} + 2^k$ is equal to   34._____

    1. 4^{2k+1} 2. 2^{2k+1} 3. $3(2^{k+1})$ 4. $3(2^k)$

35. A function, f(x), is defined as $f(x) = 2x^2 - 5$. The value of $f(f(2))$ is   35._____

    1. 13   2. 22   3. 6   4. 9

36. If $\log_2 y = 5$, then y is equal to   36._____

    1. 7   2. 10   3. 25   4. 32

37. The graph of the equation $x^2 - 4x + y^2 = 12$ is a circle with radius _____; center _____.   37._____

    1. 4, (-2, 0)
    2. 4, (2, 0)
    3. 16, (-2, 0)
    4. 16, (2, 0)

38. The total number of subsets of set a, b, c, d is   38._____

    1. 16   2. 15   3. 8   4. 4

39. If S represents the sum of the infinite geometric series $\frac{1}{4} + \frac{1}{8} + \frac{1}{16} + ...$, then   39._____

    1. S = 1   2. S<1   3. 1<S<2   4. S>2

40. A set of students' marks on a quiz worth ten points was as follows: 2, 2, 3, 3, 5, 5, 5, 7, 7, 7, 7, 9, 10.   40._____
    The arithmetic mean, median, and mode of this set of marks, arranged in *descending* order of magnitude will be

    1. mode, arithmetic mean, median
    2. median, mode, arithmetic mean
    3. arithmetic mean, median, mode
    4. mode, median, arithmetic mean

41. The number of permutations of the elements of the set $\{x_1, x_2, ..., x_n\}$, using all the elements of the set in each permutation, is

   1. 2^n 2. n^2 3. $n!$ 4. $\sum_{i=1}^{n} x_i$

42. Let R represent the set of real numbers. If a*b is defined as $\frac{a+b}{2}$ where a and b represent any two elements in R, then

   1. a*1=a
   2. a*0=0
   3. a*(2b)=(2a)*b
   4. 2+(a*b)=(2+a)*(2+b)

43. What is the abscissa of the point on the graph of $y=x^2+5x+4$ where the slope of the tangent to the graph equals 9?

   1. 18   2. 2   3. 1 2/7   4. 0

44. As x approaches 6 as a limit, the value of the fraction $\frac{x^2-36}{x-6}$ approaches

   1. zero   2. infinity   3. 12   4. 6

45. The area bounded by the x-axis and the graph of the equation $y = -x^2 + 6x$ is

   1. 108   2. 54   3. 36   4. 0

46. The locus in three dimensions of all points equidistant from two given points is

   1. a point
   2. a straight line
   3. a circle plus its center
   4. a plane

47. The implication $p \to q$ is equivalent to

   1. $q \to p$ 2. $\sim p \to \sim q$ 3. $\sim q \to p$ 4. $\sim q \to \sim p$

48. Find the solution set of $\cos 2A + 3 \cos A = -2$ where $0 \le A \le 360°$

   1. {0°, 60°, 300°}
   2. {60°, 180°, 300°}
   3. {120°, 180°, 240°}
   4. {0°, 120°, 240°}

49. A student observes that the same shaded part of a Venn diagram illustrates both sets $A \cap (B \cup C)$ and $(A \cap B) \cup (A \cap C)$
This suggests a property most closely resembling which property of real numbers?

   1. Commutative
   2. Distributive
   3. Associative
   4. Multiplicative inverse

50. In Euler's formula V+F=E+2, V represents
    1. volume
    2. magnitude of a vector
    3. number of vertices
    4. velocity in feet per second

KEY (CORRECT ANSWERS)

1. 3	11. 2	21. 1	31. 4	41. 3
2. 3	12. 2	22. 2	32. 3	42. 4
3. 1	13. 4	23. 4	33. 2	43. 2
4. 2	14. 3	24. 1	34. 4	44. 3
5. 4	15. 1	25. 1	35. 1	45. 3
6. 2	16. 1	26. 2	36. 4	46. 4
7. 2	17. 1	27. 3	37. 2	47. 4
8. 3	18. 4	28. 1	38. 1	48. 3
9. 4	19. 3	29. 2	39. 2	49. 2
10. 3	20. 3	30. 4	40. 1	50. 3

SOLUTIONS TO PROBLEMS

1. Between 5 and 10 minutes would be the maximum time that should be devoted to reviewing the multiplication of 2 decimals.
(Ans. 3)

2. A problem assigned at the beginning can be helpful for reviewing the previous day's lesson and for introducing new concepts. (Ans. 3)

3. While it is true that frequent testing will motivate learning, it is not the most valid reason. Testing helps both teacher and students to realize what concepts remain unclear. (Ans. 1)

4. Punishment for misbehavior should not include the assignment of subject matter problems. (Ans. 2)

5. The displaying of perfect test papers will definitely create resentment from those students who did poorly on these tests. (Ans. 4)

6. By studying the Roman system, one can appreciate the simplicity of the decimal system. (Ans. 2)

7. By allowing the student to choose a positive integer, say 3, he can see that $\frac{3+1}{3+2}=\frac{4}{5}\neq\frac{1}{2}$
(Ans. 2)

8. It is best to involve the whole class since there may be other students who don't realize why 4+6x3=22. A review of the order of operations would help. (Ans. 3)

9. 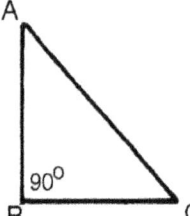 Let BC = x and AC=2x. Then $AB=x\sqrt{3}$, by the Pythagorean Theorem. Since BC is the smallest side, $\angle A$ is the smallest angle.
$\text{Tan}\angle A=\frac{x}{x\sqrt{3}}=\frac{1}{\sqrt{3}}=\frac{\sqrt{3}}{3}$. (Ans. 4)

10. First the area of a triangle should be developed, since no knowledge of circles is required. Then, before any formulas for circles can be developed, a student must learn the required terminology. (Ans. 3)

11. P = 2L+2W=18 or L=9-W. Area = LW = (9-W)(W)= 9W-W².
To maximize, find dA/dW = 9-2W and solve 9-2W = 0.
Thus, W=9/2. The maximum areas = 9(9/2) - (9/2)² = 20 1/4. (Ans. 2)

12. Let x = number of sailors sent to school. Then 2/3x graduate. Subsequently, (4/5)(2/3x) =8/15x are assigned to aircraft carriers. Finally, (3/4)(8/15x) = 2/5x = number of officers = 60. Thus x = 150. (Ans. 2)

13. The 1st pipe cost Mr. Grey $1.20 ÷ 1.20 = $1.00 (20% on cost). The 2nd pipe cost Mr. Grey $1.20 ÷ .80 = $1.50 (20% on cost). Thus, his NET LOSS was $1.00 + 1.50 - 1.20 - 1.20 = .10. (Ans. 4)   COST   SELLING PRICE LOSS

14. Average grade = $\frac{(20)(.80) + (30)(.70)}{50}$ =74%. (Ans. 3)

15. Let N=.0$\overline{4}$, so that 10N=.$\overline{4}$. Now by subtraction, 9N=.4 and N=$\frac{4}{90}$ or $\frac{2}{45}$. (Ans. 1)

16. 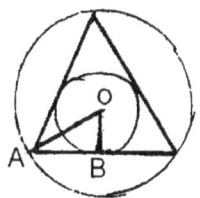 In $\triangle$OAB, $\angle$OAB=30°, $\angle$B=90°, so that OB = 1/2·OA. Thus, the ratio is 1:2. (Ans. 1)

17. 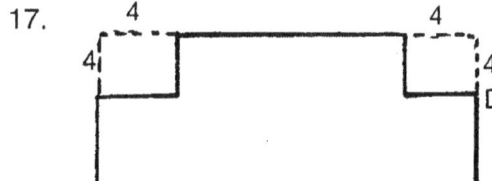 The box will have length AB=40, width CD=30, and height BE=4. Volume = (40)(30)(4) = 4800 cm^3. (Ans. 1)

18. BC^2 = 9^2 + 12^2, so BC=15. Now, CD^2=8^2+15^2, and thus CD=17. (Ans. 4)

19. One revolution = 6π feet. Since 5280 feet = 1 mile, this is equivalent to 5280 / 6π = 880 / π feet. (Ans. 3)

20. 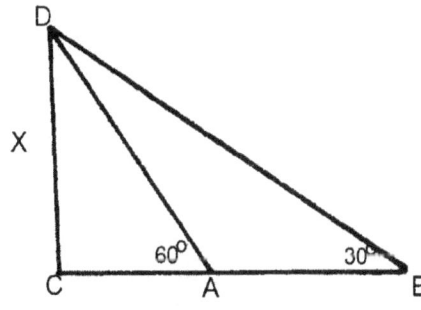 $\triangle$ADB must be isosceles, since $\angle$DAB=120° and $\angle$ADB=30°. Thus AD=AB=8. Now only consider $\triangle$ACD, $\sin 60° = \frac{x}{8}$. Finally, $x=4\sqrt{3}$. (Ans. 3)

21. Only the transitive property holds, i.e.: if x>y and y>w, then x>w. (Ans. 1)   21.____

22. $\overline{A \quad\quad\quad \overset{\cdot}{C} \quad\quad\quad B}$ In one dimension, only points A,B would be at a prescribed distance from point C. (Ans. 2)

23. Volume = (1/3)(6^2)(14) = 168 in^3. (Ans. 4)

24. 2021$_{three}$ = 2(27) + 0(9) + 2(3) + 1 = 61 in base 10. This is equivalent to 111101$_{two}$. (Ans. 1)

25. .00792 = 7.92 x .001 = 7.92 x 10^{-3}. (Ans. 1)

26. $\dfrac{2}{1+2\sqrt{3}} \cdot \dfrac{1-2\sqrt{3}}{1-2\sqrt{3}} = \dfrac{2-4\sqrt{3}}{1-12} = \dfrac{4\sqrt{3}-2}{11}$ (Ans. 2)

27. The additive inverse of c is -c and the multiplicative inverse of c is $\dfrac{1}{c}$. Now $-c+\dfrac{1}{c} = \dfrac{-c^2+1}{c} = \dfrac{(1+c)(1-c)}{c}$. (Ans. 3)

28. A = {1, 3, 5, 7, 9}, B = {2, 3, 4, 5}, then A ∩ B = {3, 5} (Ans. 1)

29. Since a+b = ab from the given information, a = ab-b or a=b(a-1), which becomes $b=\dfrac{a}{a-1}$. (Ans. 2)

30. By the Remainder Theorem, when P(x) is divided by x-R, the remainder is P(R). In this example, the remainder is P(1) = $1^3+4(1)^2+3(1)-10 = -2$. (Ans. 4)

31. Probability = $(1/2)^2 = 1/4$. (Ans. 4)

32. The roots of $x^2+3x+2=0$ are -1, -2. The negatives of these roots are 1, 2. Sum of roots = -b/1 = 3, so b = -3. Product of roots = c/1 = 2, so c=2. (Ans. 3)

33. $b^2>b$ implies b(b-1)>0. If both b>0 and b-1>0, then a solution is {b|b>1}. If b<0 and b-1<0, then a solution is {b|b<0}. Final answer: {b|b<0 or b>1}. (Ans. 2)

34. $\dfrac{2^{k+1} + 2^k(2+1)}{2} = 3(2^k)$. (Ans. 4)

35. $f(f(2)) = f(2(2^2)-5) = f(3) = 2(3^2) -5 = 13$. (Ans. 1)

36. $\log_2 y=5$ implies $2^5=y$, so y=32. (Ans. 4)

37. Rewrite as $x^2-4x+4+y^2=12+4$, which becomes: $(x-2)^2+(y-0)^2=4$. Thus, the radius is 4 and the center is (2,0). (Ans. 2)

38. Given a set with n elements, the number of subsets = 2^n. In this example, $2^n = 2^4=16$. (Ans. 1)

39. $S=\dfrac{a}{1-r}$, where a = 1st term, r = common ratio. Thus, $S=\dfrac{1}{4} \div (1-\dfrac{1}{2})=\dfrac{1}{2}$. The only correct choice is S<1. (Ans. 2)

40. Mode = 7, Mean = $\dfrac{72}{13}$ = 5.5, Median = 5. Therefore, the descending order of magnitude is mode, mean, median. (Ans. 1)

41. The number of permutations of n elements (using all elements) = n(n-1)(n-2)(...)(1) = n!. (Ans. 3)

42. $2 +(a*b) = 2+\dfrac{a+b}{2}=\dfrac{4+a+b}{2}$. Also $(2+a)*(2+b) = \dfrac{2+a+2+b}{2} = \dfrac{4+a+b}{2}$. (Ans. 4)

43. Slope $=\dfrac{dy}{dx} = 2x+5$. If $\dfrac{dy}{dx} = 9$, then $x=2$. (Ans. 2)

44. $\dfrac{x^2-36}{x-6}$ reduces to $x+6$. For all $x \neq 6$. Then $\lim\limits_{x \to 6} \dfrac{x^2-36}{x-6} = 12$.

45. $\int_0^6 (-x^2+6x)dx=(-\dfrac{x^3}{3}+3x^2)_0^6 = 36$. (Ans. 3)

46. The locus of all points in space equidistant from 2 given points is the plane which is the perpendicular bisector of the segment connecting those 2 points.

47. Using truth tables

p	q	p→q	~q→~p
T	T	T	T
T	F	F	F
F	T	T	T
F	F	T	T

    (Ans. 4)

48. Since $\cos 2A = 2\cos^2 A - 1$, the given equation becomes:
    $2\cos^2 A - 1 + 3\cos A = -2$, which will transform to: $2\cos^2 A + 3\cos A + 1 = 0$ or
    $(2\cos A+1)(\cos A+1) = 0$. From $2\cos A+1=0$, $A=120°$, $240°$ and from $\cos A+1=0$, $A=180°$.
    Final answer is $\{120°, 180°, 240°\}$. (Ans. 3)

49. The distributive property would be apparent in an example like $5\cdot(3+7) = (5\cdot3)+(5\cdot7)$.
    The $\cap$ symbol replaces $\cdot$ and the $\cup$ symbol replaces +. (Ans. 2)

50. In this formula, V=number of vertices, F=number of faces, E=number of edges. As an example, a cube has 8 vertices, 6 faces, and 12 edges. Thus $V+F = E+2$. (Ans. 3)

EXAMINATION SECTION
TEST 1

DIRECTIONS: Each question or incomplete statement is followed by several suggested answers or completions. Select the one that BEST answers the question or completes the statement. *PRINT THE LETTER OF THE CORRECT ANSWER IN THE SPACE AT THE RIGHT.*

1. With reference to the meaning of 3 + 5 x 2, John says it equals 16, while Ann says it equals 13.
   The MOST desirable action to take would be to

   1. tell the class Ann is correct and to give her extra credit
   2. involve the entire class in a review of the order of operations
   3. tell John he should be sure of his facts before he reaches a conclusion
   4. postpone discussion of this topic until another time

   1.____

2. Of the following, the BEST way to determine how well a pupil understands a principle used in solving problems is to have the pupil

   1. answer specific objective-type test questions connected with the principle taught
   2. repeat the principle orally
   3. give instances and examples involving the principle
   4. use the principle in solving unfamiliar problems in which such principles may be applied

   2.____

3. Which of the following is the LEAST desirable practice?

   1. Because such practice is psychologically sound, a mathematics teacher frequently uses a "warm-up," composed of quick, rapid drills and reviews of skills and abilities needed in the new lesson.
   2. When a new skill or concept is to be taught in mathematics, a teacher should plan on conducting a pretest to ascertain if prerequisite skills and concepts need reteaching or reinforcement.
   3. Teachers of mathematics should discourage pupils from guessing or estimating answers, because this interferes with the development of the rigorous scientific attitude inherent in the study of mathematics.
   4. Because of the frequency of changes in prices, the alert teacher should edit textbook problems before assigning them so that prices of commodities may be realistic.

   3.____

4. Students should recognize that ab + ac = a(b+c), for real numbers, involves which one of the following field postulates?

   1. Distributive   2. Commutative
   3. Associative   4. Multiplicative identity

   4.____

5. The conversion of several fractions with unlike denominators into equivalent fractions with a common denominator may be taught as an application of which one of the following properties?

   1. Commutative property for multiplication
   2. Associative property for multiplication

   5.____

3. Multiplicative identity property
4. Multiplicative inverse property

6. You are planning to teach the following three equivalents for 3/4:
   a. 3/4 = 75%   b. 3/4 = 0.75   c. 3/4 = 6/8
   Which of the following would be the BEST sequence to use?

   1. c, b, a
   2. b, c, a
   3. a, b, c
   4. c, a, b

7. A teacher presents the following problem to his mathematics class, "The length of each leg of a right triangle is 2 inches. Express the value of the cosine of an acute angle of that triangle."

   Henry writes $\dfrac{2}{\sqrt{8}}$. Jane writes $\dfrac{\sqrt{2}}{2}$.

   1. Both Henry and Jane are right.
   2. Henry is right and Jane is wrong.
   3. Henry is wrong and Jane is right.
   4. Both Henry and Jane are wrong.

8. With respect to mathematics homework, the LEAST desirable policy is to

   1. assign it regularly regardless of weekends or holidays
   2. not assign homework over weekends and holidays
   3. assign review work as well as new work
   4. assign additional drill to students for classroom infractions

9. Of the following, the BEST reason for a study of the Roman system of numeration is that such study

   1. provides good material for problems and recreations in mathematics
   2. enables students to read the dates on cornerstones of buildings
   3. reinforces an understanding of the decimal system of numeration, by contrast
   4. correlates with work in history

10. Which one of the following is the BEST motivation for a lesson on the solution of a quadratic equation?

    1. Have the student report on the history of quadratic equations.
    2. Tell the class that quadratic equations are important in science and industry.
    3. Give the class a verbal problem whose solution involves a quadratic equation.
    4. Tell the class that we have learned how to solve a linear equation and now we shall learn how to solve a quadratic equation.

11. If the distance from the earth to the moon is approximately 380,000 kilometers, then this distance, in meters, is

    1. 3.8×10^8
    2. 3.8×10^7
    3. 3.8×10^5
    4. 3.8×10^2

12. If c represents a real number and $c \neq 0$, , then the product of the additive and multiplicative inverses of c is

1. 1   2. -c   3. 1/c   4. -1

13. If 14_{five} is subtracted from 123_{four}, the result, in base ten is

    1. 18   2. 63   3. 109   4. 1299

14. For what value of k is 2 a root of the equation $2x^4 - 6x^3 + 4kx + 13 = 0$?

    1. 8/3   2. 3/8   3. -3/8   4. -8/3

15. The arithmetic mean between the roots of the equation $x^2 - 8x + 13 = 0$ is

    1. -6 1/2   2. 6 1/2   3. -4   4. 4

16. In a survey of the population of the village of Great Neck, it was found that 27% of the population needed eyeglasses, 14% of the population were lefthanded, and 5% needed eyeglasses and were also lefthanded. What percent of the population of Great Neck neither needed eyeglasses nor were lefthanded?

    1. 54   2. 59   3. 64   4. 69

17. The infinite repeating decimal of 0.02 (where 2 is repeated) is equal to

    1. 2/99   2. 11/500   3. 1/45   4. 22/999

18. The relation between the Fahrenheit and Celsius readings may be stated F = 9/5 C + 32. The numerical readings on both scales are the same when the number of degrees is

    1. -8   2. -40   3. 8   4. 40

19. Which of the following pairs of equations represent parallel lines in a rectangular coordinate system?

    1. 3x - 6y = 9
       2x + 4y = 6
    2. 3x - 6y = 9
       2x - 4y = 6
    3. 3x - 6y = 9
       x - 2y = 4
    4. 3x - 6y = 9
       x + 2y = 4

20. The graph below represents the solution set of which one of the following?
    -3 -2 -1 0 +1 +2 +3

    1. |x|<2   2. |x|≤2   3. |x|=2   4. |x|>2

21. Using the ordered pair (x, y) as an equivalent expression for x/y, the ordered pair representing the sum of (3,8) and (2,3) would be

    1. (1,5)   2. (5,11)   3. (25,24)   4. (25,6)

22. Two junior high school classes took the same test. The first class of 20 students attained an average grade of 80%. The second class of 30 students attained an average grade of 70%.
    The average grade for all students in both classes is

    1. 75%   2. 74%   3. 73%   4. 72%

23. The implication p → q is equivalent to

1. q→p 2. ~q→p 3. ~q→~p 4. ~p→~q

24. Which of the following groups of three numerals may represent the lengths of the sides of a right triangle?

    1. 9, 16, 25
    2. $\sqrt{3}, \sqrt{4}, \sqrt{5}$
    3. 1, 2, 3
    4. $\sqrt{1}, \sqrt{2}, \sqrt{3}$

25. The perimeter of a rectangle is 26. The maximum area that such a rectangle can enclose is

    1. 36 1/4   2. 42 1/4   3. 52   4. 169

26. A rectangular picture measuring x inches by y inches is surrounded by a frame of uniform width z inches. The number of square inches in the area of the frame is

    1. $2xz + 2yz + 4z^2$
    2. $xy + 2xz + 2yz + 4z^2$
    3. $2xz + 2yz + 2z^2$
    4. $2xy + 2xz + 2yz$

27. When $x^3 + 4x^2 + 3x - 10$ is divided by x-2, the remainder is

    1. 20   2. 8   3. -8   4. -10

28. Which one of the following subsets of the set of integers is closed under addition and multiplication?

    1. {0,1,2,3}   2. {0,1,2}   3. {0,1}   4. {0}

29. The total number of subsets of set {a,b,c} is

    1. 6   2. 7   3. 3   4. 8

30. Two points A and B are on the same side of a tower and in line with the center of the base of the tower. The angles of elevation of the top of the tower from A and B are equal to 60 and 30, respectively.
    If AB = 10, then the height of the tower is

    1. 5   2. $5\sqrt{3}$ 3. 10   4. $10\sqrt{3}$

31. In quadrilateral ABCD, as shown in accompanying sketch, angle A and angle C are right angles and $\overline{BD}$ is a diagonal. If BC = 15, CD = 20, and DA = 24, then the length of $\overline{AB}$ is

    1. 7
    2. 10
    3. 12
    4. 18

32. A running track is the ring formed by two concentric circles. The ring is 10 feet wide. The circumferences of the two circles differ by about _____ feet.

    1. 10   2. 30   3. 60   4. 100

33. If $0 \le x < 2\pi$, the number of elements in the solution set of the equation sin x - cos x = 0 is

    1. 1   2. 2   3. 3   4. 4

34. The intensity of illumination, I, on the page of a book, varies inversely as the square of the distance, d, between the book and the source of light.
    If I = 6 when d = 4, then the value of I when d = 8 is

    1. 24   2. 8   3. 5   4. 1.5

35. The product of two irrational numbers

    1. must be irrational
    2. must be rational
    3. may be equal to zero
    4. may be equal to an integer

36. If log4 y = 3, then y is equal to

    1. 81   2. 64   3. 12   4. 7

37. The odds AGAINST throwing an 8 in a single roll with two dice is

    1. 36 to 5   2. 5 to 1   3. 6 to 1   4. 31 to 5

38. Some properties that hold for equalities of real numbers are the
    a. reflexive property
    b. symmetric property
    c. transitive property
    Which of these properties hold true for the relation "greater than" applied to real numbers?

    1. a, c   2. b, c   3. a, b   4. c only

39. The path of a projectile is represented by the graph of $y = -x^2+8x-6$. The height of the projectile at the peak of its trajectory is

    1. 4   2. 8   3. 10   4. 42

40. The limit of $\frac{t^2-t-6}{t-3}$ as $t \to 3$

    1. is equal to 1
    2. is equal to 5
    3. is equal to 0
    4. does not exist

41. Solve for x: $4^{x-2} = 1$

    1. 1/4   2. 2   3. -2   4. 2 1/4

42. Twelve identical machines can finish a job in 8 days. The number of machines needed to finish the same job in 6 days would be

    1. 18   2. 16   3. 14   4. 9

43. A set of students' marks on a quiz worth ten points was as follows: 2, 2, 3, 3, 5, 5, 5, 7, 7, 7, 7, 9, 10.
    The arithmetic mean, median, and mode of this set of marks, arranged in DESCENDING order of magnitude, will be

1. median, mode, arithmetic mean
2. mode, arithmetic mean, median
3. mode, median, arithmetic mean
4. arithmetic mean, median, mode

44. The reciprocal of $\sqrt{3} - \sqrt{2}$ is equal to

   1. 1
   2. $\sqrt{3} + \sqrt{2}$
   3. $\dfrac{1}{\sqrt{3}} - \dfrac{1}{\sqrt{2}}$
   4. $-\sqrt{3} + \sqrt{2}$

45. The graph of the equation: $\dfrac{x^2}{9} - \dfrac{y^2}{16} = 1$ is a(n)

   1. parabola
   2. circle
   3. ellipse
   4. hyperbola

46. Find the number of cubic inches in the volume of a pyramid whose base is a square 6 inches on a side and whose altitude is 14 inches.

   1. 168
   2. 242
   3. 336
   4. 504

47. The area bounded by the x-axis and the graph of the equation $y = -x^2 + 6x$ is

   1. 0
   2. 36
   3. 54
   4. 108

48. If $18^c5 = 18^c r+2$ and $r \neq 3$, then $rc5 =$

   1. 18
   2. 462
   3. 7
   4. 13860

49. A woman who worked in the field of analytic geometry was

   1. Cavalieri
   2. Bernoulli
   3. Agnesi
   4. Cajori

50. If universal set, U, contains subsets A, B, and C, as shown in the accompanying Venn diagram, then the shaded area may be represented by

   1. $A \cap B \cap C$
   2. $(A \cap C) \cup (B \cap C)$
   3. $(A \cup C) \cap (B \cup C)$
   4. $(A \cap C) \cap C$

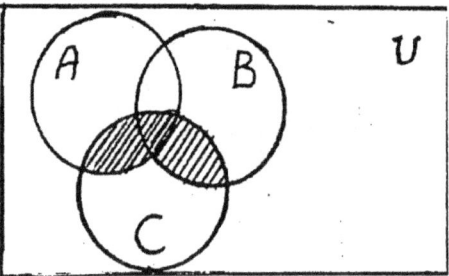

KEY (CORRECT ANSWERS)

1. 2	11. 1	21. 3	31. 1	41. 2
2. 3	12. 4	22. 2	32. 3	42. 2
3. 3	13. 1	23. 3	33. 2	43. 2
4. 1	14. 2	24. 4	34. 4	44. 2
5. 3	15. 4	25. 2	35. 4	45. 4
6. 1	16. 3	26. 1	36. 2	46. 1
7. 1	17. 3	27. 1	37. 4	47. 2
8. 4	18. 2	28. 4	38. 4	48. 2
9. 3	19. 3	29. 4	39. 3	49. 3
10. 3	20. 1	30. 2	40. 2	50. 2

SOLUTIONS TO PROBLEMS

1. A review of the order of operations would be helpful for the entire class. In this way, all students would understand that 3+5×2=3+10=13. (Ans. 2)

2. It would be best if a student can give an illustration of the principle being used. AFTER a student can give such an example, he could then attempt an unfamiliar problem employing this principle. (Ans. 3)

3. A student should not be discouraged from estimating an answer, since this practice will enable him to check the reasonableness of a final result. (Ans. 3)

4. The distributive property is usually written as: a(b+c) = ab+ac. This process is known as distributing multiplication over addition. (Ans. 1)

5. As an example: To change 3/2 into a fraction with a denominator of 8: 3/2 . 4/4 = 12/8. It can be seen that 4/4 = 1 is an identity element. (Ans. 3)

6. 3/4 = 6/8 can be shown using the identity element of 3/2. Then 3/4 = .75. can be shown by dividing 4 into 3.00. Finally, 3/4 = 75% can be taught by showing how to convert a decimal to a percent. (Ans. 1)

7. The hypotenuse $\sqrt{2^2 + 2^2} = 2\sqrt{2}$. So, cosine of either acute angle $\frac{2}{2\sqrt{2}} = \frac{1}{\sqrt{2}} = \frac{\sqrt{2}}{2}$. Note also that $\frac{\sqrt{2}}{2} \cdot \frac{\sqrt{2}}{\sqrt{2}} = \frac{2}{2\sqrt{2}} = \frac{2}{\sqrt{8}}$. Thus, both students are right. (Ans. 1)

8. Math problems should never be used for punitive purposes. (Ans. 4)

9. A student can appreciate the facility of using the decimal system after studying the Roman system's shortcomings. (Ans. 3)

10. By presenting a problem which cannot be solved by methods already learned by the students, the teacher can provide motivation to learn a new algebraic method (such as solving quadratic equations). (Ans. 3)

11. Since 1 kilometer = 1000 meters, 380,000 km = (380,000)(1000) = 380,000,000 or 3.8×10^8 m. (Ans. 1)

12. The additive, multiplicative inverses of c are -c and 1/c, respectively. Then (-c)(1/c) = -1. (Ans. 4)

13. 14_{five} = (1)(5)+4 = 9_{ten}. 123_{four} = (1)(16)+(2)(4) = 27_{ten}. The difference is 18, base 10. (Ans. 1)

14. $2(2^4) - 6(2^3) + 4k(2) + 13 = 0$. Solving, k = 3/8. (Ans. 2)

15. The sum of the roots = 8. Thus, their average =4. It should be noted that in the equation $Ax^2+Bx+C=0$, the sum of the roots is $\frac{-B}{A}$. (Ans. 4)

16. Let A = event that a person needs glasses, B = event that a person is lefthanded. Then P(A) = .27, P(B) = .14, and P(A B) = .05. Then P(A B) = .27+.14−.05 = .36. This means that 36% of the people either need glasses or are left-handed or both. Thus, 64% fall into neither category. (Ans. 3)

17. Let $N = .0\overline{2}$. Then $10N = .2\overline{2}$ and $9N = .2$. Thus, $N = \frac{.2}{9} = \frac{2}{90} = \frac{1}{45}$. (Ans. 3)

18. If F=C, then C=9/5c+32. Solving, C=−40. (Ans. 2)

19. Parallel lines have the same slope, but different y-intercepts. Both 3x−6y=9 and x−2y=4 have slopes of 1/2, but the y-intercepts are 3/2 and −2, respectively. (Ans. 3)

20. The graph translates to −2<x<2 which becomes |x|<2. (Ans. 1)

21. $\frac{3}{8} + \frac{2}{3} = \frac{25}{24}$, which corresponds to (25,24). (Ans. 3)

22. Average = $\frac{(20)(.80)+(30)(.70)}{50} = .74$ or 74%.

23. Using truth tables:

p	q	p→q	~q→~p
T	T	T	T
T	F	F	F
F	T	T	T
F	F	T	T

    (Ans. 3)

24. In any right triangle, $a^2+b^2=c^2$. Choice 4 is correct since $(\sqrt{1})^2(\sqrt{2})^2 = 3 = (\sqrt{3})^2$. (Ans. 4)

25. $2L+2W=26$ or $L+W=13$. Area$=LW=L(13-L)=13L-L^2$. Maximum area is found by setting dArea/dL=0. Thus, $13-2L=0$. So $L=6\ 1/2$. Now, $W=6\ 1/2$ and area$=(6\ 1/2)(6\ 1/2)=42\ 1/4$. (Ans. 2)

26. 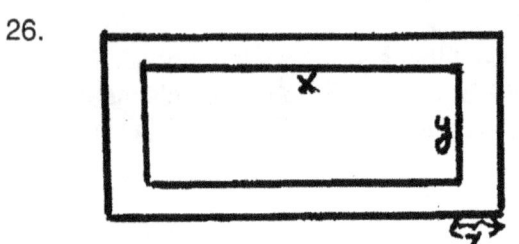 Area of frame=area of larger rectangle -area of smaller rectangle $=(x+2z)(y+2z)-xy = 2xz+4z^2$ (Ans. 1)

27. The remainder is the value of $x^3+4x^2+3x-10$ when $x=2$. Thus, $2^3+4(2^2)+3(2)-10=20$. (Ans. 1)

28. Only {0} is closed under addition and multiplication. {0,1,2,3} and {0,1,2} are open under both operations, and {0,1} is open under addition. (Ans. 4)

29. If a set has n elements, 2^n = number of subsets. Here n=3, so $2^3=8$. (Ans. 4)

30. 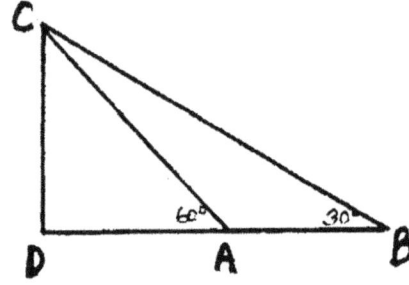 $\angle CAB =120°$ and $\angle ACB =30°$
Now, AC=AB=10
$\sin 60° = \dfrac{\sqrt{3}}{2} = \dfrac{CD}{10}$. CD$=5\sqrt{3}$. (Ans. 2)

31. BD$= \sqrt{15^2+ 20^2} = 25$. Then, AB $= \sqrt{25^2 - 24^2} = 7$. Here, the Pythagorean Theorem is being used. (Ans. 1)

32. Let d=diameter of inside circle. Then d+20=diameter of outside circle. The difference in circumferences = $= \pi (d+20) - \pi d = 20\pi$ or about 60 ft. (Ans. 3)

33. The only angles for which sin x=cos x are 45° and 225°(considering only angles between 0° and 360°). (Ans. 2)

34. $I=k/d^2$ k a constant. $6= k/16$ so k=96. Now, $I=96/d^2$. If d=8, I=96/64 =1.5. (Ans. 4)

35. As an example where the product of 2 irrational numbers may equal an integer, consider $(\sqrt{8})(\sqrt{2})=\sqrt{16} =4$. (Ans. 4)

36. $\log_4 y=3$ means $y=4^3=64$. (Ans. 2)

37. Probability of rolling an 8 = 5/36, so probability of NOT rolling an 8 = 31/36. This translates to odds of 31 to 5. (Ans. 4)
38. Let x,y be numbers. Reflexive property would say x>x, which is false. Symmetric property would say if x>y, then y>x. This is also false. But if z is a 3rd number and x>y and y>z, then x>z is true. This last statement illustrates transitivity. (Ans. 4)

39. To find maximum height, set dy/dx=0. Thus, -2x+8=0, or x=4. y=-4^2+8(4)-6=10=maximum height. (Ans. 3)

40. For all t ≠ 3, $\frac{t^2-t-6}{t-3} = t+2$. Thus, $\lim_{t \to 3} t+2 = 5$.
    (Ans. 2)

41. $4^{x-2}=1=4^0$ x-2=0. x=2. (Ans. 2)

42. Let x=# of required machines. Then 12/x = 6/8. x=16. (Ans. 2)

43. Mean=72/13 =5.54 Mode=7 Median=5. The descending order is mode, mean, median. (Ans. 2)

44. $\frac{1}{\sqrt{3}-\sqrt{2}} = \frac{1}{\sqrt{3}-\sqrt{2}} \cdot \frac{\sqrt{3}+\sqrt{2}}{\sqrt{3}+\sqrt{2}} = \frac{\sqrt{3}+\sqrt{2}}{1} = \sqrt{3}+\sqrt{2}$.
    (Ans. 2)

45. Any equation in the form $\frac{x^2}{a^2} - \frac{y^2}{b^2} = 1$ = 1 is an hyperbola. Here, a,b are constants.
    (Ans. 4)

46. V=1/3s^2h = 1/3b^2·14=168 in (Ans. 1)

47. Area = $\int_0^6 (-x^2+6x)dx = [(-\frac{x^3}{3}+3x^2)]_0^6 = 36$.
    (Ans. 2)

48. $18^C5 = \frac{18!}{5!13!}$ which $= \frac{18!}{13!5!} = 18^C13$. since = r+2 =13. r=11.
    NOW, 11^C5 = (11!)/[5! 6!] = 462.

49. By empirical knowledge.

50. Recoenize that the shaded area can be illustrated as

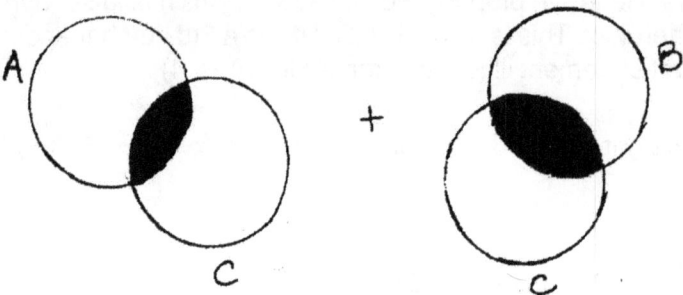

(A∩C) + (B∩C) = (A∩C) ∪ (B∩C)

EXAMINATION SECTION
TEST 1

DIRECTIONS: Each question or incomplete statement is followed by several suggested answers or completions. Select the one that BEST answers the question or completes the statement. *PRINT THE LETTER OF THE CORRECT ANSWER IN THE SPACE AT THE RIGHT.*

1. The SMALLEST integral value of k (k ≠0) that will make 8820k the cube of a positive integer is   1.____

    A. 100   B. 150   C. 1000   D. 1050

2. A wholesaler sells a certain article to the retailer at a profit of 60% of the cost. The retailer then sells this article to the consumer at a profit of 25% of his cost. The consumer pays $14.40.   2.____
The cost to the wholesaler was

    A. $7.20   B. $7.78   C. $10.80   D. $12.24

3. Two bicycles start traveling from the same point at the same time. One heads due west at 8 mph and the other heads due south at 15 mph.   3.____
In how many hours will they be 51 miles apart?
_____ hours.

    A. 2   B. approximately 2 1/4
    C. 3   D. 9

4. At the end of the first two years of school a pupil attains an average of 83% in 8 majors. The average required in 5 majors in the third year at school in order to achieve an overall average of 85% is   4.____

    A. 86.5%   B. 87%   C. 88.2%   D. 89%

5. An automobile covered the first 60 miles of its journey in 1 hour 30 minutes, and the next 87 miles in 2 hours. The *average* speed, in miles per hour, for the total trip is   5.____

    A. 41 3/4   B. 42   C. 58 4/5   D. 73 1/2

6. The standard deviation of the measures -4, 8, 0, -3, 9 is *closest to*   6.____

    A. 5.5   B. 4.8   C. 7.0   D. 1.0

7. An afternoon school study center has 36 students reporting for science, 43 for mathematics, and 44 for club activities. Of these, 20 report for both club activities and mathematics, 18 for both mathematics and science, and 13 for both club activities and science. 5 students report for all three activities.   7.____
What is the registration of the center?

    A. 75   B. 76   C. 77   D. 78

8. Which one of the following principles involving exponents that are natural numbers MOST directly suggests the definition that $x^0 = 1$?   8.____

A. $x^a \div x^b = x^{a-b}$, $x \neq 0$, $a > b$
B. $(x^a)^b = x^{ab}$
C. $x^a y^a = (xy)^a$
D. $x^a \div y^a = (\frac{x}{y})^a$, $y \neq 0$

9. The first and second terms of a geometric series are x^{-4} and x^t, and $(x \neq 0)$, respectively. If x^{52} is the eighth term of the series, t is equal to

    A. 5/2   B. 24/7   C. 4   D. 16/3

10. The resistance of a wire is directly proportional to the length and inversely proportional to the cross-sectional area. A 100-foot roll of a given size wire has a resistance of 4 ohms. A 250-foot roll of wire, whose diameter is one-third that of the wire on the first roll, will have a resistance, in ohms, of

    A. 3 1/3   B. 30   C. 54   D. 90

11. The multiplicative inverse of $1+\sqrt{2}$ is which one of the following?

    A. $1+\sqrt{2}$ B. $-1+\sqrt{2}$ C. $-1-\sqrt{2}$ D. $1-\sqrt{2}$

12.

$\otimes$	E	S	T	U
E	E	S	T	U
S	S	T	U	E
T	T	U	E	S
U	U	E	S	T

    The table at the left shows the result of the operation $\otimes$ on four elements. The element which is the inverse of $s \otimes s$ is

    A. T   B. U   C. E   D. S

13. Which one of the following describes the roots of the equation $x^2 - 2ix - 1 = 0$ (where $i = \sqrt{-1}$)?

    A. imaginary and equal
    B. imaginary and unequal
    C. rational and equal
    D. rational and unequal

14. Eliminating t from the parametric equations, $x = 1-e^t$ and $y = 1 + e^{-t}$, yields

    A. $y = \dfrac{1}{x-1}$ B. $y = \dfrac{x-2}{x-1}$ C. $y = \dfrac{2-x}{x-1}$ D. $y = \dfrac{x}{x-1}$

15. If $x \equiv 2 \pmod{7}$ and x is an integer between 0 and 12, then how many values does x have?

    A. 1   B. 2   C. 3   D. 4

16. If $|2x + 3| < 7$, then

    A. $-5 < x < -2$ B. $-2 < x < 5$
    C. $2 < x < 5$ D. $-5 < x < 2$

17. The solution set of $7x - 3 > (x+1)^2$ is which one of the following?

A. {x|x<1} ∩ {x|x>4}

B. {x|x<1} ∪ {x|x>4}

C. {x|x>1} ∩ {x|x<4}

D. {x|x>1} ∪ {x|x<4}

18. Two roots of the equation $x^3 + px + q = 0$ are -1 and 3. The third root is   18.____

    A. 1   B. -1   C. 2   D. -2

19. The ratio of $\log_2 15$ to $\log_8 225$ is   19.____

    A. 1/2   B. 2/1   C. 3/2   D. 2/3

20. If the logarithms in the equation $2 \log_{10} x - \log_{10} (30-2x) = 120$ are real numbers, then the solution set of this equation is which one of the following?   20.____

    A. {10, -30}   B. {10}   C. {-30}   D. { }

21. The determinant $\begin{vmatrix} a & 3 & 2 \\ 1 & 0 & 2 \\ 3 & 1 & -1 \end{vmatrix}$ has the value 19. The value of a   21.____

    A. -19   B. -19/2   C. -2   D. 2

22. In triangle ABC, base AB = 10 and the altitude to side AB = 8. A rhombus whose side = 7   22.____
    is inscribed in this triangle so that ∠A is common to both figures.
    The altitude of the rhombus is equal to

    A. 1.7   B. 2.4
    C. 5.6   D. None of the above

23. The longer base of an isosceles trapezoid is 2s and each of the other 3 sides is equal to   23.____
    s.
    The length of one of the diagonals is

    A. 4/3s   B. $\frac{4\sqrt{3}}{3}$s   C. $s\sqrt{2}$ D. $s\sqrt{3}$

24. Circle 0 and circle 0' are tangent internally. The diameter of circle 0' is equal to the radius   24.____
    of circle 0. From the point of tangency, T, chord TC of circle 0 is drawn intersecting circle
    0' at B.
    If TB = 8", then BC equals

    A. 8"   B. 16"   C. 24"   D. 32"

25. From external point P, tangent PA, and secant PCB are drawn to circle O. Line-segment   25.____
    AB is a diameter of the circle.
    If PC = 5" and chord CB = 4", the length of the diameter is

    A. $2\sqrt{5}$"   B. 5"   C. 6"   D. $3\sqrt{5}$"

4 (#1)

26. The line-segment joining the points (-4,1) and (8,-8) is cut by the y - axis to form two line-segments in the ratio 26._____

    A. 1:3   B. 1:2   C. 2:3   D. 2:5

27. The area of an equilateral triangle inscribed in a circle is $16\sqrt{3}$ 27._____
    The radius of the circle is

    A. $\frac{1}{3}\sqrt{3}$ B. $\frac{2}{3}\sqrt{3}$ C. $\frac{4}{3}\sqrt{3}$ D. $\frac{8}{3}\sqrt{3}$

28. If the radius of a circle is increased 50%, the area is *increased* _____%. 28._____

    A. 50   B. 125   C. 200   D. 225

29. If the lines whose equations are 2x + 3y = 7 and 3x + ay =12 intersect at an angle of 90, 29._____
    then the value of <u>a</u> is

    A. $-\frac{9}{2}$ B. $+\frac{9}{2}$ C. -2   D. +2

30. In the figure at the right, line AB is perpendicular to line 30._____
    BC. Line-segment XY slides into different positions so
    that X is always on AB, and Y is always on BC.
    If Z is the mid-point of XY, then the locus of Z is
    A. a line
    B. an arc of a circle
    C. one branch of a hyperbola
    D. an arc of an ellipse

    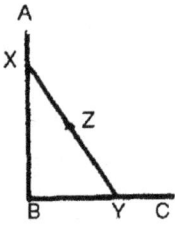

31. The area of the triangle, bounded by the lines whose equations are 5y = 4x - 5 and 2x + 31._____
    5y = 25 respectively, and the y - axis, is

    A. 10   B. 15   C. 18   D. 20

32. The coordinates of the vertex of the parabola y = x² + 8x -3 are 32._____

    A. (-8, -3)   B. (8, 125)   C. (4, 45)   D. (-4, -19)

33. If k is real and ax + by + c = 0 and dx + ey + f = 0 are the equations of two intersecting 33._____
    lines, then the equation of a system of lines passing through their intersection is

    A. (ax + by + c) + k (dx + ey + f) = 0

    B. k(ax+by+c) (dx+ey+f) = 0

    C. (ax + by + c) + (dx + ey + f) = k

    D. $k(\frac{ax+by+c}{dx+ey+f}) = 0$

34. The graph of |x| + |y| ≥ 1 includes points in quadrant(s) 34._____

    A. I but no other quadrants
    B. I and II but no other quadrants

C. I, II, and III but no other quadrants
D. I, II, III and IV

35. What is the equation of the locus of points P such that the sum of the distances from P to the two points (5, 0) and (-5, 0) is always 14 units?

   A. $24x^2 + 49y^2 = 1176$
   B. $24x^2 + 25y^2 = 600$
   C. $49x^2 + 24y^2 = 1176$
   D. $25x^2 + 24y^2 = 600$

36. If f = {(0,3),(1,5),(2,7)} and g = {(0,-1),(1,0),(2,3)}, then f - 2g is equal to

   A. {(0, 8),(1, 5),(2, 1)}
   B. {(0, 4),(1, 5),(2, 4)}
   C. {(0, 8),(1, 5),(2, 4)}
   D. {(0, 5),(-1, 5),(-2, 1)}

37. In the universe I = {-3, -2, -1, 0, 1, 2, 3}, if A = {-3, -2, -1}, B = {-1, 0, 1, 2, 3}, C = {-2, -1, 0} and C' is the complement of C, then A∪(B∩C') equals

   A. I
   B. ∅
   C. {-2, 1, 0, 1, 2, 3}
   D. {-3, -2, -1,1, 2, 3}

38. The line-segment joining A(1,-4, 3) to B(5,6,-1) in space is extended its own length through B to D.
    If the coordinates of D are (x_1, y_1, z_1), then z_1 =

   A. 5
   B. -5
   C. 1
   D. -5/2

39. The volumes of two similar polyhedrons are 8 cu.ft. and 27 cu.ft. respectively. If the total area of the first polyhedron is 112 sq. ft., how many square feet are there in the total area of the second polyhedron?

   A. 168
   B. 224
   C. 252
   D. 378

40. The center and radius of the sphere whose equation is $x^2 + 4x + y^2 - 2y + z^2 = 59$ are respectively

   A. (2, -1, 0) and 4
   B. (2, -1, 0) and 8
   C. (-2, 1, 0) and 4
   D. (-2, 1, 0) and 8

41. If a cylinder is circumscribed about a sphere, the ratio of the volume of the sphere to the volume of the cylinder is

   A. 1/3
   B. 1/2
   C. 2/3
   D. 3/4

42. If sin A = 0.8, and A is in the 1st quadrant, then sin (270° + A) is equal to

   A. -0.6
   B. 0.6
   C. -0.8
   D. 0.8

43. A body weighing 100 pounds rests on an inclined plane whose inclination is 30°. The force, in lbs., necessary to keep the body from sliding down the plane, assuming no friction, is

   A. 50
   B. $50\sqrt{3}$
   C. 100
   D. $100\sqrt{3}$

44. For what value of k is $\sin 2x = \dfrac{k \tan x}{1+\tan^2 x}$?

A. 1   B. 2   C. 3   D. $2\cos^2 x$

45. One of the cube roots of -8i is

    A. -2i   B. $\sqrt{3}+i$ C. $-\sqrt{3}+i$ D. $\sqrt{3}-i$

46. Transforming the polar equation $r = 5\sin\theta$ to an equation in rectangular coordinates yields

    A. $x^2 + y^2 = 5y$
    B. $x^2 + y^2 = 5x$
    C. $x + y^2 = 5$
    D. $x^2 + y = 5$

47. On the complex number plane, the coordinates of points' O, A and B are (0, 0), and (2, 5) and (5,2) respectively. If $\vec{OA} = \vec{OB} + \vec{OC}$, then the coordinates of point C are

    A. (7, 7)   B. (-3, 3)   C. (3, -3)   D. (3, 3)

48. Let a, b, c be the sides of an isosceles triangle with $a = b = \sqrt{2}$, $c > 2$. Then the angle opposite c

    A. is obtuse
    B. is acute
    C. may be either acute or obtuse
    D. may be a right angle

49. The number of elements in the solution set of $\sin x + \cos 2x = 1$, if the domain of x is $0 \le x < 2\pi$, is

    A. 2   B. 3   C. 4   D. 5

50. The expression $\dfrac{\sin x + \sin 3x}{\cos x + \cos 3x}$ is equal to which one of the following?

    A. $2\tan x$ B. $\tan 2x$ C. $\tan 3x$ D. $\tan 4x$

51. At a distance d from the foot of a tower the angle of elevation θ of the top of the tower is the complement of the angle of elevation of the top of a flagstaff on the tower. The length of the flagstaff is

    A. $d\cot\theta$
    B. $d(\sin\theta - \cos\theta)$
    C. $d(\tan\theta - \cot\theta)$
    D. $d(\cot\theta - \tan\theta)$

52. From a group of 5 men and 3 women a committee of 2 is chosen. What is the probability that the committee will consist of 2 men?

    A. 5/14   B. 1/3   C. 25/64   D. 2/5

53. In how many ways can six people sit in a row if two particular ones are not to sit next to each other?

    A. 240   B. 360   C. 480   D. 720

54. Given the following sets: the set of
    a. positive integers under addition
    b. integers under multiplication
    c. non-zero rational numbers under addition
    d. non-zero rational numbers under multiplication
    Which one of the above sets forms a group?

    A. a   B. b   C. c   D. d

55. The derivative of $\dfrac{1}{x\sqrt[3]{x^2}}$ with respect to x is

    A. $\dfrac{-5}{3x^2\sqrt[3]{x^2}}$ B. $\dfrac{2}{3x^2\sqrt[3]{x^2}}$

    C. $\dfrac{5}{3x^2\sqrt[3]{x^2}}$ D. $\dfrac{-5}{3\sqrt[3]{x^2}}$

56. What is the area in the first quadrant of the region bounded by the curve $y = x^3$ and the line $y = 4x$?

    A. 2   B. 3   C. 4   D. 5

57. The region bounded by $y = x^2$ and $y = 4$ is rotated about the y - axis. The volume of the solid of revolution generated by this rotation is

    A. 2π B. 4π C. 8π D. 16π

58. Assuming the use of α as a symbol for "ten" and β for "eleven", the number 283_{ten} when written in the duode-cimal system of numeration is represented by

    A. $1\beta7$ B. $1\alpha7$ C. 21β D. 21α

59. The problem of trisecting any angle with straight edge and compasses
    A. is still unsolved
    B. was proved impossible in the nineteenth century
    C. was proved impossible in Euclid's time
    D. can be done

60. Of the following, the mathematician that is generally considered to be the founder of the theory of games, is

    A. Boole   B. Poincaré   C. Von Neumann   D. Weierstrass

KEY (CORRECT ANSWERS)

1. D	16. D	31. B	46. A
2. A	17. C	32. D	47. B
3. C	18. D	33. A	48. A
4. C	19. C	34. D	49. C
5. B	20. D	35. A	50. B
6. A	21. D	36. D	51. D
7. C	22. D	37. D	52. A
8. A	23. D	38. B	53. C
9. C	24. A	39. C	54. D
10. D	25. C	40. D	55. A
11. B	26. B	41. C	56. C
12. A	27. D	42. A	57. C
13. A	28. B	43. A	58. A
14. B	29. C	44. B	59. B
15. B	30. B	45. D	60. C

SOLUTIONS TO PROBLEMS

1. $8820 = 2^2 \cdot 3^2 \cdot 5 \cdot 7^2$. In order to multiply this product by some factor so that the new number will be a perfect cube (and smallest non-zero perfect cube), the factor would be $2 \cdot 3 \cdot 5^2 \cdot 7 = 1050$. Note that $(8820)(1050) = 9,261,000$ which is $(210)^3$. (Ans. D)

2. Let c = wholesaler cost. The cost to the retailer = 1.6c and so the cost to the consumer becomes $(1.6c)(1.25) = 2c$. If $2c = \$14.40$, $c = 7.20$. (Ans. A)

3. Let h = number of hours. Then $(8h)^2 + (15h)^2 = 51^2$, since the Pythagorean Theorem can be used. Solving, h = 3. (Ans. C)

4. An average of 83% for 8 subjects means a total of 664 percentage points. Let x = average for the next 5 subjects, so that 5x = the total percentage points for these 5 subjects. To average 85% for all 13 subjects, $85\% = (664 + 5x)/13$. Solving, $x = 88.2\%$. (Ans. C)

5. Average speed = total distance/total time = 147/3.5 = 42 mph. (Ans. B)

6. Standard deviation $= \sqrt{[n\Sigma x^2 - (\Sigma x)^2]/n^2} = \sqrt{[5(170)-100]/25}$

    $= \sqrt{30} = 5.5$ (Ans. A)

7.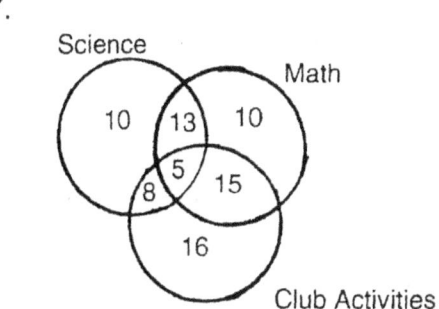

    These numbers were obtained by starting with 5 members which belong to all groups, then determining the numbers in each category. Total registration = 77. (Ans. C)

8. Since $x^a \div x^b = x^{a-b}$. Letting a=b, this can be written as $x^a \div x^a = x^0$ and $x^a \div x^a$ must be 1. Thus $x^0 = 1$. Note: The correction in selection A from a>b to a $\geq$ b. (Ans. A)

9. $x^t \div x^{-4} = x^{t+4}$ and this must be the common ratio of the geometric series. x^{52} = eighth term $= (x^{-4})(x^{t+4})^7 = x^{7t+24}$. Now, $52 = 7t + 24$ and so t=4. (Ans. C)

10. R = KL/A, where R = resistance, K = constant of proportionality, L = length, A = area. Let 9 = cross sectional area of the first wire. Since the 2nd wire has a diameter only $\frac{1}{3}$ that of the 1st wire, its area would be $\frac{1}{9}(9) = 1$. $4 = (K)(100)/9$ and K=.36. Now, resistance of 2nd wire = $(.36)(250)/1 = 90$ ohms. (Ans. D)

11. $(1 + \sqrt{2})(M) = 1$, where M = multiplicative inverse.

$M = 1/(1+\sqrt{2}) = [1/(1 + \sqrt{2})][(1-\sqrt{2})/(1-\sqrt{2})] = -1$ (Ans. B)

12. E = identity element since E⊗ any element = that element. S⊗S = T and the inverse of T is T since T⊗T = E. (Ans. A)

13. The roots of $x^2 - 2ix - 1 = 0$ are $[2i \pm \sqrt{(2i)^2 - 4(1)(-1)}]/2 = (2i \pm 0)/2 = i$ (double root). This is an imaginary root. (Ans. A)

14. Since $e^t = 1-x$, $e^{-t} = \dfrac{1}{1-x}$ So $y = 1+e^{-t} = 1+\dfrac{1}{1-x} = \dfrac{2-x}{1-x} = \dfrac{x-2}{x-1}$ (Ans. B)

15. $x \equiv 2 \pmod{7}$ and $0 \leq x \leq 12$ implies that $x=2$ and $x=9$. Thus, x can assume 2 values. (Ans. B)

16. $|2x+3|<7$ means $-7<2x+3<7$, which yields $-5<x<2$. (Ans. D)

17. $7x-3>(x+1)^2$ simplifies to $x^2-5x+4<0$ or $(x-4)(x-1)<0$. The solution is $1<x<4$, which means $\{x|x>1\} \cap \{x|x<4\}$. . (Ans. C)

18. $(-1)^3+p(-1)+q=0$ and $(3)^3+p(3)+q=0$. Solving these 2 equations yields $p = -7$ and $q^3 = -6$. The original equation becomes $x^3-7x-6=0$. Since $x^3-7x-6 = (x+1)(x-3)(x+2)$, the third root is -2. (Ans. D)

19. $\text{Log}^2 15 = x$ means $2^x = 15$. $\text{Log}_8 225 = y$ means $8^y = 225$ or $(2^3)y = 15^2$. This implies $2^{\frac{3}{2}y}$ and so $\dfrac{3}{2}y$. Thus, the ratio of $\text{Log } 15_2$ to $\text{Log}_8 225 = x/y = 3/2$.
(Ans. C)

20. $2\text{Log}_{10}x = \text{Log}_{10}x^2$. $2\text{Log}_{10}x - \text{Log}_{10}(30-2x) = \text{Log}_{10} \text{Log}_{10}(\dfrac{x^2}{30-2x})$

Now if $= \text{Log}_{10}(\dfrac{x^2}{30-2x})=120, \dfrac{x^2}{30-2x} = 10^{120}$. Thus, the solution becomes none of the given real numbers. In fact, because 30-2x must be >0, this would force x<15. Final answer is {}. (Ans. D)

21. The value of the determinant is gotten by: (a)(0)(-1) + (3)(2)(3) + (2)(1)(1) - (2)(0)(3) - (3)(1)(-1) - (a)(1)(2) and this =19. Thus, 18+2+3-2a = 19 and so a=2. (Ans. D)

11 (#1)

22.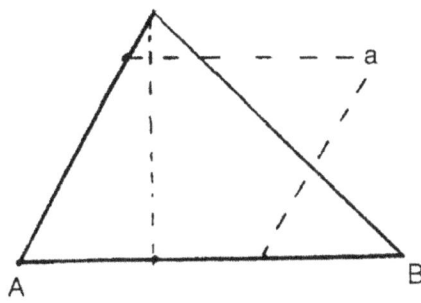

The drawing would be impossible, since the rhombus would extend beyond the bounds of the triangle. (Ans. D)

23.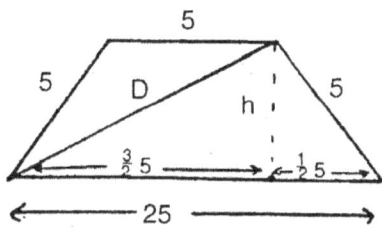

$h^2+(\frac{1}{2}s)^2=s^2$, which yields $h=s\sqrt{3}/2$

Now, $(\frac{3}{2}s)^2+(5\sqrt{3}/2)^2=D^2$. Thus, $D=s\sqrt{3}$. (Ans. D)

↓

24.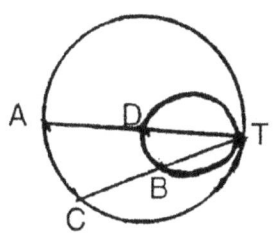

△TBD and △ACT are similar since ∠ACT = ∠DBC = 90° and both triangles contain ∠DTB. Also, $\overline{AC} \parallel \overline{DB}$ so that $\frac{TD}{DA}=\frac{TB}{BC}$. Now since $\frac{TD}{TA}=\frac{1}{2}$, $\frac{TD}{DA}=\frac{1}{1}=\frac{8}{BC}$
Thus, BC=8. (Ans. A)

25.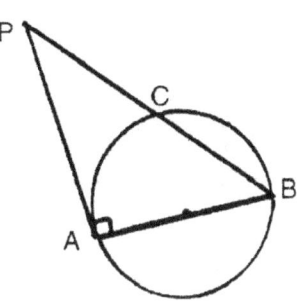

$\frac{PC}{PA}=\frac{PA}{PB}, \frac{5}{PA}=\frac{PA}{9}, PA=\sqrt{45}$. Since ∠A =90°, $(PA)^2+(AB)^2=(PB)^2$. $45+(AB)^2=81$. Thus, AB=6. (Ans. C)

26.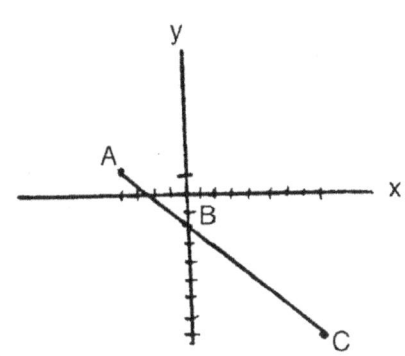

Slope of $\overline{AC}=\frac{-8-1}{8-(-4)}=-\frac{3}{4}$ B is located at (0,-2). $AB=\sqrt{4^2+3^2}=5$ and $BC=\sqrt{8^2+6^2}=10$. 5:10=1:2 (Ans. B)

27. 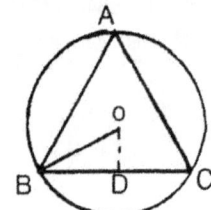 Since the area of $\triangle ABC = 16\sqrt{3}$ and this is equivalent to $\dfrac{S^2}{4}\sqrt{3}$ (s=side of $\triangle ABC$), s=8. Letting 0 = center of circle and $\overline{OD} \perp \overline{BC}$, we know that BD=4 and $\angle OBD = 30°$. So, OD = $\dfrac{1}{2}$OB. Let OB=x. $4^2 + (\dfrac{1}{2}x)^2 = x^2$. Solving, $x\sqrt{\dfrac{64}{3}} = \dfrac{8}{3}\sqrt{3}$. (Ans. D)

28. If R = original radius, area = πR^2. If new radius = 1.5R, new area = $\pi(1.5R)^2 = 2.25\pi R^2$. The area increased $1.25\pi R^2$, which represents a 125% increase. (Ans. B)

29. Two lines which intersect at 90° will have slopes which are negative inverses of each other. The slope of 2x+3y=7 is $-\dfrac{2}{3}$, and so the slope of 3x+ay=12 must be $\dfrac{3}{2}$. Thus, $-\dfrac{3}{a} = \dfrac{3}{2}$ and a=-2. (Ans. C)

30. 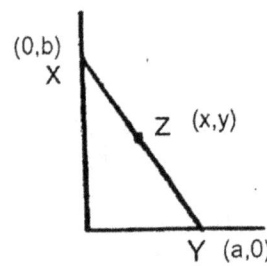 Z = midpt, distance of XY= constant. Thus, $\sqrt{a^2+b^2}$ is a constant. Now, distance of XZ = distance of YZ $\sqrt{x^2+(y-b)^2} = \sqrt{(x-a)^2+y^2}$. Simplifying, $x^2+y^2-2by+b^2 = x^2-2ax+a^2+y^2$. (I am unsure of how to find the locus of Z) (Ans. B)

31. 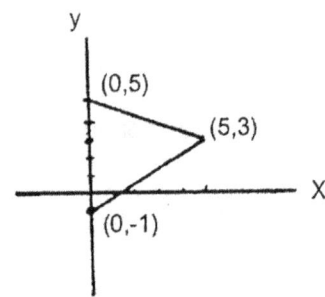 Using the segment connecting (0, -1) and (0, 5) as the base, the height would extend from (5, 3) to (0, 3). Area = (1/2)(base)(height) = $(\dfrac{1}{2})(6)(5) = 15$. (Ans. B)

32. Rewrite $y=x^2+8x-3$ as $y=(x+4)^2-19$. The vertex is (-4,-19) and this represents the lowest point of the parabola. (Ans. D)

33. Since ax+by+c=0 and dx+ey+f=0, the sum of these two equations would also be zero. Also, k(dx+ey+f)=0. Thus, (ax+by+c) + k(dx+ey+f)=0. (Ans. A)

34. 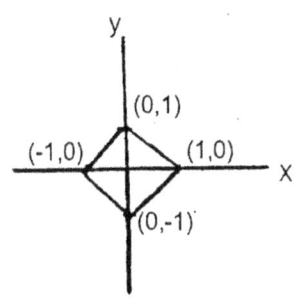 The square on the left is identified by 1x1+1y1=1. The graph of 1x1+1y1≥1 would, also include everything exterior to the square, and so would include points in all 4 quadrants. (Ans. D)

35. Let P be located at (x,y). Then $\sqrt{(x-5)^2+(y-0)^2}+\sqrt{(x+5)^2+(y-0)^2}=14$ Simplified, this equation becomes $24x^2+49y^2=1176$, which represents an ellipse. (Ans. A)

36. 2g = {(0, -2),(2, 0),(4, 6)}. Thus, f-2g = {(0, 5),(-1, 5),(-2, 1)}. (Ans. D)

37. C'={-3, 1, 2, 3}, so B∩C'={1, 2, 3}. Finally, A∪{1, 2, 3} = {-3, -2, -1, 1, 2, 3}. (Ans. D)

38. Since B is the midpoint of $\overline{AD}$, $-1=\frac{3+z_1}{2}$, $z_1=-5$. (Ans. B)

39. The volumes are in the same ratio as the cubes of any 2 corresponding sides. So, the sides are in the ratio of 2:3. The areas are in the ratio of $2^2:3^2=4:9$. Now, 4:9 = 112:x. Solving, x=252. (Ans. C)

40. Rewrite $x^2+4x+y^2-2y+z^2=59$ as $(x+2)^2+(y-1)^2+(z-0)^2=64$. The center of the sphere is (-2,1,0) and the radius = 8. (Ans. D)

41. The volume of the sphere $=\frac{4}{3}\pi R^3$ and since the cylinder has a radius and height equal to 2R, its volume = $\pi R^2(2R)=2\pi R^3$, the ratio of these two volumes is $\frac{4}{3}:2$, or 2:3. (Ans. C)

42. sin(270°+A) = -sin(90°-A) = -0.6 since 270+A lies in the fourth quadrant. (Ans. A)

43. 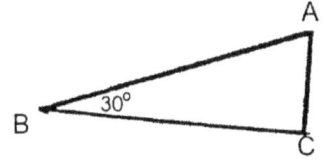 Assume the body is located at point A.
Since ∠C=90° and ∠B=30°, $AC=\frac{1}{2}AB$.
The 100 lbs. exerts a force downward. Thus,
(unknown force)(AB) = 100 $\frac{1}{2}$ (AB) =50(AB).
Finally, the unknown force =50 lbs.

44. Simplify Ktanx/(1+tan²x) to [Ksin x/cos x] ÷ sec²x, which = Ksin x cos x. Since sin 2x = 2 sin x cos x, K=2. (Ans. B)

45. Change $-8i$ to its equivalent form of $8(\cos 270° + i \sin 270°)$. The 3 cube roots are $2(\cos 90° + i \sin 90°)$, $2(\cos 210° + i \sin 210°)$, and $2(\cos 330° + i \sin 330°)$. These roots can be written as: $2i$, $-\sqrt{3}i$, and $\sqrt{3}-i$. Choice D identifies one of these roots. (Ans. D)

46. Since $r^2 = x^2 + y^2$ and $\sin\theta = y/r$, $r = 5\sin\theta$ can be rewritten as: $\sqrt{x^2+y^2} = 5(y/\sqrt{x^2+y^2})$. Simplifying, we get $x^2 + y^2 = 5y$. (Ans. A)

47. $\overline{OA} = 2 + 5i$ and $\overline{OB} = 5 + 2i$. $\overline{OA} - \overline{OB} = \overline{OC} = -3 + 3i$, which means that C is located at $(-3, 3)$. (Ans. B)

48. 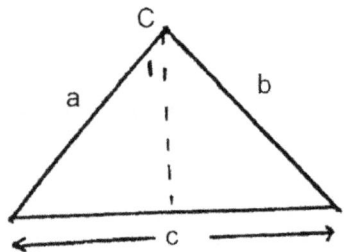 If c were equal to 2, each smaller triangle would have dimensions $1, 1, \sqrt{2}$ and so $\angle 1$ would be $45°$. This would force $\angle C$ to be $90°$. If $c > 2$, $\angle 1 > 45°$ and thus $\angle C > 90°$ and consequently is an obtuse angle. (Ans. A)

49. $\sin x + \cos 2x = 1$ can be written as $\sin x - 2\sin^2 x + 1 = 1$, which is $\sin x(1 - 2\sin x) = 0$. Solving, $\sin x = 0$ gives $0, \pi$. Solving, $1 - 2\sin x = 0$ gives $\dfrac{\pi}{6}, \dfrac{5\pi}{6}$. Thus, there are 4 answers.

50. $\sin 3x = \sin(2x+x) = \sin 2x \cos x + \sin x \cos 2x$. Further simplifying the numerator $\sin x + \sin 3x$ becomes $4\sin x \cos^2 x$. $\cos 3x = \cos(2x+x) = \cos 2x \cos x - \sin 2x \sin x$. Further simplifying the denominator $\cos x + \cos 3x$ becomes $2 \cos x \cos 2x$. Now, $4 \sin x \cos^2 x / 2 \cos x \cos 2x = (2\tan x)(\cos^2 x / \cos 2x)$. Rewriting $\cos^2 x / \cos 2x$ as $1 \div [(\cos^2 x - \sin^2 x)/\cos^2 x] = 1/(1-\tan^2 x)$, the original fraction is now written as $2\tan x/(1-\tan^2 x)$, which is equivalent to $\tan 2x$. (Ans. B)

51. 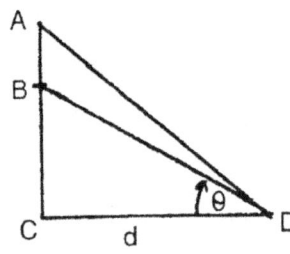 $\angle ADC = 90 - \theta$. $\tan\theta = \dfrac{BC}{d}$, so $BC = d\tan\theta$

$\tan(90-\theta) = \dfrac{AC}{d}$, so $AC = d\tan(90-\theta) = d\cot\theta$.

$AB = x = AC - BC = d\cot\theta - d\tan\theta = d(\cot\theta - \tan\theta)$. (Ans. D)

52. The total number of committees is $_8C_2 = \dfrac{8 \cdot 7}{2 \cdot 1} = 28$. The number of committees which will contain only men is $_5C_2 = \dfrac{5 \cdot 4}{2 \cdot 1} = 10$

Thus, the required probability = $\dfrac{10}{28}$ or $\dfrac{5}{14}$. NOTE: $_nC_R$ means the number of combinations of R objects from a group of n objects. Of course, $n \geq R$. (Ans. A)

53. We want to eliminate all permutations where the two individuals would be both occupying seats 1 and 2, or seats 2 and 3, or ... or seats 5 and 6. This represents $10({_4}P_4) = 240$. .
The total number of permutations $= {_6}P_6 = 6 \cdot 5 \cdot 4 \cdot 3 \cdot 2 \cdot 1 = 720$. Thus, the number of acceptable arrangements = 480. (Ans. C)

53._____

54. A group must have associativity, closure, identity element, and inverses. The non-zero rational numbers under multiplication would satisfy each requirement. The identity element = 1 and for each x, the number $\frac{1}{x}$ = inverse. (Ans. D)

54._____

55. $\frac{1}{x \cdot \sqrt[3]{x^2}} = x^{-\frac{5}{3}}$. The derivative $= \frac{-5}{3} x^{-\frac{8}{3}} = \frac{-5}{3x^2 \sqrt[3]{x^2}}$. (Ans. A)

56.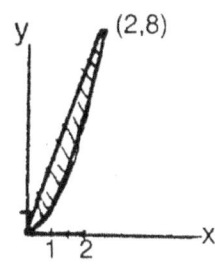

Shaded area $= \int_0^2 (4x - x^3) dx = [2x^2 - \frac{x^4}{4}]_0^2 = 8 - 4$
$= 4$. (Ans. C)

57.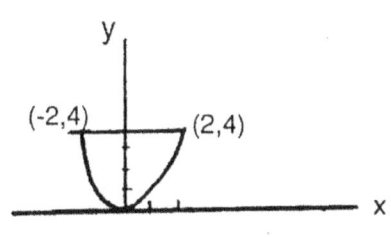

$y = x^2$ can be rewritten as $x = \sqrt{y}$. In revolving the curve $x = \sqrt{y}$ around the y axis, the volume of the solid of revolution $= \int_0^4 \pi (\sqrt{y})^2 dy = \pi [\frac{y^2}{2}]_0^4$
$= \pi(8) - \pi(0) = 8\pi$ (Ans. C)

58. The leftmost placeholder represents $12^2 = 144$. Since $\overline{283 \div 144} = 1$ with remainder of 139, the first dash = 1. The 2nd dash represents 12 and 139 consists of 11 12's with remainder of 7. Thus, the symbol for 11, β, occupies the 2nd dash. 7 must occupy the rightmost dash. The final answer = 1 β 7. (Ans. A)

58._____

59. The trisection of any angle using only a straight-edge and compass was proved impossible in the 19th century. The proof is based on Galois' theory of groups. (Ans. B)

59._____

60. A textbook entitled "Theory of Games and Economic Behavior" was developed by Von Neumann and Morgenstern. This book's first edition was published in 1944. (Ans. C)

60._____

EXAMINATION SECTION
TEST 1

DIRECTIONS: Each question or incomplete statement is followed by several suggested answers or completions. Select the one that BEST answers the question or completes the statement. *PRINT THE LETTER OF THE CORRECT ANSWER IN THE SPACE AT THE RIGHT.*

1. The statement that is mathematically CORRECT is   1.____
   1. $\sin 2x = 2 \sin x \cos x$ for all values of x
   2. $x^0 = 1$ for all values of x
   3. $\sqrt{x^2} = x$ for all values of x
   4. $\dfrac{x^2-1}{x-1} = x + 1$ for all values of x

2. Four pupils answered a question. Pupil A's answer was 37.5×10^{-6}, pupil B's answer was   2.____
   $3/8 \times 10^{-6}$, pupil C'so answer was $15/4 \times 10^{-5}$ and pupil D's answer was .000037 1/2. The answer that was NOT equivalent to the others was that of pupil

   1. A   2. B   3. C   4. D

3. In teaching a unit on reduction of algebraic fractions, a teacher is planning to include the   3.____
   study of the following fractions:

   a. $\dfrac{x^2-3x-4}{x^2-1}$

   b. $\dfrac{30x^7}{6x^3}$

   c. $\dfrac{x^3-4x}{2x^2-2x-4}$

   d. $\dfrac{15x^2-10x}{5x^2+20x}$

   The BEST sequence in which to present these factors to the class is

   1. b, d, a, c   2. d, b, a, c   3. b, a, d, c   4. b, d, c, a

4. An eleventh year mathematics class was studying operations with complex numbers.   4.____
   Asked to simplify the fraction $\dfrac{\sqrt{16}}{\sqrt{-4}}$, student A wrote: $\dfrac{\sqrt{16}}{\sqrt{-4}} = \dfrac{\sqrt{16}}{\sqrt{-4}} = \sqrt{-4} = 2i$, while

   student B wrote: $\dfrac{\sqrt{16}}{\sqrt{-4}} = \dfrac{4}{2i} = \dfrac{4i}{2i^2} = \dfrac{4i}{-2} = -2i$

   1. Student A is CORRECT and student B is INCORRECT.
   2. Student B is CORRECT and student A is INCORRECT.
   3. Both students are CORRECT.
   4. Both students are INCORRECT.

5. A teacher tied a length of string 15 cm. long between two thumbtacks 10 cm. apart. He drew a curve by moving a pencil such that it always kept the string taut. The curve he traced in this manner was a(n)

    1. ellipse
    2. catenary
    3. parabola
    4. cycloid

6. A pupil solved the equation $x+\sqrt{x-2}=4$ and got roots of 3 and 6. This solution is

    1. *Incorrect*, because one root is extraneous.
    2. *Correct*, because all radical equations have two roots.
    3. *Correct*, because both solutions give rational square roots.
    4. *Incorrect*, because the negative value of the square root was rejected.

7. A class in eleventh year mathematics studying trigonometric identities was asked to represent the binomial $\tan\theta + \cot\theta$ as a monomial. Student A obtained the result $\frac{\sec^2\theta}{\tan\theta}$ student B obtained the result $\frac{2}{\sin 2\theta}$, and student C obtained the result $\sec\theta \cos\theta$ The CORRECT answers were given by

    1. students A and B *only*
    2. students B and C *only*
    3. students A and C *only*
    4. all three students

8. A student in a tenth year mathematics class has studied the theorem stating that base angles of an isosceles triangle are congruent. He then concludes that a triangle in which no two angles are congruent must be scalene. He is reasoning

    1. *correctly*, from an inverse.
    2. *incorrectly*, from an inverse.
    3. *correctly*, from a contrapositive.
    4. *incorrectly*, from a contrapositive.

9. A teacher of tenth year mathematics is planning to teach the proofs of the following theorems to the class. What is the PROPER sequence in which these theorems should be taught?

    a. If the altitude is drawn to the hypotenuse of a right triangle, either leg of the triangle is the mean proportional between the hypotenuse and the projection of that leg on the hypotenuse.
    b. Two triangles are similar if two angles of one are congruent respectively to two angles of the other.
    c. The Pythagorean theorem.
    d. If the altitude is drawn to the hypotenuse of a right triangle, the two triangles formed are similar to the original triangle and similar to each other.

    1. c, b, d, a
    2. d, a, b, c
    3. b, a, d, c
    4. b, d, a, c

10. A pupil is given two sides and the included angle of an obtuse triangle and is asked to find the third side.
    The BEST method to use is

    1. the law of sines
    2. the law of cosines
    3. the Pythagorean theorem
    4. DeMoivre's theorem

11. The sum of the reciprocals of the roots of the equation $ax^2 + bx + c = 0$ will be

    1. -a/b   2. -b/a   3. -b/c   4. -c/b

12. A square and an equilateral triangle have equal perimeters and the area of the triangle is $9\sqrt{3}$ square inches. The length of the diagonal of the square is

    1. $\dfrac{9}{2}$ 2. $\dfrac{9\sqrt{2}}{4}$ 3. $6\sqrt{2}$ 4. $\dfrac{9\sqrt{2}}{2}$

13. If each of the statements AB< CD and AB = CD leads to a contradiction, then AB>CD. This type of reasoning is referred to as

    1. inductive   2. indirect
    3. direct   4. deductive

14. A box contains one red ball, three black balls, and five white balls. A game is played as follows: two balls are drawn in succession at random without replacement. The player wins if the two balls drawn are the same color. The probability of winning the game is

    1. 2/9   2. 1/3   3. 3/8   4. 13/36

15. A number written in base 7 is 1231_{seven}. This number written in base 5 is

    1. 3323_{five} 2. 3233_{five} 3. 1321_{five} 4. 463_{five}

16. A television console is listed in a catalog for $1,000. If the set is sold with successive discounts of 20% and 10%, the ACTUAL selling price will be

    1. $700   2. $720   3. $780   4. $850

17. A train makes a trip between two towns at the rate of <u>a</u> miles per hour and makes the return trip on the same track at the rate of <u>b</u> miles per hour. The *average* rate for the round trip is

    1. $\dfrac{2ab}{a+b}$ 2. $\dfrac{a+b}{2}$ 3. $\sqrt{ab}$ 4. $\dfrac{2(a+b)}{ab}$

18. The expressions a+bc and (a+b)(a+c) are

    1. *never* equal   2. *always* equal
    3. equal when a+b+c=1   4. equal when a+b+c=0

19. If n is an integer, then $\left(\dfrac{1}{-\sqrt{-1}}\right)^{4n+5}$ is equal to

    1. 1   2. -1   3. i   4. -i

20. If x+y=2xy, then $\dfrac{1}{x}+\dfrac{1}{y}$ equals

    1. 1   2. 2
    3. 3   4. none of these

21. If the tenth term of an arithmetic sequence is 15 and the twentieth term is 35, then the thirtieth term is

    1. 525
    2. 50
    3. 55
    4. 61

22. In a three digit number, the units digit is two more than the tens digit. The sum of the digits is 12. The number with the digits reversed is 198 less than the original number. The original number must be between

    1. 100 and 200
    2. 200 and 300
    3. 400 and 500
    4. 600 and 700

23. Two roots of the equation $x^3 + cx + d = 0$ are -1 and -2. The third root is

    1. 1
    2. -3
    3. 3
    4. -7

24. An automobile radiator contains 15 quarts of a 20% solution of antifreeze. How many quarts of the solution should be drained from the radiator and replaced with an equal amount of pure antifreeze to raise the concentration to 50%?

    1. 4 1/2
    2. 4 3/8
    3. 5 5/8
    4. 7 1/2

25. If f(x) and g(x) are two functions defined by $f(x) = 2x + 1$ and $g(x) = x^2 - 2$, then g[f(x)] is

    1. $x^2 + 2x - 1$
    2. $4x^2 + 4x - 1$
    3. $2x^2 - 3$
    4. $4x^2 + 4x + 1$

26. If $\log 4x^5 - \log x^4 + \log 5 = 4$, the value of x is

    1. 1/5
    2. 5
    3. 50
    4. 500

27. The parabola whose equation is $(y-1)^2 = 4(x+2)$ has

    1. its vertex at (2,-1)
    2. its focus at (2,1)
    3. a directrix whose equation is x-3
    4. a relative minimum point

28. If, in triangle ABC, AB > BC, which relationship is NOT possible?

    1. m<C < m<A
    2. m<C = m<B
    3. AC > AB
    4. AC = CB

29. The bases of a trapezoid are 20 and 12. If the legs are extended until they meet, the triangle formed on the shorter base has an area of 54. The area of the trapazoid is

    1. 96
    2. 240
    3. 192
    4. 150

30. 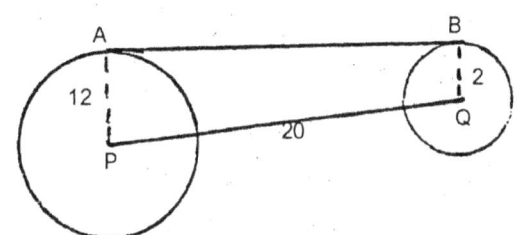 In the figure, $\overline{AB}$ is tangent to circle P at A and tangent to circle Q at B. If AP = 12, BQ = 2 and PQ = 20, then AB equals

   1. 20
   2. $10\sqrt{3}$
   3. $12\sqrt{3}$
   4. 16 1/3

31. In triangle ABC, $\overline{DE}$ is parallel to $\overline{BC}$ and $\overline{FE}$ is parallel to $\overline{DC}$. If AF=4, and FD=6, then DB is

   1. 7 1/2
   2. 10
   3. 12
   4. 15

   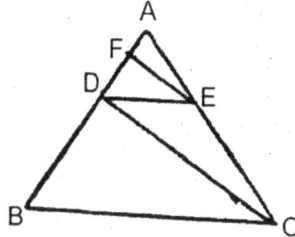

32. In right triangle ABC, $\overline{CD}$ is the median to hypotenuse $\overline{AB}$. If CD = AC, then the number of degrees in angle CAB is

   1. 67 1/2
   2. 60
   3. 45
   4. 30

33. Which of the following is equal to cos (-115)°?

   1. -sin 25°
   2. cos 25°
   3. -cos 25°
   4. sin 25°

34. When drawn on the same set of axes, what is the number of intersections of the graphs of y = sin and y = cos x as x varies from $\frac{3\pi}{2}$ to 2π radians?

   1. 1
   2. 2
   3. 3
   4. 0

35. The graph of $y = \frac{\sin 2x}{2}$ has an amplitude and a period, respectively, of

   1. $1, 2\pi$
   2. $2, \pi$
   3. $\frac{1}{2}, 2\pi$
   4. $\frac{1}{2}, \pi$

36. $\frac{\cot 150°}{\csc 210°}$ equals

   1. sin 315°
   2. tan 120°
   3. sin 135°
   4. cos 330°

37. The value of Arctan 2 + Arctan 3 is

    1. $\dfrac{2\pi}{3}$ 2. $\dfrac{3\pi}{4}$ 3. $\dfrac{5\pi}{6}$ 4. Arctan 5

38. If x and y are both acute angles, and if $\sin^2 x + \sin^2 y = 1$, then

    1. x = y
    2. x = 90° - y
    3. x = 90° + y
    4. y = 90° + x

39. Given f(x) = sin x and g(x) = cos x. Which one of the following is FALSE?

    1. $g(\dfrac{x}{2}) = \dfrac{g(x)}{2}$
    2. $f(\dfrac{\pi}{2} - x) = g(x)$
    3. f(2x) = 2 f(x)g(x)
    4. g(-x) = g(x)

40. A line is tangent to the inner circle of 2 concentric circles and intersects the outer circle at points A and B. If line segment AB is 12, then the area between the two circles is

    1. 6π 2. 12π 3. 36π 4. 144π

41. $\dfrac{x}{x^2-1} > 0$ if and only if

    1. x > 1 or -1 < x < 0
    2. x > 1
    3. |x| > 1
    4. |x| < 1

42. The domain of $f(x) = \dfrac{1}{\sqrt{9-x^2}}$, if f(x) is real, is

    1. x < 3
    2. |x| ≤ 3
    3. |x| ≤ 3
    4. |x| > 3

43. The value of $(1+i)^4$ is

    1. -4 + 8i
    2. 4 - 8i
    3. -4
    4. 4

44. The negation of p → q is

    1. p → ~q
    2. p ∧ ~q
    3. p ∨ ~q
    4. ~p → ~q

45. The equation of $x^9 + 16x^3 + 64 = 0$ has _____ positive root(s), _____ negative root(s), and _____ imaginary roots.

    1. 2, 1, 6
    2. 1, 0, 8
    3. 0, 1, 8
    4. 8, 1, 0

46. The coefficient of the fifth term of the expansion of $(x+1)^8$ is equal to

    1. 28 2. 56 3. $8C_4$ 4. $8C_5$

47. One of the cube roots of -8i is   47.____

    1. -2i
    2. $\sqrt{3}+i$
    3. $\sqrt{3}-i$
    4. $-\sqrt{3}+i$

48. The sum of one positive number and the square of a second positive number is 15. Their   48.____
    product is a MAXIMUM. The LARGER of the two numbers is

    1. $\sqrt{5}$
    2. $\sqrt{15}$
    3. 5
    4. 10

49. The area bounded by the parabolas $y = 8x - 2x^2$ and $y = 4x - x^2$ is   49.____

    1. 32/3
    2. 64/3
    3. 3.32
    4. 160/3

50. A particle moves along a straight line with acceleration 6t - 6, where t is time. At t=0, it is   50.____
    at point P and its velocity is 5. What is the distance from P and t = 2?

    1. 10
    2. 6
    3. 3
    4. 0

KEY (CORRECT ANSWERS)

1. 1	11. 3	21. 3	31. 4	41. 1
2. 2	12. 4	22. 4	32. 2	42. 2
3. 1	13. 2	23. 3	33. 1	43. 3
4. 2	14. 4	24. 3	34. 4	44. 2
5. 1	15. 1	25. 2	35. 4	45. 3
6. 1	16. 2	26. 4	36. 4	46. 3
7. 4	17. 1	27. 3	37. 2	47. 3
8. 3	18. 3	28. 1	38. 2	48. 4
9. 4	19. 3	29. 1	39. 1	49. 1
10. 2	20. 2	30. 2	40. 3	50. 2

SOLUTIONS TO PROBLEMS

1. $x^0 = 1$ is NOT true if $x = 0$, since 0^0 is undefined.

   $\sqrt{x^2} = x$ only if $x \geq 0$, and $\sqrt{x^2} = -x$ if x is negative.

   $\dfrac{x^2-1}{x-1}$ is undefined if $x = 1$. However, $\sin 2x = 2\sin x \cos x$ for all x.

2. Pupils A, C and D have answers equivalent to .0000375, whereas pupil B's answer is .000000375.

3. The MOST elementary kind of simplification of fractions is the cancellation of common monomial factors as shown in selection b. Selection d. represents common monomial factors also, but factoring is required. In selection a., the reader must recognize that there exists trial and error factoring. Finally, selection c. has both common monomial and trial and error factoring.

4. Within radical signs, one may NOT divide negative numbers. All such negative numbers must first be changed to their imaginary number form.

5. The sum of the distances between the pencil and the 2 tacks remains constant. This is a property of the ellipse.

6. 6 is an extraneous root, since $6 + \sqrt{6-2} = 6 + \sqrt{4} = 6+2 \neq 4$

   3 is a correct root.

7. To show student A is correct: $\tan\theta + \cot\theta = \tan\theta + \dfrac{1}{\tan\theta} = \dfrac{\tan^2\theta + 1}{\tan\theta} = \dfrac{\sec^2\theta}{\tan\theta}$.

   To show B is correct: $\tan\theta + \cot\theta = \dfrac{\sin\theta}{\cos\theta} + \dfrac{\cos\theta}{\sin\theta} = \dfrac{\sin^2\theta + \cos^2\theta}{\cos\theta \sin\theta} = \dfrac{1}{\frac{1}{2}\sin 2\theta} = \dfrac{2}{\sin 2\theta}$.

   To show c is correct: $\tan\theta + \cos\theta = \dfrac{\sin\theta}{\cos\theta} + \dfrac{\cos\theta}{\sin\theta} = \dfrac{\sin^2\theta + \cos^2\theta}{\cos\theta \sin\theta}$

   $= \dfrac{1}{\cos\theta \sin\theta} = \dfrac{1}{\cos\theta} \cdot \dfrac{1}{\sin\theta} = \sec\theta \cdot \csc\theta$

8. The contrapositive of the statement "If A, then B" is "If not B, than not A" and the truth of one statement implies the truth of the other.

9. Similarity properties must first be established for any 2 triangles (b). (d) then gives a special case of similarity. (a) is a direct consequence of (d). Finally, (c) can be shown, which can aid in determining the lengths of the 2 legs of the large triangle.

10. 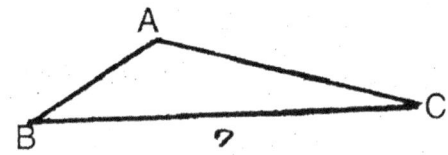 Assume AB, AC, and < A are known by the law of cosines: $(BC)^2 = (AB)^2 + (AC)^2 - 2(AB)(AC) \cos < A$. Thus, BC can be found.

11. Let R_1, R_2 be the roots. Then $\dfrac{1}{R_1}+\dfrac{1}{R_2}=\dfrac{R_2+R_1}{R_1 R_2}=\dfrac{-\tfrac{b}{a}}{\tfrac{c}{a}}=-\dfrac{b}{c}$

12. Let x = side of triangle, n = side of square. Then 3x = 4n.
    Also, area of triangle = $\dfrac{x^2}{4}\sqrt{3}=9\sqrt{3}$, from which x = 6
    (3)(6) = 4n, so n = 9/2. Diagonal of square = $n\sqrt{2}=\dfrac{9}{2}\sqrt{2}$

13. Indirect reasoning occurs when all possibilities are considered, from which it can be shown that, taken in turn, each possibility but one leads to a contradiction. The last possibility must then be correct. The critical element is that EXACTLY ONE possibility or condition must be true.

14. Given n objects of which x are a certain color, the probability of drawing 2 of that color without replacement $=\dfrac{x}{n}\cdot\dfrac{x-1}{n-1}$. In this case, the player wins if he draws either 2 black or 2 white balls. Thus, probability $=\dfrac{5}{9}\cdot\dfrac{4}{8}+\dfrac{3}{9}\cdot\dfrac{2}{8}=\dfrac{26}{72}=\dfrac{13}{36}$.

15. $1231_{seven} = (1)(343) + (2)(49) + (3)(7) + 1 = 463$
    With base 5, the right most column is ones, next column is fives next column is twenty fives, fourth column is 125's.
    Now 463 = (3)(125) + (3)(25) + (2) (5) + 3(1), so the answer is 3323_{five}.

16. Discount of 20% = ($1,000)(.80) – $800 followed by a discount of 10% = ($800)(.90) = $720 = answer.

17. Let x = distance each way. Time for 1st trip = x/a.
    Time for 2nd trip = x/6 . Average rate = Total distance ÷ total time $2x\div(\dfrac{x}{a}+\dfrac{x}{6})=2x\div([ax+bx]/ab)=2ab/(a+b)$.

18. $(a+b)(a+c) = a^2 + ab + ac + bc$. In order for this expression to equal a+bc, we need $a^2 + ab + ac = a$, which implies $a(a+b+c-1) = 0$. Now either a = 0 or a+b+c-1 = 0, i.e., a+b+c =1. Note that choice 3 does NOT give the FULL answer, but is the BEST choice.

19. $\dfrac{1}{-\sqrt{-1}} = \dfrac{1}{-i} = \dfrac{1}{-i} \cdot \dfrac{i}{i} = \dfrac{i}{-i^2} = i$ NOW, i turns in cycles of 4 as:

    $i, i^2 = -1, i^3 = -i, i^4 = 1$. If n is integral, then $4n + 5$, when divided by 4, leaves a remainder of 1. This corresponds to i.

20. $\dfrac{1}{x} + \dfrac{1}{y} = \dfrac{y+x}{xy} = \dfrac{2xy}{xy} = 2$

21. The nth term of an arithmetic progression with 1st term x and difference d is $x+(n-1)d$. Thus, $x+9d = 15$ and $x+19d = 35$. Solving, $x=-3$ and $d=2$. The 30th term is $-3+(29)(2) = 55$.

22. Any 3-digit number can be represented as $100h+10t+u$. From the conditions of the problem, we get 3 equations:
    (1) $u-t=2$ (2) $u+t+h=12$ (3) $100h+10t+u$
    $= 100u + 10t + h + 198$ which reduces to $-u + h = 2$
    Solving, $u=4, t=2, h = 6$, so the answer is 624

23. Since -1 is a root, $(-1)^3 + c(-1) + d = 0$. Also, since -2 is a root, $(-2)^3 + c(-2) + d = 0$. Solving $C = -7, d = -6$.
    Now $x^3 - 7x - 6 = (x+1)(x+2)(x-3)$; thus 3 is the last root.

24. Let x = amount of solution drained. At this point, there are 15-x quarts of the solution and 3-.20x quarts of antifreeze (recognize that for every quart of solution drained, only one-fifth of a quart of antifreeze is drained).
    Now add the x quarts of antifreeze, so that the solution again becomes 15 quarts and the amount of antifreeze = 3-.20x + x. Finally, 3-.20x + x = .50 (15), whereby x = 5 5/8.

25. $g[f(x)] = g(2x+1) = (2x+1)^2 - 2 = 4x^2 + 4x + 1 - 2 = 4x^2 + 4x - 1$

26. Log $4x^5$ = Log 4 + 5 Log x and Log x^4 = 4 Log x
    Thus, Log 4 + 5 Log x - 4 Log x + Log 5 = 4
    Log x + Log 4 + Log 5 = 4, Log 20x = 4
    This implies $10^4 = 20x$, x = 500

27. The parabola $(y-k)^2 = 4p(x-h)$ has a vertex at (h,k), directrix is $x = h-p$ and focus of (h+p, k). For the equation $(y-1)^2 = 4(x+2)$, the vertex is (-2,1), directrix is the equation $x = -3$, and focus is (-1,1).

28. In any triangle, the relative size of the angles is in the same order as the size of the sides opposite those angles. Since AB > BC, M < C > M < A.

29. The ratio of the areas of the smaller and the larger triangles is the same as the ratio of the SQUARES of corresponding sides.
    Let x = area of the larger triangle. Then, $54:x = 12^2 : 20^2$, $50x = 150$.
    Area of trapezoid = 150-54 = 96.

11 (#1)

30. Recognize that ABQP is a trapezoid with right angles at A and B. Construct a segment $\overline{QT}$ which is parallel to $\overline{AP}$ and T lies on $\overline{AB}$. TP = AP-AT = 12-2 = 10. Since $\triangle$PTQ is a right $\triangle$,
$(TQ)^2 + 10^2 = 20^2$. TQ = $10\sqrt{3}$. But AB = TQ, and also = $10\sqrt{3}$.

31. $\triangle$AFB is similar to $\triangle$ADC and $\triangle$ADE is similar to $\triangle$ABC.
For any 2 similar triangles, the ratio of corresponding sides is constant. Thus, the ratio of AE to EC is 4:6. Also, the ratio of AD to DB is 4:6. Since AD = 10, 10:DB = 4:6 and thus DB = 15.

32.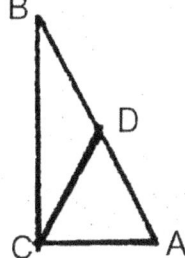
It is known that BD = DA. Since < BCA = 90°, We can show that CD = 1/2AB = AD. Since CD = AC, $\triangle$ACD is equilateral. < A = 60°.

33. cos(-115°) = -cos 65° = -sin 25° (The sign is minus, since -115° is in the 3rd quadrant, where both cosine and sine have negative values.)

34. sinx = cosx at 45°, 225°, 405°... In general, at 45°+180k°, with k an integer. $\frac{3\pi}{2}$ and 2π radians correspond to 270° and 360° respectively, and there are no intersections between 270° and 360°.

35. y = A sin Bx has a period of $2\pi/B$ and an amplitude of A. Here, A = 1/2, B = 2.

36. cot 150° = $-\sqrt{3}$ and csc 210° = -2 and the ratio = $\frac{\sqrt{3}}{2}$ = cos 330°.

37. Arctan 2 + Arctan 3 = 135°
Converting, 135° = $\frac{135\pi}{180}$ radians = $3\pi/4$

38. $\sin^2 x + \cos^2 x = 1$, thus $\cos^2 x = \sin^2 y = \cos^2(90° - y)$, if x,y < 90° Thus, x = 90° -y

39. g(x/2) = cos 1/2x, whereas g(x)/2 = cos x/2. To show that g(x/2) ≠ g(x)/2, let x = 90°. Then cos 1/2x = $\frac{1}{\sqrt{2}}$, but cos x/2 = 0.

40. 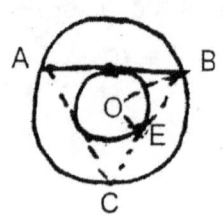 Let $\overline{AB}$ be the tangent to the inner circle. $\triangle$ ABC is equilateral. BOE is a 30 – 60 – 90 $\triangle$ with BE = 6. So OE = $2\sqrt{3}$ and OB = $4\sqrt{3}$. Area of inner circle = 12π, area of outer circle = 48π. Difference = 36π.

41. Case 1: Both x > 0 and $x^2-1>0$, satisfied by x > 1
    Case 2: Both x < 0 and $x^2-1<0$, satisfied by -1 < x < 0

42. $\sqrt{9-x^2} > 0$, in order for f(x) to be real.
    Thus $9-x^2 > 0$, solved by -3 < x < 3 or |x| < 3

43. $(1+i)^4 = 1+4i+6i^2+4i^3+i^4 = 1+4i-6-4i+1 = -4$

44. By definition, Statement 1 is the negation of Statement 2 if the individual tenth values are opposite in all cases. For this example: (T = true, F = false).

P	Q	P → Q	P ∧ ~ Q
T	T	T	F
T	F	F	T
F	T	T	F
F	F	T	F

    P → Q is equivalent to ~P V Q.
    Thus, the negation is P ∧ ~ Q.

45. Since all signs of the terms are positive, there can be no positive roots. Only choice 3 could be correct.

46. 5th coeff. = $\dfrac{8 \cdot 7 \cdot 6 \cdot 5}{1 \cdot 2 \cdot 3 \cdot 4} = 8c4$

47. $(-8i)^{\frac{1}{3}} = [8(\cos 270° + i \sin 270°)]^{\frac{1}{3}} = 2(\cos 90° + i \sin 90°)$,
    $2(\cos 210° + i \sin 210°)$, and $2(\cos 330° + i \sin 330°)$
    This leads to the 3 roots: $2i$, $-\sqrt{3}-i$, and $\sqrt{3}-i$

48. x = 1st number, y = 2nd number, $x+y^2 = 15$. Let A = xy.
    We want to maximize A. Since $x = 15-y^2$, we can write
    $A = (15-y^2)y = 15y-y^3$. To maximize, set dA/dx = 0.
    Then $15-3y^2 = 0$ and since y is positive, $y=\sqrt{5}$.
    Using $x+y^2 = 15$, we get x = 10, the larger of the 2 numbers.

49. 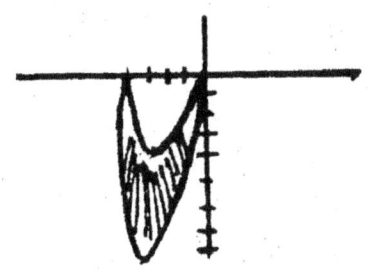 The area is found by $\int_0^4 [(8x-2x^2) - (4x-x^2)]dx = \int_0^4 (-x^2+4x)dx = [-\frac{x^3}{3}+2x^2]_0^4 = \frac{32}{3}$

50. $v = \int a\,dt = \int (6t-6)dt = 3t^2-6t+C_1$. Since at $t = 0$, $v = 5$, we know $C_1 = 5$.
Distance $= \int v\,dt = \int (3t^2-6t+5)dt = t^3-3t^2 + 5t + C_2$. But at $t = 0$, distance = 0, so $C_2 = 0$ Distance $= t^3 -3t^2 +5t$.
Now, at $t = 2$, distance = 6.

EXAMINATION SECTION
TEST 1

DIRECTIONS: Each question or incomplete statement is followed by several suggested answers or completions. Select the one that BEST answers the question or completes the statement. *PRINT THE LETTER OF THE CORRECT ANSWER IN THE SPACE AT THE RIGHT.*

1. A pupil is informed that his percentile rank on a test given to a certain group is 70. This means that   1.____

    1. his score is in the upper 30% of the test scores of the group
    2. his score is in the lower 30% of the test scores of the group
    3. he answered 70 of the items correctly
    4. he answered 70% of the items correctly

2. A pupil was asked to solve the equation $x^2 = 1$ and obtained the two roots $x = 1$ and $x = -1$. He wrote "reject" next to the negative root. The pupil was   2.____

    1. *correct*, because negative roots of quadratic equations are always rejected
    2. *incorrect*, because both answers are acceptable
    3. *correct*, because -1 is an extraneous root
    4. *incorrect*, because imaginary roots always occur in pairs

3. A pupil, given the pair of equations $y = 2x+7$ and $y = 2x-7$ to solve simultaneously, is unable to find a solution. Which is the PROPER explanation by the teacher?   3.____

    1. You have made a mistake in arithmetic. Check your work.
    2. You cannot solve this problem by the method of substitution. Try another method.
    3. These equations have no solution because they are dependent.
    4. These equations have no solution because they are inconsistent.

4. A teacher is teaching his class to solve the equation $\sin x = \cos x$. Which of the following methods would be INAPPROPRIATE for solving this equation?   4.____

    1. Confunctions
    2. Graphing
    3. Using a table of natural trigonometric functions
    4. Law of tangents

5. An eleventh year mathematics class studying positive and negative exponents examined a number of relationships in the metric system. Which of the following is NOT a correct relationship?   5.____

    1. $1 \text{ mm} = 10^{-2} \text{ cm}$
    2. $1 \text{ cm}^3 = 10^{-3} \text{ L}$
    3. $1 \text{ kg} = 10^6 \text{ mg}$
    4. $1 \text{ cm} = 10^{-5} \text{ km}$

6. In an eleventh year mathematics class studying trigonometric identities, a student wrote the following: $\sin(x + y) = \sin x + \sin y$. Of the following, the BEST procedure to follow is to   6.____

2 (#1)

1. praise the student for carefully applying the postulate of distributivity of multiplication over addition
2. suggest that the student verify his result by substitution of 0° for x and 90° for y
3. suggest that the student check his work by replacing x by 30° and y by 60°
4. suggest that the student confirm his result by substituting any acute angle for x and the negative of the same acute angle for y

7. A pupil asked the question "What is the value of the fraction 0/0?" The BEST answer is   7.____

    1. 1   2. 0
    3. indeterminate   4. infinitely large

8. Students in mathematics classes often carelessly write incorrect statements on tests and   8.____
in their homework. Identify the only one of the following statements which is mathematically CORRECT.

    1. $(x^{1/3})^2 = x^{1/9}$
    2. Only one line can be drawn parallel to a given line.
    3. $X^0 = 1$ for all values of x
    4. Two triangles are congruent if two angles and an included side of one congruent respectively to two angles and an included side of the other.

9. A tenth year mathematics class has proved the theorem   9.____
"A diagonal of a parallelogram divides the parallelogram into two congruent triangles." From this, a student concludes that if a diagonal divides a quadrilateral into two congruent triangles the quadrilateral must be a parallelogram. His conclusion is

    1. *correct*, based on reasoning from a converse
    2. *incorrect*, based on reasoning from a converse
    3. *correct*, based on reasoning from a contrapositive
    4. *incorrect*, based on reasoning from an inverse

10. An eleventh year mathematics class studying complex numbers was asked to express   10.____
the quotient $\dfrac{\sqrt{36}}{\sqrt{-9}}$ in terms of i.

Student A wrote $\dfrac{\sqrt{36}}{\sqrt{-9}} = \sqrt{\dfrac{36}{-9}} = \sqrt{-4} = 2i$

Student B wrote $\dfrac{\sqrt{36}}{\sqrt{-9}} = \dfrac{6}{3i} = \dfrac{2}{i}$

Student C wrote $\dfrac{\sqrt{36}}{\sqrt{-9}} = \dfrac{6}{3i} = \dfrac{2}{i} \cdot \dfrac{i}{i} = \dfrac{2i}{i^2} = \dfrac{2i}{-1} = -2i$

The students who expressed this *correctly* were

    1. A and B *only*   2. A and C *only*
    3. B and C *only*   4. all three

11. The expression $\dfrac{1}{a^{-1} + b^{-1}}$ equals a + b   11.____

1. a+b   2. $\dfrac{1}{-a-b}$

3. $(a+b)^{-1}$ 4. $\dfrac{ab}{a+b}$

12. In the complex number system $\dfrac{1}{i}+\dfrac{1}{i^2}+\dfrac{1}{i^3}$ equals

    1. 1   2. -1   3. 2i   4. 1-i

13. The value of $\left[1-2(2-3)^{-1}\right]^{-1}$ is

    1. -1   2. 2   3. 1/3   4. $-\dfrac{1}{3}$

14. Which of the following is a cube root of 8?

    1. -2
    2. 2i
    3. 2 (cos 240° + i sin 240°)
    4. 1 + i$\sqrt{3}$

15. The x- intercept(s) of the graph of $y = x^3 - 6x^2 + 12x - 8$ is (are)

    1. 1 and 2
    2. 2
    3. -8 and 2
    4. -8

16. The third term in the expansion of $(x-2y)^8$ is

    1. $112\, x^6 y^2$
    2. $-112\, x^6 y^2$
    3. $28 x^5 y^3$
    4. $-28 x^5 y^3$

17. If 3 fair coins are tossed, the probability that they will fall one head and two tails is

    1. 1/3   2. 2/3   3. 3/8   4. 2/9

18. How many hours does it take a train, traveling at an average rate of 30 mph between stops, to travel m miles if it makes s stops of t minutes each?

    1. $\dfrac{2m+st}{60}$ 2. $\dfrac{m+st}{60}$

    3. 30m + st   4. $\dfrac{m}{30}+st$

19. When a positive integer x is divided by a positive integer y, the quotient is w and the remainder is z where w and z are integers. The remainder ~~with~~ x + 3wy is divided by y is

    1. z   2. w   3. 3w   4. 0

20. By definition, similar polygons are polygons

    1. whose corresonding sides are in proportion
    2. which can be made to coincide
    3. whose corresponding angles are congruent

4. whose corresponding angles are congruent and whose corresponding sides are in proportion

21. Of the following, the property that the set {-1,0,1} does NOT possess is

    1. closure under addition
    2. closure under multiplication
    3. an identity element for multiplication
    4. inverse elements for addition

22. If $f(x) = 2^x$, where x is real and if f^{-1} denotes the inverse function of f, then when $a > 1$ and $b > 1$, $\dfrac{f^{-1}(a)}{f^{-1}(b)} =$

    1. $2^b/2^a$
    2. $\log_2 a - \log_2 b$
    3. $\log_2 a / \log_2 b$
    4. $2^{\frac{b}{a}}$

23. Which of the following is NOT equal to $\tan \dfrac{3\pi}{4}$?

    1. $\sin \dfrac{3\pi}{2}$
    2. $\cos \pi$
    3. $\tan \dfrac{7\pi}{4}$
    4. $\cot \dfrac{5\pi}{4}$

24. A survey of Romance Language majors at a college showd the following:

    100 students were taking Spanish
    75 students were taking French
    50 students were taking Italian
    35 students were taking French and Spanish
    25 students were taking Italian and Spanish
    15 students were taking French and Italion
    5 students were taking all three languages

    How many Romance Language majors were there altogether?

    1. 65
    2. 155
    3. 225
    4. 305

25. The LAST digit of 7^{253} is

    1. 1
    2. 5
    3. 7
    4. 9

26. The area of the circle whose equation is $x^2 + y^2 + 4x - 1 = 0$ is

    1. π
    2. 5π
    3. 16π
    4. 25π

27. The solution set of $|x + 2| \leq 6$ is

    1. $-8 \leq x \leq 4$
    2. $x \leq -8$ or $x \geq 4$
    3. $-4 \leq x \leq 8$
    4. $x \leq -4$ or $x \geq 8$

28. In a class, three times as many students passed a test as failed. The arithmetic mean of grades on the test for the entire class was double the arithmetic mean of all failures on the test.
    If the arithmetic mean of all the passing grades was 84, then the arithmetic mean of all failing grades was

    1. 32   2. 36   3. 42   4. 46

29. The measure of a side of a square is 10. The radius of the circle circumscribed around the square is CLOSEST to

    1. 5   2. 6   3. 7   4. 9

30. The measures of the angles of a triangle are represented by 2x+5, 3x+35 and 5x-10. The triangle is

    1. acute and scalene
    2. obtuse and scalene
    3. isosceles
    4. right

31. To prove a proposition by the method of indirect proof requires that we

    1. prove the converse of the proposition and infer the truth of the proposition from the truth of the converse
    2. prove the inverse of the proposition and infer the truth of the proposition from the truth of the inverse
    3. first prove a simpler related theorem which is then used to prove the proposition
    4. assume the conclusion of the proposition to be false and obtain a contradiction

32. A train takes 12 seconds to pass through the entrance of a tunnel. Fifteen seconds later, the train is completely out of the tunnel.
    Assuming that the speed of the train remains constant and the tunnel is 435 yards long, the length of the train is _____ yards.

    1. 348   2. 360   3. 372   4. 384

33. A person makes a deposit in a bank which gives 6.4% simple interest per year. After 270 days, his money has grown to 1,310 dollars from the interest.
    Assuming that the bank's interest is based on a year of 360 days, the amount that the person *initially* deposited was

    1. $1150   2. $1175   3. $1225   4. $1250

34. The solution set of the equation $\dfrac{x}{x-3} - \dfrac{1}{x+2} = \dfrac{15}{x^2-x-6}$ is

    1. ϕ 2. $\{3,-4\}$ 3. $\{3\}$ 4. $\{-4\}$

35. If the graphs of y = 2 log x and y = log 2x are drawn on the same set of axes, these graphs will

    1. not intersect
    2. intersect at one point only

3. intersect at two points only
4. coincide

36. For all x where the expressions are defined, the expression sin x is NOT equivalent to

   1. cos (90°-x)
   2. sin (180°-x)
   3. cos x tan x
   4. sin (-x)

37. The diagonal of a cube whose side is S inches long is

   1. S
   2. $S\sqrt{2}$
   3. $S\sqrt{3}$
   4. $\dfrac{S^2\sqrt{3}}{2}$

38.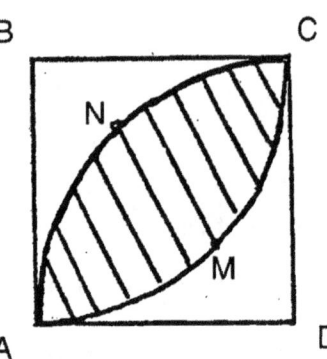
   As indicated in the diagram at left, ABCD is a square whose sides are 8. Using B as center, arc ANC is drawn as shown. The area of the shaded region is

   1. $16\pi - 32$
   2. $32 - 8\pi$
   3. $32\pi - 64$
   4. 8/3

39. One base angle of a trapezoid has a measure of 30 and its adjacent leg is x units long. If the measures of the bases are y and z, then the area of the trapezoid, in square units, is

   1. 2xy + 2xz
   2. 2y+2z/x
   3. $\dfrac{xy+xz}{2}$
   4. $\dfrac{xy+xz}{4}$

40. The diameter of the planet Earth is approximately 8,000 mi. The lenth of a longitudinal arc extending from the North Pole to the Equator is *approximately* _____ miles.

   1. 3,100
   2. 6,300
   3. 12,500
   4. 25,000

41. The measure of pne side of a rectangle is 4 and its diagonal is $\sqrt{97}$. The measure of the diagonal of a square which has the same area as this rectangle is

   1. 9
   2. $9\sqrt{2}$
   3. 6
   4. $6\sqrt{2}$

42. Parallel chords $\overline{AB}$ and $\overline{CD}$ are drawn in a circle. Chords $\overline{AD}$ and $\overline{BC}$ intersect at E. If m $(\widehat{AC})$ = 50, then m ($\angle$CED) is equal to

   1. 25
   2. 50
   3. 130
   4. 155

43. The expression $\dfrac{\sqrt{x^2+2x\sqrt{x}+x}}{2(\sqrt{x}+1)}$ in SIMPLEST form is

1. $\dfrac{\sqrt{x}}{2}$ 2. $\dfrac{\sqrt{x}+1}{3}$
3. $\dfrac{\sqrt{x}+2}{4}$ 4. $\dfrac{2\sqrt{x}-1}{x-1}$

44. One of the solutions of $(\sin x + \cos x)^2 = 2$ is   44.____

　　1. $0°$ 2. $45°$ 3. $60°$ 4. $90°$

45. The lengths of the three sides of a triangle are 3, 5 and 7. The measure of the LARGEST   45.____
　　angle of the triangle is

　　1. $60°$ 2. $120°$ 3. $135°$ 4. $150°$

46. Which of the following represents the solution set for x in the following equation: 46.____
　　$\log_8 (x-1) + \log_8 (x+1) = 1$?

　　1. {3, -3}   2. {-3}
　　3. {3}   4. {8}

47. If $\tan A = 1/6$ and $\tan B = 5/7$, then $(A+B)$ is equal to   47.____

　　1. $30°$ 2. $45°$ 3. $60°$ 4. $90°$

48. The expression $\lim\limits_{x \to \alpha} \dfrac{5x^2+3}{8-12x-3x^2}$ is equal to   48.____

　　1. -5/3   2. 3/8   3. 3/8
　　4. 5/8   5. non existent

49. $\int^2 (3x-4)^3 \, dx =$ 49.____

　　1. 5/4   2. 4/3   3. 15/4   4. 16

50. A ball is thrown vertically upward with an initial velocity of 20 ft/sec on a planet with   50.____
　　acceleration due to gravity of -6 ft/sec^2.
　　The height after 5 seconds is _____ feet.

　　1. 20   2. 25   3. 70   4. 175

KEY (CORRECT ANSWERS)

1. 1	11. 4	21. 1	31. 4	41. 4
2. 2	12. 2	22. 3	32. 1	42. 3
3. 4	13. 3	23. 4	33. 4	43. 1
4. 4	14. 3	24. 2	34. 4	44. 2
5. 1	15. 2	25. 3	35. 2	45. 2
6. 3	16. 1	26. 2	36. 4	46. 3
7. 3	17. 3	27. 1	37. 3	47. 2
8. 4	18. 1	28. 2	38. 3	48. 1
9. 2	19. 1	29. 3	39. 4	49. 1
10. 3	20. 4	30. 1	40. 2	50. 2

SOLUTIONS TO PROBLEMS

1. A percentile rank indicates the *relative* position of a score when the scores are arranged from LOWEST to HIGHEST. 70, as a percentile, means that *approximately* 70% of all the scores are LOWER and 30% of all the scores are HIGHER.

2. Unless there is a physical or logical reason to reject negative numbers, both answers are needed.

3. By subtraction, 0 = 14 is obtained, and this leads to no solution. The graphs of these two equations are parallel lines, and by definition, the equations are inconsistent.

4. The Law of Tangents states: $\dfrac{a-b}{a+b} = \dfrac{\tan\frac{1}{2}(A-B)}{\tan\frac{1}{2}(A+B)}$ where A, B are angles and a, b are sides of the same triangle. This is not appropriate here.

5. The CORRECT statement for (1) is 1 mm = 10^{-1} cm.

6. By using angles like 30° and 60°, one can see that sin (30°+60°) = sin 90° = 1, whereas sin 30° + sin 60° = .5 + .866 = 1.366.
   Thus, we have provided an example to illustrate sin(x+y) ≠ sin x + sin y.

7. A check on any division is a multiplication. For example, 10/2 = 5, verified by (2)(5) = 10. Now let 0/0 = N. Then (0)(N) = 0. But any value of N would be correct. Thus, N is indeterminate.

8. The corrections on the other statements $(1)(x^{\frac{1}{3}})^2 = x^{\frac{2}{3}}$, infinitely many lines can be drawn parallel to a given line, (3) $x^0 = 1$, if x ≠ 0.

9. The converse of "If A then B" is "If B then A." In this example, the quadrilateral could appear as:
   where AB = BC and AD = DC.

   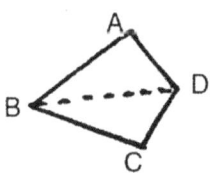

10. Only students B and C *correctly* changed $\sqrt{-9}$ to 3i first. It should be noted that student C is expressing the answer in preferred form over the form that student B is submitting.

11. $\dfrac{1}{a^{-1}+b^{-1}} = \dfrac{1}{\frac{1}{a}+\frac{1}{b}} = \dfrac{1}{\frac{b+a}{ab}} = \dfrac{ab}{b+a}$ or $\dfrac{ab}{a+b}$

12. The expression can be written as $\dfrac{i^2+i+1}{i^3} = \dfrac{i}{i^3} = \dfrac{i}{-i} = -1$

13. $[1-2(2-3)^{-1}]^{-1} = [1-2(\frac{1}{-1})]^{-1} = 3^{-1} = \frac{1}{3}$

14. To find the cube roots of $8: = 8^{\frac{1}{3}} = 8[(\cos 0° + i \sin 0°)]^{\frac{1}{3}}$, which gives three answers: $2(\cos 0° + i \sin 0°)$, $2(\cos 120° + i \sin 120°)$, and $2(\cos 240° + i \sin 240°)$. Only choice (3) matches any of these.

15. The x-intercept(s) are found by setting $y = x^3 - 6x^2 + 12x - 8 = 0$. But $x^3 - 6x^2 + 12x - 8 = (x-2)^3$. The solution of $(x-2)^3 = 0$ is 2.

16. The third term is $(8 \cdot 7/1 \cdot 2)(x)^6(-2y)^2 = 112x^6y^2$

17. The probability that the 1st coin is heads and the other 2 are tails is $(.5)(.5)(.5) = .125$. Thus, the probability of this combination for any of the coins is $3(.125) = .375 = 3/8$.

18. Total time in hours = time to travel m miles with no stops + time to make s stops of t minutes each

    $= \frac{m}{30} + \frac{st}{60} = \frac{2m+st}{60}$

19. $\frac{x}{y} = w + \frac{z}{y}$ from the given information.

    Now, $(x+3wy) \div y = \frac{x}{y} + 3w = (w + \frac{z}{y}) + 3w = 4w + \frac{z}{y}$

    Thus, z is the remainder.

20. This is self-explanatory from the definition of similar polygons. Incidentally, statement (1) would NOT be sufficient, as illustrated by:

21. Use the example $1+1 = 2$, and 2 is not an element of $\{-1, 0, 1\}$

22. To find $f^{-1}(x)$, interchange x and y and solve for y.
    Let $y = 2^x$. Change to $x = 2^y$, which is equivalent to $y = \log_2 x$
    Thus, $f^{-1}(x) = \log_2 x$. Now $\frac{f^{-1}(a)}{f^{-1}(b)} = \frac{\log_2 a}{\log_2 b}$

23. $\tan \frac{3\pi}{4} = -1$, whereas $\cot \frac{5\pi}{4} = +1$.

24. The number of students taking only Spanish = 100 - 30 - 20 - 5 = 45.
    The number of students taking only French = 75 - 30 - 10 - 5 = 30.
    The number of students taking only Italian = 50 - 20 - 10 - 5 = 15.
    The total number of students becomes 30 + 20 + 5 + 30 + 45 + 15 + 10 = 155.
    The following Vinn diagram is useful:

    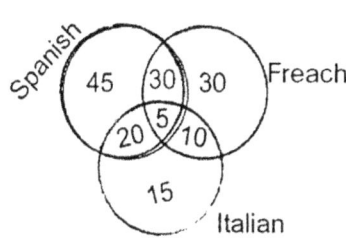

25. 7^1 ends in 7, 7^2 ends in 9, 7^3 ends in 3, 7^4 ends in 1. This cycle is repeated, so that in order to find the last digit of 7^{253}, divide 253 by 4. The remainder of this division is 1, and thus corresponds to 7^1 which ends in 7. (Note that if there were no remainder, this would have been equivalent to a remainder of 4, corresponding to 7^4 which ends in 1.)

26. Rewrite as $(x+2)^2 + y^2 = 5$, which implies that the radius SQUARED equals 5. Thus, area = 5π.

27. $|x+2| \leq 6$ is equivalent to $-6 \leq x+2 \leq 6$, which yields $-8 \leq x \leq 4$.

28. Let x = # of students who failed, 3x - # of students who passed, and y = mean of all failing grades. Now, 4x students took the test, and the mean for all 4x students is found as follows: $[(84)(3x) + (y)(x)]/4x = 63 + y/4$ Since this value is double the mean of all failures, we get: $63 + y/4 = 2y$. Thus, y = 36

29. The radius of the circumscribed circle = (1/2)(diagonal of the square) =
    $(\frac{1}{2})(10\sqrt{2}) = 5\sqrt{2} \approx 7.07$. The CLOSEST answer is 7.

30. (2x + 5) + (3x + 35) + (5x - 10) = 180, so x = 15. Thus, the angles are of measure 35, 80 and 65. The triangle is acute and scalene.

31. This is evident by the definition of the indirect proof.

32. The speed of the train is x/12, where the length of the train is x yds. Then 435 ÷ (x/12) = 15 and thus x = 348. Note that in the 12 seconds required to pass thru the tunnel's entrance, the train is traveling the distance of its own length.

33. D = initial deposit. 6.4% for a year = (6.4) (270/360) % = 4.8% for 270 days. Thus, D + .048D = 1310. D = 1250.

34. Multiplying the equation by (x-3)(x+2): x(x+2)-(x-3) = 15
    Then, $x^2 + 2x - x + 3 = 15$. Whereby (x+4)(x-3) = 0, leading to x = -4 and x = 3. However, a value of x = 3 causes two denominators to be zero, and so must be rejected. Only x = -4 can be accepted.

35. To find out if there is any intersection, set 2 Log x = Log 2x.
Since 2 Log x = Log x^2, we get $x^2 = 2x$. This statement leads to x = 0 and x = 2. However, x = 0 is rejected since Log 0 does not exist. Thus, only x = 2 is a point of intersection.

36. sin x ≠ sin (-x) Example: sin 45° = .707, but sin(-45°) = -.707

37. The diagonal of a cube can be represented at the hypotenuse of a triangle where one side is an edge and the second side is the diagonal of a face of the cube perpendicular to this edge. Then the diagonal of the cube = $\sqrt{s^2 + 2s^2} = s\sqrt{3}$.

38. Area of square ABCD = Area of sector BAMC + Area of sector DANC - area of shaded region. The area of each sector $= (\frac{1}{4})(\pi)(8^2) = 16\pi$. Thus, $64 = 16\pi + 16\pi$ - area of shaded region. This region's area = $32\pi - 64$.

39. The altitude must be 1/2 x, since it lies opposite 30° in a 30°-60°-90° triangle. Area of trapezoid = (1/2)(1/2x)(y+z) = (xy+xz)/4.

40. This longitudinal arc = (1/4)(circumference). Since circumference
    = $(2\pi)(4000) = 8000\pi$, arc = $4(8000\pi) = 2000\pi$ is *approximately* 6300.

41. The other length of the rectangle $= \sqrt{97-16} = 9$. Thus, the area of the rectangle is (9)(4) = 36. A square with this area has a side of 6 and a diagonal of $6\sqrt{2}$.

42. Since $m(\widehat{AC}) = 50$, $m(\widehat{BD}) = 50$.
$m\angle c = \frac{1}{2} m(\widehat{BD}) = 25$. $m\angle 0 = \frac{1}{2} m(\widehat{AC}) = 25$ Thus $m\angle CED$ = 180-25-25 = 130
The two theorems being used are a) An inscribed angle equals one-half its corresponding arc and (b) The sum of the angles of a triangle is 180°.

43. Simplifying the numerator:
$\sqrt{x^2 + 2x\sqrt{x} + x} = \sqrt{x(x+2\sqrt{x}+1)} = \sqrt{x(\sqrt{x}+1)(\sqrt{x}+1)} = (\sqrt{x}+1)\sqrt{x}$
Now the problem becomes $\frac{(\sqrt{x}+1)(\sqrt{x})}{2(\sqrt{x}+1)} = \frac{\sqrt{x}}{2}$

44. $(\sin x + \cos x)^2 = \sin^2 x + 2 \sin x \cos x + \cos^2 x$. Since $\sin^2 x + \cos^2 x = 1$ and $2 \sin x \cos x = \sin 2x$, the original equation reduces to sin 2x +1=2 or sin 2x = 1. One solution is found by letting 2x = 90°. Thus, x = 45°.

45. 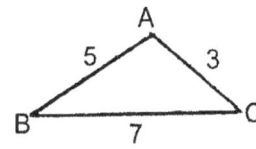 Since the LARGEST angle is opposite the LARGEST side, we are solving for $\angle A$. Using the Law of Cosines, $7^2 = 3^2 + 5^2 (2)(3)(5) \cos \angle A$. Then $\cos \angle A = -\frac{1}{2}$.

Thus, $\angle A = 120°$.

46. $\log_8(x-1) + \log_8(x+1) = \log_8(x^2-1)$. Now, $\log_8 (x^2-1) = 1$ $x^2 -1 = 8^1$. This leads to 3 and 3 as values of x. But Log (negative number) is undefined. Thus, x = 3 *only*.

47. $\text{Tan}(A+B) = (\text{Tan A} + \text{Tan B})/[1-(\text{Tan A})(\text{Tan B})]$

    $= (\frac{1}{6} + \frac{5}{7})/[1-(\frac{1}{6})(\frac{5}{7})] = 1$. Thus, $(A+B) = 45°$.

48. Rewrite $\dfrac{5x^2+3}{8-12x-3x^2}$ as $\dfrac{5+\dfrac{3}{x^2}}{\dfrac{8}{x^2}-\dfrac{12}{x}-3}$

    As $x \to \alpha, \dfrac{3}{x^2}, \dfrac{8}{x^2}$, and $12/x$ all approach 0. Thus limit of the entire expression, as $x \to \infty$, is -5/3

49. $\int_1^2 (3x-4)^3 \, dx = [\dfrac{1}{12}(3x-4)^4]_1^2 = 16/12 - 1/12 = 15/12$ or 5/4

50. a = -6, so v = -6t + C_1 At t = 0, v = 20, so C_1 = 20 v = -6t + 20. H = $-3t^2$ + 20t + C_2 Now C_2 = 0, since when t = 0, H = 0.
    Evaluate H=$3t^2$+20t when t = 5. H = 25ft. Here, a = acceleration, v = velocity, t = time, H = height.

EXAMINATION SECTION
TEST 1

DIRECTIONS: Each question or incomplete statement is followed by several suggested answers or completions. Select the one that BEST answers the question or completes the Statement. *PRINT THE LETTER OF THE CORRECT ANSWER IN THE SPACE AT THE RIGHT.*

1. Of the following, the BEST procedure for handling a student when he becomes restless or inattentive during a lesson is to

    1. stop teaching and demand that the student be attentive before you resume teaching
    2. tell the student that you are deducting 5 points from his grade for classwork
    3. continue to teach but talk louder
    4. direct a question on the lesson to the restless student

    1.____

2. The LEAST appropriate reason for using "Do Now" problems at the beginning of the period in a mathematics class is to

    1. reinforce the previous day's concepts
    2. provide motivation for the new work
    3. keep students from talking to each other
    4. provide a liaison between yesterday's work and the current lesson

    2.____

3. In teaching the solution of quadratic equations in eleventh year mathematics, what is the PROPER sequence of topics?
    (a) Quadratic formula
    (b) Factoring a quadratic trinomial
    (c) Completing the square

    1. a, b, c   2. b, c, a   3. c, a, b   4. a, c, b

    3.____

4. In order that an indirect proof in geometry be CORRECT and COMPLETE, one must prove that

    1. only one possibility is false
    2. only one possibility is true
    3. two corresponding sides (or angles) do not have equal measures
    4. all but one of all the possibilities are false and that, therefore, by elimination, the remaining possibility must be true

    4.____

5. Students in mathematics classes often give responses which contain inaccuracies. Below are listed four such responses.

    I. $\sqrt{2}$ is an irrational number because it cannot be expressed as the ratio of two numbers.
    II. x^4 means x taken as a factor four times.
    III. To bisect a line means to divide it into two equal parts.
    IV. A rectangle is defined as a parallelogram containing four right angles.
    The only one(s) which is (are) mathematically CORRECT is (are):

    1. I *only*   2. I, II
    3. II, III   4. III, IV

    5.____

97

2 (#1)

6. When proving "The sum of the measures of the angles of a triangle is equal to a straight angle," it is important to draw a(n)

    1. line parallel to a base of the triangle through the vertex of the opposite angle
    2. angle bisector
    3. median to the base
    4. congruent overlapping triangle

6.____

7. A pupil in a mathematics class wrote the following statement on a test paper:

    $\sqrt{25} = \pm 5$. This statement is

    1. *correct*, because every number has two square roots
    2. *correct*, because $(-5)^2 = 25$
    3. *incorrect*, because the symbol $\sqrt{}$ means the principal square root *only*
    4. *incorrect*, because the symbol $\sqrt{}$ means the negative square root *only*

7.____

8. A pupil in 9th year Mathematics (Algebra) reduces the fraction $\dfrac{x+1}{x+4}$ to $\dfrac{1}{4}$. The answer is

    1. *correct*, because if x is subtracted from both numerator and denominator the value of the result is 1/4
    2. *correct*, because if x is divided into the numerator and the denominator the value of the result is 1/4
    3. *incorrect*, because numerator and denominator do not have a common factor
    4. *incorrect*, because if numerator and denominator are divided by the x value, the result is 2/5

8.____

9. While teaching the solution of a quadratic by factoring, the following equation was presented:

    $x^2 + 3x = 0$

    One student divided both members of the equation by x obtaining the equation $x + 3 = 0$, where $x = -3$

    1. This is an unacceptable solution since one of the roots, x = 0, was discarded.
    2. Since every quadratic equation has 2 solutions, the student should have listed the -3 twice.
    3. This is an acceptable method yielding a correct solution.
    4. This solution is unacceptable. Since the constant is missing, the student should have used the method of "completing the square."

9.____

10. Pupil A states that π is exactly equal to $\dfrac{22}{7}$, while Pupil B states that π if is exactly equal to 3.14.

    1. Pupil A is *correct* and Pupil B is *incorrect*.
    2. Pupil B is *correct* and Pupil A is *incorrect*.
    3. BOTH Pupil A and Pupil B are *correct*.
    4. NEITHER Pupil A nor Pupil B is *correct*.

10.____

11. Given that the statement p → q is TRUE, which of the following is also true?   11._____

    1. q → p
    2. ~p → ~q
    3. ~q → ~p
    4. ~(q → p)

12. if x < b < 0 means that x and b are numbers such that x is less than b and b is less than zero, then   12._____

    1. $x^2 > bx > b^2$
    2. $x^2 < b^2 < 0$
    3. $x^2 > bx$ but $bx < 0$
    4. $x^2 - b^2 >$ but $b^2 < 0$

13. If x is positive and log then   13._____

    1. x has no minimum or maximum value
    2. the maximum value of x is 1
    3. the maximum value of x is 4
    4. the minimum value of x is 4

14. Two rectangles are similar. The measure of one side of the first is 2 and its area is 8 square units. If the measure of a diagonal of the second figure is 10, then its area, in square units, is   14._____

    1. $8\sqrt{5}$
    2. 20
    3. 40
    4. 50

15. The area of a triangle with vertices at (0,0), (5,3) and (3,7) is   15._____

    1. 11
    2. 13
    3. 16
    4. 18

16. If the third term of a geometric progression is and the seventh term is $\frac{27}{2}$, the first term is   16._____

    1. $\frac{1}{81}$
    2. $\frac{1}{72}$
    3. $\frac{1}{54}$
    4. $\frac{1}{48}$

17. Which values of x will satisfy the equation   17._____

    $$3x^2 - 7x = \left(\frac{1}{3}\right)^{4x+1}?$$

    1. $x = \dfrac{4 \pm \sqrt{5}}{2}$
    2. $x = \dfrac{3 \pm \sqrt{3}}{2}$
    3. $x = \dfrac{3 \pm \sqrt{5}}{2}$
    4. $x = \dfrac{2 \pm \sqrt{3}}{2}$

18. Which values of x satisfy the following equation involving a determinant?

$$\begin{vmatrix} x & 2 & 1 \\ -1 & 1 & -1 \\ 3 & 2 & 3x \end{vmatrix} = 0$$

   1. $x = -\frac{11}{3}, x = 1$
   2. $x = \frac{3}{4}, x = -1$
   3. $x = -\frac{7}{8}, x = 2$
   4. $x = 4, x = 3$

19. in right triangle ABC, $\angle$ B is a right angle. Point D is on AC. If $\overline{AD} \cong \overline{DC}$ and $\overline{AB} \cong \overline{BD}$, the measure of $\angle$ ACB is

   1. 30
   2. 45
   3. 60
   4. $67\frac{1}{2}$

20. A side of square ABCD has a measure of 12. A circle is drawn through vertices A and B and tangent to $\overline{CD}$.
    The measure of the radius of the circle is

   1. 6
   2. $\frac{15}{2}$
   3. $6\sqrt{2}$
   4. $\frac{15}{2}\sqrt{2}$

21. The value of cos 60° tan 45° + sin 60° tan 30° is

   1. 1
   2. 2
   3. $\frac{\sqrt{3}}{2}$
   4. $\frac{1}{2}$

22. Which of the following expresses $x^3 - 2x^2 - 5x + 6$ as the product of three linear factors?
   1. (x-1)(x-2)(x-3)
   2. (x-1)(x+2)(x+3)
   3. (x-1)(x-2)(x+3)
   4. (x-1)(x+2)(x-3)

23. Simplify the product $(256)^{.16} (256)^{.09}$
   1. 4
   2. 16
   3. 64
   4. 256

24. A regular dodecagon (twelve sided) is inscribed in a circle with a radius 4. The area of the dodecagon, in square units, is

   1. 48
   2. $36\sqrt{3}$
   3. $48\sqrt{3}$
   4. 96

25. The bisectors of the exterior angles at B and C of $\triangle$ ABC intersect at D. The measure of $\angle$ ABC is

   1. $45 - \frac{1}{2}m(\angle A)$
   2. $90 - m(\angle A)$

100

3. $90 - \frac{1}{2}m(\angle A)$ 4. $180 - m(\angle A)$

26. If $f(x) - 3^x$, then $f(x) + f(x+1) =$

    1. 4 2. $f(x)$ 3. $3f(x)$ 4. $4f(x)$

26.____

27. The number of distinct points of intersection of the relations of $x^2 + 9y^2 = 1$ and $x^2 + 9y^2 = 9$ is

    1. 1 2. 2 3. 3 4. 0

27.____

28. If x is the *smallest* positive value which satisfies the equation then

    1. $0° < x < 25°$
    2. $50° < x < 75°$
    3. $25° < x < 50°$
    4. $75° < x < 100°$

28.____

29. In quadrilateral ABCD diagonal $\overline{AC}$ is drawn. If $m(\overline{AB}) = 8$, $m(\overline{BC}) = 12$ $m(\overline{CD}) = 21$, $m(\overline{AC}) = 14$ and $\angle ABC \cong \angle ACD$, what is the measure of $\overline{AD}$?

    1. 22 1/2
    2. 24
    3. 24 1/2
    4. It cannot be determined from the information given.

29.____

30. The real values of x and y that satisfy the equation $3x + 2y + xi = 11 + 1 - 2yi$ may be described as follows:

    1. $x > 0$ and $y > 0$
    2. $x > 0$ and $y < 0$
    3. $x < 0$ and $y < 0$
    4. $x < 0$ and $y > 0$

30.____

31. A box contains 3 white balls and 2 red balls. If a ball is drawn at random and not replaced and a second ball is drawn at random, what is the probability that both balls are red?

    1. $\frac{1}{10}$ 2. $\frac{2}{25}$ 3. $\frac{2}{5}$ 4. $\frac{13}{20}$

31.____

32. A square ABCD whose side is 4 has arcs struck from opposite vertices A and C. The arcs have a radius of 4 and intersect the square at B and D.
    The area of the region bounded by the 2 arcs is

    1. $4\pi - 8$
    2. $8\pi - 16$
    3. $16 - 4\pi$
    4. 4π

32.____

33. A metal sheet in rectangular form is to be formed into an open rectangular box by cutting off squares from each corner and bending up the sides. If the sheet is 8" by 15", what is the length of the side of the squares to be cut off which will yield a box whose volume is a MAXIMUM?

    1. $\frac{1}{2}$ 2. $\frac{2}{3}$ 3. $\frac{5}{3}$ 4. $\frac{8}{3}$

33.____

34. Two of the roots of the equation $2x^3 - 12x^2 + px + q = 0$ are 2 and 3. The third root is

    1. 1 2. 2 3. -1 4. -7

35. An equation with real coefficients has 2+i, 3 and 4 among its roots. The LOWEST possible degree of the equation is

    1. 5 2. 6 3. 3 4. 4

36. The root of $x^3 = 27$ which lies in Quadrant II is

    1. $3(\cos 120° + i \sin 120°)$
    2. $27(\cos 120° + i \sin 120°)$
    3. $3(\cos 150° + i \sin 150°)$
    4. $-3(\cos 150° + i \sin 150°)$

37. When $x^3 + 3x^2 + cx + 5$ is divided by x-2 the remainder is 13. The value of c is

    1. -6 2. -2 3. 2 4. 6

38. If y = sin and y = cos x are drawn on the same set of axes from x = -π radians to x = π radians they will intersect in _____ point(s).

    1. 1 2. 2 3. 3 4. 4

39. In △ABC, a = 1, b = 2 and cos C = 1/4. The length of side c is

    1. $\sqrt{3}$ 2. 2 3. $\sqrt{5}$ 4. $\sqrt{6}$

40. A man has 5 close friends. In how many ways may he invite one or more of them to accompany him on a hunting trip?

    1. 5 2. 10 3. 31 4. 32

41. The coordinates of trapezoid OABP are 0 (0, 0), A (0, 8), B (6, 4) and P (12, y). The y-intercept of $\overline{BP}$ is

    1. -8 2. -2 3. 8 4. 16

42. The sixth term of the expansion of is

    1. $7x^6$ 2. $10x^6$
    3. $63x^7$ 4. $18x^7$

43. The values of x that satisfy the equation $|3x - 4| = |5 - 4x|$ may be described as follows:

    1. 2 values of x < 0
    2. 2 values of x > 0
    3. 1 value of x > 0, 1 value of x < 0
    4. 2 values of x > 0, 2 values of x < 0

44. Given that u and v are differentiable functions of x.

    At a point where $u \neq 0$, $v \neq 0$, the derivative of the quotient $y = \dfrac{u}{v}$ is given by

    1. $\dfrac{dy}{dx} = \dfrac{v\dfrac{du}{dx} - u\dfrac{dv}{dx}}{u^2}$
    2. $\dfrac{dy}{dx} = \dfrac{u\dfrac{dv}{dx} - v\dfrac{du}{dx}}{v^2}$
    3. $\dfrac{dy}{dx} = \dfrac{v\dfrac{du}{dx} - u\dfrac{dv}{dx}}{v^2}$
    4. $\dfrac{dy}{dx} = \dfrac{u\dfrac{dv}{dx} - v\dfrac{du}{dx}}{u^2}$

45. Evaluate the following limit $\lim\limits_{x \to \infty} \dfrac{2x^2 + 3x + 4}{3x^2 + 4x + 5}$

    1. no limit
    2. 3/4
    3. 4/5
    4. 2/3

46. The equation of the tangent to the curve $y = x^3 - x^2 + x - 1$ at the point on the curve where $x = 1$ is

    1. $y = 0$
    2. $2y + x = 1$
    3. $y = 2x + 2$
    4. $y = 2x - 2$

47. A group of boys and girls have an average (arithmetic mean) weight of 40 kg. If the average weight of the girls is 35 kg and the average weight of the boys is 50 kg, then the ratio of boys to girls is

    1. 2:3
    2. 1:2
    3. 3:2
    4. 2:1

48. The value of the product $(\log_a b)(\log_b a)$, where ($a > 1$, $b > 1$), is

    1. 1
    2. 0
    3. ab
    4. a+b

49. If $f(x) = 2x - 3$ and $g(x) = x^2 - 4$, find $f[g(x)] - g[f(x)]$

    1. $-2(x^2 - 6x + 8)$
    2. $-x^2 + 2x + 1$
    3. $x^2 - 2x - 1$
    4. $-2(x^2 + 6x + 3)$

50. A plane makes the trip from city A to city B, traveling at an average rate of 380 miles per hour. On the return trip, the plan flies at an average of 420 miles per hour. The average rate of the plane for the round trip in mph is

    1. 398
    2. 401
    3. 400
    4. 399

KEY (CORRECT ANSWERS)

1. 4	11. 3	21. 1	31. 1	41. 4
2. 3	12. 1	22. 4	32. 2	42. 1
3. 2	13. 4	23. 1	33. 3	43. 2
4. 4	14. 3	24. 1	34. 1	44. 3
5. 3	15. 2	25. 3	35. 4	45. 4
6. 1	16. 3	26. 4	36. 1	46. 4
7. 3	17. 3	27. 4	37. 1	47. 2
8. 3	18. 1	28. 2	38. 2	48. 1
9. 1	19. 1	29. 3	39. 2	49. 1
10. 4	20. 2	30. 2	40. 3	50. 4

SOLUTIONS TO PROBLEMS

1. When a student is inattentive but not disturbing anyone else, choice 4 is best. However, when a student is disruptive (even if he is attentive), choice 1 would be wiser. A person simply cannot keep teaching when a student is disruptive. If the student is only inattentive, a question which is related to the lesson ought to be directed to him.

2. "Do Now" problems could be used to keep students quiet, but this is NOT the purpose of such problems. Each of the selections 1, 2, and 4 does justify (in an educational sense) the usage of "Do Now" problems.

3. FIRST, factoring a quadratic trinomial should be taught. This method enables a student to solve a good percentage of problems involving quadratics. SECOND, for those expressions which are not factorable, the "Completing the square" method is best applicable. It can be shown that this method works for all expressions, factorable or not factorable. THIRD, the quadratic formula can be derived and appreciated for its compactness and availability to solve any quadratic equation.

4. To conduct an indirect proof, all possibilities must be considered. If n-1 out of the n possibilities are false AND it is known that one of the n possibilities MUST be true, then the remaining possibility must be true.

5. Both statements II and III are technically and mathematically correct. Correction for statement I: change "numbers" to "integers." Although statement IV is accurate, the definition of a rectangle is that it is a parallelogram with one right angle. The fact that it contains four right angles is a direct consequence.

6. 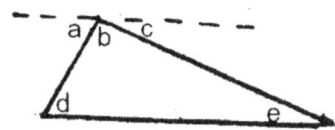 One can use a theorem that justifies $\angle a = \angle d$ and $\angle c = \angle e$.

7. $\sqrt{25} = 5$, whereas $-\sqrt{25} = -5$. The symbol $\sqrt{}$ refers to the positive value.

8. $\dfrac{x+1}{x+4}$ is irreducible since there is no common factor (other than 1) between the numerator and the denominator.

9. To solve $x^2 + 3x = 0$, rewrite as $x(x + 3) = 0$. The answers are 0 and -3.

10. Since π is irrational, it cannot be expressed as a quotient of 2 integers. Both 3.14 and $\dfrac{22}{7}$ are rational and thus serve only as approximations of π.

11. $p \to q$ is equivalent to $\sim q \to \sim p$, as can be verified by a truth table as follows:

p	q	$p \to q$	$\sim q$	$\sim p$	$\sim q \to \sim p$
T	T	T	F	F	T
T	F	F	T	F	F
F	T	T	F	T	T
F	F	T	T	T	T

12. Since $x < b < 0$, both x and b are negative numbers. Using $x < b$, if both terms are multiplied by x, the order of inequality changes; thus $x^2 > bx$. Now if both terms are multiplied by b (from $x < b$), then $bx > b^2$. Thus, $x^2 > bx > b^2$. Note that b^2, x^2, bx are all greater than 0.

13. $Log\ 2 + \frac{1}{2} Log\ x = Log\ 2 + Log\sqrt{x} = Log\ 2\sqrt{x}$. Since $x > 0$ and $Log\ x \geq Log\ 2\sqrt{x}$, we get $x \geq 2\sqrt{x}$. This implies $x^2 \geq 4x$, which would yield (normally) $x \geq 4$ or $x \leq \phi$; BUT since x is positive, the only acceptable answer is $x \geq 4$. Thus, 4 is the minimum value of x.

14. We realize that the first rectangle measures 2 by 4. Since the second rectangle is similar, let x and 2x represent 2 adjacent sides. Then, $x^2 + (2x)^2 = 10^2$, yielding $x = \sqrt{20}$ and $2x = 2\sqrt{20}$. Now, the area of the 2nd rectangle = $(\sqrt{20})(2\sqrt{20})$.

15.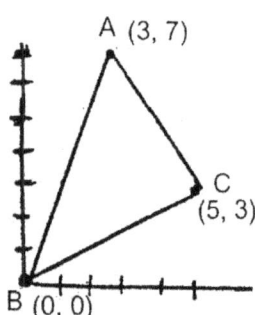

First, determine the equations of the 3 sides:

$\overline{AB}$: $y = \frac{7x}{3}$,

$\overline{BC}$: $y = \frac{3x}{5}$ and $\overline{AC}$: $y = -2x + 13$

Area of triangle = $\int_0^3 (\frac{7x}{3} - \frac{3x}{5})\ dx$

$+ \int_3^5 [(-2x + 13) - \frac{3x}{5}]\ dx =$

$[\frac{13}{15} x^2]_0^3 + [-\frac{13}{10} x^2 + 13x]_3^5 = 13$

16. $t_n = ar^{n-1}$ where t_n = nth term, a = first term, r = ratio of each term to preceding term, and n = number of terms.

$\frac{1}{6} = ar^2$ and $\frac{27}{2} = ar^6$. Divide the 2nd equation by the 1st equation to get $r^4 = 81$. Thus, r = 3 or -3. With either value of r, a = $\frac{1}{54}$.

17. Rewrite as $3^{x^2-7x} = (3^{-1})^{4x+1} = (3)^{-4x-1}$. Equating exponents, we get $x^2 - 7x = -4x - 1$ or $x^2 - 3x + 1 = 0$. Using the quadratic formula, $x = (3 \pm \sqrt{5})/2$.

18. $\begin{vmatrix} x & 2 & 1 \\ -1 & 1 & -1 \\ 3 & 2 & 3x \end{vmatrix} = 3x^2 - 6 - 2 - (3 - 2x - 6x)$
    $= 3x^2 - 8x - 11$

    Now, solving $3x^2 + 8x - 11 = 0$ to get $(3x+11)(x-1) = 0$. Thus $x = 1$ and $-11/3$.

19.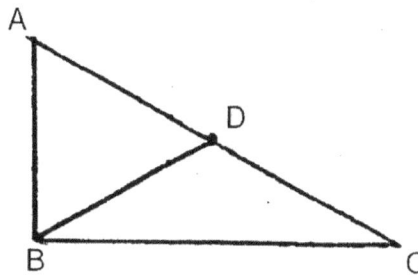

    A theorem in geometry states that a median drawn to the hypotenuse of a right triangle is equal in length to half that of the hypotenuse. Using the given information, this implies that AB=BD=AD=CD. Furthermore, since AB=1/2AC, $m\angle C = 30°$.

20.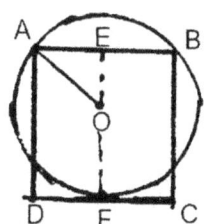

    Let r=radius $\overline{OF} \perp \overline{DC}$ and thus $\overline{OE} \perp \overline{AB}$. Now, AO = r, OE=12-r, and AE=6
    $6^2 + (12-r)^2 = r^2$ and so r=7.5.

21. cos 60° tan 45° + sin 60° tan 30° = (.5)(1) + (.866)(.577) = 1 ANOTHER METHOD: since tan 45° = 1 and tan 30° = cot 60°, rewrite as (cos 60°)(1) + (sin 60°)(cot 60°). But (sin 60°)(cot 60°) = cos 60°. Thus we have (cos 60°)(1) + cos 60° = 2 cos 60° = 1.

22. Since -2 is a solution of $x^3 - 2x^2 - 5x + 6 = 0$, x+2 is a factor.
    Likewise, the numbers 1 and 3 are solutions of $x^3 - 2x^2 - 5x + 6$; so (x-1) and (x-3) are factors. The 3 factors are (x-1), (x+2), (x-3).

23. $(256)^{.16} (256)^{.09} = 256^{.25} = \sqrt[4]{256} = 4$

24.

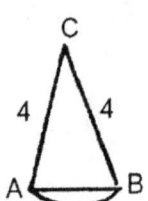

Let C = center of circle and △ABC be one of 12 triangles formed by connecting the center to each vertex. It is known that

$$\angle A = \angle B = \frac{1}{2}[180(12-2)/12] = 75°.$$

Then $\angle C = 30°$. Also, $AB^2 = 4^2 + 4^2 - (2)(4)(4)\cos 30°$. This leads to $AB \approx 2.07$. Using Hero's Formula,

area of $\triangle ABC = \sqrt{s(s-a)(s-b)(s-c)}$, where s = semiperimeter, a, b, c = lengths of sides. Substituting, we get

$\sqrt{(5.035(1.035)(1.035)(2.965)} \approx 4$.

Thus, the area of all triangles = 48.

25. Consider this diagram:

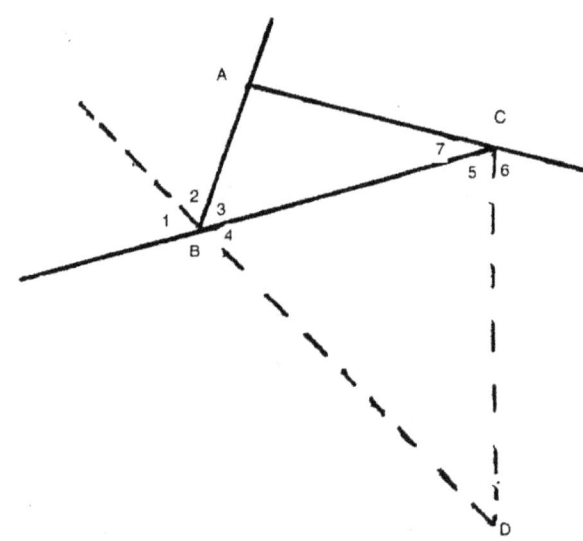

$\angle 1 = \angle 2$ and $\angle 5 = \angle 6$ since $\overline{BD}$ and $\overline{CD}$ are the exterior angle bisectors. Next, $\angle 1 = \angle 4$ by vertical angles. So $\angle 1 = \angle 4 = \angle 2$.

$\angle A + \angle 3 + \angle 7$ and $\angle D + \angle 4 + \angle 5 = 180°$. Furthermore,

(*) $\angle D + \angle 3 + \angle 4 + \angle 5 + \angle 7 + \angle A = 360°$.

Now substitute $180° - \angle 2$ for $\angle 3 + \angle 4$ and substitute $180° - \angle 6$ for $\angle 5 + \angle 7$ in the equation (*) to get:

$\angle D + (180° - \angle 2) + (180° - \angle 6) + \angle A = 360°$ which becomes $\angle D = \angle 2 + \angle 6 - \angle A$. Finally, since $\angle 2 = \angle 4$ and $\angle 6 = \angle 5$, the equation $\angle D + \angle 4 + \angle 5 = 180°$ can be transformed to $\angle 4 + \angle 5 = \angle 2 + \angle 6 = 180° - \angle D$. Now, $\angle D + \angle 2 + \angle 6 = \angle A$ becomes:

$\angle D = 180° - \angle D - \angle A$, from which we get $m\angle D = \frac{1}{2}(180 - m\angle A) = 90 - \frac{1}{2}m\angle A$

13 (#1)

26. $f(x) + f(x+1) = 3^x + 3^{x+1} = 3^x(1+3^1) = 4(3^x) = 4f(x)$

27. Substitute $x^2 = 1-9y^2$ into the second equation $(1-9y^2) + 9y^2 = 9$. This leads to $0y^2 = 8$. Thus, no solution.

28. Squaring both sides: $2\cos x + 15 = 16$. Then $\cos x = .5$ and $x = 60$. Thus, $50° < x < 75°$ is the correct inequality.

29.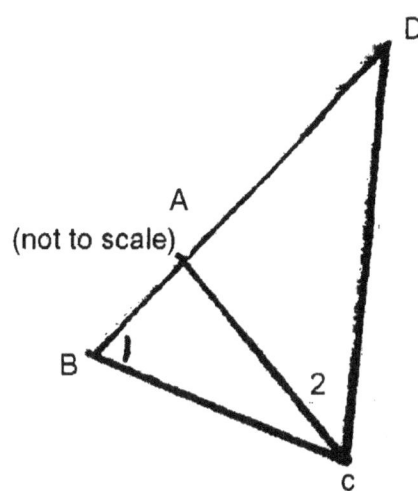

Since $\angle 1 = \angle 2$ and 2 pairs of corresponding sides which include those angles are in proportion, $\triangle ABC \sim \triangle ACD$. This can be verified since $8:14 = 12:21$. This ratio also applies to AC:AD. So, $14:AD = 4:7$ and AD $24\frac{1}{2}$.

30. If $a+bi = c+di$, then $a=c$ and $b=d$. Thus, $3x+2y = 12$ and $x=-2y$. Then $x=6$, $y=-3$. Choice 2 is correct.

31. Probability (2 red balls) $= (\frac{2}{5})(\frac{1}{4}) = \frac{1}{10}$

32.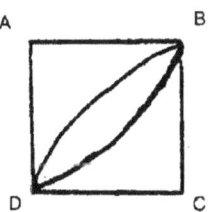

Area of sector ABD + Area of sector CDB - Area of region bounded by arcs = Area of square.

$\frac{1}{4}(16\pi) + \frac{1}{4}(16\pi) - x = 16$

Thus, $x = 8\pi - 16$

33.

After cutting off the squares with side x, length = 15-2x, width = 8-2x, height = x. Volume = $(15-2x)(8-2x)(x) = 120x - 46x^2 + 4x^3$. Next, $dV/dx = 120 - 92x + 12x^2$. Set $dV/dx = 0$ for maximum value of V. Then $x = \frac{5}{3}$ and 6. Reject x = 6, since this would force the width to be negative. Only x = is correct.

34. Since 2 is a root, $16-48+2p+q = 0$. Since 3 is also a root, $54-108+3p+q = 0$. Solving, $p=22$, $q=-12$. Now $2x^3-12x^2+22x-12 = 0$, which equals $x^3-6x^2+11x-6 = 0$ can be written as $(x-2)(x-3)(x-R) = 0$. Solving, $R=1$. Thus, 1 is the 3rd root.

35. If $2+i$ is a root, then so is $2-i$. Thus, there are at least 4 roots and 4 must be the lowest possible degree.

36. By DeMoivre's Theorem, the 3 cube roots of 27 are: $3(\cos 0° + i \sin 0°)$, $3(\cos 120° + i \sin 120°)$, and $3(\cos 240° + i \sin 240°)$.
    The second root lies in Quadrant II.

37. The polynomial $x^3 + 3x^2 + cx + 5$ must have a value of 13 when 2 is substituted for x. (Remainder Theorem) Thus, $8 + 12 + 2c + 5 = 13$. Then, $c = -6$.

38. $y = \sin x$ and $y = \cos x$ will intersect at $(-\frac{3\pi}{4}, -\frac{1}{\sqrt{2}})$ and $(\frac{\pi}{4}, \frac{1}{\sqrt{2}})$ when $-\pi \le x \le \pi$.

39. By the Law of Cosines, $c^2 = a^2 + b^2 - 2ab \cos$. $c^2 = 1 + 4 -(4)(1/4)$. Thus, $c = 2$.

40. $5C1 + 5C2 + 5C3 + 5C4 + 5C5 = 5 + 10 + 10 + 5 + 1 = 31$, where aCb means combinations of a items taken b at a time.

41. Since ABPO is a trapezoid, 2 sides must be parallel. It is NOT possible for $\overline{AD}$ to be parallel to $\overline{BP}$ because the x-coordinate of P would have to be 6. Thus, $\overline{AB} // \overline{OP}$. Slope of $\overline{AB}$ = slope of $\overline{OP}$ = $(4-8)/(6-0) = -2/3$. Equation of $\overline{OP}$: $y = \frac{2}{3}x$ and so P is located at $(12,-8)$.
    Slope of $\overline{BP}$ = $(-8-4)/(12-6) = -2$, and so the equation of $\overline{BP}$: $y = -2x + 16$. Finally, the y-intercept of $\overline{BP}$ is found by letting $x = 0$. Thus y-intercept = 16.

42. Sixth term $(9 C 5)(\frac{2}{x\sqrt{3}})^4(\frac{x^2}{2})^5 = (126)(\frac{2^4}{9x^4})(\frac{x^{10}}{2^5}) = 7x^6$

43. Either $3x-4 = 5-4x$ or $3x-4 = -(5-4x)$. The solution becomes: $x = 9/7$ and $x = 1$. Thus, we have 2 values of $x > 0$.

44. $\frac{dy}{dx} = (v\frac{du}{dx} - u\frac{dv}{dx})/v^2$

15 (#1)

45. Divide all terms by x^2 to get: $\dfrac{2+\dfrac{3}{x}+\dfrac{4}{x^2}}{3+\dfrac{4}{x}+\dfrac{5}{x^2}}$

    Limit of this fraction as $x \to 0$ is $\dfrac{2}{3}$

46. Determine $\dfrac{dy}{dx} = 3x^2 - 2x + 1$. Evaluate $3x^2 - 2x + 1$ at $x = 1$ to get 2. Thus, the tangent has a slope of 2 and passes thru (1, 0). Note that the 0 y-value was obtained by evaluating $x^3 - x^2 + x - 1$ at $x = 1$. Finally, the equation of the tangent is $y = 2x - 2$.

47. Let x = number of boys, y = number of girls. Realize that the total weight of the entire group of boys and girls can be expressed as either the total number of boys and girls times their average weight or the total weight of boys plus the total weight of the girls. Thus, $(x+y)(40) = 50x + 35y$. This reduces to $10x = 5y$ or $x:y = 1:2$.

48. Let $\text{Log}_a b = x$ so that $a^x = b$. Let $\text{Log}_b a = y$ so that $b^y = a$.
    By substitution, $a^x = (b^y)^x = b$. This implies that $xy = 1$.

49. $f[g(x)] = f(x^2-4) = 2(x^2-4)-3 = 2x^2-11$
    $g[f(x)] = g(2x-3) = (2x-3)^2 - 4 = 4x^2-12x+5$
    Now $f[g(x)] - g[f(x)] = -2x^2 + 12x - 16 = -2(x^2 - 6x + 8)$

50. Let distance from A to B be x miles. Average rate = Total distance divided by total time
    $= (x+x) \div (\dfrac{x}{380} + \dfrac{x}{420}) = 2x \div [(x)(800)/159{,}600] = 399$ mph.

EXAMINATION SECTION
TEST 1

DIRECTIONS: Each question or incomplete statement is followed by several suggested answers or completions. Select the one that BEST answers the question or completes the Statement. *PRINT THE LETTER OF THE CORRECT ANSWER IN IN THE SPACE AT THE RIGHT.*

1. A parent of a failing student comes to school for a conference. Her son failed the first three tests in tenth year mathematics. She asks what would be most helpful for her son. The LEAST desirable advice you could give her would be to

    1. send him for in-school tutoring
    2. have him drop the course and start over next semester
    3. have him do his homework and study for tests with a classmate
    4. send him to you early each day to discuss the previous day's lesson

2. On full period class tests in mathematics, there usually is clear, written indication of the credits to be assigned for each correct response. Of the following, the BEST justification for this procedure is that

    1. students will not waste time claiming more credit than is due them
    2. students can have a basis for budgeting time and making choices
    3. students can check that the mark they received was computed correctly
    4. the teacher will be able to mark the test more efficiently

3. Proof by deduction can be taught in

    1. algebra classes *only*
    2. geometry classes *only*
    3. honor classes *only,* because of its difficulty
    4. both algebra and geometry classes

4. In planning a 40 minute lesson on problem solving for your ninth year algebra class, the MOST desirable allotment of time for a final summary is _____ minutes.

    1. 4   2. 8   3. 12   4. 16

5. You find that students are continually coming late to your tenth year mathematics class. Which of the following is the LEAST desirable course of action?

    1. Call the parents of latecomers.
    2. Send notes to the teachers of previous classes requesting that they be dismissed on time.
    3. Lock the door at the late bell and refuse to admit any latecomers.
    4. Give short quizzes at the beginning of each lesson and refuse to give extra time to latecomers.

6. A pupil in your eleventh year mathematics class insists that $\sqrt{a^2+9}=a+3$. Of the following, the BEST procedure to follow is to tell the student

1. that $\sqrt{a^2+9}$ is not equal to $a+3$
2. that one must be cautious about applying the distributive law
3. that the two expressions are only equal when $a = 0$
4. to substitute a non-zero rational number for a

7. In tenth year mathematics a teacher plans to present the following topics:
   (a) The sum of the measures of the angles of a triangle is 180.
   (b) The definition of parallel lines.
   (c) The sum of the measures of the interior angles of a polygon with n sides is 180 (n-2).
   (d) If two parallel lines are cut by a transversal, the alternate interior angles are congruent.

   The BEST of the following teaching sequences is

   1. a, b, d, c
   2. a, c, b, d
   3. c, a, b, d
   4. b, d, a, c

8. An eleventh year mathematics class, studying operations _____ with complex numbers, was asked to find the product of $\sqrt{-9}$ and $\sqrt{-4}$. Student A wrote $\sqrt{-9}\sqrt{-4}=\sqrt{36}=6$. Student B maintained that $\sqrt{-9}\sqrt{-4}=(3i)(2i)=6i^2=-6$.
   Which of the following is TRUE?

   1. Both students are CORRECT.
   2. A is CORRECT and B is INCORRECT.
   3. B is CORRECT and A, is INCORRECT.
   4. Both students are INCORRECT.

9. When asked to find the solution set of $\sqrt{x+5}=2x$ an eleventh year mathematics student gave the answer $\{1\frac{1}{4}, -1\}$. His response is

   1. CORRECT
   2. INCORRECT, because he made a mistake in squaring
   3. INCORRECT, because he made a mistake in factoring
   4. INCORRECT, because he neglected to use the check as an essential part of the solution

10. In an eleventh year mathematics class, students made the following statements concerning the Law of Cosines. Which statement is INCORRECT?

    1. The law of Cosines is a generalization of the Pythagorean Theorem.
    2. The use of logarithms is often very helpful in applying the Law of Cosines.
    3. Given the magnitudes of two forces that act on an object, and given the angle between the forces, we can use the Law of Cosines to find the magnitude of the resultant.
    4. Since the Law of Cosines is developed using the distance formula, if we used the Law of Cosines to prove the Pythagorean Theorem, our reasoning would be circular.

11. The repeating decimal $0.\overline{314}$ may be represented by

    1. $\dfrac{314314}{1000000}$ 2. $\dfrac{314}{1000}$ 3. $\dfrac{314}{990}$ 4. $\dfrac{314}{999}$

12. An article was sold for m dollars at a gain of 15% on the cost. The cost in dollars of the article was

    1. $\dfrac{m}{.15}$ 2. $\dfrac{m}{1.15}$ 3. 15 m   4. 1.15 m

13. A student takes six class tests during the term. If his arithmetic average was p for the first three tests and q for the next two tests, what mark on the sixth test will give him an average of 80 for all the tests?

    1. 480 - (3p + 2q)
    2. 80 - (3p + 2q)
    3. 480 - (p + q)
    4. 80 - (p + q)

14. The sum of a number, $x \neq 0$, and its reciprocal is equal to the product of the same number and its reciprocal. Which of the following equations can be used to find this number?

    1. $x^2 + x + 1 = 0$
    2. $x^2 + x - 1 = 0$
    3. $x^2 - x + 1 = 0$
    4. $x^2 - x - 1 = 0$

15. In triangle ABC, D is the midpoint of $\overline{AB}$ and E is the midpoint of $\overline{AC}$ and $\overline{DE}$ is drawn. The ratio of the area of triangle ADE to quadrilateral BCED is

    1. 1:1   2. 1:2   3. 1:3   4. 1:4

16. The radius of a circle is increased by 3 centimeters. The number of centimeters by which the circumference is increased is

    1. 6π 2. 3π 3. 3   4. 9

17. The diagonals of a rhombus measure 6 and 8. The altitude of the rhombus measures

    1. 2.4   2. 4.8   3. 9.6   4. 12

18. At a certain college, 1/3 of all applications sent to prospective students were never returned. Of those returned, 2/5 were rejected and 1/6 of those accepted decided not to attend.
    How many applications were sent out if 1,000 freshmen were admitted?

    1. 6000   2. 2000   3. 3000   4. 4500

19. Two lines have equations ax + by + c = 0 and dx + ey + f = 0. The graphs of these lines will be perpendicular to each other if and *only* if

    1. ae - bd = 0
    2. ad - be = 0
    3. ad + be = 0
    4. ae + bd = 0

20. A certain printing press can print an edition of a newspaper in 4 hours. After this press has been at work for 1 hour, a second press also starts to print the same edition. Working together, both presses require one more hour to finish the job.
How many hours would it have taken the second press to print the edition if it had worked alone?

   1. 5   2. 2   3. 3   4. 4

21. The sum of the squares of the roots of the equation $x^2 - 6x + 4 = 0$ is

   1. 28   2. 10   3. 18   4. 23

22. The fraction $\dfrac{x^{-1} + y^{-1}}{x^{-1}}$ is equivalent to

   1. $\dfrac{x}{x+y}$ 2. $\dfrac{x+y}{x}$ 3. $1 + \dfrac{1}{y}$ 4. $1 + \dfrac{x}{y}$

23. Fifty equally spaced markers are placed on a level highway so that the distance between the first and tenth markers is 90 meters. How many meters are in the distance between the first and last marker?

   1. 441   2. 450   3. 490   4. 500

24. Which of the following functions has an inverse relation which is NOT a function?

   1. $f(x) = 1/2 - x - 2$
   2. $f(x) = x^2 + 3$
   3. $f(x) = \log_{10} x$
   4. $f(x) = \text{Arc sin } x$

25. The sides of a triangle have lengths 1, 1, $\sqrt{3}$. The measure of the LARGEST angle of this triangle is

   1. $\dfrac{\pi}{3}$ 2. $\dfrac{\pi}{2}$ 3. $\dfrac{2\pi}{3}$ 4. $\dfrac{5\pi}{6}$

26. For values of x for which $f(x)$ is defined, $f(x) = \dfrac{1 + \tan x}{\sec x + \csc x}$ is equal to

   1. sin x
   2. cos x
   3. tan x
   4. 1

27. Which one of the following is an element of the solution $2 \sin^2 x - 3 \sin x - 2 = 0$ if $0 \leq x \leq 2$?

   1. 2/3
   2. 5/6
   3. 7/6
   4. none of the above

28. On the curve $y = x$, two points P and Q are chosen having abscissas a and b respectively.

   The slope of $\overline{PQ}$ is

   1. $a + b$ 2. $a - b$ 3. $b - a$ 4. $\dfrac{a-b}{a+b}$

29. A can 3 inches in diameter contains 12 fluid ounces of water. A can filled to the same height but 4 inches in diameter contains _____ fluid ounces.

   1. 16
   2. 18
   3. $21\frac{1}{3}$
   4. $28\frac{4}{9}$

30. The solution set of $x^2 < x$, where x is a real number, is

   1. $\{x \mid x < 0\}$
   2. $\{x \mid 0 < x < 1\}$
   3. $\{x \mid x > 0\}$
   4. $\{x \mid x < 1\}$

31. If $\log V = t \log E + \log K$, then

   1. $V = (KE)^t$
   2. $V = E^t + K$
   3. $V = KE^t$
   4. $V = tE + K$

32. The number of distinct chords which can be drawn connecting 5 points on a circle is

   1. 20
   2. 15
   3. 10
   4. 5

33. The solution set for $x^3 + 27 = 0$ is

   1. $\{3, 3i, -3i\}$
   2. $\{-3, \frac{3+3i\sqrt{3}}{2}, \frac{3-3i\sqrt{3}}{2}\}$
   3. $\{-3, \frac{3+i\sqrt{3}}{2}, \frac{3-i\sqrt{3}}{2}\}$
   4. $\{3i, 3, -3\}$

34. The $\lim\limits_{x \to 3} \frac{x^2 - 9}{x - 3}$ is

   1. 6
   2. ∞
   3. 3
   4. 0

35. If * is an associative binary operation such that a*b=c, c*d=e and b*d = f, then a * f equals

   1. b
   2. c
   3. d
   4. e

36. Cos 160° is equal to all of the following EXCEPT

   1. -sin 110°
   2. sin 200°
   3. cos 200°
   4. sin 290°

37. When $x^{29} - 3x^{21} + 2$ is divided by $x - 1$, the remainder is

   1. -2
   2. 0
   3. 3
   4. 4

38. The velocity of a particle moving along the x-axis is given by the formula $v = 3t^2 + 4$. The acceleration of the particle

   1. varies *directly* as the time
   2. varies *directly* as the square of the time

3. varies *inversely* as the time
4. is constant

39. The slope of the line tangent to the circle whose equation is $x^2 + y^2 = 40$ at the point (2, 6) is

    1. -3
    2. -1/3
    3. 3
    4. 1/3

40. The equation of the axis of symmetry for the curve $y^2 = x - 6y$ is

    1. $y - 6 = 0$
    2. $2x = 3y$
    3. $x - 3 = 0$
    4. $y + 3 = 0$

41. The area bounded by the graph $f(x) = -x^2 + 5x$ and the x-axis is

    1. $\dfrac{125}{6}$
    2. $\dfrac{25}{6}$
    3. $\dfrac{25}{2}$
    4. $\dfrac{125}{3}$

42. $\overline{AB}$ and $\overline{CD}$ are parallel lines and the distance between them is 4 centimeters. Point P lies on $\overline{AB}$. In the plane determined by $\overline{AB}$ and $\overline{CD}$, the number of points 5 centimeters from P and equidistant from $\overline{AB}$ and $\overline{CD}$ is

    1. 1
    2. 2
    3. 3
    4. 4

43. The contrapositive of the statement "If it is summer, then the days are hot" is:

    1. If it is not summer, then the days are not hot.
    2. If the days are hot, then it is summer.
    3. It is summer and the days are not hot.
    4. If the days are not hot, then it is not summer.

44. A line segment is drawn from the center of a face of a unit cube to a vertex of the opposite face. The length of the line segment is

    1. $\sqrt{3}$
    2. 2
    3. $\dfrac{1}{2}\sqrt{6}$
    4. 1.5

45. A box contains only red cards and black cards. If a card is selected at random from the box, the probability that it is red is 4/7.
    Which of the statements below is CORRECT?

    1. The box contains 4 red cards and 7 black cards.
    2. If a card is selected at random from the box, the probability that it is black cannot be determined from the given information.
    3. The box contains 4 red cards and 3 black cards.
    4. If a card is selected at random from the box, the probability that it is black is 3/7

46. In Euclidean geometry, which one of the statements below is TRUE in a plane and FALSE in 3-dimensional space?

    1. Two lines parallel to the same line are parallel to each other.
    2. Two lines perpendicular to the same line are parallel to each other.

3. Through a given point not on a given line, there is one and only one line parallel to the given line.
4. Through a given point not on a given line, there is one and only one line perpendicular to the given line.

47. Which one of the following statements is FALSE? The derivative of the

   1. volume of a sphere with respect to the radius, equals the surface of the sphere.
   2. total surface of a cube with respect to an edge, equals the total length of all the edges of the cube.
   3. area of an equilateral triangle with respect to a side, equals the altitude of the triangle.
   4. volume of a cube with respect to an edge, equals the total surface of the cube.

47.____

48. The series represented by the expression $\sum_{k=1}^{n}(2k-1)$ is equal to

   1. $\dfrac{n(n+1)}{2}$
   2. n^2
   3. $(n+1)^2$
   4. $n(n+1)$

48.____

49. The graph of $|x| + |y| = 4$ is

   1. a square
   2. two intersecting lines
   3. two parallel lines
   4. one line

49.____

50. Which of the following is FALSE?

   1. A common error in inductive reasoning is "hasty generalization."
   2. Validity of conclusions reached by deduction depends on the number of cases investigated.
   3. When we use syllogisms to reach conclusions, we are using deductive reasoning.
   4. An induction assigns to a set of property found true for a certain subset.

50.____

KEY (CORRECT ANSWERS)

1. 2	11. 4	21. 1	31. 3	41. 1
2. 2	12. 2	22. 4	32. 3	42. 2
3. 4	13. 1	23. 3	33. 2	43. 4
4. 4	14. 3	24. 2	34. 1	44. 3
5. 2	15. 3	25. 3	35. 4	45. 4
6. 4	16. 1	26. 1	36. 2	46. 2
7. 4	17. 2	27. 4	37. 2	47. 4
8. 3	18. 3	28. 1	38. 1	48. 2
9. 4	19. 3	29. 3	39. 2	49. 1
10. 2	20. 2	30. 2	40. 4	50. 2

SOLUTIONS TO PROBLEMS

1. If a student has already failed 3 tests, having him drop the course and starting over next term will NOT correct the student's shortcomings. The student will probably fare no better next term.

2. It is MOST desirable that students spend time on test questions which is directly proportional to their respective values in points.

3. Deduction can be applied in many areas of mathematics, including algebra and geometry.

4. Approximately 20% of a lesson's time could be used for summarizing the material (usually). Sometimes though, only 3 or 4 minutes suffice.

5. Since students have the responsibility of coining to class on time, notes should NOT be sent to other teachers. If a student is being detained by another teacher, that student has the responsibility of attending each class on time. Choice 2 also mistakenly assumes that the cause of a student's lateness is the action of another teacher.

6. When a student substitutes the value of 2 for a, he can see that $\sqrt{2^2+9}$, which equals $\sqrt{13} \neq 5$.

7. First, parallel lines need to be defined. Second, relationships can be explained with 2 parallel lines and a transversal. Third, the proof that the angles of a triangle sum to 180 can be shown by using parallel lines and a transversal. Finally, the development of a formula for the sum of the interior angles of any polygon depends upon dividing that polygon into triangles.

8. The CORRECT procedure is to convert each radical to the "i" form before multiplying. Thus, choice 3 is correct.

9. To solve $\sqrt{x+5}=2x$, square both sides to get $x + 5 = 4x^2$. Then $(4x-5)(x+1)=0$ and $x = 5/4$ and -1. However, -1 is an extraneous root since $\sqrt{-1+5} \neq 2(-1)$. The answer is $\{1\frac{1}{4}\}$.

10. The Law of Cosines: $a^2 = b^2 + c^2 - 2bc \cos\angle A$. The use of logarithms would be of no help in this equation.

11. Let $N = 0.\overline{314}$. Then $1000N = 314.\overline{314}$ and by subtraction, $999N = 314$. Thus, $N = 314/999$.

12. Let C = cost. Then $m = C + .15C = 1.15C$. Finally, $C = m/1.15$.

13. An average of p for the first 3 tests implies a total of 3p. Likewise an average of q for the next 2 tests implies a total of 2q. Let x = score on sixth test. Now, $\frac{3p+2q+x}{6}=80$ which means x = 480 - 3p - 2q.

14. We have x + 1/x = (x)(1/x), which implies $(x^2 + 1)/x = 1$ This equation can be rewritten as $x^2 - x + 1 = 0$.

15.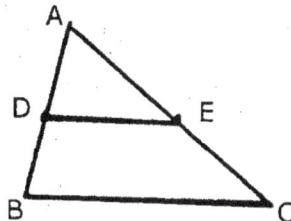
It can be proved that area of △ADE = 1/4 area of △ABC. Thus, the ratio of △ADE to quadr. BCED is 1:3.

16. Let R = original radius and R + 3 = new radius.
Then original circumference = $2\pi R$ and new circumference = $2\pi(R+3) = 2\pi R + 6\pi$.
Thus, the increase for the circumference is 6π.

17.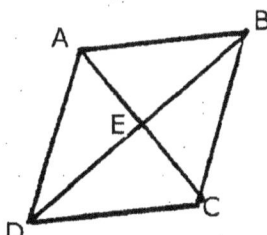
Let DB = 8, AC = 6. Since the diagonals are perpendicular bisectors of each other, the area of each of the 4 triangles = (1/2)(4)(3) = So, the area of the rhombus = 24. Also, $DE^2 + CE^2 = CD^2$. Thus $4^2 + 3^2 = CD^2$ and CD = 5.
Finally, 24 = (5)(altitude). Altitude = 4.8

18. Let x = number of applications sent out. Then $\frac{2}{3}x$ = number of applications returned; $\left(\frac{3}{5}\right)\left(\frac{2}{3}x\right)=\frac{2}{5}x$ = number of applicants accepted; $\left(\frac{5}{6}\right)\left(\frac{2}{5}x\right)=\frac{1}{3}x$ decided to attend. Thus $\frac{1}{3}x = 1000$ and so x = 3000.

19. The slope of the first line is -a/b and the slope of the second line is -d/e. In order for the 2 lines to be perpendicular to each other, the slope of one line must equal the negative reciprocal of the other line. Thus, $-\frac{a}{b}=-1/-\frac{d}{e}$ which implies that ad + be = 0.

20. Let x = number of hours the 2nd press would need if it were to work alone. In performing the present job, the 1st press will have worked 2 hours and the 2nd press will have worked 1 hour. The sum of the fractions representing the respective parts of the job done by each press equals 1. Thus, 2/4 + 1/x = 1. Consequently, x = 2 hours.

21. Let R_1, R_2 = the 2 roots. $R_1 + R_2 = 6$ and $R_1 R_2 = 4$.
    So, $(R_1+R_2)^2 = R_1^2 + 2R_1R_2 + R_2^2 = 36$. Since $2R_1R_2 = 8$,
    this means $R_1^2 + R_2^2 = 28$.

22. Rewrite the expression as $\left(\dfrac{1}{x}+\dfrac{1}{y}\right)/\dfrac{1}{x} = \dfrac{1}{x}/\dfrac{1}{x}+\dfrac{1}{y}/\dfrac{1}{x} = 1 + \dfrac{x}{y}$.

23. There is a distance of 10 meters between each marker. From the 1st marker to the last represents 49 markers in distance, which equals (49)(10) = 490 meters.

24. The inverse of $f(x) = x^2 + 3$ is $g(x) = \pm\sqrt{x-3}$, and thus $g(x)$ is NOT a function.

25.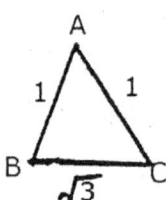

    $\angle A$ must be the largest angle of the triangle since it lies opposite the largest side.
    Now, $(\sqrt{3})^2 = (1)^2 + (1)^2 - (2)(1)(1) \cos \angle A$.
    Then $\cos \angle A = -\dfrac{1}{2}$ and $\angle A = 120°$ or $2\pi/3$ radians. (Diagram not drawn to scale.)

26. Rewrite as $\left(1+\dfrac{\sin x}{\cos x}\right)/\left(\dfrac{1}{\cos x}+\dfrac{1}{\sin x}\right) = \dfrac{\cos x + \sin x}{\cos x} / \dfrac{\sin x + \cos x}{(\cos x)(\sin x)} = \sin x$

27. Factor as $(2 \sin x + 1)(\sin x - 2) = 0$. Then $\sin x = -1/2$ and $\sin x = 2$. From $\sin x = -1/2$, we get $x = 210°$ or $7\pi/6$ radians. Since $7\pi/6 \approx 3.67$, none of the first three selections is correct. Note that $\sin x = 2$ has no solution.

28. The coordinates of $P:(a, a^2)$ and the coordinates of $Q:(b, b^2)$.
    The slope of $\overline{PQ} = (b^2-a^2)/(b-a) = b+a = a+b$.

29. Volume of 1st can = $(\pi)(\dfrac{3}{2})^2(H) = 27\pi H$ cubic inches. The volume of the 2nd can
    = $\pi(2)^2(H) = 48\pi H$ cubic inches. Thus, the ratio of volumes of the 1st can to the 2nd can is $27\pi H / 48\pi H = 9/16$. Let x = number of fluid ounces in the 2nd can.
    Then, $\dfrac{12}{x} = \dfrac{9}{16}$ and $x = 21\dfrac{1}{3}$.

30. $x^2 < x$ becomes $x^2 - x < 0$. Then $x(x-1) < 0$.
    Case 1: $x < 0$ and $x - 1 > 0$ simultaneously. This is impossible.
    Case 2: $x > 0$ and $x - 1 < 0$ simultaneously. This implies $0 < x < 1$.

31. Rewrite the right side of the equation as $\log E^t + \log K = \log (E^t)(K)$.
    Now, $\log V = \log (E^t)(K)$, so $V = KE^t$.

32. The problem resolves into $5^{(}2 = 5 \cdot 4/2 = 10$.

33. Use DeMoivre's Theorem to solve $x^3 + 27 = 0$. Rewrite $\sqrt[3]{-27}$

    $(-27+0i)^{\frac{1}{3}} = [27(\cos 180° + i \sin 180°)]^{\frac{1}{3}}$

    $= 3(\cos 60° + i \sin 60°), 3(\cos 180° + i \sin 180°),$ and $3(\cos 300° + i \sin 300°)$

    $= \dfrac{3+3i\sqrt{3}}{2}, -3$ and $\dfrac{3-3i\sqrt{3}}{2}$

34. If $x \neq 0$, $(x^2 - 9)/(x-3) = x + 3$. Thus, $\lim\limits_{x \to 3} x + 3 = 6$

35. $a*f = a*(b*d) = (a*b)*d = c*d = e$

36. $\cos 160° = -.94$, but $\sin 200° = -.34$.

37. By the Remainder Theorem, the remainder is the value of $x^{29} - 3x^{21} + 2$ when $x = 1$. Value $= 1^{29} - 3(1)^{21} + 2 = 0$

38. Acceleration $= dv/dt = 6t$, which implies that acceleration varies directly as time.

39. Differentiating the equation: $2x + 2y \dfrac{dy}{dx} = 0$, so $dy/dx = \dfrac{-x}{y}$ since dy/dx = slope, at (2,6) the slope $= -2/6 = -1/3$

40. Rewrite the equation as $x = y^2 + 6y$, which becomes $x = (y^2 + 6y + 9) - 9$ which can be written as $x = (y+3)^2 - 9$, Axis of symmetry is $y = -3$ or $y + 3 = 0$.

41.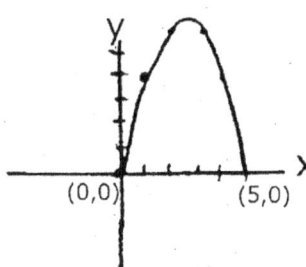

    Area $= \int_0^5 (-x^2 + 5x)dx = \left[\dfrac{-x^3}{3} + \dfrac{5x^2}{2} \right]_0^5$

    $= \dfrac{125}{6}$

42.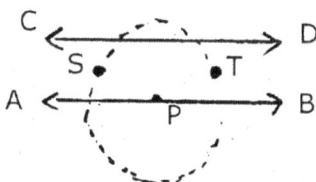

    The locus of points 5 cm. from P is a circle and the locus of points equidistant from $\overline{AB}$ and $\overline{CD}$ is a line parallel to and halfway between them. Only points S and T satisfy both conditions.

43. The contrapositive of "If p, then q" is "If not q, then not p."

44. The line of segment in question is the hypotenuse of a right triangle whose sides are 1) a line segment joining the center points of 2 opposite faces and 2) half a diagonal on the opposite face. Let x = hypotenuse. Then $x^2 = 1^2 + \left(\frac{\sqrt{2}}{2}\right)^2 = \frac{3}{2}$

    Thus $x = \sqrt{\frac{3}{2}} = \frac{1}{2}\sqrt{6}$.

45. Probability of selecting a red card and probability of selecting 4 3 a black card = 1. Thus, the required probability $= 1 - \frac{4}{7} = \frac{3}{7}$.

46. "Two lines perpendicular to the same line are parallel to each other" is true in a plane but false in 3-dimensional space.

47. Volume of a cube = e^3, where e = length of one side. dv/de = $3e^2$, whereas the total surface area = $6e^2$.

48. This summation is 1 + 3 + 5+...+ 2n-l, which is an arithmetic progression whose sum can be written as $\frac{n}{2}[1+(2n-1)] = n^2$.

49. The graph appears as

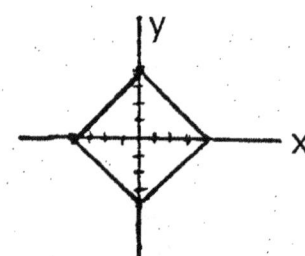

50. In using deduction, the validity of conclusions must be reached using a GENERAL case, rather than a fixed number of specific cases.

EXAMINATION SECTION
TEST 1

DIRECTIONS: Each question or incomplete statement is followed by several suggested answers or completions. Select the one that BEST answers the question or completes the statement. *PRINT THE LETTER OF THE CORRECT ANSWER IN THE SPACE AT THE RIGHT.*

1. On a uniform test at the end of tenth year mathematics (geometry), the MOST important reason for including questions requiring long answers is to

    1. check students' ability to express themselves in correct English
    2. occupy students for the entire testing period
    3. check students' ability to handle full proofs
    4. check that students have memorized proofs of required theorems

2. The INDIRECT method of proof can

    1. not be taught because it is difficult for high school students
    2. be taught in reference to everyday life situations only
    3. be taught in connection with geometric proofs only
    4. be taught in all grades of mathematics

3. A ninth year class is continuing multiplication of binomials. In a 40 minute lesson, the LEAST desirable allotment of time for motivation is _____ minutes.

    1. 4
    2. 8
    3. 15
    4. 20

4. Which of the following is the LEAST desirable procedure to use in determining the final grade for a student in a ninth year mathematics class?

    1. Rank students from top to bottom on the basis of tests and daily work. Give the top student the highest grade and each other student a lower grade in proportion to his rank.
    2. Compute the average of written tests and adjust this according to class performance.
    3. Use the arithmetic mean of all full period test marks as the grade.
    4. Give weights to homework, classwork, notebook, and test marks, and use all of these to compute the grade.

5. In preparing the plan for a developmental lesson, which of the following should be given LEAST emphasis?

    1. Key questions
    2. Lecture
    3. Motivation
    4. Summaries

6. When the term is half over, a pupil who has been "cutting" your mathematics class for two weeks returns to class and becomes a discipline problem because he cannot understand the work being done.
The BEST procedure for the teacher to follow is to

    1. report the pupil to the dean for appropriate disciplinary action
    2. arrange for make-up tutoring in school under supervision

2 (#1)

3. suggest private tutoring outside the school
4. recommend that the pupil drop the subject since he has little chance of success

7. A student in tenth year mathematics has learned that corresponding angles of congruent triangles are congruent. He then concludes that if the three angles of one triangle are congruent respectively to the three angles of a second triangle, the triangles must be congruent.
He is reasoning

   1. *correctly*
   2. *incorrectly* because he is reasoning by analogy
   3. *incorrectly* because he is assuming the truth of the converse
   4. *incorrectly* because he is assuming the truth of the contrapositive

8. As a new teacher you experience considerable difficulty in getting the attention of your mathematics class at the start of the lesson. Of the following, the BEST procedure to employ in overcoming this difficulty is to

   1. begin each lesson with a pertinent interesting activity
   2. contact the parents of all the troublemakers
   3. ask the dean to assist you in quieting the class
   4. lower the grades of the students who are inattentive after the bell rings

9. When asked to find all values of x between $0°$ and $360°$ for which $\cos^2 x + \cos x = 0$, an eleventh year mathematics student divided both sides of the equation by cos x and obtained $\cos x + 1 = 0$. He then concluded that $\cos x = -1$ and $x = 180°$.
His solution is

   1. *incorrect* because it fails to include all values of x between $0°$ and $360°$ for which $\cos x = -1$
   2. *incorrect* because it excludes zero from the range of cos x.
   3. *incorrect* because it excludes zero from the domain of x
   4. *correct*

10. In eleventh year mathematics a teacher plans to present the following topics:

    a. solving quadratic equations by use of the quadratic formula
    b. solving quadratic equations of the form $ax^2 = b$
    c. solving quadratic equations by completing the square
    d. determining the nature of the roots of a quadratic equation

    The BEST of the following teaching sequences is
    5. b, c, a, d   6. d, a, b, c
    7. a, d, c, b   8. c, b, d, a

11. Which of the following numbers is 26^9 ?

    1. 5, 011, 849, 549, 824   2. 5, 429, 503, 678, 976
    3. 5, 847, 157, 808, 128   4. 5,638, 330, 743, 552

12. A dealer sold two calculators for $15 each, one at a profit of 25% of its cost, the second at a loss of 25% of its cost. The COMBINED effect of the two transactions is

1. no gain or loss
2. a gain of $2
3. a gain of $3
4. a loss of $2

13. The repeating decimal $0.\overline{247}$ may be represented by

    1. $\dfrac{2470}{9999}$
    2. $\dfrac{247247}{1,000,000}$
    3. $\dfrac{247}{999}$
    4. $\dfrac{247}{1000}$

14. One hundred dollars is invested at a rate of interest of 8% per annum compounded semi-annually. The TOTAL value of the investment in dollars at the end of one year will one

    1. 116.64
    2. 108.16
    3. 108.08
    4. 108.00

15. Let x represent a positive real number. Consider the following statements:

    I. $\sqrt{-x} = -\sqrt{x}$
    II. $\sqrt[3]{-x} = -\sqrt[3]{x}$

    1. I and II are *false*
    2. I is *false* and II is *true*
    3. I is *true* and II is *false*
    4. I and II are *true*

16. If a and b are real numbers, then $\sqrt{a}\,\sqrt{b}$ is NOT equal to $\sqrt{ab}$ when

    1. a > 0 and b > 0
    2. a > 0 and b < 0
    3. a < 0 and b = 0
    4. a < 0 and b < 0

17. If $x^7 - 7x - 56$ is divided by $x - 2$, the remainder is

    1. 28
    2. 58
    3. 86
    4. -170

18. Which of the following equations has 0 and 1 + i as elements of its solution set?

    1. $x^2 - 2x + 2 = 0$
    2. $x^3 - 2x^2 + 2x = 0$
    3. $x^2 + 2x - 2 = 0$
    4. $x^3 + 2x^2 - 2x = 0$

19. The solution set for $x^2 - 2x - 3 < 0$ is

    1. $\{x \mid x < -1\}$
    2. $\{x \mid x > 3\}$
    3. $\{x \mid -1 < x < 3\}$
    4. $\{x \mid x < -1 \text{ or } x > 3\}$

20. If $\left|\dfrac{3(3x-5)}{2}\right| = 15$, then the solution set for x is

    1. $\{5\}$
    2. $\{5, -5\}$
    3. $\left\{-5, \dfrac{5}{3}\right\}$
    4. $\left\{5, -\dfrac{5}{3}\right\}$

21. Cos 160° is equal to each of the following EXCEPT

    1. $-\sin 110°$
    2. $\sin 200°$
    3. $\cos 200°$
    4. $\sin 290°$

22. Let r_1 and r_2 be the roots of the equation $x^2 - bx + c = 0$. If r_1^2 and r_2^2 are the roots of the equation $x^2 - dx + e = 0$, then d equals

    1. $b^2 + c^2$
    2. $b^2 + 2c$
    3. $b^2 - 2c$
    4. b^2

23. the $\lim_{x \to 3} \dfrac{x^2 - 9}{x - 3}$ is

    1. 0
    2. 6
    3. 3
    4. ∞

24. Which of the following expressions is equal to $\log_2 10$?

    1. $\dfrac{1}{\log_{10} 2}$
    2. $\dfrac{10}{\log_{10} 2}$
    3. $1 - \log_{10} 2$
    4. $-\log_{10} 2$

25. The area of a triangle having vertices whose rectangular coordinates are (0, 0), (2, 0) and (x,1)

    1. equals 1
    2. equals 2
    3. *increases* as x *increases*
    4. *decreases* as x *increases*

26. If the perimeter of a triangle is 12, the length of one side can be equal to

    1. 7
    2. $6\dfrac{1}{2}$
    3. 6
    4. $5\dfrac{1}{2}$

27. The length of a side of a rhombus is s. If s is the mean proportional between the lengths of the diagonals of the rhombus, the area of the rhombus is

    1. $\dfrac{s^2}{2}$
    2. $\dfrac{s^2}{2}\sqrt{3}$
    3. s^2
    4. $2s^2$

28. In acute triangle ABC medians $\overline{AD}$ and $\overline{BE}$ intersect in point F. The ratio of the area of triangle AFB to the area of triangle ABC is

    1. 1:6
    2. 1:4
    3. 1:3
    4. 1:2

29. A circle is inscribed in triangle ABC. AB = 8, BC = 10 and AC = 12. If D, E, and F are the points of contact of $\overline{AB}$, $\overline{BC}$ and $\overline{AC}$ respectively, the length of $\overline{AD}$ is

    1. 3
    2. 5
    3. 7
    4. 8

30. Point P is 3 centimeters from $\overline{AB}$. In the plan determined by P and $\overline{AB}$, the number of points that are 7 centimeters from P and 1 centimeter from $\overline{AB}$ is

   1. 1 2. 2 3. 3 4. 4

31. If a side of an equilateral triangle is 6, then the area of the inscribed circle is

   1. 2π
   2. 3π
   3. 12π
   4. cannot be determined from the information given

32. The measure in degrees of a central angle of a circular sector is 40. If the radius of the sector is 5, then the length of the arc of the sector is

   1. $\frac{2}{9}\pi$ 2. $\frac{4}{9}\pi$ 3. $\frac{10}{9}\pi$ 4. $\frac{20}{9}\pi$

33. Which one of the statements below is TRUE in a plane and FALSE in 3-dimensional space?

   1. Two lines parallel to the same line are parallel to each other.
   2. Two lines perpendicular to the same line are parallel to each other.
   3. Through a given point not on a given line, there is one and only one line parallel to the given line.
   4. Through a given point not on a given line, there is one and only one line perpendicular to the given line.

34. A line segment is drawn from the center of a face of a unit cube to a vertex of the opposite face. The length of the line segment is

   1. 1.5 2. 2 3. $\sqrt{3}$ 4. $\frac{1}{2}\sqrt{6}$

35. The graph of $\{(x, y)| ax^2 + by^2 = c\}$ where a, b, and c are real numbers, CANNOT be a(n)

   1. circle
   2. parabola
   3. ellipse
   4. hyperbola

36. An equation of the locus of a point whose distance from the origin is twice its distance from the point (3, 0) is

   1. $x^2 + y^2 + 8x + 12 = 0$
   2. $x^2 + y^2 - 8x + 12 = 0$
   3. $x^2 + y^2 + 12x + 18 = 0$
   4. $x^2 + y^2 = 12x + 18 = 0$

37. The slope of the line tangent to the circle whose equation is $x^2 + y^2 = 40$, at the point (2, 6), is

   1. $-\frac{1}{3}$ 2. $\frac{1}{3}$ 3. 3 4. -3

38. If $\frac{\pi}{2} < \theta < \pi$, then $\sin\theta$ and $\cos\theta$ are, respectively,

   1. $\sqrt{1-\cos^2\theta}$ and $\sqrt{1-\sin^2\theta}$
   2. $-\sqrt{1-\cos^2\theta}$ and $\sqrt{1-\sin^2\theta}$
   3. $\sqrt{1-\cos^2\theta}$ and $-\sqrt{1-\sin^2\theta}$
   4. $\sqrt{1-\cos^2\theta}$ and $-\sqrt{1-\sin^2\theta}$

39. In triangle ABC a = 6, and the measure in degrees of angle A is 30. The measure in degrees of angle B is

   1. 45 *only*
   2. 135 *only*
   3. either 45 or 135
   4. 90 *only*

40. The equations of two lines are respectively $a_1 x + b_1 y = c_1$ and $a_2 x + b_2 y = c_2$. The two lines are parallel IF and only IF

   1. $a_1 b_2 - a_2 b_1 \neq 0$ and $c_1 b_2 - c_2 b_1 \neq 0$
   2. $a_1 b_2 - a_2 b_1 \neq 0$ and $c_1 b_2 - c_2 b_1 = 0$
   3. $a_1 b_2 - a_2 b_1 = 0$ and $c_1 b_2 - c_2 b_1 \neq 0$
   4. $a_1 b_2 - a_2 b_1 = 0$ and $c_1 b_2 - c_2 b_1 = 0$

41. If n and r represent positive integers and n > r, then $\frac{n(n-1)(n-2)\ldots(n-r+1)}{1 \cdot 2 \cdot 3 \ldots r}$ is an integer

   1. *only* if n is composite
   2. *only* if r divides n
   3. *only* if n is composite and r divides n
   4. for all values of n and r

42. A particle moves along the x - axis and its directed distance from the origin at any time t > 0 is given by $x = at^3 - bt^2$ (a>0, b>0). The velocity is a minimum when

   1. $\frac{dx}{dt} = 0$
   2. $\frac{d^2x}{dt^2} = 0$
   3. $\frac{dx}{dt} = 0$ and $\frac{d^2x}{dt^2} = 0$
   4. $t = 0$

43. The area bounded by the graph of $f(x) = \dfrac{1}{x^2}$ (x>0), the x - axis and the lines x = 2 and x = 3 is

    1. $\dfrac{1}{9}$
    2. $\dfrac{1}{6}$
    3. $\dfrac{1}{4}$
    4. $\dfrac{13}{72}$

44. The function f (x) has a derivative at x = a if

    1. $\lim_{x \to a} f(x)$ exists
    2. f(x) is defined at x = a
    3. $\lim_{x \to a} \dfrac{f(x) - f(a)}{x - a}$ exists
    4. f(x) is continuous at x = a

45. Consider the four relations:

    A = {(x, y) | x + y = 6
    B = {(x, y) | x + y^2 = 6
    C = {(x, y) | x^2 + y = 6
    D = {(x, y) | x^2 + y^2 = 6

    Of the four relations, those which are also FUNCTIONS are
    1. A and B
    2. A and C
    3. A and D
    4. B and C

46. If A represents the set of algebraic numbers and R represents the set of real numbers, then a number which belongs to A ∩ R is

    1. e
    2. π
    3. i
    4. $\sqrt{5}$

47. Let us define a*b to mean $\dfrac{a - 2b}{3}$ where a and b represent integers. If a = 15, b = 6 and c = 3, then a*(b*c) equals

    1. 5
    2. 0
    3. $-\dfrac{5}{3}$
    4. -2

48. The negation of the statement "x is a positive integer, and x is odd," is equivalent to:

    1. If x is NOT a positive integer, then x is NOT odd.
    2. If x is odd, then x is a negative integer.
    3. x is NOT a positive integer, and x is NOT odd.
    4. x is NOT a positive integer or x is NOT odd.

49. Two names, each associated with a surface that can have only one side, are

    1. Euler, Jordan
    2. Jordan, Klein
    3. Klein, Moebius
    4. Moebius, Euler

50. A box contains only red cards and black cards. If a card is selected at random from the box, the probability that it is red is 3/5. Which of the statements below is CORRECT?

    1. The box contains 3 red cards and 2 black cards.
    2. The box contains 3 red cards and 5 black cards.
    3. If a card is selected at random from the box, the probability that it is black is 2/5.
    4. If a card is selected at random from the box, the probability that it is black cannot be determined from the given information.

KEY (CORRECT ANSWERS)

1. 3	11. 2	21. 2	31. 2	41. 4
2. 4	12. 4	22. 3	32. 3	42. 2
3. 1	13. 3	23. 2	33. 2	43. 2
4. 1	14. 2	24. 1	34. 4	44. 3
5. 2	15. 2	25. 1	35. 2	45. 2
6. 1	16. 4	26. 4	36. 2	46. 4
7. 3	17. 2	27. 1	37. 1	47. 1
8. 1	18. 2	28. 3	38. 3	48. 4
9. 2	19. 3	29. 2	39. 3	49. 4
10. 1	20. 4	30. 4	40. 3	50. 3

SOLUTIONS TO PROBLEMS

1. Long answers in geometry are nearly always related to providing a proof. A key objective in this type of math course is to train a student to prove an hypothesis using statements and reasons in a logical sequence.

2. The indirect proof method can be taught in any grade of high school math, since this method can be used in areas other than geometry.

3. Motivation time should be minimal.

4. Choice 1 is LEAST desirable since a number of students would have to receive low grades based on other students grades. A student's average should not suffer due to a better performance by other students.

5. The lecture is not as important as the other choices when preparing a developmental lesson. In this type of lesson, the instructor is striving to obtain active student participation in order that knowledge is imparted.

6. A student who has "cut" class and subsequently becomes a discipline problem should be reported to the school disciplinarian FIRST. If and when the student's attitude improves, then choice 2 or even choice 3 might be appropriate.

7. The student has assumed the truth of the converse, which is incorrect.

8. If a teacher has difficulty in getting the attention of the class, the use of an interesting application of math might be helpful. However, there are times when the teacher needs to remind the students of the importance of paying attention in class.

9. The range of cos x includes 0 since $\cos^2 x + \cos x = 0$ means $\cos x (\cos x + 1) = 0$. The correct answers for x are $90°$ and $180°$.

10. Easy equations like $5x^2 = 20$ should be done FIRST. Second, completing the square would be instructional. Third, a student can then appreciate the convenience of using the quadratic formula, the proof of which is based on completing the square. Finally, the student can understand the nature of the roots of any quadratic equation.

11. Any number ending in a 6 which is raised to a positive integral value will still have 6 as its last digit. Only choice 2 ends in a 6.

12. The first calculator's cost to the dealer = $15 ÷ 1.25 = $12. The second calculator's cost to the dealer = $15 ÷ .75 = $20. The combined effect for the dealer was ($15+$15)-($12+$20) = -$2, thus a loss of $2.

13. Let $N = .\overline{247}$. Then $1000N = 247.\overline{247}$. By subtraction, $999N = 247$ and so $N = 247/999$.

14. Total value at the end of one year = $\$100(1.04)^2 = \$108.16$.

15. As a numerical example, $\sqrt{-4} = 2i \neq -\sqrt{4}$ but $\sqrt[3]{-27} = -3 = -\sqrt[3]{-27}$

16. $\sqrt{a} \cdot \sqrt{b} \neq \sqrt{ab}$ when both a and b are negative.

    Example: $\sqrt{-9} \cdot \sqrt{-25} = (3i)(5i) = 15i^2 = -15 \neq \sqrt{(-9)(-25)} = \sqrt{225} = 15$.

17. By the Remainder Theorem, the remainder is the value of $x^7 - 7x - 56$ when x is replaced by 2. This value is $2^7 - 7(2) - 56 = 58$.

18. Since 1 + i is one of the roots, 1 - i must also be a root. Now, if 0, 1 + i and 1-i are the roots, then the equation with these roots can be written: x (x- [1+i])(x-[1-i]) = 0.
    This becomes $x^3 - 2x^2 + 2x = 0$.

19. $x^2 - 2x - 3 = (x-3)(x+1) < 0$.
    Case 1: x-3 < 0 and x+1 > 0 which implies -1 < x < 3.
    Case 2: x-3 > 0 and x+1 < 0 which is impossible.
    Final answer: -1 < x < 3.

20. Case 1: 3(3x-5)/2 = 15 which yields x = 5.
    Case 2: 3(3x-5)/2 = -15 from which $x = -\frac{5}{3}$. Answer: $\left\{5, -\frac{5}{3}\right\}$

21. cos 160° = -.94, whereas sin 200° = -.34.

22. Since $R_1 R_2$ are roots of $x^2 - bx + c = 0$, we know that $R_1 + R_2 = b$
    and $(R_1)(R_2) = c$. Likewise, we have R_1^2, R_2^2 are roots of $x^2 - dx + e = 0$; thus $R_1^2 + R_2^2 = d$ and
    $(R_1^2)(R_2^2) = e$.
    Now, $R_1^2 + 2R_1R_2 + R_2^2 = (R_1R_2)^2 = b^2$, and since $2R_1R_2 = 2c$, we have
    $R_1^2 + 2c + R_2^2 = b^2$ or $R_1^2 + R_2^2 = b^2 - 2c$. This means $d = b^2 - 2c$.

23. When $x \neq 3$, $(x^2-9)/x-3 = x+3$. Thus $\lim_{x \to 3} \frac{x^2 - 9}{x - 3} = 6$.

24. Let $x = \text{Log}_2 10$. Then $2^x = 10$, from which $x \text{Log}_{10} 2 = \text{Log}_{10} 10$ or $x \text{Log}_{10} 2 = 1$.
    Thus, $x = \frac{1}{\text{Log}_{10} 2}$.

25. Regardless of the value of x, the resulting triangle will have a base of 2 and a height of 1. Area = (1/2)(2)(1) = 1.

26. The sum of any 2 sides of a triangle must ALWAYS be greater than the 3rd side. If that 3rd side were 5 1/2, the other 2 sides would add to 6 1/2. This is the only correct selection.

27. Let d_1, d_2 be the lengths of the diagonals. Area of the rhombus = $(d_1)(d_2)/2$. But $s^2 = d_1 d_2$ since s is the mean proportional between d_1 and d_2. Thus, the area = $s^2/2$.

28.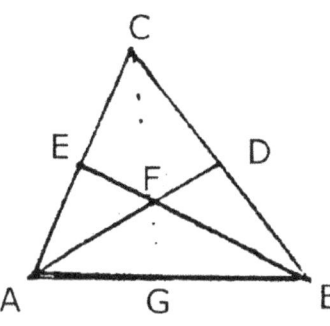
A theorem in geometry states that the medians of an acute triangle meet at a point F such that

$EF = \frac{1}{3} BE$, $FD = \frac{1}{3} AD$, and

$FG = \frac{1}{3} CG$. Also, the altitude from C to AB is 3 times the altitude from F to AB. Thus, the area of $\triangle AFB$ is 1/3 the area of $\triangle ABC$.

29. Let AD = x, so that DB = 8-x. Likewise AF = x, so that CF = 12-y. Also, BE = z, so that CE = 10-z. From a point outside a circle, the tangents drawn to that circle must be equal. Thus, x = y, 8-x = z, and 10-z = 12-y. Solving x = AD = 5.

30.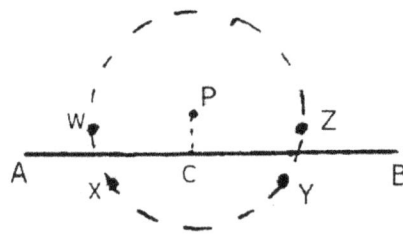
PC = 3, when $\overline{PC} \perp \overline{AB}$. Circle has radius 7. W, X, Y, Z are all 1 unit from $\overline{AB}$ and on the circle.

31. The height of the triangle is $3\sqrt{3}$, so that the radius of the inscribed circle $= (\frac{1}{3}) 3\sqrt{3} = \sqrt{3}$. Area of circle = $\pi(\sqrt{3})^2 = 3\pi$

32. Convert 40° to $\frac{2\pi}{9}$ radians. $L = R\theta$, where L = length of arc formed by a central angle, R = radius of circle, and θ = measure of the central angle in radians. Thus $L = (5)(\frac{2\pi}{9}) = \frac{10\pi}{9}$ units.

33. Two lines perpendicular to the same line are necessarily parallel to each other ONLY if all three lines lie in the same plane.

34. The required line segment is the hypotenuse of a right triangle in which one leg is a line segment joining the center points of 2 opposite faces. The other leg is half a diagonal of the opposite face. Let x = required segment. Then $x^2 = 1^2 + (\frac{\sqrt{2}}{2})^2 = \frac{3}{2}$.

So, $x = \sqrt{\dfrac{3}{2}} = \dfrac{1}{2}\sqrt{6}$.

35. In the equation of a parabola, one variable is quadratic and the other variable must be linear.

36. Let (x, y) be a general point. Then $\sqrt{x^2+y^2} = 2\sqrt{(x-3)^2+y^2}$ which reduces to $x^2+y^2-8x+12 = 0$.

37. $2x + 2y\dfrac{dy}{dx} = 0$, so $\dfrac{dy}{dx} = -\dfrac{x}{y}$ = slope. Substituting (2, 6), the slope $= -\dfrac{1}{3}$.

38. All 4 statements lead to $\sin^2\theta - \cos^2\theta = 1$, but only statement 3 illustrates that if $\dfrac{\pi}{2} < \theta < \pi$, then $\sin\theta$ is a *positive* number whereas $\cos\theta$ is a *negative* number.

39. By the Law of Sines, $\dfrac{6}{\sin 30°} = \dfrac{6\sqrt{2}}{\sin <B}$, $\sin <B = \dfrac{\sqrt{2}}{2}$.

    Then $\angle B = 45°$ or $135°$.

40. Slope of the 1st line $-\dfrac{a_1}{b_1}$. Slope of the 2nd line $-\dfrac{a_2}{b_2}$. In order for the 2 lines to be parallel, $= -\dfrac{a_1}{b_1} = -\dfrac{a_2}{b_2}$ which implies $a_1 b_2 - a_2 b_1 = 0$. since the y intercepts must be different,

    $\dfrac{c_1}{b_1} \neq \dfrac{c_2}{b_2}$. This means $c_1 b_2 - c_2 b_1 \# 0$.

41. Recognize that $\dfrac{n(n-1)(...)(n-r+1)}{(1)(2)(....)(r)} = n<r$ which is the number of combinations of n items taken r at a time, n< r must always be an integer.

42. To find the MINIMUM velocity, find d^2x/dt^2 and set it = to 0. $dx/dt = 3at^2 - 2bt$ and so $d^2x/dt^2 = 6at - 2b$. Note that when $d^2x/dt^2 = 0$, $t = b/3a$. The minimum velocity is $(3a)(b/3a)^2 - 2b(b/3a) = (b-2b^2)/3a$. Also note that velocity = dx/dt.

43. Area $= \displaystyle\int_2^3 \dfrac{1}{x^2} dx = [-\dfrac{1}{x}]_2^3 = -\dfrac{1}{3} - (-\dfrac{1}{2}) = \dfrac{1}{6}$

44. f(x) is differentiate at x = a IF $\displaystyle\lim_{x \to a} \dfrac{f(x)-f(a)}{x-a}$ exists.

45. To be a function, each value of x must correspond to exactly one y. Only equations A and C are functions.

46. Only $\sqrt{5} = 5^{\frac{1}{2}}$ is algebraic. Both e and π are transcendental. i is imaginary.

47. b*c = (b-2c) / 3 = [6-2(3)1] /3 = 0. Now a*0 = [a-2(o)/3 = (15-0) / 3 =5

48. The negation of P $\wedge$ Q is ~ (P $\wedge$ Q) = ~ P V~Q which translates to "not P or not Q." Statement 4 is the negation.

49. ----- By empirical knowledge.

50. Probability of a black card $1 - \frac{3}{5} = \frac{2}{5}$.

EXAMINATION SECTION
TEST 1
GENERAL EDUCATION

Questions 1-20.

DIRECTIONS: Each question or incomplete statement is followed by several suggested answers or completions. Select the one that BEST answers the question or completes the statement. *PRINT THE LETTER OF THE CORRECT ANSWER IN THE SPACE AT THE RIGHT.*

1. The MOST desirable type of classroom discipline is BEST attained through which one of the following practices?   1.____
    A. Encouraging traits of self-discipline
    B. Including class behavior in the final rating
    C. Establishing the idea that rules and regulations will be strictly enforced
    D. Anticipating difficulty and sending the first few minor cases of breach of discipline to the chairman or dean

2. If you find a student in one of your classes doing very poorly despite an obviously high potential, the MOST desirable procedure among the following to take is to   2.____
    A. refer the student to the guidance counselor
    B. ask the student to bring his parents to school to see you
    C. write a letter to his parents asking them to come to school to see you
    D. interview the student yourself before making any referrals or calling his parents

3. The procedure of requiring students to stand and face the class when responding is   3.____
    A. *advisable* because it discourages calling out of answers
    B. *inadvisable* because it creates an ordeal for the shy l student
    C. *advisable* because it increases audibility of answers
    D. *inadvisable* because a recalcitrant student would dispute the rule

4. Of the following, the BEST procedure for obtaining the aim of a specific lesson is   4.____
    A. for the teacher to state the aim of the lesson and write it on the blackboard so that all will be sure to have it
    B. to elicit the aim from the class and have it written on the board
    C. for the teacher to dictate the aim of the lesson so that all students can get it in their notebooks
    D. to give the aim the previous day so that the students can prepare for the lesson

5. Of the following, the BEST course of action for a new teacher who is having difficulty in presenting a particular type of lesson to take is to   5.____
    A. make an arrangement with an experienced teacher to observe his classes
    B. consult the chairman and request an opportunity for intervisitation
    C. try to adjust without outside help to avoid demonstrating weakness to colleagues
    D. discuss the problem frankly with the class and ask for suggestions from the class

6. Of the following, the BEST situation for using essay questions is where 6.____

   A. it is desired to test the ability of a pupil to organize his answers
   B. the class is made up chiefly of slow pupils
   C. *single shot* questions are needed to complete an examination
   D. it is desired to sample a large area of subject matter

7. In a lesson in which a new topic is to be taught, which one of the following is the MOST desirable principle to follow? 7.____

   A. Make certain that all difficulties encountered by pupils in doing the previous homework assignment have been corrected before beginning the new topic.
   B. Allow sufficient time to include a suitable motivation of the new material, a development, and independent pupil practice.
   C. Introduce the new topic, but require pupils to study the textbook for a complete explanation.
   D. Insist that no questions be asked by pupils until the development is completed.

8. A test may be said to be reliable when 8.____

   A. it consistently measures what it attempts to measure
   B. it adequately deals with the types of educational outcomes to be measured at proper levels of difficulty for pupils
   C. there is a high correlation between test scores and criterion measures
   D. it can be obtained on time from publishers

9. Of the following, the one which does NOT measure the concentration of scores in any set of scores or group of data is the 9.____

   A. mode   B. modulus   C. mean   D. median

10. Of the following, the GREATEST advantage of short-answer tests is the 10.____

    A. ease with which the test items can be constructed
    B. ease with which such tests can be standardized
    C. wide sampling of the subject matter of the course
    D. ease with which the test results can be interpreted

11. The MOST effective use of the talents and abilities of the able pupils in your subject area would be gained by which one of the following procedures? 11.____

    A. Give them extra homework assignments in order to earn better marks.
    B. Give them the responsibility of tutoring disadvantaged pupils.
    C. Give them monitorial duties, such as marking test papers.
    D. Excuse them from class work which they grasp easily so they do enrichment work in other subject areas.

12. The MAIN advantage of standardized tests is 12.____

    A. objectivity
    B. ease of marking for teachers
    C. marks may be compared with other groups
    D. it provides greater motivation for students

13. A percentile score of 55 is

    A. a score equivalent to the arithmetic median of the scores
    B. equaled or exceeded by 45% of the scores in the distribution
    C. equivalent to a score of 55 out of 100
    D. the accepted norm

14. The process of reviewing homework daily is time-consuming.
    Of the following suggestions made by a group of teachers, which one is MOST sound pedagogically?

    A. Do not go over the homework at all.
    B. Go over in class only the problems with which pupils had trouble.
    C. Collect the homework of only one row at a time and return it corrected the next day.
    D. Collect the homework of the whole class once a week on a specific day.

15. Which one of the following is the BEST statement about a teacher's technique of questioning?

    A. No question should be so difficult that even the slowest pupil couldn't answer it.
    B. Each lesson should have at least one question which would require the pupils to do critical thinking.
    C. There should be a series of pivotal questions to highlight the chief learnings.
    D. Each question should be simple and short.

16. Of the following, the BEST statement concerning skill in questioning is that

    A. to make sure all students hear, the teacher should often repeat her question
    B. answers should be repeated because some children sit far away from the pupil who is answering
    C. each question should be addressed to a particular pupil by giving his name before asking the question
    D. a question should be addressed to the entire class

17. Of the following, the LEAST effective method for obtaining pupil participation is to

    A. give a warm-up drill to the entire class
    B. group the class and give different assignments to each group
    C. have pupils answer in concert
    D. use experiences of pupils in the lesson development

18. A test which is too difficult will USUALLY yield scores that fall into a _____ distribution

    A. bell-shaped   B. negatively skewed
    C. positively skewed   D. bimodal

19. The MOST desirable routine procedure for going over homework is to

    A. compare answers orally with the class
    B. have students put their work on the board and explain it to the rest of the class
    C. have the teacher do each example together with the class
    D. collect it and mark it outside of class, returning it within a week

20. Of the following characteristics of a good lesson plan, the one which applies LEAST is that it

   A. forms part of a larger unit
   B. helps give direction to the lesson
   C. be adhered to even if vital side issues appear
   D. focuses on a meaningful problem

MATHEMATICS EDUCATION

Questions 21-40.

DIRECTIONS: Each question or incomplete statement is followed by several suggested answers or completions. Select the one that BEST answers the question or completes the statement. PRINT THE LETTER OF THE CORRECT ANSWER IN THE SPACE AT THE RIGHT.

21. Which one of the following was a serious logical defect in Euclid's work?

   A. No clues were given as to how his proofs were conceived.
   B. He attempted to define every term.
   C. He rigidly separated plane geometry from solid geometry.
   D. He used clumsy methods for calculation.

22. Of the following, the BEST reason for encouraging pupils in tenth year mathematics to experiment is that this procedure

   A. avoids boredom
   B. furnishes pupils with an opportunity to discover new theorems
   C. gives pupils practice in using compasses
   D. proves new theorems

23. Suppose that one of the brightest girls in the school is doing quite poorly in algebra. The LEAST plausible explanation among the following for her poor performance is that

   A. there is sibling rivalry since a younger sister does brilliantly in this area
   B. she is very much absorbed in her talent, which happens to be playing the clarinet
   C. most females do much poorer work in mathematics than males
   D. she had poor instruction in arithmetic in the early grades

24. Of the following, the MOST valid objection to the use of the *box method* for solving verbal problems is that the

   A. arrangement of the data is confusing to the student
   B. formula relating the data is not apparent to the student
   C. solution becomes too mechanized
   D. arrangement of the data is not conducive to effective checking of the answer(s)

25. Which one of the following statements would a bright tenth year student find MOST difficult to prove?

   A. If the bisectors of two angles of a triangle are equal, the triangle is isosceles.
   B. If the medians to two sides of a triangle are equal, the triangle is isosceles.

C. Two triangles are congruent if they agree in a side, an angle adjacent to that side and the altitude to that side.
D. If the diagonals of a trapezoid are equal, the trapezoid is isosceles.

26. If a teacher asks his class to find two numbers whose product is zero, then he is MOST likely preparing to teach which one of the following topics?

    A. Zero exponents
    B. Solution of a linear equation
    C. Solution of a quadratic equation
    D. Graph of a second degree equation

27. The transformation of several fractions with unlike denominators into equivalent fractions with a common denominator should be taught in each case as an application of the

    A. commutative postulate for multiplication
    B. associative postulate for multiplication
    C. multiplicative identity postulate
    D. multiplicative inverse postulate

28. A good reference book for a high school teacher of mathematics is a four volume book containing literature of mathematics, edited by James R. Newman, entitled

    A. AN INTRODUCTION TO MATHEMATICS
    B. AN INVITATION TO MATHEMATICS
    C. MATHEMATICS FOR THE MILLION
    D. THE WORLD OF MATHEMATICS

29. In solving for side b of a right △ ABC with right angle at C, when side a and ∠A are given, the class may BEST be taught to avoid division by using the

    A. cosine of the complement of ∠A
    B. sine of the complement of ∠A
    C. tangent of the supplement of ∠A
    D. tangent of the complement of ∠A

30. As a preliminary to a unit in the solution of inequalities, the teacher may introduce which one of the following axioms? (a, b, k are real numbers)

    A. If $a > b$, $a + k > b + k$
    B. If $a > b$, $ak > bk$
    C. If $a > b$, $\frac{a}{k} > \frac{b}{k}$
    D. If $a > b$, $k - a > k - b$

31. Of the following, the principal justification for teaching the process of completing the square in a second year algebra course is to develop a method for

    A. demonstrating a relationship between algebra and geometry
    B. factoring perfect square trinomials
    C. transforming equations of conic sections
    D. deriving the general quadratic formula

32. When a student solves the equation $x^2 = x$ by dividing both sides of this equation by x to obtain x = 1, it would be BEST for a teacher to follow up with which one of the following comments?

   A. This is correct.
   B. Let's check the answer.
   C. How many roots does a quadratic equation have?
   D. We should first write the equation in the form $ax^2 + bx + c = 0$.

33. Which one of the following is considered to be the MOST valid justification for the process of elimination by adding in the solution of simultaneous linear equations?

   A. If equals are added to equals, the sums are equal.
   B. If two equalities are added, member for member, and the results equated, the solution set of the resulting equality contains the common solution of the two original equalities.
   C. A quantity may be substituted for its equal.
   D. If two equalities are added, member for member, and the results equated, the new equation has the same solution set as each of the original equations.

34. The fact that the product of two negative numbers is a positive number is BEST presented to an eleventh year class as a(n)

   A. rule developed by mathematicians which students are to memorize
   B. rule which can be justified by various concrete examples
   C. application of the commutative postulate
   D. application of the distributive postulate

35. In teaching the solution of the equation $5x + 4 = 24$, a number of postulates may be used, including (a) the identity for addition, (b) the identity for multiplication, (c) the inverse for addition, (d) the inverse for multiplication.
   Which one of the following series represents the MOST appropriate sequence for solving the equation?

   A. abcd   B. cadb   C. acbd   D. cdab

36. Of the following graphs, the one that a teacher may use to illustrate a function containing the ordered pairs (x,y) is a

   A. circle of the form $x^2 + y^2 = a^2$
   B. straight line of the form $x = a$
   C. parabola of the form $y^2 = ax$
   D. straight line of the form $y = b$

37. Which one of the following topics would LEAST likely be taught in an introduction to the study of logarithms?

   A. Exponential equations   B. Significant figures
   C. Scientific notation   D. Inverse variation

38. The identity 2x + 3x = 5x should be taught as a direct application of which one of the following postulates?   38._____

    A. Associative
    B. Commutative
    C. Distributive
    D. Additive identity

39. Which one of the following areas is MAINLY emphasized in the modern mathematics programs in the high schools?   39._____

    A. Non-Euclidean geometry
    B. Algebra as a postulational system
    C. Rote learning
    D. Calculus as a required subject

40. In teaching the use of Newton's method to find an approximate value for $\sqrt{43}$, if the first step taught is to divide 43 by 6 since $6<\sqrt{43}<7$, then the next step to teach is which one of the following?   40._____

    A. $43 - (7.1)^2$
    B. $43 - 36$
    C. $\dfrac{6+7.1}{2}$
    D. $\dfrac{6+7}{2}$

KEY (CORRECT ANSWERS)

1. A	11. B	21. B	31. D
2. D	12. C	22. B	32. C
3. C	13. B	23. C	33. B
4. B	14. B	24. C	34. D
5. B	15. C	25. A	35. B
6. A	16. D	26. C	36. D
7. B	17. C	27. C	37. D
8. A	18. C	28. D	38. C
9. B	19. B	29. D	39. B
10. C	20. C	30. D	40. D

TEST 2
GENERAL EDUCATION

Questions 1-25.

DIRECTIONS: Each question or incomplete statement is followed by several suggested answers or completions. Select the one that BEST answers the question or completes the statement. *PRINT THE LETTER OF THE CORRECT ANSWER IN THE SPACE AT THE RIGHT.*

1. Of the following, the generally LEAST acceptable type of short-answer question is 1.____

   A. multiple choice
   B. completion
   C. true-false
   D. matching

2. Pupils who seem sensitive, timid, and/or immature USUALLY respond most favorably to a teacher's efforts when the teacher uses which one of the following methods? 2.____

   A. Reproves them frequently
   B. Punishes even minor infractions
   C. Urges them to enter competitions
   D. Praises even minor progress

3. Which one of the following is the MOST efficient way to distribute duplicated sheets to a class? 3.____

   A. The teacher individually hands each pupil a sheet.
   B. A monitor hands each pupil a sheet.
   C. The teacher counts off a set of papers for each column and asks the first pupil in each column to take one and pass the rest back.
   D. A monitor counts off a set of papers for each row and asks the first pupil in each row to take one and pass the rest to the side.

4. Intervisitation among teachers in a department is 4.____

   A. *unwise,* because teachers should be creative, not imitative
   B. *wise,* because teachers can gain a great deal from sharing methods and techniques
   C. *unwise,* because teachers do not like to be observed by their colleagues
   D. *wise,* because only the few *master teachers* have ideas which are good enough for the others to use

5. If a student in one of your subject classes has not done any homework for two weeks, which one of the following would be the BEST procedure to follow as an initial measure? 5.____

   A. Send him to your chairman with a note explaining the situation.
   B. Keep him after school while he makes up the homework.
   C. Discuss with him privately the reasons for his failure to do the homework.
   D. Give him a failing rating on the first report, regardless of his test average.

6. In seating your classes, it is USUALLY wisest to do which one of the following?

   A. Rearrange their seats according to marks on tests.
   B. Seat them so that the better students can assist poorer students easily.
   C. Seat them in strict alphabetical order.
   D. Let them sit wherever they wish.

7. Which one of the following is LEAST likely to succeed in sustaining the attention of slow learners? A

   A. 30-minute film
   B. 30-minute lecture
   C. change in activity every 10 minutes
   D. 20-minute laboratory exercise

8. That *practice makes perfect* is USUALLY more acceptable for

   A. slow learners than it is for rapid learners
   B. average learners than it is for slow learners
   C. rapid learners than it is for slow learners
   D. superior students than it is for average learners

9. Through which one of the following types of lessons will a teacher be MOST likely to succeed in helping children become able to learn by themselves?

   A. Supervised study
   B. Lecture-demonstration
   C. Note-giving
   D. Laboratory-demonstration

10. Of the following, which man has written a series of books on American education?

    A. Jansen   B. Pauling   C. Conant   D. Acheson

11. In connection with teaching a technical term, it is usually BEST to

    A. develop the concept before giving the term its technical name
    B. introduce the technical term and then develop the concept
    C. give the technical term and define it without follow-up discussion
    D. give the technical term, define it, and then explain the concept to the class

12. Summaries of learnings elicited during and at the end of a lesson are USUALLY

    A. a waste of time
    B. useful only to slow learners
    C. important in focusing attention on the concepts developed
    D. not as good as summaries dictated by the teacher for copying into pupils' notebooks

13. When there is some unnecessary commotion in the hallway during a lesson, the teacher should FIRST

    A. shut the door and continue with the lesson
    B. send one of the students to the administrative assistant's office and alert him
    C. step to the door to see what is the cause of the commotion so that he may take appropriate action
    D. send the students involved to the dean's office

14. Which one of the following statements about lesson plans is LEAST acceptable? They   14.____
    A. should be done anew each year even if the same subjects are to be taught
    B. continue to become less and less necessary as your years of experience increase
    C. should include the actual phraseology of pivotal questions to be asked
    D. should be prepared weekly but be flexible enough to permit daily additions and corrections

15. Of the following, the BEST approach to use in connection with the reporting of subject-class absentees who are not on the daily official class absentee list is to   15.____
    A. be very certain to send in a *cutting* slip for each missing student not on the absentee list, no matter what his record is in the subject-class
    B. select those in whom you have the least faith and send in *cutting* slips for them
    C. wait a week or so before sending in any *cutting* slips and try to use your personal influence on the students as you meet them later
    D. send in one *cutting* slip each day as an example to the others

16. When the common element in a number of experiences has been recognized and extracted by a student, then the student has MOST likely formed a(n)   16.____
    A. percept   B. concept   C. objective   D. hypothesis

17. Which one of the following is NOT the responsibility of the homeroom teacher?   17.____
    A. Encourage overage students who are doing poorly in school to drop out of school and go to work.
    B. Discuss with students the possible courses they may request for next term.
    C. Assist students to get help in handling homework difficulties in various subjects.
    D. Encourage students to join school clubs and organizations which will meet their needs.

18. Of the following possible justifications for surprise quizzes, the BEST one is that   18.____
    A. they are periodically necessary to deflate the sense of superiority of the students who ordinarily get high marks
    B. it is best to punish a class for poor discipline with these quizzes
    C. they encourage the students to study regularly
    D. they cause the students to have more respect for the teacher

19. Assume that you have just met a class for the first time and that soon after the lesson begins a boy makes a loud noise.   19.____
    Usually the BEST of the following suggestions for the immediate handling of this situation is to
    A. send him to the dean at once
    B. assign him the task of writing "*I must be a gentleman at all times*" 200 times for homework
    C. warn him about the possibility of expulsion from the school
    D. tell him to see you after class, then proceed with the lesson

20. Which one of the following statements concerning the purposes of questioning is MOST reasonable?

    A. Questions should be challenging, arouse attention, stimulate thinking, and encourage good expression in the answers given.
    B. Simple factual questions should be asked often to serve as the teacher's best evaluative device.
    C. Questions should be repeated to make sure that every student understands them.
    D. Multiple questions should be asked occasionally to encourage clear thinking in complicated situations.

21. Of the following, the one which may BEST be achieved by programmed instruction is

    A. allowing a student to proceed at his own pace
    B. reducing the number of teaching positions
    C. providing study materials for homebound students
    D. providing practice materials for students of low reading ability

22. Of the following procedures for the handling of the clarification of course objectives and daily aims to the students, the BEST one is for these objectives and aims to be

    A. clearly stated by the teacher
    B. raised by the students, discussed and accepted by them
    C. written on the blackboard before they are discussed
    D. written on the blackboard after explanation by the teacher and then copied into notebooks by the students

23. Which one of the following methods for getting a lesson started promptly is LEAST sound pedagogically?

    A. Have a challenging motivating question on the blackboard at the beginning of the period
    B. Stand near the door with the marking book and give a merit to any student who does not sit down and take out his work at once
    C. Give a quiz on the previous lesson at the beginning of the period
    D. Stand quietly in front of the room and wait for attention

24. Of the following, experience with various kinds of tests and measurements utilized for predicting academic success of pupils in advanced high school courses and honor classes in a given subject has shown that

    A. an aptitude test is the most satisfactory single instrument
    B. previous achievement represented by pupil's grades in that subject is best
    C. all other factors should be subordinated to the I.Q.
    D. the child's motivation is the paramount factor

25. It has been found that *learning by wholes,* i.e., being challenged by a total situation, is usually BEST achieved by which one of the following groups?

    A. Dull-normal pupils
    B. Girls
    C. Pupils whose attention span is small
    D. The brighter pupils

MATHEMATICS EDUCATION

Questions 26-40.

DIRECTIONS: Each question or incomplete statement is followed by several suggested answers or completions. Select the one that BEST answers the question or completes the statement. *PRINT THE LETTER OF THE CORRECT ANSWER IN THE SPACE AT THE RIGHT.*

26. Of the following, the one which states a characteristic of a good full-period mathematics test is that it should

    A. test only those exercises which involve concepts
    B. attempt to test both skills and concepts
    C. be so constructed as to make it doubtful that any student in the class could score 100%
    D. have all verbal problems worded in the way they were taught

26._____

27. In introducing the quadratic equation in the ninth-year mathematics class, it is BEST to do so by doing which one of the following?

    A. Putting such an equation on the chalkboard and presenting the steps involved in its solution
    B. Putting on the chalkboard a verbal problem which leads to a quadratic equation
    C. Plotting the graph of a quadratic equation and thus showing that it has two roots
    D. Reviewing factoring

27._____

28. In teaching a ninth-year general mathematics class, it is MOST important for the teacher to remember which one of the following?

    A. To keep students working continuously so that they do not get into mischief
    B. To make certain that students work on fundamental operations exclusively
    C. To have students develop an appreciation of mathematics and its power in our present world
    D. Not to introduce any geometric concepts, statistics, or graphs

28._____

29. Which one of the following generalizations is CORRECT?

    A. Two negatives make a positive.
    B. Two triangles are congruent if they agree in any three parts as long as one of them is a side.
    C. The formula for the area of a trapezoid, K = 1/2h (b + b'), may be used to find the area of a triangle, rectangle, or parallelogram.
    D. The set of integers is closed under all four operations.

29._____

30. Which one of the following topics is BEST saved until twelfth-year mathematics? The

    A. meaning of a postulational system
    B. definition of irrational numbers as numbers which cannot be written as the ratio of two integers
    C. use of mathematical induction as a method of proof
    D. meaning of the union and intersection of sets

30._____

31. Of the following topics, the one which normal pupils usually master MOST readily is the   31.____

    A. study of locus in tenth-year mathematics
    B. solution of literal equations
    C. solution of two linear equations in two variables
    D. solution of verbal problems

32. Of the following statements about the protractor, which one may CORRECTLY be associ-   32.____
    ated with its use in tenth-year mathematics? It should

    A. never be used
    B. be used to discover possible propositions
    C. be used to prove theorems of various types
    D. be used to prove the correctness of construction theorems

33. Of the following, the one which is the MOST important outcome of studying tenth-year   33.____
    mathematics is to develop the ability to

    A. understand and compare the meaning and advantages of inductive and postula-
       tional thinking
    B. learn the facts of Euclidean geometry in a proper sequence
    C. distinguish between Euclidean and non-Euclidean geometry
    D. understand the superiority of deductive over inductive thinking

34. If, in reviewing order of operations, John said, "3 + 2.5 = 25", which one of the following   34.____
    ways of correcting him is LEAST defensible?

    A. What operations are called for in the expression 3 + 2.5, and in what order?
    B. The answer is 13. Can you rewrite the expression so that the answer would be 25,
       John?
    C. Look in your notebooks for our agreement on the order of operations.
    D. No, it is not 25. What is it, Mary?

35. If a student in a ninth-year general mathematics class appears unable to remember the   35.____
    multiplication tables, the one of the following procedures which would be LEAST defensi-
    ble is to

    A. have him do nothing but study the tables until he knows them perfectly
    B. have him use a printed table in many multiplication applications
    C. have him study applications involving multiplication incidental to other operations
    D. explain to him various number combination facts

36. Which one of the following cases of variation can be taught using the relation D = RT?   36.____
    I.   Joint
    II. Inverse
    III. Direct

    A. I, III   B. II, III
    C. I, II   D. I, II, III

37. In a tenth-year mathematics class, if the teacher starts the course with constructions, she should make certain of which one of the following? That the

   A. conclusions are proved by the use of a straight-edge and protractor
   B. students label this experience as experimental, not deductive
   C. conclusions are proved on the basis of measurements
   D. students accept the conclusions now, on the basis that later in the term they'll be able to prove them

38. In developing the formula for the area of a circle in a tenth-year mathematics class, which one of the following formulas should the teacher review? The area of

   A. an equilateral triangle in terms of its side
   B. a regular hexagon in terms of its side
   C. a regular polygon in terms of its apothem and perimeter
   D. triangle in terms of two sides and the included angle

39. In teaching radical equations, the teacher assigned this example for homework:

   $\sqrt{x-1}=-1$. The next day, all but one student agreed that $x = 2$. The dissenter claimed that there was no solution because the one root is *extraneous*.
   Of the following, the BEST way for the teacher to handle this answer is to

   A. say that every equation must have at least one root
   B. say that extraneous roots are gotten in radical equations only when the degree of the equation is raised as a result of squaring both sides of the equation
   C. substitute for x the value 2 to show the rest of the class that the dissenter was right; then develop understanding of the concept of extraneous roots
   D. substitute for x the value 2, and show the dissenter why the rest of the class was right

40. In teaching a ninth-year mathematics class the unit on the addition of algebraic fractions, a teacher finds that her pupils have forgotten how to add arithmetic fractions. The BEST one of the following procedures in this case is to

   A. practice the addition of arithmetic fractions exclusively for two or three lessons
   B. take some arithmetic fractional addition examples and go over every step involved. Teach the algebraic addition the next day.
   C. assign several examples dealing with the addition of arithmetic fractions for homework. Postpone the topic of addition of algebraic fractions to the next day.
   D. recall with the class the steps involved in addition of arithmetic fractions, having the students do several of these. Then follow up with the addition of algebraic fractions, pointing out carefully the analogous procedures.

KEY (CORRECT ANSWERS)

1. C	11. A	21. A	31. C
2. D	12. C	22. B	32. B
3. D	13. C	23. B	33. A
4. B	14. B	24. B	34. D
5. C	15. A	25. D	35. A
6. B	16. B	26. B	36. D
7. B	17. A	27. B	37. B
8. A	18. C	28. C	38. C
9. A	19. D	29. C	39. C
10. C	20. A	30. C	40. D

EXAMINATION SECTION
TEST 1

Questions 1-15.

DIRECTIONS: Each question or incomplete statement is followed by several suggested answers or completions. Select the one that BEST answers the question or completes the statement. *PRINT THE LETTER OF THE CORRECT ANSWER IN THE SPACE AT THE RIGHT.*

1. The prescribed procedure for recording the attendance in the official class is that it

   A. may be recorded in the roll book by a reliable pupil, with the clear understanding that the teacher assume full responsibility for the accuracy of the report
   B. may be recorded in the roll book by a pupil, provided the teacher checks daily
   C. must be recorded in the roll book by the teacher daily since it is a legal document the accuracy of which is imperative
   D. may be kept on a card and, in a day or so, be recorded in the roll book after errors have been corrected, excuse passes obtained, etc., to avoid having corrections frequently made in the roll book itself

   1.____

2. Which one of the following would be the LEAST effective procedure for insuring a prompt start of a lesson?

   A. Give a quiz as the initial step in the lesson.
   B. Assign pupils to blackboard work while others copy the next assignment.
   C. Take attendance and call for attention.
   D. Have pupils copy the new assignment and start on a *warm-up* exercise.

   2.____

3. During a supervised study period on an assignment, the teacher should NOT

   A. grade test papers and prepare reports
   B. confer quietly with individual pupils about proper study habits
   C. note the common errors made and the difficulties encountered by several pupils and conduct a quiet discussion with these pupils
   D. note the general quality and quantity of the pupils' work and modify plans for subsequent lessons if necessary

   3.____

4. Which one of the following is the MOST desirable way of economizing on time during a subject-class period?

   A. Review the homework only occasionally.
   B. Establish definite routines for the pupils.
   C. Use the blackboard sparingly.
   D. Discourage the asking of questions by students.

   4.____

5. If, soon after the start of a new term, a pupil in one of your academic classes should refuse to do the class work, which one of the following procedures would, as a general rule, be the BEST one to follow in such a case?

   A. Send the pupil to your chairman immediately.
   B. Assert your authority at once and let him know who is *boss*.

   5.____

155

C. Speak to him after class to ascertain the cause of his behavior.
D. Ignore the pupil but give him a failing mark at the end of the term.

6. Of the following possible criteria for evaluating the success of the teaching of reluctant learners in *second track* courses, the LEAST significant is

   A. achievement on standardized tests
   B. improvement in social behavior
   C. improvement in work habits
   D. improvement over past performance

6.____

7. Which one of the following statements about lesson plans is pedagogically sound? They

   A. should be made up at least a month in advance and adhered to strictly so that nothing is neglected
   B. are not needed by the experienced teacher
   C. should be made up week by week, according to the special needs of each class and be used flexibly
   D. need not include pivotal questions

7.____

8. The PRIMARY aim of assigning homework should generally be to

   A. review for class and term tests
   B. drill
   C. develop habits of working hard
   D. instill concepts

8.____

9. The daily homework assignment should USUALLY

   A. not include exercises on the new work if the class understands it
   B. have part devoted to review and part based on the new lesson
   C. consist, at least in part, of reading ahead in the new work to be taught
   D. be patterned after Regents-type questions

9.____

10. Of the following, the one which is a disadvantage of grouping bright students together is that

    A. the standard high school curriculum will be covered too quickly
    B. in being with other bright students, these talented pupils become too humble
    C. the teachers with special talents have to be assigned to the bright group at the expense of the rest of the students
    D. it tends to deprive them of leadership opportunities

10.____

11. If a class as a whole does very poorly on a full-period unit test, the MOST effective of the following procedures is to

    A. return the papers and warn the pupils they must improve
    B. give another test on the same unit after clarifying the main concepts with which the students had had difficulty and providing remedial instruction
    C. go over the test and then have each pupil bring in two copies of the correct solution of every problem he failed to work correctly
    D. discard the test papers and proceed to the next topic, resolving to deal with it more effectively

11.____

12. Of the following, the one which is usually the LEAST important purpose for giving a quiz is that it

    A. is often part of the learning process
    B. often provides a basis for remedial work
    C. gives an opportunity for additional review and drill
    D. provides objective evidence on which to base marks

13. Which one of the following principles of learning is the LEAST acceptable?

    A. Concepts and processes should be developed from concrete and familiar situations in the life of the pupil.
    B. The pupils should always understand the reason for a process.
    C. Drill may occasionally be conducted effectively in preparation for understanding.
    D. When a rule is developed, it should be as far as possible the pupil's own generalization on the way he solves a problem.

14. Of the following, the LEAST desirable function of a school club is to

    A. promote interest in a subject and develop a broader understanding of its nature
    B. select bright pupils for a subject team, thus providing opportunities to coach them
    C. discuss with interested students the many applications of the subject
    D. foster special interests and talents along subject lines

15. Which one of the following practices regarding the use of the *review book* is LEAST desirable? Using it

    A. as early as possible to help get pupils started in preparing for the Regents examination
    B. as a supplementary text after the work of the first term is well under way
    C. early in the second term of the work
    D. in the middle of the second term for Regents review

Questions 16-40.

DIRECTIONS: Each question or incomplete statement is followed by several suggested answers or completions. Select the one that BEST answers the question or completes the statement. *PRINT THE LETTER OF THE CORRECT ANSWER IN THE SPACE AT THE RIGHT.*

16. Of the following, the MOST important outcome of studying the unit on formulas in algebra is

    A. manipulating formulas with facility
    B. substituting numerical values accurately
    C. recognizing and memorizing formulas
    D. understanding dependence and variation

17. Of the following outcomes of the teaching of algebra, the one we should seek to make MOST lasting for those who do not continue the study of mathematics is the retention of

    A. manipulative skills   B. the knowledge of formulas
    C. mathematical concepts   D. the ability to apply formulas

4 (#1)

18. The following topics, which appear in the four-year high school mathematics curriculum, are normally introduced in which one of the indicated orders?
    I. Calculus
    II. Similarity proofs
    III. Arithmetic progressions
    IV. Trigonometry of the right triangle
    The CORRECT answer is:

    A. IV, I, II, III
    B. IV, II, III, I
    C. IV, II, I, III
    D. III, II, I, IV

19. Which one of the following statements dealing with the teaching of geometry is LEAST acceptable pedagogically?

    A. The transition from the intuitive to the demonstrative method
    B. The chief aim of the teaching of geometry is the mastery of proofs of required theorems
    C. The teaching of demonstrative geometry may at times employ the method of experimentation as an approach to a new theorem
    D. Blackboard constructions, in a geometry class, should be made with an unmarked straight-edge and a pair of compasses.

20. Of the following questions, which one would be MOST effective in furthering thought in a mathematics classroom?

    A. "Henry, which of these two methods of factoring is easier to use here?"
    B. "We should substitute y for x, should we not?"
    C. "How can we make sure that this answer is correct?" (Pause) "John."
    D. "Now, class, what can you tell me about the area of an equilateral triangle?"

21. On the ninth-year level, a teacher of remedial arithmetic can BEST motivate the class by doing which one of the following?

    A. Reteaching and drilling on the various techniques in arithmetic
    B. Having pupils memorize every operation that must be learned
    C. Combining drill work and memory work
    D. Presenting interesting problems which involve various arithmetical computations

22. Which one of the following is pedagogically the LEAST desirable motivation for the teaching of a theorem in a tenth-year mathematics class?

    A. Relating an historical anecdote connected with the theorem
    B. Informing the pupils that this theorem has appeared many times as a question in Regents examinations
    C. Presenting a puzzle whose solution involves the use of this theorem
    D. Displaying an instrument, the explanation of the operation of which is based on this theorem

23. In connection with the teaching of advanced algebra, the MOST significant of the following comments is:

    A. The main aim is to have the pupils become proficient in manipulating symbols
    B. Pupils in this course need not master the techniques of algebra

C. The goal is to bring pupils to realize that the processes and procedures are means of recording and working with ideas
D. It is not necessary to review previous work, since the pupils who elect to take this course are the superior mathematics pupils

24. In the teaching of arithmetic in a general mathematics course in the ninth year, there is need for regular recurrent testing and practice on the various basic arithmetical operations.
Which one of the following is the LEAST important reason for systematic attention to these operations? To

   A. discuss and correct inadequacies before they become serious
   B. raise each skill to a higher level of competence
   C. use each process in a continually more mature problem situation
   D. make sure that these slower students are kept busy and *on their toes*

25. An extended unit on *Consumer Mathematics* would be MOST suitable for a class in which one of the following?

   A. Ninth-year algebra
   B. Tenth-year mathematics
   C. Ninth-year general mathematics
   D. Intermediate algebra - one year

26. In tenth-year mathematics, the statement, *"Two triangles are congruent if the corresponding sides are equal,"* is a

   A. definition   B. theorem   C. postulate   D. corollary

27. Of the following, which one is the LEAST important reason for replacing the separate intermediate algebra and trigonometry courses with the eleventh-year mathematics course?

   A. More time will be available for extended review of ninth-year algebra.
   B. Topics that are duplicated in intermediate algebra and trigonometry are combined in the eleventh-year course.
   C. Algebraic manipulations that are learned are applied immediately to trigonometric functions.
   D. The eleventh-year course permits a better utilization of time than that which is available through a combination of a term of the longer intermediate algebra course and a term of the shorter trigonometry course.

28. Of the following, the MOST desirable culminating activity in a review lesson on the topic of angle measurement by use of arcs in a bright tenth-year mathematics class is to

   A. have each theorem studied several times to make sure that each pupil has mastered it
   B. drill on the numerical applications of the theorems
   C. drill on the complete proofs of the theorems
   D. derive a single general theorem for all cases of angle measurement by means of arcs

29. The *distributive law* is FIRST applied in high school mathematics in the _____ year. 29.___

   A. ninth   B. tenth   C. eleventh   D. twelfth

30. Of the groups listed below, the one that has been experimenting PRIMARILY with seventh- and eight-year mathematics programs is 30.___

   A. University of Illinois Committee on School Mathematics
   B. University of Maryland Mathematics Project
   C. School Mathematics Study Group
   D. The Secondary School Curriculum Committee, National Council of Teachers of Mathematics

31. In teaching the topic of subtraction of signed numbers in ninth-year mathematics, which one of the following procedures is LEAST desirable? 31.___

   A. Start with the rule: *"Change the sign of the subtrahend and proceed as in addition"* and then apply the rule.
   B. Lead the pupils by a series of numerical illustrations to discover that every subtraction of the form (a) - (b) yields the same answer as the corresponding addition example of the form (a) + (-b).
   C. Use a scale of thermometer readings as a visual aid.
   D. Derive the generalization: Subtraction can be thought of as asking *"How far and in what direction must we go from the subtrahend to get to the minuend?"*

32. In connection with the use of experimentation and deduction in tenth-year mathematics, which one of the following statements is UNACCEPTABLE? 32.___

   A. Experimentation may be used to discover new facts.
   B. Deduction may be used to discover new theorems and to explain why a theorem is true.
   C. Experimentation should generally precede deduction.
   D. The main value of deduction is to show that experimentation is unreliable.

33. In teaching the topic *"Proof of Identities"* in eleventh-year mathematics, which one of the following procedures is the LEAST desirable? (Assume that x is the only angle that appears in the identity.) 33.___

   A. If there are fractions in the original identity and
   B. x appears in a denominator, always clear the equation of fractions first.
   C. Transform the expression on the left side to a form identical with the expression on the right side.
   D. Transform the expression on the right side to a form identical with the expression on the left side.
   E. Transform the expression on each side separately until identical forms are reached.

34. Which one of the following is the BEST check for the answer to a word problem? See 34.___

   A. whether the answer is plausible
   B. whether the answer satisfies all the conditions stated in the problem
   C. whether the answer satisfies the equation used to solve the problem
   D. that there are no fractions in the answer

35. The following topics are taught in tenth-year mathematics:
    I. the area of the segment of a circle
    II. the area of a triangle
    III. the area of a sector
    IV. the definition of area
    The order in which these topics should normally be presented to students is

    A. I, II, III, IV
    B. II, IV, I, III
    C. IV, II, III, I
    D. IV, I, II, III

36. When learning the topic of simultaneous linear equations in two unknowns in the ninth year, which one of the following procedures should NOT be used by the pupils?

    A. Checking the answers in both of the original equations
    B. The method of double elimination if the answer obtained for the first unknown is a complicated fraction
    C. Eliminating either one of the two unknowns
    D. If one equation is used to obtain the answer for the second unknown, using only the other equation to check the answers

37. According to the state syllabus in tenth-year mathematics, each of the three statements listed below should be classified and presented as one of the following: a(n)
    I. theorem
    II. definition
    III. postulate
    IV. incorrect statement

    "Two triangles are congruent if they agree in two sides and the included angle." (SAS)

    "Two triangles are congruent if they agree in two angles and the side opposite one of these angles." (SAA)

    "Two triangles are congruent if they agree in two sides and the angle opposite one of these sides." (SSA)

    When the above statements are properly classified (using the letters I, II, III, and IV, these classifications listed in order should be

    A. II, I, I
    B. III, I, IV
    C. III, III, IV
    D. I, I, IV

38. In teaching the topic of scale drawing as a method of indirect measurement in a ninth-year class for slow students, the LEAST suitable application among the following would be finding the

    A. height of a flag pole
    B. distance across a river
    C. distance between two inaccessible points about 100 ft. apart
    D. maximum range of vision on the earth from an airplane with a given altitude

39. A form of indirect proof is employed if, when asked to prove: *"If two angles of a triangle are unequal, the sides opposite these angles are unequal,"* we prove instead which one of the following?

    A. If two angles of a triangle are equal, the sides opposite them are equal.
    B. If two sides of a triangle are equal, the angles opposite them are equal.
    C. If two sides of a triangle are unequal, the angles opposite them are unequal.
    D. Both (A) and (B) above

39.____

40. To prove the locus theorem relating to the points equally distant from the sides of an angle, it is

    A. sufficient to prove: "Any point on the bisector of an angle is equally distant from the sides of an angle"
    B. necessary and sufficient to prove the statement quoted in (A) above, and also to prove its contrapositive
    C. necessary and sufficient to prove the converse of the statement quoted in (A) above, and also to prove the inverse of the statement in (A)
    D. sufficient to prove the statement quoted in (A) above and its converse

40.____

KEY (CORRECT ANSWERS)

1. C	11. B	21. D	31. A
2. C	12. D	22. B	32. D
3. A	13. C	23. C	33. A
4. B	14. B	24. D	34. B
5. C	15. A	25. C	35. C
6. A	16. D	26. C	36. D
7. C	17. C	27. A	37. B
8. D	18. B	28. D	38. D
9. B	19. B	29. A	39. B
10. D	20. C	30. B	40. D

TEST 2

Questions 1-25.

DIRECTIONS: Each question or incomplete statement is followed by several suggested answers or completions. Select the one that BEST answers the question or completes the statement. *PRINT THE LETTER OF THE CORRECT ANSWER IN THE SPACE AT THE RIGHT.*

1. Which one of the following questions asked by a teacher is MOST acceptable?

    A. "The answer to question 5 is what?"
    B. "Mary, is her answer to question 5 right?"
    C. "What is your answer to question 5, George?"
    D. "Class, tell George the answer to question 5!"

2. The technique of using a team teaching design which includes a master teacher, regular teachers, and teacher aides is based MOST directly upon which one of the following concepts?

    A. Teachers who have served faithfully deserve master teacher status.
    B. Teaching is a complex art requiring different levels of competence and training.
    C. The conservation of public funds is a moral obligation.
    D. Teacher aides are often more knowledgeable and skillful than teachers.

3. In conducting a developmental lesson, the usually MOST desirable way, among the following, of responding to a student's correct answer to your question is to

    A. enter a grade in your record book
    B. call on another pupil to answer the same question
    C. follow up with another question
    D. elaborate on the pupil answer

4. Which one of the following procedures is MOST acceptable to use in class when several pupils make flagrant errors in grammar and usage?

    A. Correct the students unobtrusively and proceed with your lesson
    B. Take a few minutes to explain since every teacher is a teacher of English
    C. Ignore the errors since such deviations are time-consuming and interfere with covering the required course of study
    D. Write a note to each pupil's English teacher to inform him of the errors

5. When a parent complains to you that you are underrating her son, the BEST procedure, among the following, for you to follow is to

    A. tell the parent that you alone have the moral and legal responsibility for assigning the marks
    B. refer the parent to the principal
    C. agree to raise the grades in the future
    D. explain the grading system and review the pupil's grades with the parent

6. Which one of the following statements would BEST describe procedures of note-taking in a class of slow learners?

   A. They should have few or no notes at all since they have limited verbal ability.
   B. Mimeographed notes should be given to them since note-taking is frustrating for them.
   C. Notes, of a simple kind, should be developed cooperatively by pupils and teacher.
   D. A few short notes should be copied directly from the textbook to insure accuracy and reinforce reading skills.

7. In THE AMERICAN HIGH SCHOOL TODAY, James B. Conant proposes that

   A. the four-year high school should be a comprehensive high school
   B. the present curriculum in the fourth year of high school is more appropriate for a *community junior college*
   C. *social living* courses should be added in all high schools to provide better life adjustment in our atomic era
   D. standardized achievement tests, such as State Regents, have outlived their usefulness

8. The SIMPLEST way, among the following, to exhibit a newspaper clipping to an entire class at one time is to

   A. make a slide for a slide projector
   B. make a highly enlarged photostat;
   C. use the overhead projector
   D. use an opaque projector

9. Of the following, which combination of activities is LEAST suitable as a homework assignment in preparation for a full-period test?

   A. "Study and review all work since (date)."
   B. "Skim through chapters 16 and 17. Study your class notes since (date). Review your homework since (date)."
   C. "Re-read chapters 16 and 17. Look over the questions at the end of each chapter."
   D. "Review all class notes and homework since (date). Do the practice mimeo test distributed today."

10. In selecting the aim for a developmental lesson, the MOST important among the following considerations is the

    A. content of the previous day's lesson
    B. motivation to be used
    C. decision as to which knowledges, attitudes, or skills should be taught next
    D. content of the syllabus

11. The validity of intelligence tests as instruments for evaluating native ability has been questioned because these tests tend to

    A. lack reliability, especially for gifted children
    B. lack reliability, especially for pupils of low motor coordination who consequently have a poor sense of spatial relations

C. place too much emphasis on mathematical and scientific aptitude
D. have an experiential base which is foreign to culturally different children in poverty areas

12. Of the following, the MAJOR aim for giving a standardized test to classes at the beginning of a new course is probably to

    A. discover weaknesses of previous teaching
    B. discover interests, aptitudes, and previous learnings in this area
    C. give teachers and supervisors a basis for deciding upon the regrouping of classes in terms of ability
    D. arouse pupil curiosity and provide a base for motivation

13. Of the following terms, the one MOST closely associated with the sum total of response patterns and abilities possessed by the learner at any given time is

    A. adaptation   B. readiness
    C. reinforcement D. response

14. If 48% of your class failed a unit test, the BEST procedure to follow is to

    A. develop a normal curve on a graph and adjust the grades
    B. ask your Chairman to evaluate your test; if he agrees it is fair, re-teach parts of the unit, then review and give a new test
    C. chastise the failing pupils sternly and write notes to the parents, if your Chairman agrees your test is fair
    D. give an *extra credit* test to the failing pupils to raise their grades

15. Of the following reasons for giving homework, the LEAST acceptable reason is that it

    A. extends the learning process beyond the classroom
    B. provides practice in the art of self-study
    C. increases the chances of retentivity
    D. trains the pupils in habits of doing hard work

16. Which one of the following sets of statements BEST explains the occurrence of disciplinary infractions among adolescents in secondary schools?

    A. Adolescents tend to resist authority; they seek the admiration of their peers; they are not convinced that poor self-control is necessarily harmful to future success.
    B. Syllabi are teacher-imposed; rules of conduct in secondary schools are unrealistic.
    C. Adolescents undergo rapid physical growth; their span of attention is short; they are incapable of abstract thoughts.
    D. Adolescence has been extended by modern society; rules of conduct do not parallel chronological age; there is a wide-spread lack of pre-vocational meaningful study.

17. If you are appointed in mid-year and are assigned a class which has fallen hopelessly behind the time schedule for the course of study in your department, which one of the following procedures would probably be MOST acceptable?

A. With the aid of your Chairman, re-plan the balance of the schedule to include the most vital topics.
B. Speed up your teaching each period; double the assignments; omit audio-visual aids; reduce the number of tests.
C. With the aid of your Chairman, develop copious mimeographed notes for pupils to study at home; test pupils; catch up as you go.
D. Proceed at your usual pace; inform your Chairman; explain that these pupils are getting excellent training on fewer topics and will fare better even though you will not be able to go through the whole course of study.

18. Of the following, the MAIN reason why psychologists warn against over-emphasis of the *rewards and punishment* motivation in teaching is that this type of motivation

    A. ignores the more effective stimulus of inner satisfaction
    B. inevitably leads to a listless class atmosphere
    C. has little or no influence with the bright child
    D. often leads by easy stages to corporal punishment

19. Pragmatism, as an educational philosophy, was stressed by

    A. Dewey   B. Terman   C. Binet   D. Pestalozzi

20. A boy has scored 57% on a test in a modified (slow) class.
    Which one of the following comments by the teacher is MOST likely to stimulate him towards sustained scholastic improvement?

    A. Why didn't' t you study harder?
    B. Some of your answers showed very good understanding.
    C. You will have to work much harder to get out of the slow class.
    D. I had hoped that you would prove that we had been wrong in putting you into the slow class.

21. Of the following, the MOST acceptable measure for encouraging students to speak loudly enough for the class to hear is to

    A. call only upon those students who speak loudly enough to be heard
    B. have students stand up and face the class whenever they are called upon for an answer
    C. use a demerit system for prodding all students to talk in audible tones
    D. stop any student who is speaking too quietly and have him begin again but in a louder voice

22. Of the following, the BEST way to start a class promptly is to

    A. have one row put the homework on the board
    B. put a class problem on the board
    C. have a monitor put the homework assignment for the next day on the board while the rest of the class copies it
    D. take class attendance

23. Which one of the following statements concerning the aim of a lesson is MOST valid? 23._____

    A. The teacher should write the aim on the blackboard at the beginning of each lesson.
    B. The aim should be an outgrowth of and developed from the motivation.
    C. Each child should write the aim of each lesson in his notebook each day.
    D. The teacher should announce the aim of the lesson to the class at the beginning of each period.

24. If a class you inherit from another teacher is poorly motivated and many of the students talk to one another during lessons, you should NOT 24._____

    A. teach carefully planned lessons daily for those who listen and try to ignore the others
    B. look up records of each member of the class and consult the guidance counselor where appropriate
    C. plan lessons in which students change activity every 15 minutes from written work to oral work to reading, etc.
    D. rearrange the seating, so that groups who talk to one another are separated as far as possible

25. Among the following, the MOST obvious fact that faces the teacher of a ninth grade class is that the 25._____

    A. future doctors, chemists, engineers, and nurses can be accurately identified
    B. boys are generally more talented in science and math than are the girls
    C. girls are generally more mature than the boys
    D. girls prefer the biological aspects of science, while the boys prefer the physical aspects of science and mathematics

Questions 26-40.

DIRECTIONS: Each question or incomplete statement is followed by several suggested answers or completions. Select the one that BEST answers the question or completes the statement. *PRINT THE LETTER OF THE CORRECT ANSWER IN THE SPACE AT THE RIGHT.*

26. Of the following errors, which do tenty-year students commit MOST frequently? 26._____

    A. Reasoning from a generalization
    B. Reasoning from an inverse
    C. Reasoning by analogy
    D. Circular reasoning

27. Of the following, which one can properly be considered a conceptual weakness of Euclid's geometry? 27._____

    A. He made many tacit assumptions which were not formally postulated.
    B. He proved theorems by the method of superposition.
    C. His fifth postulate is a theorem which should have been proven.
    D. He restricted the instruments for constructions to the straight-edge and compasses.

28. Because of the crowded syllabi in the high school mathematics courses, economy of time is essential.
    Of the following, the BEST way to save time is to

    A. combine two lessons into one
    B. have pupils study certain required topics on their own and hold them responsible for these topics
    C. review only those homework examples that gave the class the most difficulty
    D. lecture to the class so there will be a minimum of questions asked

29. Which one of the following should NOT be a regular feature of the homework assignment?

    A. Honor problems
    B. Reading in the textbook on the work covered that day
    C. Reading in the textbook on the work to be covered the next day
    D. Review problems

30. Of the following, the MOST valid reason for having a testing program in a math class is to

    A. be able to justify the grade a pupil receives
    B. prepare the pupils in the techniques of test-taking so they will be better qualified to pass the Regents examination
    C. evaluate the teaching and determine those areas in which more review will be needed
    D. terminate each unit of work presented

31. Of the following, which is the BEST motivation for introducing a lesson on the solution of a quadratic equation by completing the square?

    A. Announce to the class, "Today, we will learn a new method of solving quadratic equations."
    B. Present a quadratic equation whose roots are imaginary.
    C. Present a simple verbal problem which leads to a quadratic equation which cannot be solved by factoring.
    D. Begin with simple equations which are solved by taking the square roots of both members. Gradually introduce more difficult equations until the method is developed.

32. The use of the *discovery method* in the teaching of tenth-year mathematics involves getting the pupil to

    A. associate a theorem with the mathematician who made the discovery
    B. discover the procedure by which a theorem has been proved
    C. recognize when to use a direct or an indirect method of proof
    D. make and test conjectures of his own

33. Of the following objectives of a ninth-year algebra course, the one which has been introduced MOST recently is the

    A. ability to translate verbal problems into equation form
    B. ability to solve inequalities as well as equations

C. understanding of dependence and functional relationships
D. understanding of the postulates of the four fundamental operations as applied to the solution of equations

34. Of the following topics in tenth-year mathematics, the one students usually find MOST difficult is

    A. coordinate geometry
    B. angle measurement
    C. geometric constructions
    D. locus

35. When a pupil combines two fractions with different denominators, he should understand that he is making use of which one of the following?

    A. Commutative and associative postulates for addition
    B. Multiplicative identity and distributive postulates
    C. Additive identity and additive inverse postulates
    D. Multiplicative identity and multiplicative inverse postulates

36. Of the following, the STRONGEST criticism of the teaching of modern mathematics is that

    A. it is too difficult for the children to handle
    B. parents are unable to help their children to overcome difficulties
    C. many of the topics covered should be delayed until the students are in college
    D. many teachers have not been adequately trained to teach the new mathematics

37. The principle $a \cdot 1 = a$ can be used to explain each of the following EXCEPT the

    A. simplification of a complex fraction
    B. simplification of radicals
    C. rationalizing of a fraction with an irrational denominator
    D. conversion of the measure of an angle from degrees to radians

38. While discussing polygons, a student asks for the name of a polygon of seven sides. The teacher has forgotten but thinks that a likely answer would be *septagon*.
Of the following, the BEST reply for the teacher to make would be

    A. "I believe it's septagon."
    B. "It is not important, because 7 is not an exact divisor of 360."
    C. "I don't know. Let's continue with the lesson."
    D. "I don't recall. Let us both look it up and report to the class."

39. Of the following, the BEST reason why a student should study academic mathematics is that

    A. it is necessary for college entrance
    B. modern technology is such that a pupil needs such background to better understand and contribute to the world in which we live
    C. a good mind needs to be challenged
    D. traditionally such subjects have been part of the education of college bound

40. A student asks why is it necessary to study *required* theorems in tenth-year mathematics.
    Of the following, the BEST reason is that the study of *required* theorems

    A. is mandated by the state Board of Regents
    B. is a result of the regular inclusion of a required theorem in the tenth-year mathematics Regents examination
    C. makes students aware of the principle of sequence in tenth-year mathematics
    D. affords good training in memorization

40.____

KEY (CORRECT ANSWERS)

1. C	11. D	21. D	31. C
2. B	12. B	22. B	32. D
3. C	13. B	23. B	33. B
4. A	14. B	24. A	34. D
5. D	15. D	25. C	35. B
6. C	16. A	26. D	36. D
7. A	17. A	27. A	37. B
8. D	18. A	28. C	38. D
9. A	19. A	29. C	39. B
10. C	20. B	30. C	40. C

EXAMINATION SECTION
TEST 1

DIRECTIONS: Each question or incomplete statement is followed by several suggested answers or completions. Select the one that BEST answers the question or completes the statement. *PRINT THE LETTER OF THE CORRECT ANSWER IN THE SPACE AT THE RIGHT.*

1. The BEST procedure among the following for introducing the subtraction of a mixed number from a whole number is to

    A. cut a piece of ribbon 1 3/4 feet long from a piece 3 feet long
    B. use a yardstick to show that 1 3/4 feet added to 1 1/4 feet are equal to 3 feet
    C. use a yardstick drawn on the board to illustrate the subtraction as it takes place
    D. use fractional discs to illustrate subtraction of 1 1/4 from 3

    1.____

2. In teaching the bar graph, the one point among the following to emphasize is that the

    A. scale for the lengths of the *bars* must start at zero
    B. *bars* must extend vertically
    C. longest *bar* should be placed in the center of the graph
    D. bar graph is most useful in representing a linear relation

    2.____

3. In order for pupils to make a correct graph of the formula, C = 10p, where C represents the cost, in cents, of a number of pencils, p, when each pencil costs 10 cents, they MUST understand that the domain of p is the set of

    A. real numbers
    B. integers
    C. rational numbers
    D. non-negative integers

    3.____

4. In a 20 item test, the 5 pupils who scored the highest marks nevertheless failed to get 3 items right.
   The SOUNDEST procedure among the following for the teacher to adopt next is to

    A. assume that the 3 items develop concepts too difficult for his class
    B. go to his chairman and ask him to help solve the teaching problem
    C. analyze each wrong answer given to the 3 items by the class
    D. give further application and drill in the concepts included in the 3 items

    4.____

5. Of the following, the BEST way for a mathematics teacher who is new to a school to start acquainting himself with the filmstrips appropriate to mathematics at his school is by

    A. studying the school's collection of mathematics filmstrip synopses carefully
    B. previewing the mathematics filmstrips available in the school
    C. incorporating all appropriate filmstrips as soon as possible into class lessons so he may view them
    D. asking his experienced colleagues for advice on filmstrips

    5.____

6. Of the following suggestions concerning the teaching of mathematics to disadvantaged children, the BEST one is that

    6.____

A. if they are retarded in mathematics, no new topic should be taught until they have mastered the fundamental operations
B. the basic concepts for the particular grade should be taught using special approaches, procedures, and materials
C. the simplest mathematical concepts for the grade should be selected and taught
D. only those concepts in mathematics relevant to the problems in living in areas of poverty should be taught

7. In introducing a unit on measurement, the BEST starting procedure among the following is to

   A. provide each pupil with a table showing the conversion of smaller units into larger ones (i.e., feet to yards)
   B. provide each pupil with a ruler with which he measures the sizes of common objects around the classroom
   C. discuss with the class the historic origin of the inch, foot, and yard
   D. have each pupil estimate and verify by measurement one inch, one foot, and one yard, and then estimate and verify, where convenient, the sizes of common objects

8. By frequent assignment of mathematics homework as punishment, a teacher is likely to

   A. have the pupil react to the subject with emotional overtones
   B. improve the behavior of the pupils so punished
   C. improve the behavior of all the pupils in the class
   D. secure the cooperation of the parents of the class, because they like to see their children do homework

9. A mathematical system consists of which one of the following groupings selected from I, II, III, IV?

   I. undefined terms
   II. axioms
   III. defined terms
   IV. theorems

   The CORRECT answer is:

   A. III, IV   B. I, III, IV
   C. I, II   D. all of the above

10. In the initial teaching of how to find the area of a rectangle, the BEST method among the following is that

    A. the area formula be presented by the teacher and pupils be assigned to do many practice problems
    B. pupils be involved in experiences with rectangle area measure and that they then develop the formula with the guidance of the teacher
    C. pupils be assigned to study a workbook development of the rectangle area formula
    D. pupils read the text development aloud to the class

11. Each of the following causes serious difficulty for students who are learning to solve problems EXCEPT

    A. failure to identify the unknown
    B. failure to use the *box* arrangement

C. weakness in translation from the English sentence or sentences to the algebraic equation or equations
D. failure to make proper use of the given data in the problem

12. A pupil responds to a question involving the multiplication of a number by 100 by stating that he would add two zeros to the number.
This is NOT acceptable because of which one of the following reasons?

    A. He should be required to write out all steps of the computation.
    B. He should state what the product is, rather than how to obtain it.
    C. His method would not always yield the correct product.
    D. He should be discouraged from using *shortcuts*.

13. In general, a pupil's ability to solve problems in reasoning is MOST closely related to which one of the following?

    A. His chronological age
    B. His previous school experience
    C. His mental age
    D. The skill of his previous mathematics teachers

14. The BEST teaching procedure of the following for discovering that the sum of the angles of a triangle is equal to a straight angle would be:

    A. The teacher uses a protractor to measure the angles of a triangle on the blackboard and obtains the sum of the three angles
    B. a bright pupil uses the procedure described in (A)
    C. each pupil has his own protractor and uses the procedure in (A) while working at his desk
    D. each pupil has his own cardboard triangle, tears off the angles of his triangle, and places them properly on his desk to find their sum

15. Assume that a teacher asks the class, "Give an example of an equation whose solution set is the empty set," and a pupil responds "$x^2 + 4 = 0$".
Which one of the following BEST describes the question and the answer? The question is worded _____, the answer is worded _____.

    A. properly, correctly
    B. properly, incorrectly
    C. improperly, correctly
    D. improperly, incorrectly

16. A student attempts to simplify $\frac{5x + 6}{2}$ and obtains the answer 5x+3.
His error is probably a result of INCORRECT use of the _____ law.

    A. distributive
    B. associative
    C. commutative
    D. multiplicative inverse

17. Of the following, the aim that is *modern* in the teaching of mathematics in junior high school is that the properties of the number system should be taught to

    A. lay a foundation for algebra
    B. strengthen skills acquired in elementary school
    C. illustrate the postulational nature of mathematics
    D. provide skills for the solution of problems in daily life

18. Of the following, a type of problem GENERALLY associated with the term Social Arithmetic is the   18._____

    A. solution of mixture problems
    B. writing of numbers in bases other than ten
    C. performance of calculations in the metric system
    D. computation of insurance commission

19. The BEST educational procedure of the following for motivating a pupil in mathematics is to   19._____

    A. develop a competitive spirit in each class
    B. start each lesson with a problem
    C. test frequently, particularly at the end of each teaching sequence
    D. start teaching each concept with a real mathematical experience

20. Which one of the following is the LEAST desirable application of percentage for use in teaching a seventh grade class?   20._____

    A. Allocation of items in federal budget
    B. Class' own record of attendance
    C. Pupils' own test scores
    D. Baseball averages

KEY (CORRECT ANSWERS)

1.	A	11.	B
2.	A	12.	C
3.	D	13.	C
4.	C	14.	D
5.	B	15.	B
6.	B	16.	A
7.	D	17.	C
8.	A	18.	D
9.	D	19.	D
10.	B	20.	A

TEST 2

DIRECTIONS: Each question or incomplete statement is followed by several suggested answers or completions. Select the one that BEST answers the question or completes the statement. *PRINT THE LETTER OF THE CORRECT ANSWER IN THE SPACE AT THE RIGHT.*

1. Of the following errors, which do tenth-year students commit MOST frequently? 1.____

    A. Reasoning from a generalization
    B. Reasoning from an inverse
    C. Reasoning by analogy
    D. Circular reasoning

2. Of the following, which one can properly be considered a conceptual weakness of Euclid's geometry? 2.____

    A. He made many tacit assumptions which were not formally postulated.
    B. He proved theorems by the method of superposition.
    C. His fifth postulate is a theorem which should have been proven.
    D. He restricted the instruments for constructions to the straight edge and compasses.

3. Because of the crowded syllabi in the high school mathematics courses, economy of time is essential. 3.____
   Of the following, the BEST way to save time is to

    A. combine two lessons into one
    B. have pupils study certain required topics on their own and hold them responsible for these topics
    C. review only those homework examples that gave the class the most difficulty
    D. lecture to the class so there will be a minimum of questions asked

4. Which one of the following should NOT be a regular feature of the homework assignment? 4.____

    A. Honor problems
    B. Reading in the textbook on the work covered that day
    C. Reading in the textbook on the work to be covered the next day
    D. Review problems

5. Of the following, the MOST valid reason for having a testing program in a math class is to 5.____

    A. be able to justify the grade a pupil receives
    B. prepare the pupils in the techniques of test-taking so they will be better qualified to pass the Regents examination
    C. evaluate the teaching and determine those areas in which more review will be needed
    D. terminate each unit of work presented

6. Of the following, which is the BEST motivation for introducing a lesson on the solution of a quadratic equation by completing the square?

   A. Announce to the class, "Today we will learn a new method of solving quadratic equations."
   B. Present a quadratic equation whose roots are imaginary.
   C. Present a simple verbal problem which leads to a quadratic equation which cannot be solved by factoring.
   D. Begin with simple equations which are solved by taking the square roots of both members. Gradually introduce more difficult equations until the method is developed.

6.____

7. The use of the *discovery method* in the teaching of tenth year mathematics involves getting the pupil to

   A. associate a theorem with the mathematician who made the discovery
   B. discover the procedure by which a theorem has been proved
   C. recognize when to use a direct or an indirect method of proof
   D. make and test conjectures of his own

7.____

8. Of the following objectives of a ninth-year algebra course, the one which has been introduced MOST recently is the

   A. ability to translate verbal problems into equation form
   B. ability to solve inequalities as well as equations
   C. understanding of dependence and functional relationships
   D. understanding of the postulates of the four fundamental operations as applied to the solution of equations

8.____

9. Of the following topics in tenth year mathematics, the one students usually find MOST difficult is

   A. coordinate geometry   B. angle measurement
   C. geometric constructions D. locus

9.____

10. When a pupil combines two fractions with different denominators, he should understand that he is making use of which one of the following?

    A. Commutative and associative postulates for addition
    B. Multiplicative identity and distributive postulates
    C. Additive identity and additive inverse postulates
    D. Multiplicative identity and multiplicative inverse postulates

10.____

11. Of the following, the STRONGEST criticism of the teaching of modern mathematics is that

    A. it is too difficult for the children to handle
    B. parents are unable to help their children to overcome difficulties
    C. many of the topics covered should be delayed until the students are in college
    D. many teachers have not been adequately trained to teach the new mathematics

11.____

12. The principle "a.1 = a" can be used to explain each of the following EXCEPT the

    A. simplification of a complex fraction
    B. simplification of radicals

12.____

C. rationalizing of a fraction with an irrational denominator
D. conversion of the measure of an angle from degrees to radians

13. While discussing polygons, a student asks for the name of a polygon of seven sides The teacher has forgotten but thinks that a likely answer would be *septagon.*
Of the following, the BEST reply for the teacher to make would be

   A. "I believe it's septagon."
   B. "It is not important, because 7 is not an exact divisor of 360."
   C. "I don't know. Let's continue with the lesson."
   D. "I don't recall. Let us both look it up and report to the class."

14. Of the following, the BEST reason why a student should study academic mathematics is that

   A. it is necessary for college entrance
   B. modern technology is such that a pupil needs such background to better understand and contribute to the world in which we live
   C. a good mind needs to be challenged
   D. traditionally, such subjects have been part of the education of college bound

15. A student asks why it is necessary to study *required* theorems in tenth year mathematics. Of the following, the BEST reason is that the study of *required* theorems

   A. is mandated by the state Board of Regents
   B. is a result of the regular inclusion of a required theorem in the tenth year mathematics Regents examination
   C. makes students aware of the principle of sequence in tenth year mathematics
   D. affords good training in memorization

KEY (CORRECT ANSWERS)

1. D
2. A
3. C
4. C
5. C

6. C
7. D
8. B
9. D
10. B

11. D
12. B
13. D
14. B
15. C

TEST 3

DIRECTIONS: Each question or incomplete statement is followed by several suggested answers or completions. Select the one that BEST answers the question or completes the statement. *PRINT THE LETTER OF THE CORRECT ANSWER IN THE SPACK AT THE RIGHT.*

1. Of the following, the BEST reason for a short warm-up exercise at the start of the mathematics period is that it

    A. keeps the pupils busy so that the teacher may take the attendance
    B. gives the pupil a chance to quiet down so that the lesson can begin promptly
    C. provides the teacher with additional valid marks for the pupil
    D. is an opportunity to prepare for the new teaching in the lesson

    1.____

2. Lattice points can be used to do which one of the following?

    A. Graph equations
    B. Illustrate proportion
    C. Find the power of cardinal numbers
    D. Find non-denumerable sets

    2.____

3. Of the following, the one which BEST illustrates the use of the concept of relative primes is teaching

    A. pupils to reduce fractions to lowest terms
    B. pupils least common multiple
    C. the Pythagorean Theorem
    D. quadratic equations

    3.____

4. Developmental mathematics includes the following four steps:
    I. thinking through
    II. real experiences
    III. written computation
    IV. application to problems

    Which one of the following is the BEST sequence to use in teaching mathematics?

    A. I, II, III, IV
    B. IV, III, II, I
    C. II, IV, III, I
    D. II, I, III, IV

    4.____

5. In multiplication, the factors may be grouped in any manner without affecting their product.
    This is an illustration of which one of the following?

    A. Commutative law of multiplication
    B. Distributive law
    C. Associative law of multiplication
    D. Existence of an identity in multiplication

    5.____

6. Among the justifications for the use of programmed material, the POOREST one is which one of the following?

    A. Supplementary homework can be assigned to faster students.
    B. It can be used for corrective and remedial instruction.

    6.____

C. It can help relieve the teacher shortage in mathematics.
D. It breaks down the work in mathematics into a hierarchy of simple items.

7. Practice is most successful if all EXCEPT which one of the following suggestions is followed?

   A. Practice should be given on a known process
   B. The more practice assigned, the greater the improvement
   C. Practice material should be corrected
   D. Practice is necessary to make some skills automatic

8. The pantograph is a teaching aid which may BEST be used in teaching which one of the following?

   A. Graphs
   B. Drawing to scale
   C. Geometric formulas
   D. Relationship of area of a circle to that of a rectangle

9. Of the following, the one man NOT paired with an area of mathematics in which he specialized is

   A. Napier - Logarithms
   B. Boole - Logic
   C. Rieman - Non-Euclidean Geometry
   D. Lobachevsky - Analytic Geometry

10. To build a clear understanding of division, a teacher should BEST teach which one of the following first?

    A. That division is the opposite of multiplication
    B. The definitions of divisor, dividend, and quotient
    C. Finding the first quotient figure
    D. That division is repeated subtraction

11. The use of a place value diagram is MOST helpful in teaching _____ fractions.

    A. decimal
    B. reduction of
    C. addition of
    D. multiplication of

12. When pupils conclude after much computation that *even numbers + even numbers equal even numbers,* it is an illustration of which one of the following?

    A. Inductive generalization
    B. Mathematical proof of these statements
    C. Deductive generalization
    D. Accepting false premises

13. Which one of the following methods is the BEST one to be used by a mathematics teacher in helping to improve reading?

    A. Photocopy a list of basic mathematics vocabulary to be distributed to each pupil
    B. Devote some part of each lesson to improvement in mathematical reading
    C. Lower mathematics grades for poor spelling on tests
    D. Stress the reading of puzzle problems as a hobby

14. Of the following, the BEST reason for giving a homework assignment in mathematics is that it is a technique for

   A. teaching and learning
   B. keeping parents informed of what the school is teaching
   C. achieving proper mental discipline
   D. keeping the pupils busy

15. Practice and theory of rounding off numbers should precede the teaching of which one of the following?

   A. Estimation
   B. Mixed numbers
   C. Negative numbers
   D. Formulae

16. At the start of mathematics, a system of fundamental statements are offered. These are called which one of the following?

   A. Corollaries
   B. Intuitionalisms
   C. Foundations
   D. Postulates

17. The subject of set theory may be considered as having originated with which one of the following?

   A. Gauss
   B. Leibnitz
   C. Cantor
   D. Haussdorf

18. The teaching of which one of the following topics would be helped the LEAST by the use of *Venn Diagrams*?

   A. Inequalities
   B. Closed sentences
   C. Numeration systems
   D. Operations on sets

19. Which one of the following aids would BEST be used in the initial teaching of the area of a rectangle?

   A. Square material
   B. Pegboard
   C. 36" ruler
   D. Hypsometer

20. In teaching factoring, the sequence of skills includes:
   I. Find common factors of pairs of numbers
   II. Determine whether or not a number is a factor of another given number
   III. Multiplication and division are inverse processes

   Which one of the following represents the BEST sequence in teaching the topic of factoring?

   A. I, II, III
   B. I, III, II
   C. III, II, I
   D. II, I, III

21. Many reforms have been suggested to improve the teaching of mathematics. Which one of the following is LEAST valid as a reason for such reforms?

   A. The mathematics programs in many schools do not treat adequately the advances made in mathematics during the past 150 years.
   B. Traditional mathematics has lost its mental discipline values.
   C. The mathematics needs of people in our modern society are not met by the traditional program.
   D. Many topics of our traditional mathematics program are obsolete.

22. Of the following, the one MOST effective step in teaching the basic number facts is to have the pupils 22._____

    A. repeat the facts many times until recall is automatic
    B. write the facts in many different forms
    C. meet the number facts in many different situations
    D. see the facts as represented by real objects

23. Having discovered a few bright pupils interested in mathematics in a *normal* class, the teacher should do which one of the following? 23._____

    A. Guide them in studying additional material
    B. Leave them alone to work on their own
    C. Let them help by marking papers
    D. Assign extra homework to them

24. The mathematician who made use of the ordered nature of numbers to develop a graphic system was 24._____

    A. Newton   B. Descartes
    C. Kronecker   D. Russell

25. Of the following, the device for showing the properties and characteristics of a trapezoid is the 25._____

    A. extensible quadrilateral
    B. ruler
    C. squared materials
    D. simplified transit

KEY (CORRECT ANSWERS)

1.	D	11.	A
2.	A	12.	A
3.	A	13.	B
4.	D	14.	A
5.	C	15.	A
6.	C	16.	D
7.	B	17.	C
8.	B	18.	C
9.	D	19.	A
10.	D	20.	C

21. B
22. C
23. A
24. B
25. A

TEST 4

DIRECTIONS: Each question or incomplete statement is followed by several suggested answers or completions. Select the one that BEST answers the question or completes the statement. *PRINT THE LETTER OF THE CORRECT ANSWER IN THE SPACE AT THE RIGHT.*

1. Of the following statements, select the one which is NOT consistent with present thinking. 1.____

   A. All pupils can be expected to discover mathematical relationships completely on their own initiative.
   B. Drilling pupils on the solution of problems of the same type offers them limited experience in problem-solving.
   C. In general, success in problem-solving depends, in part, upon finding a relationship between the known and the unknown.
   D. Not every textbook exercise is a problem.

2. Of the following statements concerning methods of teaching mathematics, the one which is NOT correct is: 2.____

   A. In the lecture method, there may well be a great deal of teaching but little learning
   B. In the laboratory method, students weigh, count, draw, measure, compare, and analyze.
   C. Teachers who tend to move on rapidly may not provide sufficient time for experimentation and for self-discovery.
   D. An important method in the development of mathematical concepts is the use of a workbook

3. Mathematics bulletins suggest that within each cycle, there also be a cyclical arrangement for teaching the sequence of topics. 3.____
   According to current thinking, which one of the following is NOT a strong argument for such an arrangement? To

   A. provide for continuous development and reinforcement of the content of each topic throughout the year
   B. sustain interest
   C. present the simpler aspects of each topic first
   D. help maintain school schedules providing time allotments for the teaching of mathematics

4. Of the following, which one is the MOST acceptable procedure for spurring pupils to greater effort in their mathematics work? 4.____

   A. Have each pupil keep a graph of his test marks.
   B. Read all test scores aloud in class.
   C. Give pupils test marks without returning test papers to them.
   D. Return test papers to pupils without informing them of the test grades.

182

5. Which one of the following is the MOST effective way of allowing for individual rates of progress in class work?

   A. Omit difficult and time-consuming topics
   B. Teach all topics with variations of depth and intensity
   C. Concentrate on review of arithmetic fundamentals
   D. Have slow learners work principally with workbook assignments to give them greater drill opportunities

6. Of the following, which one is the BEST statement of the students' aim for a certain one-period lesson in an average junior high school class? To

   A. learn about parallelogram area
   B. learn about quadrilateral area
   C. learn about the parallelogram formula
   D. work out and learn to apply the formula for the area of a parallelogram

7. In planning drill for mathematics classes, which one of the following procedures should be adhered to?

   A. Every pupil in a class should be assigned the same drill exercises.
   B. An entire lesson period should frequently be devoted to drill exercises.
   C. Drill should be individualized according to pupil need.
   D. The teacher should consistently use the same drill technique.

8. Which one of the following is the LEAST effective way of enriching mathematics courses for bright pupils?

   A. Assembling bibliographies of mathematics and science books in the school library and encouraging wide reading
   B. Publishing a mathematics departmental magazine each year
   C. Arranging a mathematics section in the school's annual science fair.
   D. Making sure that the bright pupils complete all of the more difficult exercises and problems of each set in the assigned text

9. The standard junior high school mathematics curriculum does NOT include a unit of

   A. numerical trigonometry
   B. statistics
   C. similarity of geometric figures
   D. logarithms

10. Which one of the following visual aids is usually MOST helpful in clarifying the concept of place value?

    A. Discs   B. Circles on a flannel board
    C. Pocket chart   D. Pegboard

11. Which one of the following visual aids is usually MOST effective in explaining common fractions?

    A. Circle sectors on a flannel board
    B. Abacus
    C. Squared material
    D. Pegboard

12. For which one of the following topics is a number line usually a useful teaching technique?

    A. Multiplication of polynomials
    B. Graph of a linear equation
    C. Signed numbers
    D. Tangent ratio

13. Which one of the following items is usually the MOST educationally valuable for display on a mathematics bulletin board in the school corridor?

    A. Pupil-made mathematics charts and posters related to a single theme
    B. Teacher-made mathematics charts and posters related to a single theme
    C. Pupil papers from recent examinations
    D. Commercial circulars obtainable from book publishers

14. Which one of the following is an INACCURATE characterization of mathematical recreations? They

    A. arouse curiosity about number relations
    B. tend to restore lost confidence
    C. are used principally to fill in any extra time which otherwise would be wasted
    D. create a more social setting because they provoke discussion

15. Developmental mathematics, in its teaching-learning pattern, involves four steps:
    I. Written computation
    II. Real experiences
    III. Thinking through
    IV. Application to problems

Which one of the following represents the MOST educationally sound order for usually employing these steps?

    A. III, IV, II, I   B. II, IV, III, I
    C. II, III, I, IV   D. II, IV, I, III

16. In reviewing addition of fractions, examples of the following types would be included:
    I.   7/9
       +2/3
    II. 1/5
       +2/5
    III. 1/6
       +2/3
    IV. 1 1/3
       +2 5/6

The MOST effective gradation would require their consideration in which one of the following orders?

    A. II, III, I, IV   B. I, II, IV, III
    C. II, III, IV, I   D. IV, I, III, II

17. Which one of the following is the MOST acceptable sequence in the development of areas of geometric figures?

    A. Right triangle, parallelogram, rectangle
    B. Rectangle, right triangle, oblique triangle, parallelogram
    C. Trapezoid, parallelogram, triangle
    D. Parallelogram, rectangle, oblique triangle, right triangle

17.____

18. Which one of the following will most likely contribute LEAST to pupil discovery of the generalization concerning volume of a cube?

    A. Making paper cubes from a pattern
    B. Studying wooden models of cubes
    C. Fitting one inch cubes into a carton having a cubical shape
    D. Pointing out the logical connection between the formula for the area of a square and that for the volume of a cube

18.____

19. Which one of the following usually represents the MOST pedagogically sound initial step in teaching the area of a circle formula, $A = \pi r^2$? Teacher

    A. gives pupils the formula and shows them how to apply it in several examples
    B. has a discussion on the meaning of the constant, π
    C. has pupils read aloud, in turn, from text material on circle area
    D. has pupils construct several circles with different radii on squared paper for approximate computation of their areas

19.____

20. Study of the relationship between snapshots and their enlargements is MOST valuable for which one of the following topics?

    A. Signed Numbers   B. Ratio
    C. Area of a Triangle   D. Circle Graphs

20.____

21. Of the following statements concerning the teaching of graphs, the one which is INCORRECT is:

    A. A graph is a pictorial representation showing the relationship of values
    B. Lengths of lines and areas of surfaces are used to represent numerical values
    C. The data involved do not affect the choice of type of graph used
    D. The type of graph used is, at least in part, dependent upon the purpose to which the graph is to be put

21.____

22. Which one of the following is an acceptable approach for an eighth grade teacher to take in helping pupils who have difficulty in reading verbal problems in the available textbooks?

    A. Avoid giving verbal problems on homework assignments
    B. Postpone problem-solving until later in the school year
    C. Omit verbal problems from this class' work
    D. Duplicate worksheets containing verbal problems constructed by teacher and pupils

22.____

23. Which one of the following is usually the BEST book to give a bright, seventh-grade pupil   23._____
    for research and outside reading on mathematics?

    A. THE WORLD OF MATHEMATICS - Newman
    B. HOW MUCH AND HOW MANY - Bendick
    C. MATHEMATICS IN WESTERN CULTURE - Kline
    D. ELEMENTARY MATHEMATICS FROM AN ADVANCED VIEWPOINT - Klein

24. A teacher should be LEAST concerned with which one of the following in making a rec-   24._____
    ommendation for possible adoption of a new mathematics textbook?

    A. Clarity of print and attractiveness of illustrations and diagrams
    B. Reading level of material in text
    C. Lack of availability of an answer key in back of book
    D. Comprehensiveness of the review and test sections

25. Of the following, the BEST reason for the inclusion of *modern mathematics* in the junior   25._____
    high school curriculum is that

    A. the most important mathematics is that which has been discovered and developed recently
    B. traditional mathematics is incorrect
    C. a better foundation is thus provided for understanding mathematics
    D. number systems in bases other than 10 often require fewer digits in computations

KEY (CORRECT ANSWERS)

1. A	11. A
2. D	12. C
3. D	13. A
4. A	14. C
5. B	15. C
6. D	16. A
7. C	17. B
8. D	18. D
9. D	19. D
10. C	20. B

21. C
22. D
23. B
24. C
25. C

TEST 5

DIRECTIONS: Each question or incomplete statement is followed by several suggested answers or completions. Select the one that BEST answers the question or completes the statement. *PRINT THE LETTER OF THE CORRECT ANSWER IN THE SPACE AT THE RIGHT.*

1. Of the following, the problems which are of LEAST value in stimulating real thinking are those   1.____

   A. which pupils solve in many ways
   B. which pupils solve in one way which has been thoroughly practiced
   C. in which pupils encounter extraneous data
   D. which pupils cannot solve because of insufficient data

2. Of the following, select the suggestion LEAST likely to help a pupil having difficulty in finding the solutions to a verbal problem.   2.____

   A. Generalize the problem by using letters instead of numbers.
   B. Estimate the answer.
   C. Use round numbers.
   D. Use diagrams or representations.

3. In order to implement the aims and objectives of the junior high school, the mathematics teacher should NOT   3.____

   A. make certain to study each child as an individual and provide for the normal bright, and slow learners
   B. encourage and help pupils to explore and sample the fields of algebra, geometry, and trigonometry
   C. assist all pupils in acquiring competence in independent study through effective study habits
   D. encourage all pupils to go on to college

4. Of the following, the one that LEAST describes a principle of classroom motivation is that   4.____

   A. the motivation should be brief
   B. the motivation should be related to the new work being introduced
   C. the motivation should be related to the experiences of the pupils
   D. interest in the subject for its own sake is always an adequate motivation

5. The CORRECT order of teaching-learning pattern which involves the following processes: 5.____

   I. application of problems
   II. computation
   III. experiences
   IV. thinking through

   is in the sequence:

   A. I, II, III, IV   B. III, IV, II, I
   C. II, III, IV, I   D. IV, I, II, III

6. Select the one of the following principles of learning mathematics which is INCORRECT: 6.____

   A. Pupils learn as individuals even though they are taught in groups
   B. It should be expected that all pupils can master all elements of mathematics at the same grade and age
   C. Individual instruction in mathematics is occasionally or even often necessary
   D. Each pupil tends to learn only in terms of his active interest and participation

7. When teaching a new topic, the teacher should 7.____

   A. make sure that all homework difficulties have been corrected before teaching the new material
   B. allow sufficient time for a full presentation of the new material
   C. teach the new material before any discussion of the homework
   D. warn pupils that they will be tested on the new material the next day

8. In a comparison of the developmental and lecture method of teaching, which one of the following statements is *most nearly* CORRECT? 8.____

   A. In the lecture method, the teacher readily checks the progress of learning.
   B. There is greater pupil participation in the developmental method.
   C. Greater pupil attention is insured in the lecture method.
   D. There is less need for review at the beginning of a developmental lesson.

9. A benefit resulting from the introduction of numbers in other bases than 10 into the curriculum of junior high school mathematics is that 9.____

   A. this results in better understanding of the number system in base 10
   B. there is a better basis for problem solving
   C. computation is simpler with numbers in bases other than 10
   D. fewer digits are required for numbers in bases other than 10

10. Of the following, the statement concerning deductive proofs which is CORRECT is that they 10.____

    A. have no place in the junior high school mathematics curriculum
    B. help junior high school pupils to understand and to appreciate the sequential nature of mathematics
    C. can be used only in geometry
    D. should not be used before a pupil reaches the 9th grade

11. Temperature, sea level, stocks, and bonds all provide concrete illustrations for teaching which one of the following topics in mathematics? 11.____

    A. The metric system of measurement
    B. Exponents
    C. Signed numbers
    D. Radicals

12. In presenting the unit in informal geometry, the teacher should guard against 12.____

    A. a predominance of telling the pupils the properties of geometric figures
    B. developing inductively the relationships and properties of geometric figures

C. relating the geometric figures to pupils' experiences
D. developing mensurational formulas inductively

13. Pupils should be encouraged to make their own measuring instruments because of which one of the following?

    A. These are superior to the manufactured ones.
    B. It is a useful way of consuming time while some of the slower youngsters are being drilled.
    C. This practice develops a keener understanding of measurement.
    D. This practice aids in developing skill in fundamentals.

14. Of the following, in presenting the solution of equations in the junior high school, a modern mathematics approach

    A. compares the equation to a scale that is in balance
    B. makes use of the concept of equivalent equations
    C. makes use of the rule that the same thing can be done to both sides of the equation
    D. avoids the concept of solution set

15. Of the following, the statement concerning modern mathematics which is CORRECT is that it

    A. attempts to present modern applications of mathematics to science, business, and technology
    B. includes material developed only in the 20th century
    C. attempts to organize arithmetic and algebra on a firm postulational basis
    D. should be taught only to gifted students

16. Of the following statements concerning consumer education, select the one which is INCORRECT:

    A. Because prices change frequently, the teacher must be on guard constantly to keep materials up-to-date
    B. The backgrounds (wages, social security, etc.) of the topic should be left to the social studies teacher in order to save time
    C. Pupils should be encouraged to bring to class actual invoices, tax tables, payroll sheets, etc.
    D. Pupils should be encouraged to discuss their own experiences in part-time work

17. Which one of the following statements dealing with the topic of fractions is NOT true?

    A. Groups of pupils who used manipulative materials in learning to understand the meaning of fractions showed no marked difference over other groups which did not use such aids.
    B. Fractions have several meanings rather than only one meaning.
    C. Of the fractions used in social situations, an exceptionally large, number have these denominators: 2, 3, 4, 5, 6, 10, 12, and 16.
    D. To expand the number system to include fractions took many centuries.

18. Pupils should be encouraged to keep a mathematics notebook because it 18.____
    A. can be used as the principal basis for report card ratings
    B. is a convenient source of paper for tests
    C. provides the pupil with a record of work done in class
    D. makes it convenient for the teacher to assign practice work to the class

19. Of the following, the MOST suitable topic for a junior high school mathematics publication is: 19.____
    A. NON-EUCLIDEAN GEOMETRY   B. SPHERICAL TRIGONOMETRY
    C. COMPUTING MACHINES   D. SYMBOLIC LOGIC

20. Of these practices employed by teachers in the utilization of bulletin boards, which one is the LEAST desirable? 20.____

    A. The teacher posts a list of the standing in the class of every pupil in every class as a motivational device.
    B. Pupils may be encouraged to use a class bulletin board as a clearinghouse for the exchange of problems or puzzles.
    C. A select group of pupils may use the bulletin board as a showcase for the display of materials resulting from group research.
    D. Clippings from current periodicals posted on the bulletin board enable pupils to sense the wide ramifications of numbers.

KEY (CORRECT ANSWERS)

1.	B	11.	C
2.	A	12.	A
3.	D	13.	C
4.	D	14.	B
5.	B	15.	C
6.	B	16.	B
7.	B	17.	A
8.	B	18.	C
9.	A	19.	C
10.	B	20.	A

MATHEMATICAL RELATIONSHIPS AND CONCEPTS

1. SOLVING LINEAR EQUATIONS

When solving simple linear equations, the goal is to rewrite the equation in the form *variable = constant* or *constant = variable*. To achieve the goal, you generally need to add the same quantity to both sides of the equation or to multiply both sides of the equation by the same quantity. Thus, to solve $3x - 6 = 14$, we would add 6, the opposite of -6, to both sides, obtaining $3x = 20$. We would then multiply both sides by 1/3, the *opposite* or *inverse* of 3, to obtain the final answer.

$$3x = 20$$
$$\frac{1}{3} \cdot 3x = \frac{1}{3} \cdot 20$$
$$x = \frac{20}{3} \text{ or } 6\frac{2}{3}$$

Notice that the equation has been reduced to the form *variable = constant*, that is $= 6\frac{2}{3}$. Here is another example. Solve for x:

Add -7 (the opposite of 7) to both sides	$\frac{2}{3}x + 7 = 18$
This reduces to	$-7 \quad -7$
	$\frac{2}{3}x = 11$
Multiply both sides by $\frac{3}{2}$ because	$\frac{3}{2} \cdot \frac{2}{3}x = \frac{3}{2} \cdot \frac{11}{1}$
$\frac{3}{2}$ is the inverse of $\frac{2}{3}$	$x = \frac{33}{2} \text{ or } 16\frac{1}{2}$

Some equations have variables on both sides of the equality symbol.

Problem: Solve for x: $3x + 7 = 5x - 11$
Solution:

Add -3x to both sides	$3x + 7 = 5x - 11$
This reduces to:	$-3x \quad\quad -3x$
Add 11 to both sides: This reduces to:	$7 = 2x - 11$
	$+ 11 \quad\quad + 11$
Multiply both sides by $\frac{1}{2}$:	$18 = 2x$
The answer is:	$\frac{1}{2} \cdot 18 = \frac{1}{2} \cdot 2x$
	$9 = x$

Problem: Solve for t: $4 + 3(t-2) = t + 1$

Solution: When equations contain parentheses, always remove the parentheses first and then proceed as usual. Here, $3(t-2)$ is equivalent to $3t - 6$. Thus,

	4	+ 3t	− 6	=	t	+ 1
	3t	+ 4	− 6	=	t	+ 1
Reordered:		3t	− 2	=	t	+ 1
Reduced:	−t			=	−t	
Add -t to both sides:						
The result is:	2t	− 2		=	1	
Add 2 to both sides:		+ 2			+2	
The result is:	2t			=	3	
Multiply both sides by 1/2 :	$\frac{1}{2} \cdot 2t = \frac{1}{2} \cdot 3$					
The answer is:	$t = \frac{3}{2}$					

Problem: Solve for x: 0.17x + 1.2 = 6.3

Solution: Sometimes you must multiply both sides by an appropriate power of ten in order to remove the decimals. Because the equation above has as many as two digits to the right of the decimal point, we multiply both sides by 10^2 or 100.

$$100(0.17x + 1.2) = 100(6.3)$$
$$17x + 120 = 630$$
$$17x = 510$$
$$x = 30$$

EXERCISES

1. Solve for x:
   A. 2x − 3 = 15
   B. 5x + 8 = 20
   C. 15 = 3x − 6
   D. $\frac{2}{3}x - 7 = 4$
   E. 3/5x + 4 = 12

2. Solve for x:
   A. 3x + 5 = 6x − 1
   B. 4x − 5 = 12 − 9
   C. 4 − 2x = 6x + 5
   D. $12 - x = \frac{3}{2}x = 2$
   E. 300 − 140x = 3860x − 20

3. Solve for the variable:
   A. 2x − 5 = 4(3x+l) − 2
   B. 10t + 1 = 2(3t+5) − 1
   C. 2(x+2) = 1 + 3(1−x)
   D. 5 − (11 − 2x) = 7x + 7

4. Solve for the variable:
   A. $0.42x - 1.2 = 7.2$
   B. $1.1a + 3 = 0.712$
   C. $-6.54 = 1.48t - 3.062$
   D. $\dfrac{1}{a} + 1 = 3$

2. EVALUATING ALGEBRAIC EXPRESSIONS

Evaluating algebraic expressions is mostly a matter of replacing variables with numbers. You may need to use your equation-solving knowledge to complete the process.

Problem: Find the value of y when x= 3 if $x = 3y - 6$.

Solution: $x = 3y - 6$
Replace x by 3 $3 = 3y - 6$
$$\begin{array}{r} +6 \quad\quad +6 \\ \hline 9 = 3y \end{array}$$
$$\dfrac{1}{3} \times 9 = \dfrac{1}{3} \times 3y$$
The answer is: $3 = y$

EXERCISES

5. Evaluate the following when a=2, b=3, c=2:
   A. $-3a + 5b$
   B. $a(b+c)$
   C. $3a + 2b + 4c$

6. Find the value of y when $x = 3$ if
   A. $y = 3x - 9$
   B. $x + y = 11$
   C. $2x + 3y = 7$
   D. $5 - (x+y) = 11$
   E. $3y = 2x$

7. Solve for y if $x = 20$:
   A. $y = \dfrac{2}{3}x - 4$
   B. $y = \dfrac{9}{5}x + 32$
   C. $\dfrac{1}{3}y + \dfrac{1}{4}x = \dfrac{1}{5}$

8. Interest (I) equals principal (P) multiplied by the interest rate per unit of time (r) multiplied by the number of the time periods (t) of the loan: I = Prt. What is the rate per year if an invested principal of $2000 earns $320 interest over a 2-year period?

9. What is the value of a if b = 0.2 and 3.2 + a + 0.3b = 0.25?

3. SOLVING LITERAL EQUATIONS

A literal equation is one involving more than one variable; for example, 3x + 2y = 6 or d = rt. Often literal equations need to be solved for one or another of the variables in the equation. Thus, d = rt is in a form where d is the solution. To *solve for* r, we may divide both sides of the equation by t to obtain $\frac{d}{t} = \frac{rt}{t}$ or $\frac{d}{t} = r$. We might also divide both sides by r to obtain $\frac{d}{r} = t$.

Thus, we have three *equivalent* equations: $d = rt; \frac{d}{t} = r; \frac{d}{r} = t$.

Solving literal equations involves our usual equation-solving techniques: We add (or subtract) the same quantity to both sides of the equation, and we multiply (or divide) both sides by the same quantity.

Problem: Rewrite 2x + 9y - 18 = 0 in terms of y:

Solution:
$$2x + 9y - 18 = 0$$
$$+18 \quad +18$$
$$2x + 9y = 18$$
$$-2x \quad\quad -2x$$
$$9y = 18 - 2x$$

now divide both sides by 9:
$$\frac{9}{9}y = \frac{18 - 2x}{9}$$
$$y = \frac{18 - 2x}{9}$$

Problem: Solve the following for c: $F = \frac{9}{5}C + 32$

Solution:
$$F = \frac{9}{5}C + 32$$
$$-32 \quad\quad\quad -32$$
$$F - 32 = \frac{9}{5}C$$

$$\frac{5}{9}(F - 32) = \frac{5}{9} \times \frac{9}{5}C$$
$$\frac{5}{9}(F - 32) = C$$

Problem: Solve for x: $y = 14 - 8x$

Solution:
$$y = 14 - 8x$$
$$\underline{-14 \qquad -14}$$
$$y - 14 = -8x$$
$$\frac{y-14}{-8} = \frac{-8x}{-8}$$

Multiply numerator and denominator by -1 to eliminate the negative denominator

$$\frac{y \; 14}{8} = x$$

$$\frac{14 \; y}{8} = x$$

EXERCISES

10. Solve the equations in terms of y
    A. $3x + y = 12$
    B. $xy = 8$
    C. $A = bry$
    D. $4x + 3y = 12$
    E. $4x - 13y = 17$
    F. $3x = 6y$

11. Rewrite $I = Prt$ in terms of P

12. Solve $s = a + (n - 1)d$ for d

13. Rewrite $L = a(l + ct)$ in terms of c

14. Suppose $x\,y\,z = 10$. Solve for x and then for y

15. Give two equivalent forms of the equation $7x - 2y = 14$ by solving for x and for y

4. DIRECT AND INVERSE VARIATION

If the numbers involved are simple, direct and inverse variation problems can be done mentally.

Consider this problem: Suppose y varies directly as x. If y is 8 when x is 2, what is y when x is 3?

To say, *y varies directly as x* means y is a multiple of x. Now, if y is 8 when x is 2, what multiple of x must y be? Clearly, 8 is 4 times 2 so y must be 4 times x: $y = 4x$. At this point, you can answer the question, *What is y when x is 3?* Since $y = 4x$, it follows that when x is 3, y is 12.

Consider this problem: Suppose y varies directly as x. When $y = 5$, then $x = 10$. What is the value of y when $x = 6$? The variable y varies directly as x. This means that y is a multiple of x. What do you multiply the x-value of 10 by to get the y-value 5? The multiplier is 1/2 because $1/2 \cdot 10 = 5$. Thus, if $x = 6$, then $y = 1/2 \cdot 6 = 3$.

EXERCISES

16. Solve these direct variation problems. In each case, y varies directly as x.
    A. If y is 3 when x is 1, then y = _____ when x = 6.
    B. If y is 10 when x is 2, then y = _____ when x = 4.
    C. If y is 2 when x is 4, then y = _____ when x = 9.
    D. If y is 5 when x is 15, then y = _____ when x = 9.
    E. If y is 3 when x is 2, then y = _____ when x = 10.
    F. If y is 12 when x is 4, then y = 15 when x = _____.
    G. If y is 3 when x is 9, then y = 4 when x = _____.
    H. If y is 3/2 when x is 1, then y = 6 when x = _____.
    I. If y is 5 when x is 2, then y = _____ when x = 6.

Although many variation problems can be solved or approximated mentally, there are mechanical, rote methods for solving such problems.

Consider problem 16I above: If y is 5 when x is 2, then y = _____ when x = 6. Some people might reason this way: *So y = 5 when x 2. That means that y equals two and a half times x. So if x = 6, then two and a half x's make 6 + 6 + 3 = 15, so when x = 6, then y = 15.*

Here is a mechanical way to do the same problem. Since y varies directly as x, y is a multiple of x: y = kx. By substituting the known values 5 and 2 for y and x respectively, you can solve for k. We know that y = kx, 5 = k.2. Therefore, 5/2 = k. If y = 5/2x and if x = 6, then y = 5/2.6 = 15. Thus, we have this procedure:

Use formula y = kx where $\dfrac{\text{Known y-value}}{\text{Known x-value}}$

EXERCISES

17. Solve these direct variation problems by using the formula y = kx. In each case, y varies directly as x. For each problem, identify the value of k you used and the value that goes in the blank.
    A. If y is 6 when x is 2, then y = _____ when x = 10.
    B. If y is 6 when x is 3, then y = _____ when x = 18.
    C. If y is 12 when x is 1/3, then y = _____ when x = 5.
    D. If y is 28 when x is -4, then y = _____ when x = 7.
    E. If y is 12 when x is 4, then y = 12.36 when x = _____.
    F. If y is 459 when x is 17, then y = 27 when x = _____.
    G. If y is 100 when x is -10, then y = -10 when x = _____.
    H. If y is 1.4 when x is 7, then y = 10 when x = _____.

18. The salary of an hourly worker varies directly with the number of hours she works per week. According to the records, she worked 24 hours last week and made $108. How many hours would she need to work this week to make $45?

19. The weight of a collection of machine screws varies directly as the number of screws in the collection. If 110 screws weigh 1.1 kg, how many screws are in a collection weighing 0.56 kg.?

By now you have noticed that y varies directly as x, when x increases so does y and when x decreases so does y. For instance, if x doubles then y also doubles. For inverse variations, however, if x doubles, then y decreases by half! Overall, for inverse variations one variable moves in the opposite direction from the other.

Direct Variation: If y = 8 when x = 4, then when x = 8, y = 16.
Inverse Variation: If y = 8 when x = 4, then when x = 8, y = 4.

Direct Variation: If y = 15 when x = 3, then when x = 9, y = 45.
Inverse Variation: If y = 15 when x = 3, then when x = 9, y = 5.

Suppose y is inversely related to x. Then if x doubles, y is 1/2 its former value. If the value of x is multiplied by 3, then the y-value is multiplied by 1/3, and so forth.

EXERCISES

20. Solve these inverse variation problems mentally. In each case, assume that y varies inversely as x.
    A. If y = 6 when x = 8, then y = _____ when x = 16.
    B. If y = 6 when x = 8, then y = _____ when x = 24.
    C. If y = 6 when x = 8, then y = _____ when x = 2.
    D. If y = 10 when x = 10, then y = _____ when x = 5.
    E. If y = 10 when x = 10, then y = _____ when x = 2.
    F. If y = 24 when x = 6, then y = 12 when x = _____.
    G. If y = 24 when x = 12, then y = 2 when x = _____.
    H. If y = 15 when x = 12, then y = 10 when x = _____.
    I. If y = 1 when x = 1, then y = 1/3 when x = _____.

As is the case with direct variation, there is also a formula (if you need it) for solving inverse variation problems:

$$y = \frac{k}{x} \text{ where } k = \text{(known x-value)} \cdot \text{(known y-value)}$$

Let us solve problem 20C by means of the formula. In this problem, k = 8·6 = 48. Thus, $y = \frac{48}{x}$. So, to find y when x = 2, we calculate y = 48/x = 48/2 = 24.

Let us use the formula to solve 20G. Here, k = 12·24 = 288. So the formula is $y = \frac{288}{x}$. If y = 2, then to find x we proceed as follows:

$$y = \frac{288}{x}.$$
$$2 = \frac{288}{x}$$
$$2x = 288$$
$$x = 144$$

21. Solve these inverse variation problems by using the formula $y = \dfrac{k}{x}$. In each case, y varies inversely as x. For each problem, identify the value of k you used and then the value that goes in the blank.
    A. If y is 12 when x = 2, then y = _____ when x = 1.
    B. If y is 6 when x = 2, then y = _____ when x = 3.
    C. If y is 2 when x = -3, then y = _____ when x = 1/2.
    D. If y is 6 when x = 4, then y = _____ when x = 3.
    E. If y is 3 when x = 2, then y = 1 when x = _____.
    F. If y is 10 when x = 9, then y = 45 when x = _____.

22. The pressure of a gas varies inversely as its volume. If the pressure is 21 pounds per square inch when the volume is 350 cubic inches, find the pressure when the volume is 70 cubic inches.

In place of phrases *varies directly as* or *varies inversely as,* you may encounter terms like *is directly proportional to* or *is inversely proportional to*. Problems 23-26 use this alternate wording.

23. The time required to heat water to a given temperature is directly proportional to the volume of water being heated. If 1 1/2 gallons of water take 12 minutes to heat, how many minutes will 2 gallons take to heat?

24. The scaled score on a particular test is directly proportional to the raw score. Lee had a scaled score of 500 and a raw score of 40. If Carlos had a scaled score of 375, what was his raw score?

25. The time required to travel one lap on a racetrack is inversely proportional to a car's average speed. A car averaging 90 mph takes 2 minutes to complete one lap. How long will it take to complete one lap at 120 mph?

26. A sociologist has developed a test for measuring *teaching anxiety* among junior high school teachers. She estimates that test scores are inversely related to years of teaching experience. If a teacher with 3 years experience scores 60, how many years experience has a teacher who scores 15?

5. RATIO AND PROPORTION

Ratio may be considered to be another word for *fraction*. The ratio of x to y is written x/y or x:y. Just as the fractions 2/4 and 1/2 are equal, we consider the ratio 2:4 to be the same as 1:2.

Thus, if an office employs 18 men and 15 women, we might report the ratio of men to women as 18:15, but more likely we would use 6:5 (dividing both terms by 3). On the other hand, the ratio of women to men would be 5:6. Watch out for the order of the numbers when writing ratios. The order of terms should match the order of groups or things to which they refer.

EXERCISES

27. Give the ratios required (using lowest terms).
    A. An office employs 10 female employees and 3 males. What is the ratio of males to females?
    B. A rectangle has length 20 and width 15. What is the ratio of length to width?
    C. John spends $200 a month for food and $300 a month for rent. What is the ratio of the amount he spends for food to the amount he spends for rent?
    D. A TV station airs 40 drama shows in a given week and 24 news/sports shows. What is the ratio of news/sports to drama for the TV station?

A proportion is a statement that two ratios are equal. Proportions are commonly used to solve ratio problems. Consider this problem: Bill needs to paint 3 identical bedrooms. He needs 5 gallons of paint for 2 of the rooms. How much paint will he need for all 3 rooms? We express the relationship this way

$$\frac{5}{2} = \frac{x}{3}$$ (Read 5 is to 2 as x is to 3) or this way

$$\frac{2}{5} = \frac{3}{x}$$ (Read 2 is to 5 as 3 is to x)

Note that both proportions will yield the same solution for x.

To solve a proportion, simply multiply as follows and solve the resulting equation:

Product: 15 $\quad\quad\quad$ Product: 2x

$$\frac{5}{2} = \frac{x}{3}$$

Thus, $\quad$ 15 = 2x
$\quad\quad$ 7 1/2 = x

So, 7 1/2 gallons are needed for 3 rooms.

Here is a second problem: 3 is to 7 as 8 is to what?

$$\frac{3}{7} = \frac{8}{x}$$
$$3x = 7 \times 8$$
$$3x = 56$$
$$x = \frac{56}{3}$$

28. A park ranger counts 16 trout out of 30 fish sampled in a given lake. If the lake contains 2000 fish in all, how many would you predict should be trout?

29. The ratio of a person's weight on Mars to the person's weight on Earth is 2:5. How much would a 120-pound Earth person weigh on Mars?

30. A map of your hometown has a scale that reads, *1 inch equals 6 miles.* If two locations on the map are 4 1⁄2 inches apart, what is the distance between them in miles?

31. Gerry's car burns 1 1/2 quarts of oil on a 700-mile trip. How much oil will be needed for a 3000-mile trip?

32. If a 6-foot person casts a 4-foot shadow, how tall is a tree that casts a 25-foot shadow?

33. The ratio of male to female faculty members in the Delendo School system is 2:5. If there are 36 male faculty, how many female faculty are there?

34. A collection of miniature dinosaur replicas are all constructed on the same scale. One dinosaur, whose length is estimated at 12 feet, measures 4 inches. Another measures 6 inches. Estimate its length in feet.

35. It is estimated that student scores on two different physical skills tests are proportional. John got 20 on the first test and 32 on the second. If Maria got 6 on the first test, estimate her score on the second.

6. PERCENT PROBLEMS

What is 10% of 60? Many percent problems, such as this one, can be done mentally:

10% of 60 becomes 1/10 of 60 or 6
10% of 90 is 9
10% of 463 is 46.3, etc.

More complicated problems involve changing percents to decimals and manipulating the resulting numbers.

23% of 187 becomes 0.23 x 187 or 43.01
102% of 16 becomes 1.02 x 16 or 16.32

Proportions can be used to solve many percent problems. Consider this question: *50 is 25% of what number?* Since 25% = 1/4, you could determine the answer in this way: 50 is 1/4 of 200. But you could also set up a proportion: 50 is to x as 25 is to 100.

$$\frac{50}{x} = \frac{25}{100}$$

or 50 . 100 = 25x

200 = x

Problem: 10 is 30% of what number?

Solution: $\frac{10}{x} = \frac{30}{100}$

1000 = 30x

$$\frac{1000}{30} = x$$

$33.3 = x$ (rounding the answer)

So, 10 is 30% of 33.3 (rounded).

Problem: 25 is what percent of 60?

Solution: $\frac{25}{60} = \frac{x}{100}$

$41.67 = x$ (rounding the answer)

So, 25 is approximately 41.67% of 60.

EXERCISES

36. What is:
    A. 10% of 50
    B. 1% of 50
    C. 20% of 50
    D. 21% of 50
    E. 25% of 40
    F. 50% of 160
    G. 100% of 86
    H. 150% of 50

37. What is:
    A. 17% of 80
    B. 12% of 116
    C. 8% of 21
    D. 7.5% of $15.60

38. Solve the following:
    A. 16 is 25% of what number?
    B. 13 is 86% of what number?
    C. 10 is what percent of 18?
    D. 17 is what percent of 51?

39. Solve the following:
    Example: A shirt that regularly sells for $15 is on sale for $12. What is the percent of the discount?
    The discount is $3 out of $15. 3 is what percent of 15?

    $3 = x \cdot 15$

    $$\frac{3}{15} = x$$

    $0.2 = x$

So, $x = 20\%$. The discount is 20%.

Example: The sign says that all merchandise is marked down 12%. What should one pay for a dress normally priced $28? 12% of $28 becomes 0.12 m . $28 or $3.36. Thus, the sale price of the dress is $28 - $3.36 or $24.64.

- A. The price of a $32 shirt has just increased by 16%. What does it cost now?
- B. A used car is marked $6200, but the salesman claims that he can deduct another 15%. What would the new price be?
- C. A movie ticket that usually sells for $4 now costs $5. What is the percent of the mark-up?
- D. A tire selling for $60 has just been reduced to $56. What is the percent of the discount?

40. Three grapefruits weighing 14 oz. each were combined with seven oranges weighing 8 oz. each. What percent of the total weight was provided by
    - A. the grapefruits?
    - B. the oranges?

7. EXPRESSING RELATIONSHIPS SYMBOLICALLY

Consider this problem: In Academy School there are twenty times as many students as there are teachers. Express this fact symbolically, letting S represent the number of students and T, the number of teachers. Which of the following answers is correct?

- A. $T = S + 20$
- B. $S = T + 20$
- C. $T = 20S$
- D. $S = 20T$

The Academy School problem illustrates what is meant by *expressing relationships symbolically*. When you have taken a relationship expressed in words and have expressed it by means of an equation or formula, it is a good idea to create an example to test your answer to see if it is correct.

Consider the Academy School problem. There are twenty times as many students as teachers at the school. If Academy School had, for example, one teacher, how many students would there be? There would be 20. So, if $T = 1$, $S = 20$. If you take the number of teachers (T) and multiply it by 20, you will identify the number of students (S): $20T = S$. Therefore, choice D above is the correct answer.

Notice how choices A, B, C fail when you substitute $T = 1$, $S = 20$ in the equations. By testing your answer, you can avoid incorrect responses. A person who thought $T = 20S$ was the correct equation should discover the error by responding in this way: *I know that for 20 students I should have one teacher. If I let $S = 20$ in the equation $T = 20S$, I would get $T = 20 . 20 = 400$. Four hundred teachers for 20 students? Something is wrong!*

Problem: An item regularly sells for R dollars but is on sale for S dollars. Which expression gives the percent discount?

A. $\dfrac{(R-S)(100)}{R}$

B. $\dfrac{100S}{R}$

C. $\dfrac{R-S}{100}$

D. $(R-S)100$

Solution: How do we find percent discounts? Suppose something that normally sells for $10 is on sale for $8. This discount is $2 out of $10 or 2/10, 0.20, or 20%. The strategy used was this: The sale price (S) was subtracted from the regular price (R), then the answer was divided by the regular price (R) to get 2/10 or 0.20. We then moved the decimal point two places to the right to get the answer, 20%. This is the same as multiplying by 100. Thus, the formula is identified this way: R-S/R . 100. The answer is A.

Only practice and some familiarity with frequently encountered situations can help improve formula and equation-writing skills. Remember, if you have any difficulty at all with these problems, begin by creating an example to test your answer. We did this with both problems above.

EXERCISES

41. If 100 pounds of scrap metal cost p dollars, how much is 2 tons worth at the same rate? (Note: 2000 pounds = 1 ton)

    A. 2p   B. $\dfrac{100-p}{2}$ C. 40p   D. $\dfrac{2-p}{100}$

42. An item regularly sells for p dollars but is marked 25% *off*. Which of the following is not a correct expression for the sale price?

    A. $\dfrac{3}{4}p$ B. $(1-0.25)p$ C. $p - 1/4p$ D. $p - 25$

43. Given a car's odometer reading S at the start of a trip, the reading F at the trip's finish, and the elapsed time t, write an expression for the trip's average speed V.

44. The regular price p of an item has been increased by 20%. Write an expression for the new price.

45. If x is positive and increasing in value, then y = 1/x is
    A. increasing and always positive
    B. increasing and always negative
    C. decreasing and always positive
    D. decreasing and always negative
    E. none of the above

46. If x is positive and increasing in value, then $y = \dfrac{1}{x}$ is

    A. increasing and always positive
    B. increasing and always negative
    C. decreasing and always positive
    D. decreasing and always negative
    E. none of the above

47. Write an expression that gives the total number of jars we need if each jar holds 0.5 liters and we need T liters in all. (Create an example to test your answer.)

48. Louise is trying to write an equation involving P, Q, and R. She has created an example showing that when P and Q are both 1, R must be 4. Which one or more of the following equations indicates this relationship?

    A. R = 5P - Q
    B. $1 = \dfrac{P+Q+R}{6}$
    C. R = 5(P-Q)
    D. 4Q = PR

49. Which of the following have the property that when x is positive and decreasing, y is positive and increasing?

    A. y = 4 - 1/x
    B. y = (4+x) 100
    C. xy = 1
    D. 1/x + 1/y = 3

50. Textbooks you plan to order cost $P. However, you receive a 20% discount on each book after the first 100 ordered. Which of the following will express your dollar cost if you order T textbooks, where T is larger than 100?

    A. 100P + 0.8(T-100)
    B. (100-0.20)PT
    C. 20P + 0.8PT
    D. 100P + 0.8PT

51. Suppose that personal income is taxed at a 15% rate for the first $20,000 and 28% for all income over that amount. Write an expression for the total tax paid on an income of D dollars, where D is larger than $20,000.

8. GRAPHS AND TABLES

For most people, reading graphs and tables is a matter of attention to detail and common sense. Carelessness is the most frequent cause of error. The exercises below will give you some idea of the most frequently encountered ways of displaying data and relationships pictorially.

52.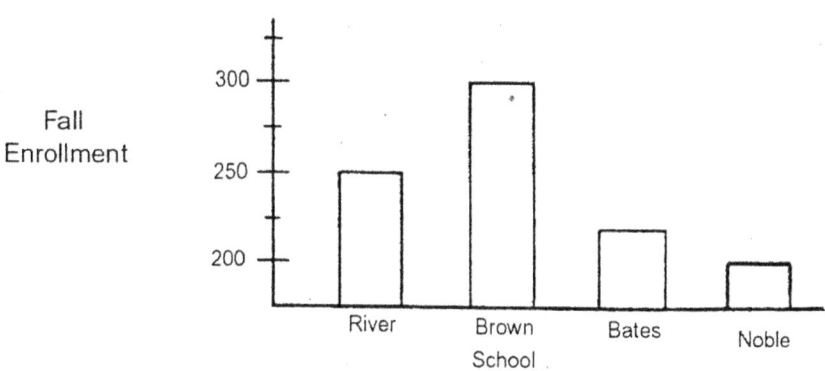

   A. What is the total enrollment at the four schools?
   B. What, approximately, is the ratio of the enrollment at Noble School to that at River School?
   C. How many times greater is enrollment at Brown School than at Noble School?

53. This graph shows spending for the town of Amsden last year. What percentage went for police and fire protection?

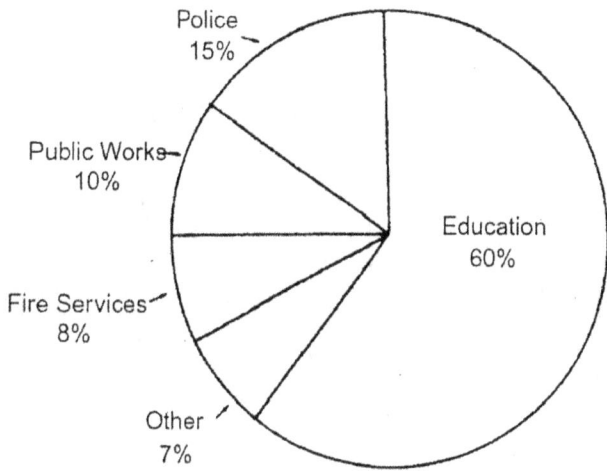

54. The graph below represents milk production for three counties last year. (Each symbol represents 10,000 gallons.) What was the approximate milk production in Balch County last year?

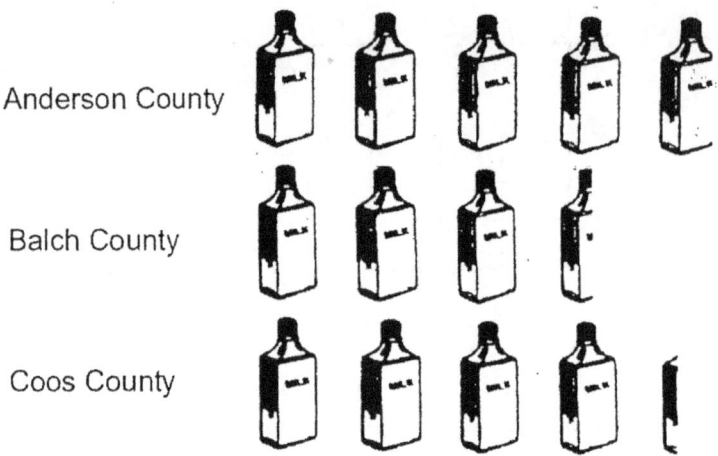

55. Mrs. Menon's mathematics group has been working independently on some lesson units. Mrs. Menon's record book is shown below. She enters S on the day a student starts Unit 1. On the day a student completes a unit, she enters that unit's number in her book.

DAY

	1	2	3	4	5	6	7	8	9	10	11	12	13
Andrew	S	1		2			3		4		5		6
Susan		S	1		2			3			4	5	
Louts				S		1	2		3		4		5
Tomas			S	1		2		3	4		5		6
Fran					S	1	2		4		5		6

UNITS COMPLETED

A. Susan took 11 days to complete units 1-5. How many days did Louis take to complete the same units?
B. At the end of the 11th day, which student had been working at the most rapid pace?

56. The distance (d) a person walks varies directly with time (t). Which graph best represents this situation?

A.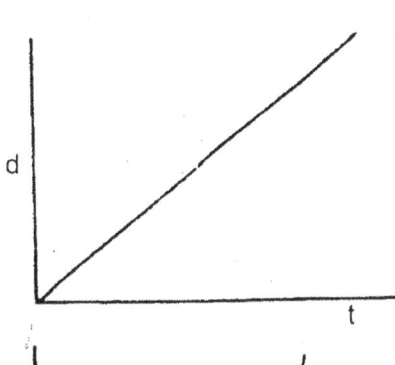

B.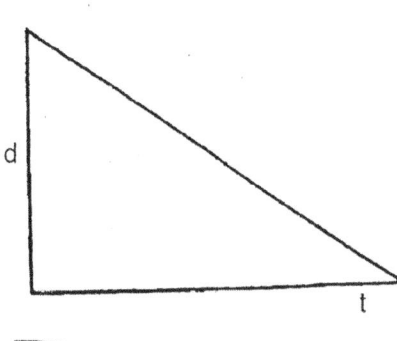

C.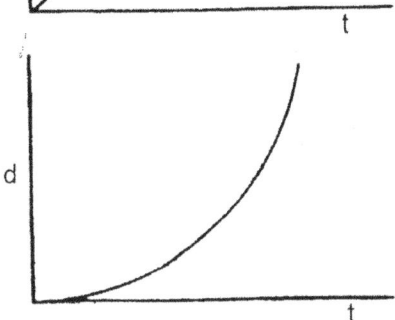

D.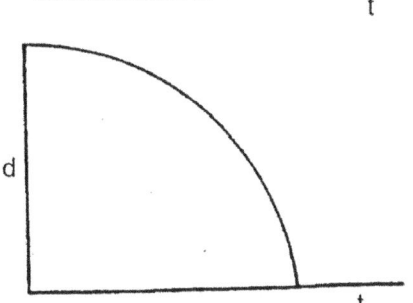

57. Which graph best represents the number of hours (T) from sunrise to sunset in Hartford, Connecticut, from January of one year to January of the next?

A.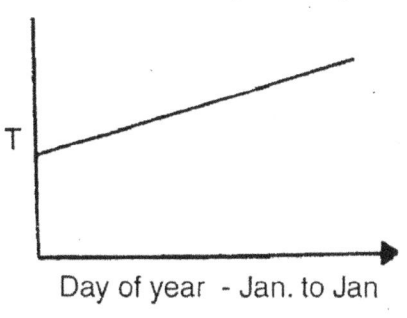
Day of year - Jan. to Jan

B.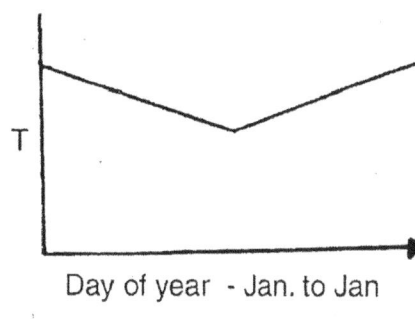
Day of year - Jan. to Jan

C.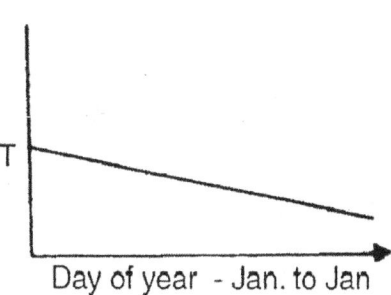
Day of year - Jan. to Jan

D.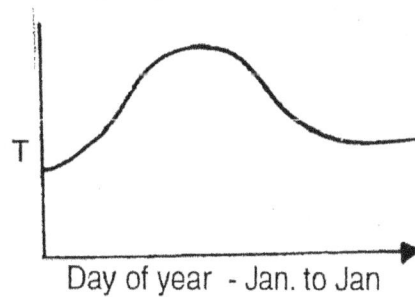
Day of year - Jan. to Jan

58.

City	TEMPERATURE Noon	6 PM
A	72°	54°
B	80°	70°
C	62°	50°
D	90°	66°

A. In which city did the temperature drop the most rapidly between noon and 6 P.M.?
B. Assuming an equivalent decrease in temperature per hour, what was the rate of temperature decrease in city A between noon and 6 P.M.?

59. Lee has been studying designs for picnic tables as shown below. Which design gives Lee the greatest surface area per dollar?

Design	Surface Area of Table	Cost of Materials
#1	20 square feet	$48.00
#2	18 square feet	$44.00
#3	24 square feet	$60.00

60. Ms. Haddad's 30 students took a standardized examination. The data below indicate the quartile in which each of her students' scores lie.

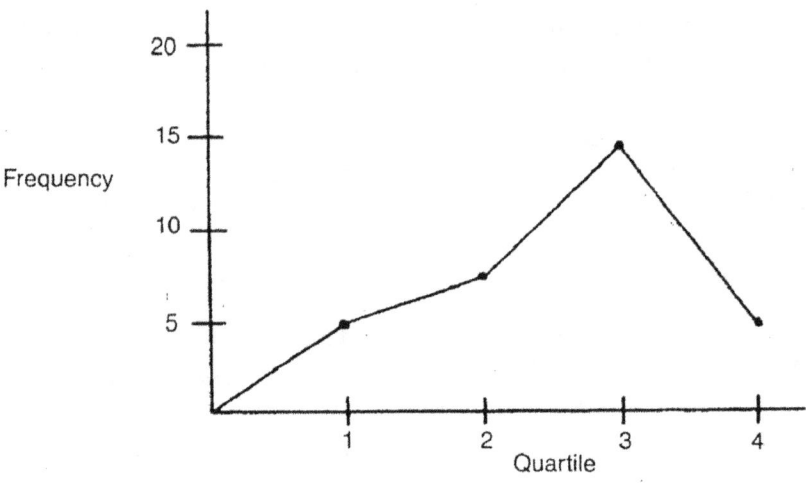

A. Approximately how many students have scores in the 4th quartile?
B. What quartile contains more of Ms. Haddad's students' scores than any other?

61. Use the table below to respond to the statements that follow.

SMOKERS BY FAMILY INCOME AND SEX

Family Income	Male	Female
Under $5,000	40%	32%
$5,000 - $14,999	36%	32%
$15,000 - $24,999	36%	30%
$25,000 or more	32%	26%

		Yes	No	Cannot Tell From Table Data
A.	60% of males with family incomes of under $5,000 are non-smokers	___		___
B.	58% of the people with family incomes of $25,000 or more are smokers	___	___	___
C.	Among those with family incomes of $25,000 or more, more males than females smoke.	___	___	___
D.	36% of those with family incomes of under $5,000 smoke.	___	___	___
E.	Among 600 females with family incomes in the $15,000-$24,999 range, there are about 180 smokers.	___	___	___

9. BASIC PROBABILITY CONCEPTS

When a student says, *The probability that I will pass the examination tomorrow is 2/3,* what does that student mean? She means that, were she to find herself in that situation many times, on about 2/3 of those occasions she would pass the exam. On about 1/3 of the occasions she would not pass.

Imagine a person playing a game which involves rolling a die. When he says, *The probability that I will roll a three is 1/6,* what does he mean? In this case, he means that of the six possible out-comes when rolling a die (1, 2, 3, 4, 5, 6), one possible outcome out of six is three. It is also true that, were he to roll that die a large number of times, about 1/6 of the times he would roll a three. (Thus, in 600 rolls, he would expect to get approximately 100 three's.)

Problem: The names of 5 students - Deborah, Andrew, Thomas, Jose, and Maria - are placed in a hat. One name is withdrawn at random. What is the probability that
    A. Deborah's name is chosen?
    B. The name chosen is either Deborah's or Andrew's?
    C. A boy's name is chosen?

Solution:
    A. Deborah's name is 1 of 5. Thus, the answer to A is 1/5.
    B. 2/5
    C. 3/5

Problem: Consider the data below on 100 different students.
If we choose one student at random from the 100 students shown on the chart, what is the probability of choosing
    A. a boy?
    B. a girl?
    C. a student with glasses?
    D. a girl with glasses?

	Glasses	No Glasses
Boys	15	45
Girls	10	30

Solution:
A. Of the 100 students, 15 + 45 = 60 are boys. Thus, the probability of choosing a boy is 60/100 = 6/10 = 3/5.
B. There are 10 + 30 = 40 girls. Thus, 40/100 = 2/5 is the probability of choosing a girl. You could also reason this way: The probability of choosing a boy is 3/5. The probability of not choosing a boy is, therefore, 1 - 3/5 = 2/5.
C. 15 + 10 = 25 out of 100 students. Thus, the answer is 25/100 = 1/4.
D. 10/100 or 1/10.

EXERCISES

62. A hat contains six tickets numbered 1, 1, 2, 2, 3, 3, respectively. One ticket is withdrawn at random. What is the probability that the ticket drawn
    A. is a 1?
    B. has an even number on it?
    C. is either a 2 or 3?
    D. has a 5 on it?
    E. has a number less than 3 on it?

63. Kim keeps records of his hens' daily egg production for 3 weeks and identifies the results listed in the table below. Based on these data, answer the questions that follow.

Eggs Laid Per Day	Number of Days
1	//
2	////
3	++++ //
4	/
5	///
6	//
7	//

    A. What is the probability of getting 5 or more eggs on a given day?
    B. What is the probability of not getting exactly 4 eggs on a given day?

64. Here are some data on student test performance at a particular school. Based on the data, answer the questions that follow.

	Above Mean	Below Mean
Boys	246	54
Girls	280	20

    A. What is the probability that a randomly chosen student scored above the mean?
    B. What is the probability that a randomly chosen female student scored below the mean?

65. The science students at our school have kept records indicating that the probability of rain at noon on a given day is 1/3 during the month of October.
    A. We have 21 school days this October. How many of rainy-days-at-noon do we anticipate?
    B. What is the probability of no rain at noon during October?
    C. Suppose that the probability of the sun shining at noon is 1/6 during October. What is the probability of neither rain nor sun at noon during October?

66. Here is a summary of student performance on a statewide test. Based on the data, answer the questions that follow.

Class	Number Passed	Number Failed
Ms. Adams	20	5
Ms. Blake	18	6
Ms. Gomez	22	2

    A. What is the probability that a randomly chosen student has passed the exam?
    B. What is the probability that a student who has failed belongs to Ms. Adams' class?

67. Based on statewide test data, here are probabilities of scoring in certain categories:

Score	Probability
0-50	0.16
51-60	0.24
61-70	0.30
71-80	0.20

    A. If 5,000 students took the test, how many would you predict had scores below 51?
    B. Eighty students at School A took the test. Fifteen students scored 50 or below. Is this better or worse than the state as a whole?
    C. Overall, what was the probability of scoring above 80 on the statewide test?

10. NEEDED AND EXTRANEOUS INFORMATION IN PROBLEM SOLVING

Problems with missing or with extra information are very common in real-life situations, but relatively rare in textbooks. These problems may not be necessarily difficult, but they often trap unwary readers whose schooling has led them to expect that all school problems and test problems contain precisely the information needed for a solution. But that is not always so. It is important to read problems carefully and use your common sense; imagine you are not faced with a *mathematics* problem on a test, but have encountered the problem in your daily life. Ask yourself, what information would you need to solve it?

EXERCISES

68. Pedro wants to tile a rectangular floor measuring 7.2 m by 5.4 m. Tiles cost 35¢ each at a store. What additional information will Pedro need before he can tell how much he needs to spend on tiles at a store?

69. Consider this situation: A manager bought 100 identical video cameras for $2,568. He sold them for $5,042. This situation includes three numerical pieces of information, not all of which may be needed to answer the questions below. What are the answers? What information is extraneous in each case?

	Answer	Extraneous Data
A. What was the total profit?	_____	_____
B. What was the selling price of each camera?	_____	_____
C. What did the manager pay for the cameras?	_____	_____
D. What was the manager's profit per camera?	_____	_____

70. Identify the additional information, if any, needed for each of the following problems.
    A. When mixing concrete for a patio, a contractor uses sand and gravel in a ratio of 3 to 4. How many cubic yards of gravel did the contractor use?
    B. The distance from Ampex to Bodwick is 38 miles. The distance from Bodwick to Cranmore is 20 miles. How far is it from Ampex to Cranmore?
    C. Ten percent of Ms. Mora's fourth graders failed the state's mastery test in reading. Four percent of Mr. Gomez's class failed. What was the total number of failing students in the two classes?
    D. All the rooms in Lauren's house are the same size. To paint two of those rooms she needs three gallons of paint. How many gallons does she need to paint all her rooms?
    E. A team wins 105 games. This is 70% of the games they played. How many games did they lose?

71. Identify any extraneous data.
    A. Of 180 class days last year, Lisa missed 9. If the probability of her missing school that year was 1/20, what was the probability of her being in school on a given day?
    B. The 30 students in Ms. Gate's class paid an average of $12.50 each during the year for special class materials, fees, etc. How much more, on the average, would each student need to pay for the class average to be $14 per student?
    C. A car averaged 20 miles per hour traveling from point A to point B. On the return trip, it averaged 40 miles per hour and took 2 1/2 hours. How far did the car travel for the entire trip?
    D. Tickets to the student production of OUR TOWN sell for $3 each. Yesterday, 30 students and 7 teachers bought tickets. Today $123 worth of tickets were sold, including another 30 student tickets. How many nonstudents bought tickets these two days?

KEY (CORRECT ANSWERS)

1.
   A. $x = 9$
   B. $x = \dfrac{12}{5}$
   C. $x = 7$
   D. $\dfrac{2}{3}x = 11$, so $x = \dfrac{3}{2} \cdot \dfrac{11}{1} = \dfrac{33}{2}$
   E. $\dfrac{3}{5}x = 8$, so $x = \dfrac{5}{3} \cdot \dfrac{8}{1} = \dfrac{40}{3}$

2.
   A. $x = 2$
   B. $x = 2$
   C. $x = x = -\dfrac{1}{8}$
   D. $x = 4$
   E. $x = \dfrac{320}{4000} = \dfrac{2}{25}$

3.
   A. $x = -\dfrac{7}{10}$
   B. $t = 2$
   C. $x = 0$
   D. $x = -\dfrac{13}{5}$

4.
   A. $x = 20$
   B. $a = -\dfrac{52}{25}$ or -2.08
   C. $t = -\dfrac{3478}{1480} = -\dfrac{47}{20}$
   D. $\dfrac{1}{a} = 2$, so $a = \dfrac{1}{2}$

5.
   A. 9
   B. 10
   C. 20

6.
   A. 0
   B. 8
   C. 1/3
   D. -9
   E. 2

7. A. $\dfrac{28}{3}$
    B. 68
    C. $-\dfrac{72}{5}$

8. $320 = \$2000 \times r \times 2$, so $r = \dfrac{320}{4000} = \dfrac{32}{400} = \dfrac{8}{100} = 8\%$

9. $a = -\dfrac{301}{100} = -3.01$

10. A. $Y = 12 - 3X$
    B. $y = \dfrac{8}{x}$
    C. $y = \dfrac{A}{br}$
    D. $y = \dfrac{12-4x}{3} = 4 - \dfrac{4}{3}x$
    E. $y = \dfrac{17-4x}{-13} = \dfrac{4x-17}{13}$
    F. $y = \dfrac{3x}{6} = \dfrac{1}{2}x$

11. $P = \dfrac{I}{rt}$

12. $\dfrac{s-a}{n\,1} = d$

13. $L = a + act;\ L - a = act;\ \dfrac{L-a}{at} = C$

14. $x = \dfrac{10}{yz};\ y = \dfrac{10}{xz}$

15. $x = \dfrac{14+2y}{7};\ y = \dfrac{14-7x}{-2}$ or $y = \dfrac{7x-14}{2}$

16. A. 18   D. 3   G. 12
    B. 20   E. 15   H. 4
    C. 4 1/2   F. 5   I. 15

17. A. $k = \frac{6}{2} = 3$, so y = 3x and y = 30

    B. $k = \frac{6}{3} = 2$, so y = 2x and y = 36

    C. $k = 12 \div \frac{1}{3} = 12 \times \frac{3}{1} = 36$, so y = 36x and y = 180

    D. $k = \frac{28}{4} = -7$, so y = -7x and y = -49

    E. $k = \frac{12}{4} = 3$ so y = 3x and 12.36 = 3x. Therefore, x - 4.12

    F. $k = \frac{459}{17} = 27$, so y = 27x and 27 = 27x. Therefore, x = 1

    G. $k = \frac{100}{10} = -10$, so y = -10x and -10 = -10x. Therefore, x = 1

    H. $k = \frac{14}{7} = 0.2$, so y = .2x and 10 = .2x. Thus, 100 = 2x and x = 50

18. $k = \frac{\text{known y-value}}{\text{known x-value}} = \frac{24}{108} = \frac{2}{9}$, so $y = \frac{2}{9}x$. If x = 45, then $y = \frac{2}{9} \cdot \frac{45}{1} = \frac{90}{9} = 10$.
    She needs to work 10 hours this week. If you reversed the x's and y's, you should have obtained $k = \frac{108}{24} = \frac{9}{2}$, so, $y = \frac{9}{2}x$. When y = 45, we have $45 = \frac{9}{2}x$ and, multiplying both sides by $\frac{2}{9}$, we get $\frac{2}{9} \cdot \frac{45}{1} = x$, so x = 10.

19. If y = 110 when x = 1.1, then what is y when x = .56?
    $K = \frac{110}{1.1} = \frac{1100}{11} = 100$ and y = 100x. So, when x = .56, then y = 100 × .56 = 56.

20. A. 3
    B. 2
    C. 24
    D. 20
    E. 50
    F. 12
    G. 144
    H. The value of y has been multiplied by 2/3. The value of x will therefore be multiplied by 3/2 (or 1 1/2). Since x = 12 and 1 1/2 twelves are 18, the answer is x = 18.
    I. 3

21. A. $k = 12 \times 2 = 24$, so $y = y = \dfrac{24}{x}$. Thus when $x = 1$, $y = 24$.

    B. $k = 6 \times 2 = 12$, so $y = \dfrac{12}{x}$. Thus when $x = 3$, $y = 4$.

    C. $k = 2(-3) = -6$, so $y = -\dfrac{6}{x}$. Thus when $x = \dfrac{1}{2}$, $y = -6 \div \dfrac{1}{2} = -\dfrac{6}{1} \times \dfrac{2}{1} = -12$

    D. $k = 6 \cdot 4 = 24$, so $y = y = \dfrac{24}{x}$. Thus when $x = 3$, $y = 8$.

    E. $k = 3 \cdot 2 = 6$, so $y = y = \dfrac{6}{x}$ Thus if $y = 1$, we have $1 = \dfrac{6}{x}$ and $x = 6$.

    F. $k = 10 \cdot 9 = 90$, so $y = \dfrac{90}{x}$. Thus if $y = 45$, we have $45 = \dfrac{90}{x}$ and $x = 2$.

22. If y is 21 when x = 350, then what is y when x = 70?
$k = 21 \cdot 350$, so $y = \dfrac{21 \cdot 350}{x}$. If $x = 70$, then $y = \dfrac{21 \cdot 350}{70}$ $21 \cdot 5 = 105$ pounds per square inch.

23. If y = 1 1/2 when x = 12, then when y = 2, what is x?
Here, $1\,1/2 \cdot 8 = 12$, so $2 \cdot 8 = 16$. Therefore, $x = 16$ when $y = 2$.

24. Let y represent the scaled score and x represent the raw score. Then,
$k = \dfrac{500}{40} = \dfrac{25}{2}$, so $y = \dfrac{25}{2}x$. Thus, if $y = 375$, we have $375 = \dfrac{25}{2}x$. Therefore, $x = \dfrac{2}{25} \cdot 375 = 30$.

25. Let y represent the speed and x the number of minutes. Notice that 90 plus one-third of 90 is 120. So, since y has increased by $1\dfrac{1}{3}$ (or $\dfrac{4}{3}$), x will decrease by $\dfrac{3}{4} \cdot \dfrac{3}{4} \cdot 2 = \dfrac{6}{4} = \dfrac{3}{2}$ so the answer is 3/2 minutes, or 1 1/2 minutes.

26. Going from 60 to 15 represents a decrease by a factor of 1/4. Thus, the years of experience will increase by a factor of 4, and the answer is 12.

27. A. three to ten or $\dfrac{3}{10}$ or 3:10

    B. $\dfrac{20}{15} = \dfrac{4}{3}$ or 4:3 or four to three

    C. $\dfrac{200}{300} = \dfrac{2}{3}$ or 2:3 or two to three

    D. $\dfrac{24}{40} = \dfrac{3}{5}$ or 3:5 or three to five

28. 16 trout out of 30 fish. How many trout out of 2000 fish?
    $\dfrac{16}{30} = \dfrac{x}{2000}$, so $16 \times 2000 = 30x$ and $x = \dfrac{32000}{30}$ trout. Since $\dfrac{32000}{30} = 1066.7$, the ranger would estimate that roughly 1067 trout are in the lake.

29. $\dfrac{\text{Mars}}{\text{Earth}} = \dfrac{2}{5} = \dfrac{x}{120}$ so $240 = 5x$, and $x = 48$ pounds.

30. $\dfrac{1}{6} = \dfrac{4\tfrac{1}{2}}{x}$, so $x = 6 \times 4\tfrac{1}{2} = 27$ miles.

31. $\dfrac{1\tfrac{1}{2}}{700} = \dfrac{x}{3000}$, so $1\tfrac{1}{2} \times 3000 = 700x$ or $4500 = 700x$ and $x = \dfrac{45}{7} = 6\tfrac{3}{7}$ quarts.

32. $\dfrac{6}{4} = \dfrac{x}{25}$ and $6 \cdot 25 = 4x$. Therefore, $x = \dfrac{150}{4} = 37\tfrac{1}{2}$ feet

33. $\dfrac{2}{5} = \dfrac{36}{x}$, so $2x = 180$ and $x = 90$ females.

34. $\dfrac{12 \text{ feet}}{4 \text{ inches}} = \dfrac{x \text{ feet}}{6 \text{ inches}}$, so $12 \cdot 6 = 4x$, and $x = 18$ feet.

35. $\dfrac{20}{32} = \dfrac{6}{x}$, so $20x = 192$ and $x = \dfrac{192}{20} = 9.6$.

36. A. 5   D. 10.5   G. 86
    B. 0.5   E. 10   H. 75
    C. 10   F. 80

37. A. 13.6   C. 1.68
    B. 13.92   D. $1.17

38. A. Mental solution: 16 is 1/4 of what? Answer: 4 x 16 or 64 Algebraic solution:
$\frac{16}{x} = \frac{25}{100}$; 1600 = 25x, therefore $x = \frac{1600}{25} = 64$

   B. $\frac{13}{x} = \frac{86}{100}$; 1300 = 86x, so $x = \frac{1300}{86}$ or approximately 15.1

   C. $\frac{10}{18} = \frac{x}{100}$, so $x = \frac{1000}{18} = 55.55....$ Thus, x is approximately 55.6%

   D. $\frac{17}{51} = \frac{x}{100}$, so $x = \frac{1700}{51}$ 33.33.... Thus, x is approximately 33.3% (or exactly 33 1/3%).

39. A. 16% of $32 = 0.16 x 32 = $5.12. The shirt now costs $32 + $5.12 or $37.12
    B. 15% of $6200 = 0.15 x 6200 = $930. The new price would be $6200 - $930 = $5270
    C. The mark-up is $1. The percent mark-up is $1 out of a price of $4 or 1/4 = 0.25 = 25%
    D. The discount is $4 out of a price of $60 or 4/60 = 0.0666... or approximately 6.7%

40. A. The total weight is 3 x 14 + 7 x 8 = 98 oz. Of the total, the grapefruits provide 42/98 = 0.4285...or approximately 43%
    B. If the grapefruits provide 43% of the total weight, then the oranges must provide the rest: 57% because 43% + 57% = 100%

41. C

42. D

43. We use the formula d = rt, except that we are interested in the rate of travel r. Thus, r = d/t. In terms of this problem, r is denoted by V and we have V = F-S/t

44. p + 0.2p or 1.2p

45. C

46. e. Let x be 1/2, 1, 2. The corresponding y values are -1 1/2, 0, 1 1/2. The expression x - 1/x is always increasing but it is negative when x is less than 1 and positive when x is larger than 1.

47. T/0.5 or 2T

48. If you let P = 1 and Q = 1, then R = 4 for equations a, c, d

49. b, d (Try substituting some positive, decreasing values for x; for example, x = 10, 2, 1. What happens to y?)

50. Total Cost

$$100 \times P$$
$$+ (T - 100) \cdot .8P$$
$$\overline{100P + (T - 100) \cdot .8P}$$

$p each for 100 books 80% of P (.8P) for each book over 100 (T-100)

$$100P + (T-100).8P = 100P + T \times .8P - 100 \times .8P$$
$$= 100P + .8TP - 80P$$
$$= 20P + .8TP$$

Therefore, c is the correct response.

51. $.15 \times 20,000 + .28 \times (D-20,000)$
   $= 3000 + .28D - .28 \times 20,000$
   $= 3000 + .28D - 5600$
   $= .28D - 2600$

52. A. approximately 975 students
    B. 200 to 250 or 4:5
    C. 1 1/2

53. 23%

54. 35,000 gallons

55. A. 10 days
    B. Fran

56. Choice A is correct: If t doubles, d doubles, etc.

57. Choice D

58. A. City D
    B. 18 degrees/6 hours = 3 degrees per hour
       (The rate of decrease for city D was 4 degrees per hour.)

59. #1 gives 20/48 square feet per dollar (20/48 = 5/12)
    #2 gives 18/44 square feet per dollar (18/44 = 9/22)
    #3 gives 24/60 square feet per dollar (24/60 = 2/5)
    Comparing the order of these fractions, 2/5 is less than 9/22, which is less than 5/12.
    Thus, 5/12 square feet per dollar is the best Lee can do. Choice #1 is best.

60. A. 5
    B. The third quartile

61. A. Yes
    B. No. The correct figure will lie somewhere between 26% and 32%, depending on the ratio of men to women. Suppose, for example, that there are 200 males and 100 females in the $25,000 plus category. Of the males, 32% or 64 smoke. Of the females, 26% or 26 smoke. Altogether 90 out of 300 smoke, that is, 90/300 = 30/100 = 30%. Thus, 26% of the females are smokers, 32% of the males are smokers,

and 30% of the entire group smokes. (Note that 30% is closer to the male percentage of 32% than it is to the female percentage of 26%. This is because there are more males than females in the entire population.)

C. You cannot tell. A higher percentage of males are smokers, but the absolute number of males who smoke could be smaller. Perhaps there are 300 people in this category; for example, 100 males and 200 females. 32% of 100 means 32 males smoke. 26% of 200 means 52 females smoke.

D. You cannot tell. The correct figure will lie somewhere between 32% and 40%, but will not be 36% unless the number of males equals the number of females in the under $5,000 category. (See the answer to B above)

E. Yes.

62.
- A. 2/6 or 1/3
- B. 2/6 or 1/3
- C. 4/6 or 2/3
- D. 0/6 or 0
- E. 4/6 or 2/3

63.
- A. On 7 of the 21 days, egg production was 5 or more dozen. Thus, the probability is 7/21 or 1/3.
- B. The probability of getting exactly 4 dozen eggs is 1/21. The probability of not getting 4 dozen is 20/21.

64.
- A. There are 600 students in all (246 + 54 + 280 + 20 = 600). Of these, 246 + 280 = 526 scored above the mean. The probability would be 526/600 (or 263/300).
- B. 20/300 or 1/15

65.
- A. 7
- B. 2/3
- C. The probability of either rain or sun is 1/3 + 1/6 = 1/2. The other half of the time you get neither rain nor sun. The probability of neither rain nor sun is 1/2.

66.
- A. 60 out of 73 students passed: 60/73
- B. 5/13

67.
- A. 0.16 × 5000 = 800
- B. 15/80 = .1875, which is larger than the statewide figure of .16. Since a score below 51 is presumably not good, your students did worse than the state as a whole.
- C. The probability of scoring in the 0-80 range is .16 + .24 + .30 + .20 = .90. The missing .10, therefore, must have scores above 80.

68. He needs to know the size of a tile so that he can decide how many tiles he needs.

69.
- A. $2474; 100 cameras
- B. $50.42; $2568
- C. $2568; 100 and $5042
- D. $24.74; no extraneous data

70. A. How many cubic yards of sand did the contractor use or how many cubic yards of both sand and gravel did the contractor use?
    B. We need to know where Ampex and Cranmore are in relation to Bodwick. Do the three towns lie on a line with Bodwick in the middle (Figure 1) or with Cranmore in the middle (Figure 2)?

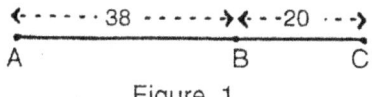
Figure 1

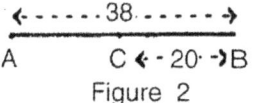
Figure 2

    Do the three towns form the vertices of a right triangle, etc.?
    C. What is the number of students in each class?
    D. How many rooms are in that house?
    E. No information is needed. $105 = .70x$ so $1050 = 7x$ and $x = 150$. The team played 150 games and won 105. They lost 45 games.

71. A. The information in the first sentence is extraneous. Alternately, if you use the information in the first sentence, then 1/20 is extraneous.
    B. The 30 is not needed.
    C. The first sentence is irrelevant.
    D. We don't need to know that yesterday 30 students bought tickets; only the non-student data are relevant.

BASIC FUNDAMENTALS OF MATHEMATICS

PRINCIPLES AND APPLICATIONS

CONCISE TEXT

WITH PROBLEMS AND ANSWERS

* ARITHMETIC
* ALGEBRA
* LOGARITHMS
* GEOMETRY
* TRIGONMETRY

BASIC FUNDAMENTALS OF MATHEMATICS

CHAPTER 1
INTRODUCTION

1. **PURPOSE AND SCOPE**

    a. Purpose. This section provides the basic mathematics required by students and candidates in all fields, including beginning and advanced students.

    b. Scope. This section covers those principles and applications of arithmetic, algebra, logarithms, geometry, and trigonometry that are required for practical understanding.

2. **MATHEMATICS AND TESTING**

    Skill in the use of mathematics, particularly arithmetic, algebra, and trigonometry, is essential in all fields of testing, including mental and general ability, school, college entrance, aptitude, achievement, civil service, professional, and advanced or graduate examinations.

BASIC FUNDAMENTALS OF MATHEMATICS

		Paragraphs	Page
Chapter 1.	INTRODUCTION	1, 2	2
2.	PERCENTAGE	3–12	3
3.	RATIO AND PROPORTION		5
Section I.	Ratio	13–15	
II.	Proportion	16–21	7
Chapter 4.	POWERS AND ROOTS	22–25	9
5.	ALGEBRA		
Section I.	Introduction	26–31	
II.	Positive and negative numbers	32–42	
III.	Fundamental operations	43–50	
IV.	Factoring	51–61	
V.	Algebraic fractions	62–69	
VI.	Exponents and radicals	70–76	
VII.	Imaginary and complex numbers	77–79	
VIII.	Equations	80–86	
IX.	Quadratic equations	87–94	
Chapter 6.	GRAPHS		
Section I.	Basic characteristics of graphs	95–99	29
II.	Graphing equations	100–103	32
Chapter 7.	POWERS OF TEN	104–111	34
8.	LOGARITHMS	112–127	38
9.	PLANE GEOMETRY	128–142	43
10.	TRIGONOMETRY		
Section I.	Basic trigonometric theory	143–153	
II.	Natural trigonometric functions	154–164	
III.	Trigonometric laws	165–173	59
Chapter 11.	RADIANS	174–176	61
12.	VECTORS	177–181	62

ANSWERS TO PROBLEMS

CHAPTER 2
PERCENTAGE

3. General

a. Definition. Percentage is the process of computation in which the basis of comparison is a *hundred*. The term *percent*—from *per*, *by*, and *centum*, hundred—means *by* or *on the hundred*. Thus, 2 percent of a quantity means two parts of every hundred parts of the quantity.

b. Symbol. The symbol of percentage is %. Percent may also be indicated by a fraction or a decimal. Thus, $5\% = \frac{5}{100} = .05$. Figure 1 shows the relationship between fractions, decimals, and percentage.

c. Base, Rate, and Percentage.

(1) The *base* is the number on which the percentage is computed.

(2) The *rate* is the amount (in hundredths) of the base to be estimated.

(3) The *percentage* is a part or portion of a whole expressed as so many per hundred. Percentage is the portion of the base determined by the rate.

4. Conversion of Decimal to Percent

To change a decimal to percent, move the decimal point two places to the right and add the percent symbol.

Example: Change .375 to percent.
Move decimal point two places to right: 37.5
Add percent symbol: 37.5%

5. Conversion of Fraction to Percent

To convert a fraction to percent, divide the numerator by the denominator and convert to a decimal. Then, convert the decimal to percent (par. 4).

Example: Change fraction $\frac{5}{8}$ to percent.
Divide numerator by denominator: $5 \div 8 = .625$
Convert decimal to percent: $6.25 = 62.5\%$
Thus, $\frac{5}{8} = 62.5\%$.

6. Conversion of Percent to Decimal

To change a percent to a decimal, omit the percent symbol and move the decimal point two places to the left.

Example 1: Change 15% to a decimal.
Omit percent symbol: 15 becomes 15
Move decimal point two places to the left: 15 becomes .15
Thus, $15\% = .15$.

Example 2: Change 110% to a decimal.
Omit percent symbol: 110% becomes 110
Move the decimal point two places to the left: 110 becomes 1.10.
Thus, $110\% = 1.10$.

7. Conversion of Percent to Fraction

To change a percent to a fraction, first change the percent to a decimal (par. 6) and then to a fraction. Reduce the fraction to its lowest terms.

Example 1: Change 25% to a fraction.
Change to a decimal: $25\% = .25$
Change to a fraction: $.25 = \frac{25}{100}$
Reduce fraction to lowest terms: $\frac{25}{100} = \frac{1}{4}$
Thus, $25\% = \frac{1}{4}$.

Example 2: Change 37.5% to a fraction.
Change to a decimal: $37.5\% = .375$
Change to a fraction: $.375 = \frac{375}{1000}$
Reduce fraction to lowest terms: $\frac{375}{1000} = \frac{3}{8}$
Thus, $37.5\% = \frac{3}{8}$.

8. Finding Percentage

a. General. To find the percent of a number, write the percent as a decimal and multiply the number by this decimal. In this case, the *base* and *rate* are given. The problem is to find the *percentage*.

Example 1: Find 5% of 140 (140 is the base, 5% is the rate, and the product is the percentage).
5% of $140 = .05 \times 140 = 7$

Example 2: Find 5.2% of 140.
5.2% of $140 = .052 \times 140 = 7.28$

Example 3: Find 150% of 36.
150% of $36 = 1.50 \times 36 = 54$

Example 4: Find $\frac{1}{2}\%$ of 840.
$\frac{1}{2}\% = .5\%$
$.5\%$ of $840 = .005 \times 840 = 4.20$
Thus, $\frac{1}{2}\%$ of $840 = 4.20$.

b. Application of Percentage. In communications-electronics, typical applications of percentage computation are used in determining tolerance values of resistors or in determining the efficiencies of motors and generators.

9. Finding Rate

To find the percent one number is of another, write the problem as a fraction, change the fraction to a decimal, and write the decimal as a percent. In this case, the *percentage* and *base* are given. The problem is to find the *rate*.

Example 1: 3 is what percent of 8? (3 is the percentage, 8 is the base, and the quotient is the rate.)
$\frac{3}{8} = .375$

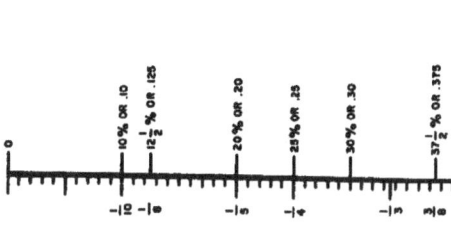

Figure 1. Relationship between fractions, decimals, and percentage.

$.375 = 37.5\% = 37\frac{1}{2}\%$

Therefore, 3 is $37\frac{1}{2}\%$ of 8.

Example 2: What percent of 542 is 234?

$\frac{234}{542} = .4317 +$ (round off)

$.432 = 43.2\%$

Therefore, 234 is 43.2% of 542.

Example 3: 125 is what percent of 50?

$\frac{125}{50} = 2.50$

$2.50 = 250\%$

Therefore, 125 is 250% of 50.

10. Finding Base Numbers

To find a number when a percent of the number is known, first find 1% of the number, and then find 100% of the number. In this case, the *percentage* of the number and the *rate* are given. The problem is to find the *base*.

Example 1: 42 is 12% of what number?

12% (base number) = 42

1% (base number) = $\frac{42}{12} = 3.50$

100% (base number) = $100 \times 3.50 = 350$

Therefore, the base number is 350.

Example 2: 45 is 150% of what number?

150% (base number) = 45

1% (base number) = $\frac{45}{150} = .3$

100% (base number) = $100 \times .3 = 30$

Therefore, the base number is 30.

11. Expressing Accuracy of Measurements in Percent

a. Relative error is the accuracy of a measurement expressed in percent of the total measurement. In determining the relative error, it is first necessary to establish the *limit of error*.

b. The *limit of error* is the difference between the *true value* and the *measured value*. Assume that the reading on a scale, to the nearest tenth of an inch, is 2.2 inches. If the true value is 2.15 inches, the limit of error is the difference between 2.15 and 2.20, or .05 inch.

c. Relative error is computed by solving the ratio $\frac{\text{LIMIT OF ERROR}}{\text{MEASURED VALUE}}$, and expressing the result as a percent. In the scale reading above, the relative error $= \frac{.05}{2.2} = 2.27\%$, or 2.3%.

12. Review Problems—Percentage

a. Show each of the following in three forms—as a fraction or mixed number, as a decimal, and as a percent:

(1) $\frac{3}{5}$
(2) 50%
(3) .375
(4) $\frac{1}{4}$
(5) $62\frac{1}{2}\%$
(6) .6
(7) $\frac{3}{10}$
(8) 70%
(9) 2.25
(10) $1\frac{7}{8}$
(11) .08
(12) $\frac{3}{50}$
(13) .18
(14) $1\frac{1}{4}\%$
(15) .025
(16) .05
(17) $8\frac{1}{3}\%$
(18) $37\frac{1}{2}\%$
(19) 105%
(20) 4%

b. Evaluate the following:

(1) 250% of 60
(2) 125% of 40
(3) 200% of 2
(4) 225% of 400

c. What percent of a number is—

(1) 1.5 times the number?
(2) $2\frac{3}{4}$ times the number?
(3) $\frac{3}{2}$ times the number?
(4) $5\frac{1}{2}$ times the number?

d. Find the following:

(1) $\frac{2}{5}\%$ of 410
(2) $\frac{3}{5}\%$ of 416,000
(3) $\frac{2}{5}\%$ of 85
(4) 5.2% of 85

e. Solve the following problems:

(1) Find the relative error for a limit of error of .05 inch in measuring 24.2 inches.
(2) Find the relative error for a limit of error of 2 inches in measuring 200 yards.

f. Find the number when—

(1) 12% of the number is 52
(2) 15% of the number is 375
(3) 32% of the number is 166.4
(4) 8% of the number is 16
(5) 84% of the number is 168

CHAPTER 3
RATIO AND PROPORTION

Section I. RATIO

13. Understanding Ratio

It is often desirable, for the purpose of comparison, to express one quantity in terms of another quantity of the same kind. One way to express this relationship is by means of a *ratio*. For example, if one resistor has a resistance of 800 ohms and another has a resistance of 100 ohms, the first resistor has 8 times as much resistance as the second. In other words, the ratio between the resistors is 8 to 1.

14. Expressing Ratio

Ratio can be expressed in four different ways. For example, the ratio of 12 to 3 can be expressed as follows: 12 to 3, 12:3, 12 ÷ 3, or $\frac{12}{3}$. The numbers 12 and 3, which are the terms of the ratio, are called the *antecedent* and the *consequent*, respectively. The antecedent is the dividend or the numerator; the consequent is the divisor or denominator.

15. Obtaining Value of Ratio

Both terms of any ratio may be multiplied and divided by the same number without changing the value of the expression. In the ratio $\frac{12}{3}$, for example, the 12 is divided by 3, giving the value of 4. This means that the ratio 12:3 is equal to the ratio 4:1.

Example 1: What is the ratio of 6:2?
$$\frac{6}{2} = 3, \text{ or } 3:1$$

Example 2: What is the ratio of 7:3?
$$\frac{7}{3} = 2\frac{1}{3} \text{ or } 2\frac{1}{3}:1$$

Example 3: Find the ratio of the areas (par. 26) of two squares the sides of which are 6 and 8 inches, respectively. The areas of similar figures are in the same ratio as the squares of their like dimensions.
$$8^2:6^2 = 64:36$$
$$\frac{64}{36} = 1\frac{28}{36} = 1\frac{7}{9} \text{ or } 1\frac{7}{9}:1$$

Thus, the second square (8 inches on a side) is $1\frac{7}{9}$ times as large as the first square (6 inches on a side).

Section II. PROPORTIONS

16. Understanding Proportion

A proportion is a statement of equality between two ratios. If the value of one ratio is equal to the value of another ratio, they are said to be in proportion. For example, the ratio 3:6 is equal to the ratio 4:8. Therefore, this can be written 3:6 :: 4:8 or 3:6 = 4:8. In any proportion, the first and last terms are called the *extremes*; the second and third terms are called the *means* (fig. 2).

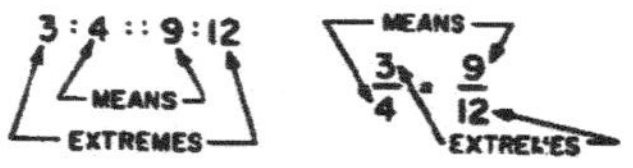

Figure 2. Terms of proportion.

17. Rules of Proportion

There are three rules of proportion used in determining an unknown quantity.

They also can be used to prove that the proportion is true.

a. In any proportion, *the product of the means equals the product of the extremes.*

Example 1: 3:4 :: 9:12.
$3 \times 12 = 36$ (product of extremes)
$4 \times 9 = 36$ (product of means)

Example 2: $\frac{3}{4} = \frac{9}{12}$.

Note. When the proportion is expressed in fractional form, the numerator of one fraction is multiplied by the denominator of the other fraction. This process is called *cross-multiplication*.

$3 \times 12 = 36$ (product of extremes)
$4 \times 9 = 36$ (product of means)

b. In any proportion, *the product of the means divided by either extreme gives the other extreme.*

Example: 6:8 :: 18:24.
$8 \times 18 = 144$ (product of means)
$144 \div 6 = 24$ (one extreme)
$144 \div 24 = 6$ (other extreme)

c. In any proportion, *the product of the extremes divided by either mean gives the other mean.*

Example: 5:7 :: 15:21
$5 \times 21 = 105$ (product of extremes)
$105 \div 7 = 15$ (one mean)
$105 \div 15 = 7$ (other mean)

18. Solving for Unknown Term

As demonstrated in paragraph 49, the unknown term of a proportion can be determined if the other three terms are known.

Example 1: In the proportion $\frac{5}{10} = \frac{10}{y}$, solve for y (the unknown quantity). Find the product of the means:
$$10 \times 10 = 100$$
Find the product of the extremes: $5 \times y = 5y$

The products of the means and extremes are equal: $5y = 100$
Divide both sides by 5:
$$\frac{5y}{5} = \frac{100}{5}$$
$$y = 20$$
Therefore, $\frac{5}{10} = \frac{10}{20}$.

Example 2: In the proportion 6:12 :: 24:y, solve for y. Write the proportion in fractional form:
$$\frac{6}{12} = \frac{24}{y}$$
Cross-multiply.
$6y = 288$
Divide both sides by 6.
$$\frac{6y}{6} = \frac{288}{6}$$
$y = 48$
Therefore, 6:12 :: 24:48.

Example 3: In the proportion $\frac{5}{10} = \frac{z}{20}$, solve for z.
Cross-multiply.
$10z = 100$
Divide both sides by 10:
$$\frac{10z}{10} = \frac{100}{10}$$
$z = 10$
Therefore, $\frac{10}{20} = \frac{5}{10}$.

19. Stating Ratios for Problems in Proportion

When setting up a proportion problem, be sure to state the ratios correctly. Analyze each problem carefully to determine whether the unknown quantity will be greater or lesser than the known term of the ratio in which it occurs. Arrange the terms of the ratio as shown below, and solve for the unknown quantity as explained in paragraph 18.

$$\frac{\text{LESSER}}{\text{GREATER}} = \frac{\text{LESSER}}{\text{GREATER}}, \text{ or LESSER : GREATER :: LESSER : GREATER}$$

Example: The weight of 15 feet of iron pipe is 8 pounds. What is the weight of 255 feet of the same pipe? Let the unknown quantity be represented by the letter y. Since ratios must express a relation between quantities of the same kind, one ratio must be between feet and feet and the other between pounds and pounds.

Study the problems; 255 feet of pipe will weigh more than 15 feet of pipe. Arrange the first ratio in the order LESSER to GREATER—15 feet:

255 feet, or $\frac{15}{255}$.

Arrange the second ratio in the same order—LESSER to GREATER—8 pounds: y pounds, or $\frac{8}{y}$.

Write the proportion and solve.

15:255 = 8:y, or
$$\frac{15}{255} = \frac{8}{y}$$
$$15y = 255 \times 8$$
$$15y = 2040$$
$$y = \frac{2040}{15}$$
$$y = 136 \text{ pounds}$$

20. Inverse Proportion

a. The ratio 2:3 is the inverse of the ratio 3:2. In proportion, when a second ratio is equal to the inverse of the first ratio, the elements are said to be *inversely proportional.*

b. Two numbers are inversely proportional when one increases the other decreases. In this case, their product is always the same. In problems dealing with pulleys, the speeds of different size pulleys connected by belts are inversely proportional to their diameters. A smaller pulley rotates faster than a larger pulley.

Example 1: A pulley 30 inches in diameter is turning at a speed of 300 revolutions per minute. If this pulley is belted to a pulley 15 inches in diameter (fig. 3), determine the speed at which the smaller pulley is turning.

Let the speed of the smaller pulley be represented by y. Study the problem; the first ratio will be between inches and the second will be between revolutions per minute (rpm). Also note that the second pulley is smaller than the first and must make more revolutions than the first. Therefore, the answer will be a number larger than 300.

Arrange the ratios in the order LESSER to GREATER.

First ratio:

15:30, or $\frac{15}{30}$

Second ratio:

300:y, or $\frac{300}{y}$

The proportion:

15:30 = 300:y, or $\frac{15}{30} = \frac{300}{y}$

Solve the proportion:
$$\frac{15}{30} = \frac{300}{y}$$
$$15y = 300 \times 30$$
$$15y = 9000$$
$$y = \frac{9000}{15}$$
$$y = 600 \text{ rpm}$$

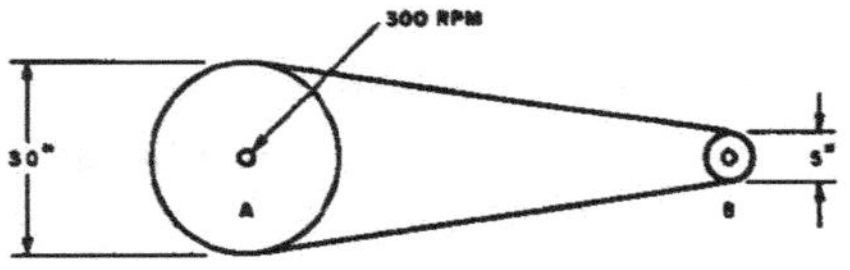

Example 2: A 24-inch pulley is fixed to a drive shaft that is turning at the rate of 400 rpm. This pulley is belted to a 6-inch pulley. Determine the speed of the smaller pulley in revolutions per minute. Driving pulley (400 rpm, 24 inches in diameter). Driven pulley (y rpm, 6 inches in diameter).

$$\frac{6}{24} = \frac{400}{y}$$
$$6y = 400 \times 24 = 9,600$$
$$y = 1,600 \text{ rpm}$$

21. Problems Using Proportion

a. A steel plate ½ inch thick, 12 inches wide, and 9 feet long weighs 183.6 pounds. What is the weight of a piece of steel plate of the same thickness and width if it is 16 feet 6 inches long?

b. If three men complete a certain job in 8 days, how many days would it take seven men to complete the same job, considering that they will work at the same speed?

c. If 3 resistors cost 25 cents, find the cost of 60 resistors at the same rate?

d. If the upkeep on 62 trucks for a year is $3,100, what would be the upkeep on 28 such trucks for 1 year at the same rate?

e. At a given temperature, the resistance of a wire increases with its length. If the resistance of a wire per 1,000 feet at 68°F is .248 ohm, what is the resistance of 1,500 feet; of 1,200 feet; of 1,850 feet; of 3,600 feet?

f. If 21-gage wire weighs 2.452 pounds per 1,000 feet, what is the weight of 1,150 feet; 1,540 feet; 1,680 feet; 349 yards?

g. The speeds of gears running together are inversely proportional to the number of teeth in the gears. A driving gear with 48 teeth meshes with a driven gear with 16 teeth. If the driving gear turns at the rate of 100 rpm, how many rpm are made by the driven gear?

h. A 36-tooth gear running at a speed of 280 rpm drives another gear with 64 teeth. What is the speed of the other gear?

Figure 3. Pulleys and inverse ratio.

CHAPTER 4
POWERS AND ROOTS

22. Powers

There are many times in mathematics when a number must be multiplied by itself a number of times, such as $4 \times 4 \times 4 \times 4$. This is written as 4^5 and is described as 4 raised to the fifth power. A number multiplied by itself once is said to be raised to the second power (squared). Thus, 5×5 is written 5^2. The number 2, written to the right and above the number 5, is the *exponent*; the number 5 is the *base*. The base number is a *factor* of a number written in exponential form because the product is evenly divisible by the base.

23. Roots

The root of a number is that number which, when multiplied by itself a given number of times, will equal the given number. The square root of 25 is 5, since 5×5 or 5^2 equals 25. The third root (cube root) of 216 is 6, since $6 \times 6 \times 6$ or 6^3 equals 216. The fourth root of 81 is 3, since $3 \times 3 \times 3 \times 3$ or 3^4 equals 81. Extraction of a root is generally indicated by placing, in front of the number, a *radical sign* ($\sqrt{}$). A small figure is placed in the angle at the front of the sign to indicate the root to be taken. If the small figure is omitted, it is understood that the operation required is square root.

Thus,

$\sqrt{25} = 5$
$\sqrt[3]{216} = 6$
$\sqrt[4]{81} = 3$

24. Finding Square Root of a Number

a. Finding Square Root by Mental Calculation. In some instances, the square root can be determined mentally from a knowledge of common multiplication. For example, $\sqrt{25}$ is 5, since 5×5 or $5^2 = 25$. Similarly, $\sqrt{144}$ is 12, since 12×12 or $12^2 = 144$.

b. Finding Square Root by Arithmetical Process. In most cases, the square root of a number must be determined by a mathematical process. If the number is a perfect square, the square root will be an integral number; if the number is not a perfect square, the square root will be a continued decimal.

Example 1: Evaluate $\sqrt{3398.89}$.

Step 1. Starting at the decimal point, mark off the digits in pairs in both directions.

$\sqrt{33\ 98.89}$

Step 2. Place the decimal point for the answer directly above the decimal point that appears under the radical sign.

$\sqrt{33\ 98.89}$

Step 3. Determine by inspection the largest number that can be squared without exceeding the first pair of digits—33. The answer is 5, since the square of any number larger than 5 will be greater than 33. Place the 5 above the first pair of digits.

$\begin{array}{r} 5 \\ \sqrt{33\ 98.89} \end{array}$

Step 4. Square 5 to obtain 25, and place it under 33. Subtract 25 from 33 and obtain 8. Bring down the next pair of digits—98.

$\begin{array}{r} 5 \\ \sqrt{33\ 98.89} \\ 25 \\ \hline 898 \end{array}$

Step 5. Double the answer, 5, to obtain a trial divisor of 10. Divide the trial divisor into all but the last digit of the modified remainder. It will go into 89 eight times. Place the 8 above the second pair of digits, and also place the 8 to the right of the trial divisor. Thus, the true divisor is 108. Multiply 108 by 8 and obtain 864. Subtract 864 from 898 to obtain 34. Bring down the next pair of digits—89.

$\begin{array}{r} 5\ 8. \\ \sqrt{33\ 98.89} \\ 25 \\ \hline 898 \\ 864 \\ \hline 3489 \end{array}$

$2 \times 5 = 10\ \boxed{8}$
$\boxed{8} \times 108 =$
864

Note. With each new successive digit in the answer:

1. Place the digit in the answer above the pair of digits involved.
2. Place the same digit to the right of the trial divisor to obtain the true divisor.
3. Multiply the digit by the true divisor. (Do not use the square boxes in actual problems.)

Step 6. Double the answer, 58, to obtain a trial divisor of 116. Divide the trial divisor into all but the last digit of the remainder. It will go into 348 three times. Place the 3 above the third pair of digits, and also place the 3 to the right of the trial divisor. Thus, the true divisor is 1163. Multiply 1163 by 3 to obtain 3489. Subtract 3489 from 3489. There is no remainder. Therefore 3398.89 is a perfect square and its square root is 58.3.

$\begin{array}{r} 5\ 8.\ 3 \\ \sqrt{33\ 98.89} \\ 25 \\ \hline 898 \\ 864 \\ \hline 3489 \\ 3489 \end{array}$

$2 \times 58 = 116\ \boxed{3}$
$\boxed{3} \times 1163 = 3489$

Step 7. Check the answer by squaring $58.3 - 58.3^2 = 3398.89$. The complete calculation is shown below:

$\begin{array}{r} 5\ 8.\ 8 \\ \sqrt{33\ 98.89} \\ 25 \\ \hline 898 \\ 864 \\ \hline 3489 \\ 3489 \end{array}$

$5 \times 5 = 25$
$2 \times 5 = 10\ \boxed{8}$
$\boxed{8} \times 108 = 864$
$2 \times 58 = 116\ \boxed{3}$
$\boxed{3} \times 1163 = 3489$

Example 2: Evaluate $\sqrt{786.808}$.

Step 1. Starting at the decimal point, mark off the digits in pairs in both directions.

$\sqrt{07\ 86.80\ 80}$

Note. The extreme left-hand group may have only one digit. However, there must be an even number of digits to the right of the decimal point. If necessary, add a zero.

Step 2. Place the decimal point for the answer directly above the decimal point that appears under the radical sign.

Step 3. Determine the largest number that can be squared without exceeding the first digit—7. The answer is 2, since the square of any whole number larger than 2 will be greater than 7. Place the 2 above the 7.

$\begin{array}{r} 2 \\ \sqrt{07\ 86.80\ 80} \end{array}$

Step 4. Square 2 to obtain 4 and place it under 7. Subtract 4 from 7 to obtain 3. Bring down the next pair of digits—86.

$\begin{array}{r} 2 \\ \sqrt{07\ 86.80\ 80} \\ 4 \\ \hline 386 \end{array}$

Step 5. Double the answer, 2, to obtain a trial divisor of 4. Divide the trial divisor into all but the last digit of the modified remainder. It will go into 38 nine times. Place the 9 above the second pair of digits, and also place the 9 to the right of the trial divisor. The true divisor is 49. Multiply 49 by 9 to obtain 441. However,

Step 6. 441 cannot be subtracted from 386, so the next lower digit must be tried. Substitute 8 for 9 in both the answer and the divisor and multiply 48 by 8 to obtain 384. Subtract 384 from 386 to obtain a remainder of 2. Bring down the next pair of digits—80.

$$\begin{array}{r} 2\;9. \\ \sqrt{07\;86.80\;80} \\ 4 \\ \overline{386} \\ 441 \end{array}$$

$2 \times 2 = 4\;\boxed{9}$
$\boxed{9} \times 49 =$

$$\begin{array}{r} 2\;8. \\ \sqrt{07\;86.80\;80} \\ 4 \\ \overline{386} \\ 384 \\ \overline{280} \end{array}$$

$4\;\boxed{8}$
$\boxed{8} \times 48 =$

Step 7. Multiply 280 by 2 to obtain a trial divisor of 560. Divide the trial divisor into all but the last digit of the remainder. It will go 5 times. Place the 5 above the fourth pair of digits, and also place the 5 to the right of the trial divisor. Thus, the true divisor is 5605. Multiply 5605 by 5 to obtain 28025. Subtract 28025 from 28080. There is a remainder of 55. Thus, the square root of 786.808 is 28.05, with a remainder of 55. A more exact answer can be obtained by adding pairs of zeros and continuing the square root process.

$$\begin{array}{r} 2\;8.\;0\;5 \\ \sqrt{07\;86.80\;80} \\ 4 \\ \overline{386} \\ 384 \\ \overline{28080} \\ 28025 \\ \overline{55} \end{array}$$

$2 \times 280 = 560\;\boxed{5}$
$\boxed{5} \times 5605 =$

Check the answer by squaring 28.05 and adding the remainder $(28.05^2 + .0055)$. Place the extreme right digit of the remainder under the extreme right digit of the squared number. The complete calculation is shown below:

$$\begin{array}{r} 2\;8.\;0\;5 \\ \sqrt{07\;86.80\;80} \\ 4 \\ \overline{386} \\ 384 \\ \overline{28080} \\ 26025 \\ \overline{55} \end{array}$$

$2 \times 2 = 4\;\boxed{8}$
$\boxed{8} \times 48 =$
$2 \times 280 = 560\;\boxed{5}$
$\boxed{5} \times 5605 =$

25. Review Problems—Square Root

a. Solve the following:

(1) $\sqrt{441}$
(2) $\sqrt{1089}$
(3) $\sqrt{2500}$
(4) $\sqrt{8.40}$
(5) $\sqrt{2510.01}$
(6) $\sqrt{4901.4001}$
(7) $\sqrt{7482.25}$
(8) $\sqrt{5759.2921}$

b. Solve the following to nearest thousandth.

(1) $\sqrt{5}$
(2) $\sqrt{7}$
(3) $\sqrt{11}$
(4) $\sqrt{13}$
(5) $\sqrt{15}$
(6) $\sqrt{17}$

c. The current (in amperes) flowing through a resistor can be determined by taking the square root of the quotient obtained by dividing the value of power supplied to the resistor (in watts) by the value of the resistance (in ohms). Thus, if a resistance of 300 ohms is absorbing 60 watts of power, it is drawing a current of $\sqrt{\dfrac{60}{300}}$ amperes. This equals about .447 ampere. In the same manner, find the value of current for each of the following values of power and resistance:

	Power (watts)	Resistance (ohms)	Current (amperes)
(1)	25	1,000	?
(2)	50	7,000	?
(3)	40	500	?
(4)	75	60	?

CHAPTER 5
ALGEBRA

Section I. INTRODUCTION

26. General

a. Algebra is an extension of arithmetic. All of the four basic operations of arithmetic—addition, subtraction, multiplication and division—apply also to algebra. Arithmetic deals only with particular numbers; algebra may also employ letters or symbols to represent numbers.

b. Algebra is often referred to as the shorthand language of mathematicians. The simplest example of the algebraic language is the formula, in which letters are used to represent words or numbers. For example, the area (A) of a rectangle can be determined by multiplying the length (l) by the width (w). Algebraically, this is stated as $A = lw$.

27. Algebraic Expressions and Terms

a. An *algebraic expression* is the representation of any quantity in algebraic signs and symbols; for example, $2x - 7$. A *numerical algebraic expression* consists entirely of numerals and signs, such as $8 - (6 \times 2)$. A *literal algebraic expression* contains only letters and symbols, such as $ax - ay$.

b. Each algebraic expression contains two or more terms, separated by one of the signs of operation ($+$, $-$, $\div$, $\times$). The expression $3x - 4xy - 2y$, for example, contains three terms: $3x$, $4xy$, and $2y$. If the terms have the same letters and exponents, such as $3a^2x$, $9a^2x$, and $12a^2x$, they are called *similar terms*. Terms that do not contain the same letters and exponents, such as $3ab^2$, $3a^2b$, and $3x^2y$, are *dissimilar terms*.

c. If an algebraic expression contains one term, such as $3abc$ or $5a^2z^2$, it is called a *monomial*; if it contains two terms, such as $x - y$,

it is called a *binomial*; and if it contains three terms, such as $5x^2 - 3xy - 2y^2$, it is called a *trinomial*. A more general rule of algebraic expressions states that any expression containing more than one term is called a *polynomial*.

28. Signs of Operation

In algebra, the conventional signs of operation ($+$, $-$, $\times$, and $\div$) retain the same meaning as in arithmetic. In algebra, however, certain other signs may be used.

a. Multiplication may be indicated as follows:

Arithmetic	Algebra
$a \times b$	ab
$a \times b$	$a \cdot b$
$a \times b$	$(a)(b)$

b. Division may be indicated as follows:

Arithmetic	Algebra
$x \div y$	$\dfrac{x}{y}$
$(a + b) \div (a - b)$	$\dfrac{a+b}{a-b}$

c. The arithmetical signs for both *addition* and *subtraction* are retained in algebra.

Arithmetic	Algebra
$4 + 5$	$4 + 5$
$a - b$	$a - b$

29. Coefficients

Any factor of a product is known as a coefficient of the remaining factors. In the term πf, 2 is the numerical coefficient of πf, f is the coefficient of 2π, and π is the coefficient of $2f$. However, it is common practice to speak of the numerical part of the term as the coefficient. If a term contains no numerical coefficient, the number 1 is understood. Thus, abc is $1\,abc$, and xyz is $1\,xyz$.

30. Subscripts

In expression such as $R_t = R_1 + R_2 + R_3$, the small numbers or letters written to the right and below the literal terms are called subscripts. Subscripts are used to designate different values of a variable quantity. They are read: R sub 1, R sub 2, etc.

31. The Radical Sign

The radical sign ($\sqrt{}$) has the same meaning in algebra as in arithmetic (ch. 5). Thus, the expression $z = 2\sqrt{R^2 + x^2}$ states that z is equal to 2 times the square root of $R^2 + x^2$.

Section II. POSITIVE AND NEGATIVE NUMBERS

32. Signed Numbers

Only positive numbers are used in arithmetical operations, but both *positive* and *negative* numbers may appear in algebraic expressions. The plus sign ($+$) is used to indicate a positive number and the minus sign ($-$) to indicate a negative number. If the sign is omitted, the number is understood to be positive. Positive and negative numbers are called *signed numbers*.

33. Need for Negative Numbers

The need for negative numbers may be seen from the succession of subtraction below:

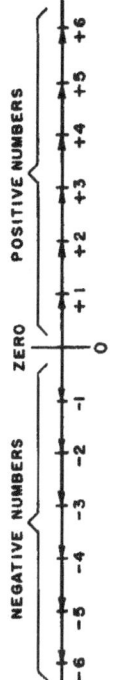

When the subtrahend is greater than the minuend, the difference becomes less than zero and the negative sign is placed before the difference. Thus, a negative number may be defined as a number less than zero.

34. Application of Positive and Negative Numbers

In technical work, many scales are calibrated above and below (or to the right and left of)

a center point designated 0 (zero). For example, the degrees of temperature indicated on a thermometer scale are measurements of distance taken on a scale in opposite directions from some point chosen to represent a reference or zero point. Temperature is always so many degrees above or below zero. In mathematics, it is convenient to indicate that a temperature is so many degrees above or below zero by prefixing the reading with a positive or negative sign. Thus, 45° above zero is $+45°$ and 15° below zero is $-15°$. Similarly, in electronic and electrical measuring instruments, scales are often calibrated to read positive numbers on one side of a zero and negative numbers on the other.

35. Graphical Representation of Positive and Negative Numbers

a. Principle. Positive and negative numbers may be represented graphically as shown in figure 4. The zero is the reference point. This graph can be used to illustrate both addition and subtraction.

b. Addition. To add numbers graphically, start at the zero reference point and mark off the first number, going to the right if the number is positive, or to the left if the number is

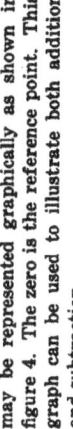

Figure 4. Graphical representation of positive and negative numbers.

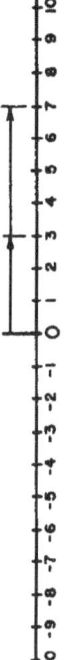

Figure 5. Graphical representation of addition of positive numbers.

Figure 6. Graphical representation of addition of negative numbers (—3 and —2).

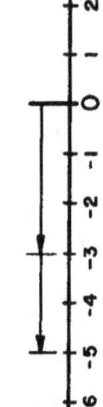

Figure 7. Graphical representation of addition of negative numbers (—1 and —5).

negative. From this new point, mark off the second number, again going to the right if the number is positive, or to the left if it is negative. The number of units between zero and the final point is the sum of the two numbers. This procedure can be continued for more than two numbers. Figure 5 shows graphical addition of positive numbers; figures 6 and 7 show graphical addition of negative numbers; and figure 8 shows the addition of a combination of a positive and a negative number. Figures 6 and 7 show that the order in which the negative numbers are taken does not affect the answer.

c. *Subtraction.* To subtract numbers graphically, change the sign of the subtrahend (number to be subtracted) and proceed as for addition. Figure 9 shows the subtraction of $+3$ from $+5$ to obtain the difference of $+2$.

36. Absolute Value of a Number

The numerical value of a number, without regard to its sign, is called the *absolute value* of the number. Thus, the absolute value of —3 or $+3$ is 3. This is written $|3|$.

37. Addition of Positive and Negative Numbers

a. *Positive Numbers.* To add two or more positive numbers, find the sum of their absolute values and prefix the sum with a plus sign. When there is no possibility of misunderstanding, the plus sign is usually omitted.

Example: Add $+4$, $+5$, and $+6$
$+4 + (+5) + (+6) = +15$ or 15

b. *Negative Numbers.* To add two or more negative numbers, find the sum of their absolute values and prefix the sum with a minus sign.

Example: Add -4, -5, and -6
$-4 + (-5) + (-6) = -15$

c. *Positive and Negative Numbers.* To add a positive and a negative number, find the difference between their absolute values and prefix the sum with the sign of the number that has the greater absolute value. When three or more positive and negative numbers are to be added, first find the sum of all positive numbers, and then the sum of all negative numbers. Add these sums algebraically as above.

Example 1: Add $+6$ and -9.
$+6 + (-9) = -3$

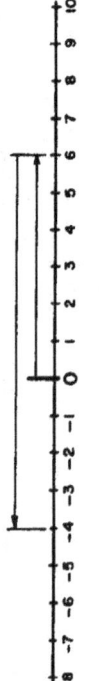

Figure 8. Graphical representation of addition of positive and negative numbers.

Figure 9. Graphical representation of subtraction of positive numbers.

Example 2: Add $+5$, -8, $+12$, and -6.
$+5 + (+12) = +17$
$-8 + (-6) = -14$
$(+17) + (-14) = +3$

38. Subtraction of Positive and Negative Numbers

To subtract positive and negative numbers, change the sign of the subtrahend and proceed as in addition (par. 37).

a. *Positive Numbers.*

Example 1: Subtract $+2$ from $+5$.
$+5 - (+2) = +5 - 2 = +3$ or 3

Example 2: Subtract $+5a^2$ from $+6a^2$.
$+6a^2 - (+5a^2) = +6a^2 - 5a^2$
$= +1a^2 = a^2$

b. *Negative Numbers.*

Example 1: Subtract -3 from -5.
$-5 - (-3) = -5 + 3 = -2$

Example 2: Subtract $-4a$ from $-2a$.
$-2a - (-4a) = -2a + 4a =$
$+2a$ or $2a$

c. *Positive and Negative Numbers.*

Example 1: Subtract -2 from $+5$.
$+5 - (-2) = +5 + 2 = +7$ or 7.

Example 2: Subtract $-3x^2$ from $+5x^2$.
$+5x^2 - (-3x^2) = +5x^2 + 3x^2$
$= +8x^2$ or $8x^2$

39. Multiplication of Positive and Negative Numbers

a. *Numbers Having Like Signs.* If the two numbers to be multiplied have the same signs, the product is positive.

Example 1: Multiply $+5$ by $+3$.
$(+5)(+3) = +15$ or 15

Example 2: Multiply -5 by -3.
$(-5)(-3) = +15$ or 15

b. *Numbers Having Unlike Signs.* If the two numbers to be multiplied have unlike signs, the product is negative.

Example 1: Multiply -5 by $+3$.
$(-5)(+3) = -15$

Example 2: Multiply $+5$ by -3.
$(+5)(-3) = -15$

c. *Several Positive and Negative Numbers.* To multiply several positive and negative numbers, multiply the numbers in groups of two in the order in which they appear.

Example 1:
Multiply $(-5)(+3)(+7)(-2)(-4)$.
$(-5)(+3) \quad (+7)(-2) \quad (-4)$
$= \quad (-15) \quad \quad (-14) \quad \quad (-4)$
$= \quad \quad \quad (+210) \quad \quad \quad (-4)$
$= \quad \quad \quad \quad \quad -840$

Example 2:
Multiply $(+7)(+2)(-5)(-3)(-1)(-4)$.
$= (+7)(+2) \quad (-5)(-3) \quad (-1)(-4)$
$= \quad (+14) \quad \quad (+15) \quad \quad (+4)$
$= \quad \quad \quad (+210) \quad \quad \quad (+4)$
$= \quad \quad \quad \quad \quad 840$

40. Division of Positive and Negative Numbers

a. *Numbers Having Like Signs.* The quotient of two numbers that have the same signs is positive.

Example 1: Divide -15 by -5.
$-15 \div -5 = +3$ or 3

Example 2: Divide $+24$ by $+6$.
$+24 \div +6 = +4$ or 4

b. *Numbers Having Unlike Signs.* The quotient of two numbers that have opposite signs is negative.

Example 1: Divide 35 by -7.
$+35 \div -7 = -5$

Example 2: Divide $-8{,}988$ by 28.
$-8988 \div 28 = -321$

41. Order of Signs

When only addition and subtraction signs appear in a series of terms, addition and subtraction procedures may be performed in any order. However, when multiplication and division signs appear in the same series with addition and subtraction signs, the multiplication and division must be performed first, and then the addition and subtraction.

Example 1: Evaluate $15 + 5 - 3 + 4 - 8$.

Step 1. Add the + terms:
$15 + 5 + 4 = 24$

Step 2. Add the − terms:
$(-3) + (-8) = -11$

Step 3. Add the + terms and − terms algebraically:
$24 - 11 = 13$.

Example 2: Evaluate $9 \times 4 + 6 - 3 + 5 \times 2$.

Step 1. Perform the multiplication first:
$(9 \times 4) + 6 - 3 + (5 \times 2) = (36) + 6 - 3 + (10)$

Step 2. Add the + terms:
$36 + 6 + 10 = 52$

Step 3. Add the − terms:
-3

Add the + terms and − terms algebraically:
$52 - 3 = 49$

Example 3: Evaluate $81 \div 9 - 3 + 6 - 15 + 4 \times 5$.

Step 1. Perform the division:
$(81 \div 9) - 3 + 6 - 15 + (4 \times 5) = (9) - 3 + 6 - 15 + (4 \times 5)$

Step 2. Perform the multiplication:
$9 - 3 + 6 - 15 + (4 \times 5) = 9 - 3 + 6 - 15 + (20)$

Step 3. Add the + terms:
$9 + 6 + 20 = 35$

Step 4. Add the − terms:
$(-3) + (-15) = -18$

Step 5. Add the + terms and − terms algebraically:
$35 - 18 = 17$.

42. Review Problems—Positive and Negative Numbers

a. Add the following:

(1) 23 and −6
(2) 21 and 37
(3) −54 and 33
(4) −43° and −96°
(5) 682 volts and −934 volts

b. Subtract the following:

(1) −104 amperes from 147 amperes
(2) −37 volts from −45 volts
(3) $.64cy$ from $.0025cy$
(4) $21.36ax^2$ from $-10.63ax^2$
(5) $-.986x^2y$ from $.824x^2y$

c. Find the product of the following:

(1) −6.4 and 2.8
(2) 3, −6, and 4
(3) $-\frac{2}{3}$, $\frac{6}{7}$, and $\frac{2}{5}$
(4) 3.01, −.02, and −1.26
(5) −.0025, 150, −.10, and .075
(6) −2, 5, 3, −1, and 4

d. Divide:

(1) 36 by 4
(2) $-\frac{5}{7}$ by $\frac{3}{4}$
(3) −5.6 by −.008
(4) −750 by −3
(5) $\frac{1}{3}$ ampere by $\frac{1}{2}$ ampere
(6) −.3750 by 150

e. Evaluate the following:

(1) $2 + 3 - 9$
(2) $3 + 4 + 2 \times 5 - 3$
(3) $2 - 3 \times 9$
(4) $3 \times 4 + 2 \times 5 - 3$
(5) $5 + 3 \times 7 - 2 \times 11 + 7$
(6) $28 \div 14 - 8 + 16 + 3 \times 2$
(7) $46 - 18 + 3 \times 4 - 8 + 12$
(8) $5 - 3 + 6 \times 4 + 40$
(9) $8 - 16 + 4 \times 3 - 10 \times 5$
(10) $15 \div 5 - 3 + 2 \times 10 - 2$

Section III. FUNDAMENTAL OPERATIONS

43. Addition and Subtraction of Algebraic Expressions

a. General. Only similar algebraic terms—those that are exactly alike in all respects other than numerical coefficients—may be added or subtracted. For example, the sum of $3x^2y$ and $5x^2y$ is $8x^2y$. Dissimilar terms cannot be added or subtracted directly, but the processes of addition or subtraction can be indicated by the use of plus or minus signs. For example, the sum of $4x^2y$ and $2xy^2$ is $4x^2y + 2xy^2$.

b. Procedure. To add or subtract algebraic expressions, arrange the terms so that like terms are in the same vertical column, and preferably in descending order of powers. Add or subtract the terms according to the rules of signed numbers (pars. 37 and 38).

Example 1: Add $x^3 - 3x^2 + 1$, $x^2 + x - 3$, and $x^2 + x + 1$.

$$\begin{array}{r} x^3 - 3x^2 + 1 \\ x^2 + x - 3 \\ x^2 + x + 1 \\ \hline 2x^3 - 2x^2 + 2x - 1 \end{array}$$

Example 2: Subtract $x^3 + 3x^2 + x - 1$ from $x^4 + x^3 - x + 2$.

$$\begin{array}{r} x^4 + x^3 - x + 2 \\ -(x^3 - 3x^2 - x + 1) \end{array}$$

Remove parentheses and change signs.

$$\begin{array}{r} x^4 + x^3 - x + 2 \\ -x^3 - 3x^2 - x + 1 \\ \hline x^4 - 3x^2 - x + 3 \end{array}$$

44. Multiplication and Division of Monomials

a. Multiplication. In multiplying monomials, multiply the numerical coefficients and write this result as the coefficient of the product. After the coefficient, write each literal factor with an exponent equal to the sum of all the exponents of that letter in the original factors.

For example, $3a^n \cdot 2a^m = 6a^{n+m}$.

Example 1: Multiply x^3 by x^5.
$x^3 \cdot x^5 = x^{3+5} = x^8$

Example 2: Multiply x, x^3, and x^{10}.
$x^1 \cdot x^3 \cdot x^{10} = x^{1+3+10} = x^{14}$

Example 3: Multiply x^2y^4 by $3xy^3$.
Step 1. Multiply the coefficients:
$1 \cdot 3 = 3$

Step 2. Multiply the two factors having the base x:
$x^2 \cdot x = x^{2+1} = x^3$

Step 3. Multiply the two factors having the base y:
$y^4 \cdot y^3 = y^{4+3} = y^7$

Step 4. The product is:
$x^2y^4 \cdot 3xy^3 = 3x^3y^7$

Example 4: Multiply x^2y^2z and wx^3y^5.
$x^2y^2z \cdot wx^3y^5 = wx^{2+3}y^{2+5}z^{1+5}$
$x^{2+3} = x^5$
$y^{4+1} = y^5$
$z^{1+5} = z^6$
Therefore, $x^2y^2z \cdot wx^3y^5 = wx^5y^5z^6$.

b. Division. In dividing a monomial by a monomial, divide the numerical coefficient of the dividend by the coefficient of the divisor and write the result as the coefficient of the quotient. After the coefficient, write each literal factor with an exponent equal to its exponent in the dividend minus its exponent in the divisor. Thus, to divide $6a^n$ by $3a^m$ (n greater than m), $\frac{6a^n}{3a^m} = 2a^{n-m}$.

Example 1: Divide x^3 by x^2.
$\frac{x^3}{x^2} = x^{3-2} = x^1 = x$

Example 2: Divide $5x^5y^2z^3$ by $6x^2z^2$.
$\frac{5x^5y^2z^3}{6x^2z^2} = \frac{5}{6} x^{5-2}yz^{3-2}$
$= \frac{5}{6} x^3yz$ or $\frac{5x^3yz}{6}$

c. Removal of Parentheses and Brackets.

(1) In multiplying a quantity in parentheses by a given factor, multiply each term inside the parentheses by that factor and drop the parentheses. If the factor is a negative quantity, the sign of every term inside the parentheses is changed. For example, $-5(a - b + c) = -5a + 5b - 5c$.

(2) When an algebraic expression, such as $5x - 4[x - 2(x - 3)]$, has more than one grouping symbol (parentheses and brackets), remove the inside grouping symbol first and then successively remove the outer grouping symbols.

Example 1: Simplify $5x - 4[x - 2(x-3)]$.
$5x - 4[x - 2(x-3)] = 5x - 4[x - 2x + 6]$
$= 5x - 4x + 8x - 24$
$= 9x - 24$
$= 3(3x - 8)$

Example 2: Simplify $4a - \{6a - 2b + 2[2a - b + 42] - (c + 2b)\}$.
$4a - \{6a - 2b + 2[2a - b + 42] - (c + 2b)\}$
$= 4a - \{6a - 2b + 4a - 2b + 84 - c - 2b\}$
$= 4a - 6a + 2b - 4a + 2b + 84 + c + 2b$
$= -6a + 6b + c + 84$

Example 3: Simplify $-(-1[-(x - y - z) + 29] - 39 + 2y - z)$.
$-\{-1[-(x - y - z) + 29] - 39 + 2y - z\}$
$= -\{-1[-x + y + z + 29] - 39 + 2y - z\}$
$= -\{+x - y - z - 29 - 39 + 2y - z\}$
$= -x + y + z + 29 + 39 - 2y + z$
$= -x - y + 2z + 68$

45. Raising Algebraic Functions to Powers

To raise an algebraic function to a power, multiply the exponents. Thus, $(a^n)^m = a^{nm}$.

Example 1: Simplify $(5^3)^4$.
$(5^3)^4 = 5^{3 \cdot 4} = 5^{12}$

Example 2: Simplify $(2ab)^3$.
$(2ab)^3 = 2ab \cdot 2ab \cdot 2ab = 8a^3b^3$
or $2^{1 \cdot 3} a^{1 \cdot 3} b^{1 \cdot 3} = 8a^3b^3$

Example 3: Simplify $(ax^3)^5$.
$(ax^3)^5 = a^{1 \cdot 5} x^{3 \cdot 5} = a^5 x^{15}$

Example 4: Simplify $[(x^3)^4]^5 = [x^{12}]^5 = [x^{12}]^5 = x^{12 \cdot 5} = x^{60}$

Example 5: Simplify $\left(\frac{2}{x^3}\right)^5$.
$\left(\frac{2}{x^3}\right)^5 = \frac{2^{1 \cdot 5}}{x^{3 \cdot 5}} = \frac{2^5}{x^{15}} = \frac{32}{x^{15}}$

46. Negative Exponents

The rule for dividing monomials (par. 44b) also holds when the exponents of the denominator is greater than the exponent of the numerator. For example, $a^3 \div a^5 = a^{3-5} = a^{-2}$; however, a quantity such as a^{-2} may be written as $\frac{1}{a^2}$.

Example: Multiply x^2, x^{-1}, and $\frac{1}{x^3}$.

Step 1. Write down the factors of the multiplication:
$x^2 \cdot x^{-1} \cdot \frac{1}{x^3}$

Step 2. Place all factors in the numerator:
$x^2 \cdot x^{-1} \cdot x^{-3}$

Step 3. Multiply the factors (add their exponents):
$x^{2-1-3} = x^{-2}$

47. Zero Exponents

The zero power of any quantity is equal to 1. For example $x^3 \cdot x^{-3} = x^0$ when the exponents are added. However, x^{-3} can also be written $\frac{1}{x^3}$; in this case, $x^3 \cdot x^{-3} = \frac{x^3}{x^3} = 1$.

Therefore, $x^0 = 1$. Any number (except zero) raised to the zero power is equal to 1.

Example: Solve $\frac{x^2y^3}{z} \cdot \frac{z^4}{xy} \div \frac{x^2y^3}{z^3}$.

$\frac{x^2y^3}{z} \cdot \frac{z^4}{xy} \div \frac{x^2y^3}{z^3} = \frac{x^2y^3z^4}{xyz} \div \frac{x^2y^3}{z^3} = \frac{x^2y^3z^4}{xyz} \cdot \frac{z^3}{x^2y^3}$

$= \frac{x^2y^3z^7}{x^3y^3z} = x^{2-3}y^{3-3}z^{7-1}$

$= x^{-1}yz^6 = x^{-1} \cdot 1 \cdot z^6 = \frac{z^6}{x}$

48. Multiplication of Polynomials

a. By a Monomial. To multiply a polynomial by a monomial, multiply each term in the polynomial separately by the monomial and add the products. Observe the rules for the multiplication of signed numbers (par. 39) and exponents (par. 44a).

Example 1: Multiply $3a + 2ab + 5c$ by $2b$.
$3a + 2ab + 5c$
$\underline{\quad\quad 2b\quad\quad}$
$6ab + 4ab^2 + 10bc$

Example 2: Multiply $ad - ae + af$ by $3a^2$.
$ad - ae + af$
$\underline{\quad\quad 3a^2\quad\quad}$
$3a^3d - 3a^3e + 3a^3f$

Example 3: Multiply $3x^2y^3 - 2xy^3 + 5x^2y$ by $4x^3y$.
$3x^2y^3 - 2xy^3 + 5x^2y$
$\underline{\quad\quad 4x^3y\quad\quad}$
$12x^5y^4 - 8x^4y^4 + 20x^5y^2$

b. By a Polynomial. To multiply a polynomial by another polynomial, multiply each term of one polynomial by each term of the other and add the products.

Example 1: Multiply $(a + b)$ by $(a + b)$.
$a + b$
$\underline{a + b}$
$a^2 + ab$
$\underline{\quad\quad ab + b^2}$
$a^2 + 2ab + b^2$

Example 2: Multiply $2x + 3y$ by $2z + 3z$.
$2x + 3y$
$\underline{2x + 3z}$
$4x^2 + 6xy$
$\underline{\quad\quad + 6xz + 9yz}$
$4x^2 + 6xy + 6xz + 9yz$

Example 3: Multiply $5x^2 - 6xy + 3y^2$ by $x + y$.
$5x^2 - 6xy + 3y^2$
$\underline{x + y}$
$5x^3 - 6x^2y + 3xy^2$
$\underline{\quad\quad + 5x^2y - 6xy^2 + 3y^3}$
$5x^3 - x^2y - 3xy^2 + 3y^3$

49. Division of Polynomials

a. By a Monomial. To divide a polynomial by a monomial, divide each term of the polynomial by the monomial.

Example 1: Divide $3a^2 + 4ab + 5ac$ by a.
$\frac{3a^2 + 4ab + 5ac}{a} = 3a + 4b + 5c$

Example 2: Divide $7x^2 + 14xy - 21ax^2$ by $7x$.
$\frac{7x^2 + 14xy - 21ax^2}{7x} = x + 2y - 3ax$

Example 3: Divide $4r(s+t) - r^4(s+t)^2 + qr^2(s+t)^3$ by $r^2(s+t)$.
$\frac{4r(s+t) - r^4(s+t)^2 + qr^2(s+t)^3}{r^2(s+t)}$
$= \frac{4r(s+t)}{r^2(s+t)} - \frac{r^4(s+t)^2}{r^2(s+t)} + \frac{qr^2(s+t)^3}{r^2(s+t)}$
$= \frac{4}{r} - r(s+t) + q(s+t)^2$

b. By a Polynomial. To divide a polynomial by a polynomial, just arrange the dividend and the divisor according to descending powers of one variable, starting with the highest powers at the left. Then proceed as shown in the examples below. If there is a remainder, write it as the numerator of a fraction the denominator of which is the divisor.

Example 1: Divide $ab + ac + db + dc$ by $a + d$.

Step 1. Divide the first term of the divisor, a, into the first term of the dividend, ab. The quantity a is contained in the first term, ab, b times. Write b as the first term of the quotient.

$$\begin{array}{r} b \\ a+d\overline{)ab+ac+db+dc} \end{array}$$

Step 2. Multiply both terms of the divisor by b:

$$\begin{array}{r} b \\ a+d\overline{)ab+ac+db+dc} \\ ab \quad\quad + db \end{array}$$

Step 3. Subtract the result from the original dividend:

$$\begin{array}{r} b \\ a+d\overline{)ab+ac+db+dc} \\ \underline{ab \quad\quad + db} \\ ac \quad\quad + dc \end{array}$$

Step 4. Divide the first term of the divisor into the first term of the remainder. It is contained in the first term, ac, c times. Write c as the second term of the quotient.

$$\begin{array}{r} b+c \\ a+d\overline{)ab+ac+db+dc} \\ \underline{ab \quad\quad + db} \\ ac \quad\quad + dc \end{array}$$

Step 5. Multiply both terms of the divisor by c and subtract. There is no remainder:

$$\begin{array}{r} b+c \\ a+d\overline{)ab+ac+db+dc} \\ \underline{ab \quad\quad + db} \\ ac \quad\quad + dc \end{array}$$

Step 6. Therefore,
$$\frac{ab+ac+db+dc}{a+d} = b+c.$$

Example 2: Divide $x^2 + 2xy + y^2$ by $x + y$.

$$\begin{array}{r} x+y \\ x+y\overline{)x^2+2xy+y^2} \\ \underline{x^2 + xy} \\ xy + y^2 \\ \underline{xy + y^2} \end{array}$$

Therefore,
$$\frac{x^2+2xy+y^2}{x+y} = x+y.$$

Example 3: Divide $6a^2 - ab - 27ac - 15b^2 + 7bc + 30c^2$ by $3a - 5b - 6c$.

$$\begin{array}{r} 2a+3b-5c \\ 3a-5b-6c\overline{)6a^2-ab-27ac-15b^2+7bc+30c^2} \\ \underline{6a^2 - 10ab - 12ac} \\ 9ab - 15ac - 15b^2 + 7bc + 30c^2 \\ \underline{9ab - 15b^2 - 18bc} \\ -15ac \quad\quad + 25bc + 30c^2 \\ \underline{-15ac \quad\quad + 25bc + 30c^2} \end{array}$$

50. Review Problems—Fundamental Operations

a. Add the following algebraic expressions:

(1) $2a^4 + 3a^2b^2 + 5b^4$, $a^4 - 5a^2b^2 - 2b^4$, and $3a^4 - 2a^2b^2 + b^4$.

(2) $3E - 2RI - 15ZI$, $6RI + 24ZI$, and $-2E - RI + 11ZI$.

(3) $10w - 4x + 3y + 6z$, $2z - 5w + y$, $3z - 2x - y$, and $6y - 4w - z + 5x$.

b. Subtract the following algebraic expressions:

(1) $-7ax - 2by + cz$ from $12ax + 15by - 8cz$.

(2) $10w - 3y - 4z + 6z$ from $3x + 5y - 2z - 15w$.

(3) $8a^2 + 10ab - 4b^2$ from $12a^2 - 24ab + 2b^2$.

c. Simplify:

(1) $7a^0$

(2) $(5x + 9)^0$

(3) $(3x^2 + 7x + 1)^0$

d. Perform the indicated operations:

(1) $t^6 \cdot t^4$

(2) $y^a \cdot y^b$

(3) $y^{a+1} \cdot y^{a-1}$

(4) $\dfrac{r^{10}}{r^4}$

(5) $(R^3)^m$

(6) $\dfrac{r^{m+5}}{r^4}$

e. Express with positive exponents:

(1) $4x^{-3}$

(2) $r^{-3}x^{-4}$

(3) $(6z)^{-10}$

(4) $I^{-2}R^{-1}$

(5) $2^{-2}a^3b^{-3}$

(6) $\dfrac{3EI^{-2}R^{-1}}{4}$

f. Perform the indicated operations:

(1) $(5ab)(2a^2 - 3ab + 7b^2)$

(2) $4a(a^2 + 3a + 1)$

(3) $(i^2 + 3i + 9)(i - 3)$

(4) $(2z^2 + 3xy - y^2)(z^2 + xy + y^2)$

(5) $(3x^2 - 2xy - 5y^2)(3x^2 + 2xy - 5y^2)$

(6) $[(x-1)a - (x-1)c] \div [(x-1)ac]$

(7) $(3rL - rR^2) \div rR$

(8) $(5a^4b - 10a^6b^3 + 15a^3b^4) \div 5a^3b$

(9) $(1 + 2z^4 + 4z^3 - z^3 + 7z) \div (3 + z^2 - z)$

(10) $(100b^3 - 13b^2 - 3b) \div (3 + 25b)$

Section IV. FACTORING

51. Understanding Factoring

Factoring is the breaking up of an expression into the *factors* or *individual parts* of which it is composed. In other words, to factor an algebraic expression means to find two or more expressions which, when multiplied together, will result in the original expression. For example, since $3 \cdot 5 = 15$, 3 and 5 are the factors of 15; since $4 \cdot a \cdot b = 4ab$, 4, a, and b, are the factors of $4ab$; since $a(x+y) = ax + ay$, a and $(x+y)$ are the factors of $ax + ay$.

52. Factors of Positive Integers

It is often difficult to determine at a glance the factors of which a number is composed. For example, consider the numerical expression 36. There are many different combinations of numbers that would result in an answer of 36; for example, the desired factors for 36 in a certain problem might $36 \cdot 1$, $18 \cdot 2$, $12 \cdot 3$, $9 \cdot 4$, $6 \cdot 6$, $2 \cdot 2 \cdot 9$, $4 \cdot 3 \cdot 3$, $2 \cdot 3 \cdot 6$, and so on.

53. Factors of a Monomial

Because the factors of a monomial are evident, usually a monomial is not separated into its prime factors. The factors of a^3b^2c are $a \cdot a \cdot a \cdot b \cdot b \cdot c$, and the factors of $15a^2b^3$ are $3 \cdot 5 \cdot a \cdot a \cdot b \cdot b \cdot b$.

54. Square Root of a Monomial

The square root of an algebraic expression is one of its two equal factors. Thus, the square root of 49 is 7, the square root of 81 is 9, the square root of a^2 is a, and the square root of x^2y^2 is xy. As discussed in paragraph 31, the radical sign is used to indicate the square root of a number. Actually, every number has two square roots, one positive and one negative. If no sign precedes the radical, the positive or *principal root* is understood. For example, $\sqrt{9} = +3$. If a negative sign *precedes the radical*, however, the negative root is intended. Thus, $-\sqrt{9} = -3$. When dealing with literal terms, the values of the various factors often are unknown. Therefore, *when extracting the square root of a monomial, extract the square root of the numerical coefficient, divide the exponents of the literal terms by 2, and prefix the square root with the plus or minus ($\pm$) sign,* which denotes that either the positive or negative root may be the correct one.

Example 1: $\sqrt{x^2 y^4} = \pm x^2 y^2$.
Example 2: $\sqrt{49 a^2 b^2} = \pm 7 a^2 b$.

55. Cube Root of a Monomial

The cube root of a monomial is one of its three equal factors. The index 3 in the angle of the radical sign ($\sqrt[3]{\ }$) indicates cube root (par. 31). *To extract the cube root of a monomial, extract the cube root of the numerical coefficient, divide the exponents of the literal terms by 3, and prefix the cube with the same sign as that of the monomial.*

Example 1: $\sqrt[3]{a^3 y^3} = a^2 y$.
Example 2: $\sqrt[3]{27 x^{12} y^6 z^9} = 3x^4 y^2 z^3$.
Example 3: $\sqrt[3]{-64 r^{21} s^3} = -4 r^7 s$.

56. Factors of a Polynomial

a. Common Monomial Factor. In an algebraic expression, the type of factor which can be recognized most easily is the monomial factor (single letter or number) which is common to each term in the expression. For instance, in the expression $xa + xb + xc$, the x is a factor common to each of the terms. Thus, the expression $xa + xb + xc$ can be written $x(a + b + c)$. This relationship is shown pictorially in figure 10. Since the area of a rectangle is equal to its base multiplied by its altitude (par. 136b), the area of the uppermost rectangle in figure 10 is x times a, or xa. The areas of the center and lower rectangles are xb and xc, respectively. The area of the large rectangle formed by the three small rectangles is equal to its base x times its altitude $(a + b + c)$, or $x(a + b + c)$. Since the area of the large rectangle is equal to the sum of the areas of the three smaller rectangles, then $x(a + b + c)$ is equal to $xa + xb + xc$. This shows that the factor x can be removed from $xa + xb + xc$ and the expression written $x(a + b + c)$. Accuracy of factoring can be checked by multiplying the two factors together—the product should be the original expression. Thus, $x(a + b + c) = xa + xb + xc$. *To factor a polynomial the terms of which have a common monomial factor, determine the largest factor common to all of the terms, divide the polynomial by this factor, and write the quotient in parentheses preceded by the monomial factor.* The first factor contains all that is common to all of the terms; it may consist of more than one literal number and may be to a power higher than the first.

Example 1: Factor $x^3 - 7x^2 + 4x$.
$x^3 - 7x^2 + 4x = x(x^2 - 7x + 4)$.

Example 2: Factor $abx + aby - abz$.
$abx + aby - abz = ab(x + y - z)$.

Example 3: Factor $2ax^3 - 4bx^2 + 6cx^2 = 2x^2(a - 2^2 + 3^c)$.

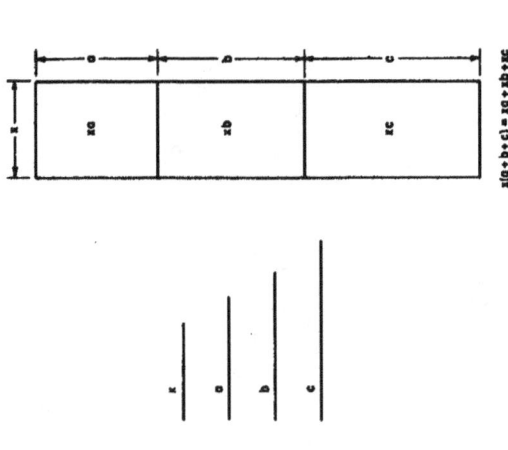

Figure 10. Common monomial factors.

b. Binomial Factors. Sometimes binomial factors are not immediately apparent, and an algebraic term may appear to have no common factors. For example, the expression $am + bm + an + bn$ may seem to have no factors in common. However, the first pair, $am + bm$, has a common factor, m, and the second pair, $an + bn$, has a common factor, n. Factoring out the common factors, the expression becomes $m(a + b) + n(a + b)$. Since there are two terms containing a common factor $(a + b)$, this factor can be removed to make the expression $(a + b)(m + n)$. Thus, the factors are $(a + b)$ and $(m + n)$. This relationship is shown pictorially in figure 11. Starting with the upper left-hand rectangle and going clockwise, the areas of the four rectangles are am, bm, and bn. The area of the large rectangle formed by the four smaller rectangles is its base $(m + n)$ times its altitude $(a + b)$, or $(m + n)(a + b)$. Since the area of the large rectangle is equal to the sum of the areas of the four smaller rectangles, then $(m + n)(a + b)$ is equal to $an + am + bm + bn$. This shows that the expression $am + bm + an + bn$ can be factored into $(m + n)$ and $(a + b)$. To check the factoring, multiply $(a + b)$ by $(m + n)$; the product is $am + bm + an + bn$. Since the addition of terms can be expressed in any order, the factoring is correct.

Example 1: Factor $py - pz - qy + qz$.
$py - pz - qy + qz = p(y - z) - q(y - z)$
$= (p - q)(y - z)$

Example 2: Factor $4xa - 8zb - 6ya - 4xb + 8za + 6yb$.
$4xa - 8zb - 6ya - 4xb + 8za + 6yb - 8zb$
$= 2a(2x - 3y + 4z) - 2b(2x - 3y + 4z)$
$= (2a - 2b)(2x - 3y + 4z)$
$= 2(a - b)(2x - 3y + 4z)$

Example 3: Factor $da + db - dc - ea - eb + ec + fa + fb - fc$.
$da + db - dc - ea - eb + ec + fa + fb - fc$
$= d(a + b - c) - e(a + b - c) + f(a + b - c)$
$= (d - e + f)(a + b - c)$

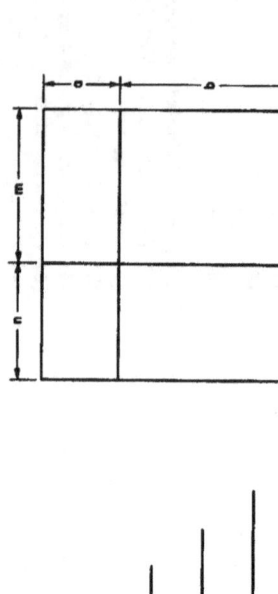

Figure 11. Binomial factors.

57. Factors of the Square of a Binomial

a. Square of Sum of Two Numbers. The square of the sum of two numbers is a special product that should be readily recognized to aid in factoring algebraic expressions. *The square of the sum of two numbers equals the square of the first, plus twice the product of the first and second, plus the square of the second.* To illustrate, $(a + b)^2 = a^2 + 2ab + b^2$. Conversely, the factors of $a^2 + 2ab + b^2$ are $(a + b) (a + b)$ or $(a + b)^2$. This relationship is shown in figure 12. The areas of the four rectangles, as shown on the figure, are a^2, ab, ab, and b^2. The area of the large rectangle formed by the four smaller rectangles is equal to its base $(a + b)$ times its altitude $(a + b)$, or $(a + b)^2$. Since the area of the large rectangle is equal to the sum of the areas of the four smaller rectangles, then $(a + b)^2$ is equal to $a^2 + ab + ab + b^2$, or $a^2 + 2ab + b^2$. This shows that the expression $a^2 + 2ab + b^2$ can be factored into $(a + b) (a + b)$, or $(a + b)^2$. Figure 13 shows a similar relationship in which nine small rectangles form one large rectangle.

In this case, the area of the large rectangle is $(a + 2b)^2$ and the sum of the areas of the nine smaller rectangles is $a^2 + 4ab + 4b^2$; consequently, $(a + 2b)$ and $(a + 2b)$ are factors of $a^2 + 4ab + 4b^2$. Thus, the factors of the square of one number, plus twice the product of the first and second number, plus the square of the second number are the square of the sum of the two numbers.

Example: Factor $4b^2 + 16db + 16d^2$.

$$4b^2 + 16db + 16d^2 = (2b + 4d)(2b + 4d)$$
$$= (2b + 4d)^2$$
$$= [2(b + 2d)]^2$$
$$= 2^2 (b + 2d)^2$$

To prove the factoring:
$$(2b + 4d)^2 = (2b)^2 + 2(2b)(4d) + (4d)^2$$
$$= 4b^2 + 16db + 16d^2$$

Note that 4 (that is, 2^2) may be removed before factoring the rest of the expression—this often simplifies computation.

$$4(b^2 + 4bd + 4d^2) = 4(b + 2d)^2$$

b. Square of Difference of Two Numbers. The square of the difference of two numbers equals the square of the first, minus twice the product of the first and second, plus the square of the second. For example, $(a - b)^2 = a^2 - 2ab + b^2$. The factors of $a^2 - 2ab + b^2$ are $(a - b) (a - b)$ or $(a - b)^2$. This relationship is shown pictorially in figure 14. The area of the large rectangle formed by the four small rectangles is a^2. The areas of the four smaller rectangles are shown on the illustration. The area of the upper left-hand rectangle is $(a - b)^2$. It is also equal to the area of the large rectangle minus the areas of the other three rectangles, or $a^2 - b(a - b) - b(a - b) - b^2$. This can be further simplified as follows:

$$a^2 - b(a - b) - b(a - b) - b^2$$
$$a^2 - 2b(a - b) - b^2$$
$$a^2 - 2ab + 2b^2 - b^2$$
$$a^2 - 2ab + b^2$$

Therefore, $(a - b)^2 = a^2 - 2ab + b^2$, and $(a - b)$ and $(a - b)$ are factors of $a^2 - 2ab + b^2$. Thus, the factors of the square of one number, minus twice the product of the first and the second, plus the square of the second are the square of the difference of the two numbers.

Example:
Factor $9b^2 - 12bd + 4d^2$.
$$9b^2 - 12bd + 4d^2 = (3b - 2d)(3b - 2d)$$
$$= (3b - 2d)^2$$

To prove the factoring:
$$(3b - 2d)^2 = (3b)^2 - 2(3b)(2d) + (2d)^2$$
$$= 9b^2 - 12bd + 4d^2$$

58. Factors of Difference of Two Squares

The product of the sum and difference of two numbers is equal to the difference of their squares. Thus, $(a + b)(a - b) = a^2 - b^2$. To factor the difference of two squares, extract the square roots, then write the sum of the roots as one factor and the difference of the roots as the other factor. Thus, the factors of $a^2 - b^2$ are $(a + b)(a - b)$.

Example:
Factor $4x^2 - 9y^4$.
$$4x^2 - 9y^4 = (2x + 3y)(2x - 3y)$$

To prove the factoring:
$$(2x + 3y)(2x - 3y)$$
$$= (2x)^2 + (2x)(3y) - (2x)(3y) - (3y)^2$$
$$= 4x^2 - 9y^4$$

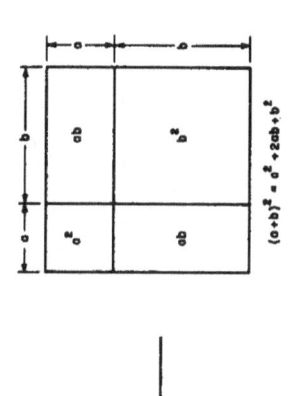

Figure 12. Square of sum of two numbers.

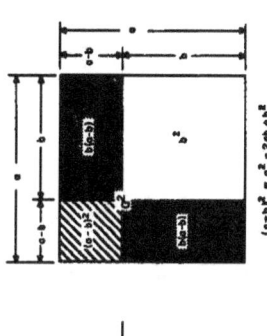

Figure 14. Square of difference of two numbers.

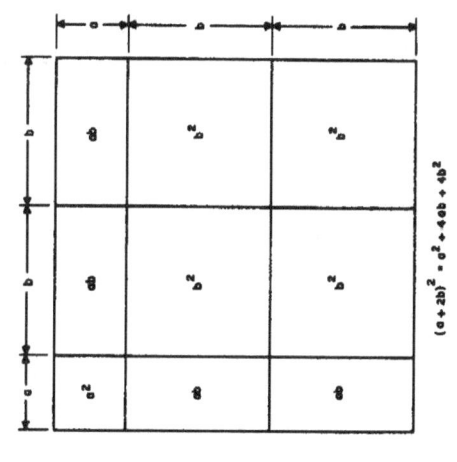

Figure 13. Factors of square of positive binomial.

59. Factors of Trinomials

a. Trinomials Such as $x^2 + x(a + b) + ab$. The factors of a trinomial consisting of the square of the common term, the product of the common term and the algebraic sum of the unlike terms, and the product of the unlike terms are two binomials that have one term in common and the other term unlike. Thus, the factors of $x^2 + x(a + b) + ab$ are $(x + a)(x + b)$ where x is the common term, and a and b are the unlike terms. As proof, the product of $(x + a)(x + b)$ is $x^2 + xa + xb + xb + ab$. By factoring the two terms which have a common factor, x, the original trinomial $x^2 + x(a + b) + ab$ is obtained.

Example: Factor $9r^2 + 6r(s + t) + 4st$.

$9r^2 + 6r(s + t) + 4st = (3r + 2s)(3r + 2t)$

To prove the factoring:

$(3r + 2s)(3r + 2t) = (3r)^2 + (3r)(2s) + (3r)(2t) + (2s)(2t)$
$= 9r^2 + 6rs + 6rt + 4st$
$= 9r^2 + 6r(s + t) + 4st$

b. Trinomials Such as $x^2 + 6x + 8$. To factor a trinomial of the form $x^2 + 6x + 8$, $x^2 - 6x + 8$, $x^2 + 6x - 8$, or $x^2 - 6x - 8$, much of the work is done by trial and error. The problem is to find two factors of the final term which, when added together, will give the coefficient of the middle term. Taking the first of the trinomials above, the factors of 8 are $8 \cdot 1$ and $4 \cdot 2$. Since $4 + 2 = 6$ and $8 + 1 = 9$, the factors that will be used are 4 and 2. With regards to signs, *if the signs of the final term is positive, the signs of the two factors are alike and will be the same as the sign of the middle term.* Thus, the factors $x^2 + 6x + 8$ are $(x + 4)$ and $(x + 2)$, and the factors of $x^2 - 6x + 8$ are $(x - 4)$ and $(x - 2)$. *If the sign of the final term is negative, however, the signs containing the two terms of each binomial factor are unlike; the larger factor will take the sign of the middle term.* For example, the factors of $x^2 + 2x - 8$ are $(x + 4)$ and $(x - 2)$, and the factors of $x^2 - 2x - 8$ are $(x - 4)$ and $(x + 2)$.

Example 1: Factor $y^2 + 12y + 32$.
$y^2 + 12y + 32 = (y + 8)(y + 4)$

Example 2: Factor $z^2 - 11z + 30$.
$z^2 - 11z + 30 = (z - 6)(z - 5)$

Example 3: Factor $r^2 + 4r - 12$.
$r^2 + 4r - 12 = (r + 6)(r - 2)$

Example 4: Factor $s^2 - s - 20$.
$s^2 - s - 20 = (s - 5)(s + 4)$

c. Trinomials Such as $6a^2 - 11a - 10$. The procedure used to factor trinomials of this type is an extension of the procedure described in *b* above and as shown in the example below.

Example: Factor $6a^2 - 11a - 10$.

Step 1. Find two numbers that, when multiplied together, form the left-hand term, $6a^2$.

$(6a)(a) = 6a^2$
$(2a)(3a) = 6a^2$

Step 2. Find two numbers that, when multiplied together, form the right-hand term, -10.

$(10)(-1) = -10$
$(5)(-2) = -10$
$(-10)(1) = -10$
$(-5)(2) = -10$

Step 3. By trial and error, set up two binomial expressions containing factors from step 1 in the left-hand term and factors from step 2 in the right-hand term. The proper selection of factors should give the middle term of the trinomial when the binomials are multiplied.

$(2a + 5)(3a - 2)$ (first trial)
$6a^2 + 15a - 4a - 10 = 6a^2 + 11a - 10$ (multiplying out)

The middle term obtained does not match the middle term of the given trinomial. The numerical value is correct, but the sign is wrong. Make a second trial with the signs in the binomials changed.

$(2a - 5)(3a + 2)$
$6a^2 - 15a + 4a - 10 = 6a^2 - 11a - 10$

Since the second trial results in the correct trinomial, the factors of $6a^2 - 11a - 10$ are $(2a - 5)$ and $(3a + 2)$.

Note. The method of trial and error used above may not work in every case. Other arrangements of factors and signs must be tried until the correct results are obtained.

60. Factors of Two Cubes

a. Sum of Two Cubes. The factors of the sum of two cubes, such as $x^3 + y^3$, are $(x + y)$ and $(x^2 - xy + y^2)$. In this case, the binomial is an expression of the sum of the primes times the sum of the squares of the primes minus the product of the primes. This is seen readily by dividing $x^3 + y^3$ by $x + y$.

Thus,

$$\begin{array}{r} x^2 - xy + y^2 \\ x + y \overline{\smash{)}x^3 + y^3} \\ \underline{x^3 + x^2y} \\ -x^2y \\ \underline{-x^2y - xy^2} \\ xy^2 + y^3 \\ \underline{xy^2 + y^3} \end{array}$$

Example 1: Factor $z^3 + 8$.
$z^3 + 8 = (z + 2)(z^2 - 2z + 4)$

To prove the factoring:

$$\begin{array}{r} z^2 - 2z + 4 \\ z + 2 \overline{\smash{)}z^3   + 8} \\ \underline{z^3 + 2z^2} \\ -2z^2 \\ \underline{-2z^2 - 4z} \\ 4z + 8 \\ \underline{4z + 8} \end{array}$$

b. Difference of Two Cubes. The factors of the difference of two cubes, such as $x^3 - y^3$, are $(x - y)(x^2 + xy + y^2)$. These factors are an expression of the difference of the primes times the sum of the squares plus the product of the primes. As in the sum of two cubes, the factoring can be proved by dividing the product by the binomial factor.

Example 1: Factor $a^3 - b^3$.

$a^3 - b^3 = (a - b)(a^2 + ab + b^2)$

To prove the factoring:

$$\begin{array}{r} a^2 + ab + b^2 \\ a - b \overline{\smash{)}a^3   - b^3} \\ \underline{a^3 - a^2b} \\ a^2b \\ \underline{a^2b - ab^2} \\ ab^2 - b^3 \\ \underline{ab^2 - b^3} \end{array}$$

Example 2: Factor $z^3 - 27$.

$z^3 - 27 = (z - 3)(z^2 + 3z + 9)$

To prove the factoring:

$$\begin{array}{r} z^2 + 3z + 9 \\ z - 3 \overline{\smash{)}z^3   - 27} \\ \underline{z^3 - 3z^2} \\ 3z^2 \\ \underline{3z^2 - 9z} \\ 9z - 27 \\ \underline{9z - 27} \end{array}$$

Example 2:

Factor $r^3 + 125z^3$.
$r^3 + 125z^3 = (r + 5z)(r^2 - 5rz + 25z^2)$

To prove the factoring:

$$\begin{array}{r} r^2 - 5rz + 25z^2 \\ r + 5z \overline{\smash{)}r^3   + 125z^3} \\ \underline{r^3 + 5r^2z} \\ -5r^2z \\ \underline{-5r^2z - 25rz^2} \\ 25rz^2 + 125z^3 \\ \underline{25rz^2 + 125z^3} \end{array}$$

Example 3: Factor $64s^3 - 216t^3$.
$64s^3 - 216t^3 = (4s - 6t)(16s^2 + 24st + 36t^2)$

To prove the factoring:

$$\begin{array}{r} 16s^2 + 24st + 36t^2 \\ \underline{4s - 6t} \\ 64s^3 + 96s^2t + 144st^2 \\ \underline{- 96s^2t - 144st^2 - 216t^3} \\ 64s^3 - 216t^3 \end{array}$$

61. Review Problems—Factoring

a. Factor:
(1) $25 + 5 - 30$
(2) $8 + 4 - 32$
(3) $9 - 18 + 21$
(4) $7r - 21r + 35r$
(5) $10x + 8y + 6z$

b. Find the values of the indicated powers:
(1) $(7xy^3)^2$
(2) $(-2w^5)^2$
(3) $(8a^2b^4)^2$
(4) $(9a^3x)^3$
(5) $(-3bz^4)^3$

c. Find the value of each of the following:
(1) $\sqrt{5^8}$
(2) $\sqrt{4^8}$
(3) $\sqrt{a^2b^6}$
(4) $\sqrt{36y^2z^4}$
(5) $\sqrt{100a^2b^{10}}$
(6) $\sqrt{16a^2} \cdot 5^2$
(7) $\sqrt[3]{-27}$
(8) $\sqrt[3]{-x^{-3}}$
(9) $\sqrt[3]{(-8)^2}$
(10) $\sqrt[3]{125z^{12}y^{16}z^5}$

d. Factor:
(1) $3x + 6$
(2) $5a^2 + 15a$
(3) $10x^3 - 14x^2 - 2x$
(4) $6azy + 9bzx - 12cz$
(5) $m^3 + m^2 - 5mx$
(6) $3a^5 - 6a^4b - 3a^6b^5$
(7) $7ry^3 - 14ry^3 + 21ry^3$
(8) $12x^2am + 14za^2m + 16zam^2$
(9) $\pi r_1^2 + \pi r_2^2$
(10) $\frac{1}{4}c^2d - \frac{1}{8}c^2d^3 + \frac{1}{16}cd^3$

Section V. ALGEBRAIC FRACTIONS

62. General

Algebraic fractions play an important part in equations for electrical and electronic circuits. These fractions can be added, subtracted, multiplied, and divided in the same manner as arithmetical fractions.

63. Changing Signs of Fractions

a. The sign preceding a fraction is the sign of the fraction. It refers to the fraction as a whole and not to either the numerator or the denominator. In addition, the numerator and denominator each has a sign. For example, in the fraction $-\frac{3a}{5b}$, the sign of the fraction is minus, the sign of the numerator is plus, and the sign of the denominator is plus. Any two of the three signs can be changed without changing the value of the fraction.

Thus, $-\frac{3a}{5b} = \frac{-3a}{5b} = \frac{3a}{-5b}$.

Therefore, the sign of the fraction is not changed if the signs of both the numerator and the denominator are changed. Also, the sign of the fraction must be changed if the sign of either the numerator or denominator, but not both, is changed.

b. If the numerator or denominator is a polynomial, the sign of each term should be changed, not just the first sign. For example,

$$-\frac{a-b}{c-d} = +\frac{-(a-b)}{c-d} = \frac{-a+b}{c-d} = \frac{b-a}{c-d}.$$

c. If the numerator or denominator is in factored form, change only the sign of one of the factors, not both. Thus,

$$-\frac{(x-y)(x-2y)}{x+y} = \frac{(x+y)(x-2y)}{x+y} = \frac{(y-x)(x-2y)}{x+y}.$$

64. Changing Form of Algebraic Fractions

In algebra, as in arithmetic, any fraction can be changed to an equivalent fraction by multiplying or dividing both the numerator and denominator by the same term or number except zero. This will not change the value of the fraction. For example, to change the fraction $\frac{3}{5}$ to a fraction with 10 as its denominator, multiply both the numerator and the denominator by 2. Thus,

$$\frac{3}{5} = \frac{3 \cdot 2}{5 \cdot 2} = \frac{6}{10}.$$

Similarly, to change the fraction $\frac{x}{y}$ to a fraction with yz as its denominator, the denominator is changed to yz by multiplying by z; the numerator also is multiplied by z to become xz. Thus,

$$\frac{x}{y} = \frac{x \cdot z}{y \cdot z} = \frac{xz}{yz}.$$

Example 1: Change $\frac{4}{a-3}$ to a fraction with $a^2 - 9$ as its denominator.

$$\frac{4}{a-3} = \frac{4 \cdot (a+3)}{(a-3)(a+3)} = \frac{4(a+3)}{a^2-9}$$

Example 2: Change $\frac{4r-3}{6r}$ to a fraction with $18r^2s$ as its denominator.

$$\frac{4r-3}{6r} = \frac{(4r-3) \cdot 3rs}{6r \cdot 3rs} = \frac{3rs(4r-3)}{18r^2s}$$

65. Reducing Fractions to Lowest Terms

As in arithmetic, when the numerator and denominator of a fraction have no common factor other than 1, the fraction is said to be in its lowest terms. The fraction $\frac{3}{8}$, $\frac{a}{b}$, and $\frac{p+q}{p-q}$, therefore, are in their lowest terms since the numerator and denominator of each fraction have no other factor except 1. The fractions $\frac{6}{12}$ and $\frac{3a}{9a^2}$ are not in their lowest terms. The fraction $\frac{6}{12}$ can be reduced to its lowest term by dividing both the numerator and denominator by 6. Similarly, the fraction $\frac{6y}{15y^2}$ can be reduced to $\frac{1}{3y}$ by dividing the numerator and denominator by $5y$. Thus, to reduce a fraction to its lowest terms, factor the numerator and denominator into prime factors and cancel the factors common to both (since they are equal to $\frac{1}{1}$).

Example 1: Reduce $\frac{6y}{8y^2}$ to lowest terms.

$$\frac{6y}{8y^2} = \frac{2y(3)}{2y(4y)} = \frac{3}{4y}$$

Example 2: Reduce $\frac{xab^2}{xcb}$ to lowest terms.

$$\frac{xab^2}{xcb} = \frac{xb(ab)}{xb(c)} = \frac{ab}{c}$$

Example 3: Reduce $\dfrac{a^2-b^2}{4a+4b}$ to lowest terms.

$$\dfrac{a^2-b^2}{4a+4b}=\dfrac{(a+b)(a-b)}{4(a+b)}=\dfrac{a-b}{4}$$

Example 4: Reduce $\dfrac{2a^2+4ab+2b^2}{2a+2b}$ to lowest terms.

$$\dfrac{2a^2+4ab+2b^2}{2a+2b}=\dfrac{2(a+b)(a+b)}{2(a+b)}=\dfrac{a+b}{1}=a+b$$

66. Finding Lowest Common Denominator

The lowest common denominator (LCD) of two or more fractions is the smallest term or number that is divisible by each of the denominators. Inspect to find this term or number, divide the LCD by the denominator of each fraction, and multiply both the numerator and denominator by the quotient. For example, when changing the fractions $\tfrac{2}{3}$ and $\tfrac{4}{5}$ to fractions which have an LCD, inspection shows that 15 is the smallest number which is divisible by both 3 and 5. Thus, the fractions $\tfrac{2}{3}$ and $\tfrac{3}{5}$ become $\tfrac{10}{15}$ and $\tfrac{9}{15}$. Similarly, the LCD of $\tfrac{4xy}{3a^2}$ and $\tfrac{6z}{4ab}$ is $12a^2b$ because this is the smallest term that is divisible by both $3a^2$ and $4ab$. Thus, the fraction $\tfrac{4xy}{3a^2}$ and $\tfrac{6z}{4ab}$ become $\tfrac{16xyb}{12a^2b}$ and $\tfrac{18za}{12a^2b}$, respectively. When fractions have factors with exponents in the denominators, the highest power of each distinct factor is used to form the LCD. For example, consider the problem of finding the LCD of fractions having the following denominators: x^2y^2z, $x^2y^4z^3$, y^4z^3, x^2y^4. The LCD is $x^2y^4z^3$ because x^2, y^4, and z^3 are the highest powers of x, y, and z in any one denominator.

Example: Change $\dfrac{3a}{a^2-b^2}$ and $\dfrac{4b}{a^2-ab-2b^2}$ to equivalent fractions having an LCD.

$$\dfrac{3a}{a^2-b^2}=\dfrac{3a}{(a+b)(a-b)}$$

$$\dfrac{4b}{a^2-ab-2b^2}=\dfrac{4b}{(a+b)(a-2b)}$$

Step 1. Factor each denominator into its prime factors:

Step 2. The lowest common multiple of the denominators is the LCD:

$$(a+b)(a-b)(a-2b)$$

Step 3. Divide the LCD by the denominators:

$$(a+b)(a-b)(a-2b)\div(a+b)(a-b)=a-2b$$
$$(a+b)(a-b)(a-2b)\div(a+b)(a-2b)=a-b$$

Step 4. Change $\dfrac{3a}{(a+b)(a-b)}$ into a fraction having $(a+b)(a-b)(a-2b)$ as its denominator:

$$\dfrac{3a}{(a+b)(a-b)}=\dfrac{3a(a-2b)}{(a+b)(a-b)(a-2b)}$$

Step 5. Change $\dfrac{4b}{(a+b)(a-2b)}$ into a fraction having $(a+b)(a-b)(a-2b)$ as its denominator.

$$\dfrac{4b}{(a+b)(a-2b)}=\dfrac{4b(a-b)}{(a+b)(a-b)(a-2b)}$$

Step 6. Therefore, $\dfrac{3a}{a^2-b^2}=\dfrac{3a(a-2b)}{(a+b)(a-b)(a-2b)}$

and $\dfrac{4b}{a^2-ab-b^2}=\dfrac{4b(a-b)}{(a+b)(a-b)(a-2b)}$

67. Addition and Subtraction of Algebraic Fractions

a. Addition. The addition of algebraic fractions is similar to the corresponding operation in arithmetic. To add two or more fractions having a common denominator, add the numerators and place the result over the common denominator. If the fractions have different denominators, convert them to fractions with an LCD. The sum of the fractions is equal to the algebraic sum of the numerators divided by the LCD. Simplify the numerator and reduce the result to its lowest terms. If possible, factor or combine for further simplification.

Example: Find the sum of $\dfrac{2x}{x+y}$ and $\dfrac{2y}{x-y}$.

The LCD is $(x+y)(x-y)$. Therefore,

$$\dfrac{2x}{x+y}+\dfrac{2y}{x-y}=\dfrac{2x(x-y)}{(x+y)(x-y)}+\dfrac{2y(x+y)}{(x+y)(x-y)}$$
$$=\dfrac{2x(x-y)+2y(x+y)}{(x+y)(x-y)}$$
$$=\dfrac{2x^2-2xy+2xy+2y^2}{(x+y)(x-y)}$$
$$=\dfrac{2x^2+2y^2}{(x+y)(x-y)}$$
$$=\dfrac{2(x^2+y^2)}{x^2-y^2}$$

b. Subtraction. To subtract two fractions having a common denominator, subtract the numerator of the subtrahend from the numerator of the minuend and place the result over the common denominator. If the denominators are different, find the LCD and subtract, as shown below.

Example: Subtract $\dfrac{8}{x^2+6x-16}$ from $\dfrac{9}{x^2+7x-18}$.

The LCD is $(x-2)(x+8)(x+9)$. Therefore,

$$\dfrac{9}{x^2+7x-18}-\dfrac{8}{x^2+6x-16}$$
$$=\dfrac{9(x+8)}{(x-2)(x+8)(x+9)}-\dfrac{8(x+9)}{(x-2)(x+8)(x+9)}$$
$$=\dfrac{9(x+8)-8(x+9)}{(x-2)(x+8)(x+9)}$$
$$=\dfrac{9x+72-8x-72}{(x-2)(x+8)(x+9)}$$
$$=\dfrac{x}{(x-2)(x+8)(x+9)}$$

68. Multiplication and Division of Algebraic Fractions

a. Multiplication. The process of multiplication of algebraic fractions is the same as in arithmetic. The product of two or more fractions is the product of the numerators divided by the product of the denominators. The operation may be simplified by dividing common factors in the numerator and denominator by the same factor.

Example 1: Multiply $\frac{6a^2b}{7x}$ by $\frac{21x^2y}{24a^3b}$.

The first numerator and the second denominator are divisible by $6a^2b$; the first denominator and the second numerator are divisible by $7x$. Therefore:

$$\frac{\overset{1}{6a^2b}}{\underset{1}{7x}} \cdot \frac{\overset{3xy}{21x^2y}}{\underset{4}{24a^3b}} = \frac{3xy}{4}$$

Example 2: Multiply $\frac{a^2+2ab+b^2}{a-b}$ by $\frac{a^2-2ab+b^2}{a+b}$.

$$\frac{a^2+2ab+b^2}{a-b} \cdot \frac{a^2-2ab+b^2}{a+b} = \frac{(a+b)(a+b)}{a-b} \cdot \frac{(a-b)(a-b)}{a+b}$$

$$= \frac{\overset{1}{(a+b)}(a+b)\overset{1}{(a-b)}(a-b)}{\underset{1}{(a-b)}\underset{1}{(a+b)}}$$

$$= (a+b)(a-b)$$

$$= a^2 - b^2$$

b. Division. To divide algebraic fractions, multiply the dividend by the reciprocal of the divisor. Thus, to divide by x, multiply by the reciprocal of x, that is $\frac{1}{x}$. In other words, invert the divisor and proceed as in multiplication.

Example 1: Divide $\frac{2a+2b}{a-3}$ by $\frac{a^2-b^2}{2a-6}$.

$$\frac{2a+2b}{a-3} \div \frac{a^2-b^2}{2a-6} = \frac{2a+2b}{a-3} \cdot \frac{2a-6}{a^2-b^2}$$

$$= \frac{2(a+b)}{a-3} \cdot \frac{2(a-3)}{(a+b)(a-b)}$$

$$= \frac{2 \cdot 2}{a-b}$$

$$= \frac{4}{a-b}$$

Example 2: Divide $\frac{z^2-z-6}{z^2-25}$ by $\frac{z^2+z-12}{z^2-z-20}$.

$$\frac{z^2-z-6}{z^2-25} \div \frac{z^2+z-12}{z^2-z-20} = \frac{z^2-z-6}{z^2-25} \cdot \frac{z^2-z-20}{z^2+z-12}$$

$$= \frac{(z-3)(z+2)}{(z-5)(z+5)} \cdot \frac{(z-5)(z+4)}{(z+4)(z-3)}$$

$$= \frac{z+2}{z+5}$$

69. Review Problems—Algebraic Fractions

a. Changing Signs of Fractions. Solve for the unknown.

(1) $\frac{4x+3}{6} - \frac{x-9}{4} = 5$

(2) $\frac{x-2}{4} - \frac{1}{2} =$

(3) $\frac{r+4}{3} - \frac{r-2}{5} = 2$

(4) $\frac{4x-3}{6x} - \frac{4x+5}{3x} = 2$

(5) $\frac{7t+2}{3} = 3$

(6) $\frac{x-4}{3} + \frac{2x-5}{6} = 3$

(7) $\frac{2r+3}{2} - \frac{3r+2}{4} = 2$

(8) $\frac{7x-4}{3} + \frac{x-5}{5} = \frac{1}{5}$

b. Equivalent Fractions. Supply missing terms.

(1) $\frac{4}{8} = \frac{?}{16}$

(2) $\frac{1}{c} = \frac{?}{cx}$

(3) $\frac{3}{r-s} = r^2 - s^2$

(4) $\frac{a-8}{1} = \frac{?}{3}$

(5) $\frac{l-6}{l-3} = \frac{?}{(l-3)(l-9)}$

(6) Change $\frac{4E^2}{R}$ into an equivalent fraction of which the denominator is $21^2 R$.

(7) Change $\frac{1}{3\pi fc}$ into an equivalent fraction of which the denominator is $6\pi f^2 c$.

c. Lowest Common Denominator. Reduce to equivalent fractions having an LCD.

(1) $\frac{1}{R}, \frac{1}{Ri}, \frac{1}{r}$

(2) $\frac{1}{a+1}, \frac{x}{a-1}$

(3) $\frac{b}{2x}, \frac{c}{3x}$

(4) $\frac{y}{2}, \frac{y}{2y+6}$

(5) $\frac{2}{c}, \frac{3}{c+1}$

(6) $\frac{i}{e-5}, \frac{i}{2e-10}$

(7) $\frac{y}{c^2-d^2}, \frac{z}{c-d}$

d. Addition and Subtraction of Fractions. Perform the indicated operations.

(1) $\frac{1}{a} + \frac{4}{a} + \frac{7}{a}$

(2) $\frac{s}{t} + \frac{s+4}{2t} + \frac{s+3}{4t}$

(3) $\frac{3a}{4x^2y} + \frac{5b}{6xy^3}$

(4) $\frac{2}{z^2-1} + \frac{4}{z^2-4}$

(5) $\frac{3c-2d}{4cd^2} + \frac{2c-3d}{3c^2d}$

(6) $\frac{(r+1)(r-3)}{r^2+2r-15} + \frac{(r-2)(r+5)}{r^2+2r-15}$

(7) $3y - \frac{1}{4}$

(8) $\frac{a+b}{a-b} - \frac{a-b}{a+b}$

(9) $\frac{32}{25q^2} - \frac{16}{5q}$

(10) $\frac{3t-2t}{4t v^3} - \frac{2t-3t}{3t^2 v}$

e. Multiplication and Division of Fractions. Perform the indicated operations.

(1) $\frac{9y^2}{16} \cdot \frac{2}{3}$

(2) $\frac{a^3}{b^4} \cdot \frac{a^6}{b^2}$

(3) $\frac{3x^2}{49y^2} \cdot \frac{7yz^2}{9xm}$

(4) $\left(\frac{1}{r} - \frac{1}{s}\right)\left(r - \frac{r^2}{s}\right)$

(5) $\frac{2x^2-5xy-3y^2}{z^2-9y^2} \cdot \frac{3x+9y}{10x^2+5xy}$

(6) $\frac{a^2+2ab+b^2}{a^2-b^2} \cdot \frac{a+b}{a^2-2ab+b^2} \div \frac{a+b}{a^3}$

(7) $3z \div \frac{1}{5}$

(8) $\frac{5ba^2}{6cd} \div 5b$

(9) $\frac{12s^2t}{20uv} \div \frac{3st}{4u^2v}$

(10) $\left(e+2-\frac{3}{e}\right) \div \left(e+1-\frac{2}{e}\right)$

Section VI. EXPONENTS AND RADICALS

70. General

Chapter 4 presents exponents and roots consisting only of whole numbers. However, to use exponents and radicals to solve many equations and formulas, a knowledge of additional operations is required.

71. Fractional Exponents

a. General. A fractional exponent is merely another way of expressing the root of a number. For example, the cube root of x usually is written $\sqrt[3]{x}$; however, it also can be written $x^{\frac{1}{3}}$. Similarly, $\sqrt{2}$ also can be written $2^{\frac{1}{2}}$.

b. Application. Fractional exponents have a practical value in simplifying algebraic problems. They follow the same rules as exponents that consist of integers, and can be added, subtracted, multiplied, or divided in the same way; thus

$$a^{\frac{1}{2}} \cdot a^{\frac{1}{2}} = a^{\frac{1}{2}+\frac{1}{2}} = a^1 = a, \text{ and } a^{\frac{1}{3}} \cdot a^{\frac{1}{3}} \cdot a^{\frac{1}{3}} = a^{\frac{1}{3}+\frac{1}{3}+\frac{1}{3}} = a^1 = a.$$

In other words, $a^{\frac{1}{2}}$ is one of two equal factors of a or the square root of a, and $a^{\frac{1}{3}}$ is two of three equal factors of a or the square cube root of a; therefore, $a^{\frac{1}{2}} = \sqrt{a}$ and $a^{\frac{1}{3}} = \sqrt[3]{a}$.

c. Changing from Radical Form to Exponential Form. To change a radical expression to exponential form, remove the radical sign and annex a fractional exponent to the radicand (number under the radical sign). The numerator of the fractional exponent is the power of the radicand, and the denominator is the index of the root.

Example 1: Change $\sqrt{a^3}$ to exponential form and simplify.

$$\sqrt{a^3} = (a^3)^{\frac{1}{2}}$$

Multiplying exponents and simplifying:

$$(a^3)^{\frac{1}{2}} = a^{3 \cdot \frac{1}{2}} = a^{\frac{3}{2}} = a^{1\frac{1}{2}} = \sqrt{a}$$

Therefore, $\sqrt{a^3} = \sqrt{a}$.

Example 2: Change $\sqrt[3]{8a^2b^3}$ to exponential form and simplify.

$$\sqrt[3]{8a^2b^3} = \sqrt[3]{2^3a^2b^3} = (2^3a^2b^3)^{\frac{1}{3}} = 2^{3 \cdot \frac{1}{3}}a^{2 \cdot \frac{1}{3}}b^{3 \cdot \frac{1}{3}} = 2^1 a^{\frac{2}{3}}b^1 = 2b (a^2)^{\frac{1}{3}} = 2b\sqrt[3]{a^2}$$

d. Changing from Exponential Form to Radical Form. To change an expression with a fraction exponent to a radical form, make the base of the fractional exponent the radicand, the numerator of the exponent the power of the radicand, and the denominator of the exponent the index of the root.

Example 1: Change $4^{\frac{1}{2}}$ to radical form.

$$4^{\frac{1}{2}} = \sqrt{4}$$

Example 2: Change $3^{\frac{2}{3}}$ to radical form.

$$3^{\frac{2}{3}} = \sqrt[3]{3^2} = \sqrt[3]{9}$$

Example 3: Change $(5a^2b)^{\frac{2}{3}}$ to radical form.

$$(5a^2b)^{\frac{2}{3}} = \sqrt[3]{(5a^2b)^2} = \sqrt[3]{25a^4b^2}$$

72. Simplification of Radicals

a. Removing a Factor from the Radicand. The form in which a radical expression is written may be changed without altering its numerical value. Sometimes there is a question as to what actually is the simplest form for an expression. For instance, consider the simplification of an expression such as $\sqrt{1250}$: $\sqrt{1250} = \sqrt{2.5^4} = 5^2\sqrt{2} = 25\sqrt{2}$. The expression $25\sqrt{2}$ usually is accepted as being simpler than $\sqrt{1250}$. As a general rule, the fewer the factors under the radical sign, the simpler the expression. Thus, a radicand may be separated into two factors, one of which is the greater power whose root can be taken. The root of this factor may then be written as the coefficient of a radical of which the other factor is the radicand.

Example 1: Simplify $\sqrt{50}$.

$$\sqrt{50} = \sqrt{25 \cdot 2}$$
$$= \sqrt{25}\sqrt{2}$$
$$= 5\sqrt{2}$$

Example 2: Simplify $\sqrt[4]{32a^7b^5}$.

$$\sqrt[4]{32a^7b^5} = (2^5 a^7 b^5)^{\frac{1}{4}}$$
$$= 2^{\frac{5}{4}} a^{\frac{7}{4}} b^{\frac{5}{4}}$$
$$= 2^{1\frac{1}{4}} a^{1\frac{3}{4}} b^{1\frac{1}{4}}$$
$$= 2a \sqrt[4]{2a^3b^5}$$

b. Rationalizing Denominator. Rationalizing a denominator containing a radical means to eliminate the radical in the denominator. For example, to rationalize the expression $\frac{1}{\sqrt{2}}$, first change the denominator into an expression having a fractional exponent; thus, $\frac{1}{\sqrt{2}} = \frac{1}{2^{\frac{1}{2}}}$; then multiply the denominator by a number that will make its exponent equal to 1. This operation eliminates the radical sign below the line. In this case, $2^{\frac{1}{2}}$ is such a factor; thus $2^{\frac{1}{2}} \cdot 2^{\frac{1}{2}} = 2^1 = 2$. Such multiplication can be performed without changing the value of the fraction if the numerator also is multiplied by the same number; thus $\frac{1}{2^{\frac{1}{2}}} \cdot \frac{2^{\frac{1}{2}}}{2^{\frac{1}{2}}} = \frac{2^{\frac{1}{2}}}{2^{\frac{1}{2}+\frac{1}{2}}} = \frac{2^{\frac{1}{2}}}{2}$. Finally, changing the numerator into radical form, $\frac{\sqrt[3]{2^2}}{2} = \frac{\sqrt[3]{4}}{2}$. Therefore, to rationalize a denominator, multiply both the numerator and the denominator by a number that will make the exponent in the denominator equal to 1; then simplify the radical in the numerator. The examples below illustrate the method of rationalizing a few different types of denominators.

Example 1: Rationalize $\frac{1}{3^{\frac{1}{2}}}$.

$$\frac{1}{3^{\frac{1}{2}}} = \frac{1}{3^{\frac{1}{2}}} \cdot \frac{3^{\frac{1}{2}}}{3^{\frac{1}{2}}} = \frac{3^{\frac{1}{2}}}{3} = \frac{\sqrt[3]{3^2}}{3} = \frac{\sqrt[3]{9}}{3}$$

Example 2: Rationalize $\frac{1}{\sqrt{8}}$.

First simplify $\sqrt{8}$.

$$\sqrt{8} = \sqrt{4 \cdot 2} = \sqrt{4} \cdot \sqrt{2} = 2 \cdot 2^{\frac{1}{2}}$$
$$\frac{1}{\sqrt{8}} = \frac{1}{2 \cdot 2^{\frac{1}{2}}} = \frac{2^{\frac{1}{2}}}{2 \cdot 2^{\frac{1}{2}} \cdot 2^{\frac{1}{2}}} = \frac{\sqrt{2}}{4}$$

Example 3: Rationalize $\frac{1}{\sqrt{7}}$.

Here the square root in the denominator is being multiplied by itself, making the number a perfect square.

$$\frac{1}{\sqrt{7}} = \frac{1}{\sqrt{7}} \cdot \frac{\sqrt{7}}{\sqrt{7}} = \frac{\sqrt{7}}{\sqrt{7}\sqrt{7}} = \frac{\sqrt{7}}{7}$$

c. Practical Application. The processes of the simplification of radicals and rationalization of denominators are useful when computing decimals. It is necessary to know, however, that $\sqrt{2} = 1.414$, $\sqrt{3} = 1.732$, etc. For example, consider the problem of evaluating $\frac{1}{\sqrt{2}}$. One way of evaluating this problem is to divide 1 by 1.414. This evaluation is a long-division problem of some length, however. A much more simple way is to rationalize—thus $\frac{1}{\sqrt{2}} = \frac{\sqrt{2}}{2}$, and dividing 1.414 by 2 gives the result, 0.707.

73. Addition and Subtraction of Radicals

As discussed in paragraph 27b, terms that are alike in all respects, except for their coefficients, are called *similar terms*. Similarly, radicals that have the same index and the same radicand and differ only in their coefficients are called *similar radicals*. For example, $-5\sqrt{3}$, $2\sqrt{3}$, and $\sqrt{3}$ are similar radicals. Similar radicals may be added or subtracted in the same way that similar terms are added and subtracted. However, if the radicands are not alike and cannot be reduced to a common radicand, they are dissimilar and addition and subtraction can only be indicated; thus to add or subtract radicals, reduce them to their simplest form, then combine similar radicals, and indicate the addition or subtraction of dissimilar radicals.

Example 1: Perform the indicated operations.
$$4\sqrt{6} - 5\sqrt{6} - \sqrt{6} + 10\sqrt{6} = 8\sqrt{6}$$

Example 2: Add.
$$\sqrt{48a} + \sqrt{\frac{a}{3}} + \sqrt{3a} = 4\sqrt{3a} + \tfrac{1}{3}\sqrt{3a} + \sqrt{3a}$$
$$= \frac{16}{3}\sqrt{3a}$$

Example 3: Perform the indicated operations.
$$\sqrt[3]{16r^2} - r\sqrt[3]{4r} + \sqrt[9]{64r^3} = \sqrt[3]{(4r)^2} - r\sqrt[3]{4r} + \sqrt[9]{(4r)^3}$$
$$= (4r)^{\frac{2}{3}} - 4(4r)^{\frac{1}{3}} + (4r)^{\frac{3}{9}}$$
$$= \sqrt[3]{4r} - r\sqrt[3]{4r} + \sqrt[3]{4r}$$
$$= \sqrt[3]{4r}\,(2 - r)$$

Example 4: Perform the indicated operations.
$$2\sqrt{6} + \sqrt[9]{\frac{2}{3}} - \sqrt[4]{36} = 2\sqrt{6} + \sqrt[9]{\frac{2}{3}\cdot\frac{3}{3}} - \sqrt{6.6}$$
$$= 2\sqrt{6} + \sqrt[9]{\frac{9}{3}}\sqrt{6} - \sqrt{6^2}$$
$$= 2\sqrt{6} + 3\sqrt{6} - \sqrt{6}$$
$$= 4\sqrt{6}$$

74. Multiplication of Radicals

a. Radicals With Same Indexes. Radicals can be multiplied and combined under the same radical sign even though they differ in value, provided the index of the radicals are the same. To multiply a radical expression when radicals are of the same order, first multiply the coefficients, then multiply the radicands, and then simplify, if possible. For example, $2\sqrt{3}\cdot 3\sqrt{5} = 6\sqrt{15}$. If the radicand is a perfect square, simplify the result by extracting the square root. Remember that there are two square roots, one positive and one negative; thus, $6\sqrt{3}\cdot 4\sqrt{3} = 24\sqrt{9} = 24(\pm 3) = \pm 72$. When polynomial expressions, either or both of which involve radicals, are to be multiplied, proceed in the same manner as with literal polynomial expressions (par. 48). For example, $(\sqrt{3}+2\sqrt{5})\times(\sqrt{3}-2\sqrt{5}) =$

$$\begin{array}{r}\sqrt{3}+2\sqrt{5}\\ \sqrt{3}-2\sqrt{5}\\ \hline \sqrt{9}+2\sqrt{15}\\ -2\sqrt{15}-4\sqrt{25}\\ \hline \sqrt{9}\qquad -4\sqrt{25}=\pm 3\;\pm 20\\ =\pm 3\;\pm 20\\ = 3\;\pm 20\text{ or }-3\;\pm 20\\ =\pm 17\text{ or }\pm 23\end{array}$$

Example 1: Multiply $2\sqrt[3]{3a}$, $5\sqrt[3]{4a}$, and $3\sqrt[3]{18a}$.
$$2\sqrt[3]{3a}\cdot 5\sqrt[3]{4a}\cdot 3\sqrt[3]{18a} = 2\cdot 5\cdot 3\cdot\sqrt[3]{3a}\cdot\sqrt[3]{4a}\cdot\sqrt[3]{18a}$$
$$= 30\sqrt[3]{216a^3}$$
$$= 30\cdot 6a$$
$$= 180a$$

Example 2: Multiply $\sqrt[4]{8t^3}$ and $\sqrt[4]{4t^5}$.
$$\sqrt[4]{8t^3}\cdot\sqrt[4]{4t^5} = \sqrt[4]{32t^8}$$
$$= \sqrt[4]{2^4\cdot 2\cdot t^4\cdot t\cdot 8}$$
$$= 2t\sqrt[4]{2t\,8}$$

b. Radicals With Different Indexes. To multiply radicals when the indexes are different, first express them as radicals with a common index (or common fractional exponent) and proceed as in *a* above. The common index is the lowest common multiple of the indexes of the original radicals.

Example 1: Multiply $\sqrt{2}\cdot\sqrt[3]{4}$.
$$\sqrt{2}\cdot\sqrt[3]{4} = \sqrt{2}\cdot\sqrt[3]{2^2}$$
$$= 2^{\frac{1}{2}}\cdot 2^{\frac{2}{3}}$$
$$= 2^{\frac{3}{6}}\cdot 2^{\frac{4}{6}}$$
$$= 2^{\frac{7}{6}}$$
$$= 2\cdot 2^{\frac{1}{6}}\text{ or }2\sqrt[6]{2}$$

Example 2: Multiply $\sqrt[3]{4x}\cdot\sqrt[4]{8x^3}$.
$$\sqrt[3]{4x}\cdot\sqrt[4]{8x^3} = \sqrt[12]{(4x)^4}\cdot\sqrt[12]{(8x^3)^3}$$
$$= \sqrt[12]{(2^2x)^4}\cdot\sqrt[12]{(2x^4)^3}$$
$$= \sqrt[12]{2^8\cdot 2^9\cdot x^4\cdot x^9}$$
$$= \sqrt[12]{2^{17}\cdot x^{13}}$$
$$= 2x\sqrt[12]{2^5\cdot x}$$
$$= 2x\sqrt[12]{32x}$$

75. Division of Radicals

a. Monomial Radical Expressions. The division of radicals is essentially the opposite of multiplication. When radicals are of the same order, the division of two radicals may be expressed under one radical sign—for example, $\dfrac{\sqrt{4}}{\sqrt{2}} = \sqrt{\dfrac{4}{2}} = \sqrt{2}$. When radicals are of different orders, they must be expressed as radicals having the same index or be changed to fractional exponents.

Example 1: Divide $\sqrt{15}$ by $\sqrt{5}$.
$$\frac{\sqrt{15}}{\sqrt{5}} = \sqrt{\frac{15}{5}} = \sqrt{3}$$

Example 2: Divide $\sqrt[3]{x^2y}$ by $\sqrt[3]{y^7}$.
$$\frac{\sqrt[3]{x^2y}}{\sqrt[3]{y^7}} = \sqrt[3]{\frac{x^2y}{y^7}}$$
$$= \sqrt[3]{\frac{x^2}{y^6}}$$
$$= \frac{x}{y^2}\sqrt[3]{x^2}$$

Example 3: Divide $\sqrt{35}$ by $\sqrt{15}$.
$$\frac{\sqrt{35}}{\sqrt{15}} = \sqrt{\frac{35}{15}}$$
$$= \sqrt{\frac{7}{3}}$$
$$= \frac{1}{3}\sqrt{21}$$

Example 4: Divide $\sqrt{4ab}\cdot\sqrt[3]{2ab}$ by $\sqrt[6]{4a^5b^3}$.
$$\frac{\sqrt{4ab}\cdot\sqrt[3]{2ab}}{\sqrt[6]{4a^5b^3}} = \frac{\sqrt[6]{(4ab)^3}\cdot\sqrt[6]{(2ab)^2}}{\sqrt[6]{4a^5b^3}}$$
$$= \sqrt[6]{\frac{64a^3b^3\cdot 4a^2b^2}{4a^5b^3}}$$
$$= \sqrt[6]{64b^2}$$
$$= \sqrt[6]{2^6b^2}\text{ or }(2b^2)^{\frac{1}{6}}$$
$$= 2\sqrt[3]{b}$$

b. Binomial Expressions With Radical in Divisor. When the divisor is a binomial in which one or more of the terms contains a square root, division is performed by first rationalizing the divisor. Multiply the numerator and denominator of the fraction by the denominator with the sign between the terms changed; then simplify the numerator and the denominator.

Example 1: Divide 3 by $4+\sqrt{6}$.
$$\frac{3}{4+\sqrt{6}} = \frac{3}{4+\sqrt{6}}\cdot\frac{4-\sqrt{6}}{4-\sqrt{6}}$$
$$= \frac{3(4-\sqrt{6})}{16-6}$$
$$= \frac{3}{10}(4-\sqrt{6})$$

243

Example 2: Divide $\sqrt{1+x} - \sqrt{1-x}$ by $\sqrt{1+x} + \sqrt{1-x}$.

$$\frac{\sqrt{1+x}-\sqrt{1-x}}{\sqrt{1+x}+\sqrt{1-x}} = \frac{\sqrt{1+x}-\sqrt{1-x}}{\sqrt{1+x}+\sqrt{1-x}} \cdot \frac{\sqrt{1+x}-\sqrt{1-x}}{\sqrt{1+x}-\sqrt{1-x}}$$

$$= \frac{(1+x)-2\sqrt{1-x^2}+(1-x)}{(1+x)-(1-x)}$$

$$= \frac{2-2\sqrt{1-x^2}}{2x}$$

$$= \frac{1-\sqrt{1-x^2}}{x}$$

76. Review Problems—Exponents and Radicals

a. Simplify.

(1) $2^{\frac{-1}{3}} \cdot 2^{\frac{2}{3}}$
(2) $2^{\frac{2}{3}}(8^{\frac{1}{3}})$
(3) $(8^{\frac{1}{3}})^2$
(4) $\sqrt{50}$
(5) $\sqrt[3]{\frac{1}{16}}$
(6) $\sqrt{18x-9}$
(7) $\sqrt[n]{\frac{6z^{2n}}{y^n}}$
(8) $(x^{10}y^5)^{\frac{1}{5}}$
(9) $(de^4)^{\frac{3}{4}}$
(10) $\left(\frac{64r^4}{s^8}\right)^{\frac{3}{2}}$
(10) $(a^5b^3)^{\frac{1}{6}}$

b. Express with radical signs.

(1) $4^{\frac{1}{3}}$
(2) $\frac{3}{a^2b^{\frac{2}{3}}}$
(3) $\frac{2}{6^{\frac{3}{5}}}$
(4) $(8f)^{\frac{1}{12}}$
(5) $5x^{-5}$
(6) $\frac{1}{a^4c^{1.5}}$
(7) $\frac{1}{6r^4}$
(8) $(8a^{26}s^8)^{\frac{1}{3}}$
(9) $(2r_1 + 3r_2)^{\frac{1}{2}}$
(10) $3(x^4y^8)^{\frac{1}{2}}$

c. Express with fractional exponents.

(1) $\sqrt[4]{a^3}$
(2) $\sqrt[3]{6z}$
(3) $6z\sqrt[3]{a^7}$
(4) $\sqrt[5]{z^2}$
(5) $\sqrt[5]{3a^2b^3}$
(6) $y^3\sqrt[3]{a^3}$
(7) $8\sqrt[3]{3e}$
(8) $9\sqrt[4]{g^7}$
(9) $3b\sqrt[5]{cd^2}$
(10) $\sqrt[n]{(x-y)^{12}}$

d. Simplify by removing suitable factors from radicand.

(1) $\sqrt{12}$
(2) $\sqrt{63}$
(3) $\sqrt{63x^5}$
(4) $2\sqrt{72x^{2}b^4}$
(5) $\sqrt{605d^7}$
(6) $\sqrt{81^2R}$
(7) $3\sqrt{63p^2z^7}$
(8) $2d^{x2}\sqrt{108d^7r^8}$
(9) $5a\sqrt{81a^2b}$
(10) $16a^2z\sqrt{98u^4z^{3}y^3z}$

e. Rationalize denominators.

(1) $\frac{1}{\sqrt{50}}$
(2) $\frac{1}{\sqrt{4x}}$
(3) $\frac{2a}{\sqrt{5a}}$
(4) $\frac{1}{\sqrt[3]{x}}$
(5) $\frac{1}{\sqrt[4]{8ax^2}}$
(6) $\frac{1}{\sqrt[3]{3}-2x}$
(7) $\frac{a+b}{\sqrt[3]{a^2}}$
(8) $\frac{a}{\sqrt[4]{a^3bc}}$
(9) $\frac{1}{\sqrt[3]{(s+1)^2}}$
(10) $\frac{i+3}{\sqrt[4]{(i+3)^2}}$

f. Simplify.

(1) $6\sqrt{4} - 3\sqrt{4} + 2\sqrt{4}$
(2) $6\sqrt{45} - 2\sqrt{20}$
(3) $x - \sqrt[5]{\frac{3x^2}{4}}$
(4) $\frac{a}{2} + \sqrt{\frac{9a^2}{2}}$
(5) $r\sqrt{rst} + rt\sqrt{\frac{s}{rt}}$
(6) $\sqrt{\frac{x+y}{z-y}} - \sqrt{\frac{x-y}{z+y}}$
(7) $\sqrt{5} + 3\sqrt{x} + 5\sqrt{x}$
(8) $7\sqrt{a} - 4\sqrt{5} - 2\sqrt{6}$
(9) $4\sqrt{x-y} + 3\sqrt{x+y} - 8\sqrt{x-y}$
(10) $3\sqrt{125a^5b^4} + b\sqrt{20a^7} - \sqrt{500a^6b^3}$

g. Find product and simplify.

(1) $3\sqrt{5} \cdot 4\sqrt{2}$
(2) $2\sqrt[3]{9} \cdot 3\sqrt[3]{3}$
(3) $4\sqrt[3]{a^2b^4} \cdot 2\sqrt[3]{ab^2}$
(4) $\sqrt[4]{a^2x^2} \cdot x\sqrt[3]{3x^4}$
(5) $\sqrt[4]{4x^2y^2} \cdot \sqrt[3]{2x^2y^2} \cdot \sqrt[4]{4xy^3}$
(6) $2\sqrt[3]{2pq^4r} \cdot \sqrt[4]{4pq^4r^3} \cdot 3\sqrt[3]{8pq^4r^2}$
(7) $(\sqrt{a} + \sqrt{b} + \sqrt{c})^2$
(8) $a\sqrt{x}(a\sqrt{ax} + x\sqrt{ax} + \sqrt{ax})$
(9) $\sqrt{9} - \sqrt{11} \cdot \sqrt{9} + \sqrt{11}$
(10) $\sqrt[4]{x^3y^2}\sqrt{256a^8}$

h. Divide and simplify.

(1) $\frac{\sqrt{12}}{\sqrt{3}}$
(2) $\frac{\sqrt[3]{625y}}{\sqrt[3]{5y}}$
(3) $\frac{\sqrt[3]{16x^2}}{\sqrt[3]{2x}}$
(4) $\frac{3zy}{\sqrt{zu}}$
(5) $\frac{\sqrt{5}-2}{2}$
(6) $\frac{\sqrt{30a}\sqrt[3]{24c^2}\sqrt[3]{72a}}{\sqrt{5a}}$
(7) $\frac{\sqrt{2}+\sqrt{c}}{\sqrt{c}+2\sqrt{2}}$
(8) $\frac{4\sqrt{3}-3\sqrt{2}}{\sqrt{6}} \div \frac{\sqrt{10}}{4\sqrt{3}+3\sqrt{2}}$
(9) $\frac{\sqrt{e^2+f^2+1}}{\sqrt{e^2+f^2-f}}$
(10) $\frac{2b+\sqrt{1-4b^2}}{2b-\sqrt{1-4b^2}}$

Section VII. IMAGINARY AND COMPLEX NUMBERS

77. Imaginary Numbers

a. Indicated Square Root of Negative Numbers.

(1) In the study of roots to this point, only the roots of positive numbers have been considered. Sometimes a negative expression will appear under the radical. Such an expression originally was given the designation *imaginary number* to distinguish it from real numbers. In electricity and electronics, however, so-called imaginary numbers are used for real physical calculations—the reactance of a large capacitor or inductor must be calculated by using this type of number.

(2) In multiplication, when a real number is multiplied by itself the result is always positive. For example, $+5 \cdot +5 = 25$, and $-5 \cdot -5 = 25$. Therefore, any number raised to a power having an even exponent will be positive because like signs are being multiplied. However, this is not true for the interpretation of an expression such as $\sqrt{-9}$. Any negative number can be regarded as the product of a positive number of the same absolute value and -1, and the square root of a negative

244

number can be written as the square root of a positive number times $\sqrt{-1}$; thus, $\sqrt{-9} = \sqrt{9}\sqrt{-1} = 3\sqrt{-1}$, with $\sqrt{-1}$ being the imaginary number. Most mathematics texts represent the imaginary number $\sqrt{-1}$ by the letter i. However, the letter I or i means current in electrical formulas; therefore, the letter j, commonly called the *operator j*, is used in electronics.

Example 1: Multiply $\sqrt{-36}$ and $\sqrt{-4}$.
$$\sqrt{-36} = \sqrt{(-1)36} = \sqrt{-1} \cdot \sqrt{36} = \sqrt{-1} \cdot 6 = j6$$
$$\sqrt{-4} = j^4 \cdot j^2 = j^28 = (-1)8 = -8$$

Example 2: Multiply $\sqrt{-Z^2}$ and $\sqrt{-4}$.
$$\sqrt{-Z^2} = \sqrt{(-1)Z^2} = \sqrt{-1} \cdot \sqrt{Z^2} = \sqrt{-1} \cdot Z = jZ$$

Example 3: $-\sqrt{-9a^2} = -\sqrt{(-1)9a^2} = -\sqrt{-1} \cdot \sqrt{9a^2} = -\sqrt{-1} \cdot 3a = -j3a$

b. Powers of Operator j. Imaginary numbers follow the fundamental laws of addition, subtraction, multiplication, and division. They also can be raised to a power; thus, $j^3 = j^2 \cdot j = -1(j) = -j$, and $j^4 = j^2 \cdot j^2 = -1(-1) = 1$. The values of the powers of j are obtained as follows:

$$j^2 = j \cdot j = \sqrt{-1} \cdot \sqrt{-1} = -1;$$
$$j^3 = j \cdot j \cdot j = \sqrt{-1} \cdot \sqrt{-1} \cdot \sqrt{-1} = -1\sqrt{-1} = -j;\text{ and}$$
$$j^4 = j \cdot j \cdot j \cdot j = \sqrt{-1} \cdot \sqrt{-1} \cdot \sqrt{-1} \cdot \sqrt{-1} = -1 \cdot -1 = 1;\text{ but}$$
$$j^5 = j \cdot j \cdot j \cdot j \cdot j = j^4 \cdot j = j^1 = \sqrt{-1},\text{ and the whole cycle starts over again. Therefore, } j^4$$

can be eliminated as many times as it is contained in an expression, reducing the quantity to j, j^2, or j^3 and getting its value from the following:

$$j \cdot j = \sqrt{-1}$$
$$j^2 = -1$$
$$j^3 = -j$$
$$j^4 = 1$$

Example 1: Simplify j^{13}.
$$j^{13} = j^{12} \cdot j = j = \sqrt{-1}$$

Example 2: Simplify j^{27}.
$$j^{27} = j^{24} \cdot j^3 = j^3 = -j = -\sqrt{-1}$$

c. Addition and Subtraction of Imaginary Numbers. These numbers may be added or subtracted in the same manner that any algebraic expression is added or subtracted (par. 44). First change the expression to the j form; then treat the j as any other letter in an algebraic expression.

Example 1: Add $\sqrt{-25}$, $\sqrt{-36}$, and $\sqrt{-9}$.
$$\sqrt{-25} + \sqrt{-36} + \sqrt{-9} = j5 + j6 + j3 = j14$$

Example 2: Add $6\sqrt{-2} + 5\sqrt{-8} + 8\sqrt{-18}$.
$$6\sqrt{-2} + 5\sqrt{-8} + 8\sqrt{-18} = j^2\sqrt{2} + j^5\sqrt{8} + j^8\sqrt{18}$$
$$= j^6\sqrt{2} + j(5 \cdot 2)\sqrt{2} + j(8 \cdot 3)\sqrt{2}$$
$$= (j^6 + j^{10} + j^{24})\sqrt{2}$$
$$= j^{40}\sqrt{2}$$

Example 3: Subtract $\sqrt{-64}$ from $\sqrt{-36}$.
$$\sqrt{-36} - \sqrt{-64} = j^6 - j^8 = -j^2$$

Example 4: Subtract $4\sqrt{-8}$ from $6\sqrt{-18}$.
$$6\sqrt{-18} - 4\sqrt{-8} = j(6 \cdot 3)\sqrt{2} - j(4 \cdot 2)\sqrt{2}$$
$$= (j^{18} - j^8)\sqrt{2}$$
$$= j^{10}\sqrt{2}$$

d. Multiplication of Simple Imaginary Numbers. When multiplying two imaginary numbers, remember that $j^2 = -1$, $j^3 = -j$, and $j^4 = 1$ (b above); then, proceed as with any problem in multiplication (par. 45).

Example 1: Multiply $\sqrt{-16}$ and $\sqrt{-4}$.
$$\sqrt{-16} \cdot \sqrt{-4} = j^4 \cdot j^2 = j^28 = (-1)8 = -8$$

Example 2: Multiply $\sqrt{-81}$, $\sqrt{-25}$, and $\sqrt{-49}$.
$$\sqrt{-81} \cdot \sqrt{-25} \cdot \sqrt{-49} = j^9 \cdot j^5 \cdot j^7 = j^3315 = (-j)315 = -j315$$

e. Division of Single Imaginary Numbers. In the division of two simple imaginary numbers, when both the dividend and divisor contain operator j, divide both by j and proceed as with ordinary integers. If a j remains in the denominator, the denominator must be rationalized because the j represents a radical expression. To rationalize, multiply both the numerator and denominator by the imaginary number.

Example 1: Divide $\sqrt{-100}$ by $\sqrt{-16}$.
$$\frac{\sqrt{-100}}{\sqrt{-16}} = \frac{j \cdot 10}{j \cdot 4} = 2\tfrac{1}{2}$$

Example 2: Divide 12 by $\sqrt{-6}$.
$$\frac{12}{\sqrt{-6}} = \frac{12}{j\sqrt{6}} = \frac{12 \cdot j\sqrt{6}}{j\sqrt{6} \cdot j\sqrt{6}} = \frac{j12\sqrt{6}}{j^26} = \frac{j2\sqrt{6}}{-1} = -j2\sqrt{6}$$

Example 3: Divide $\sqrt{-3}$ by $\sqrt{-4}$.
$$\frac{\sqrt{-3}}{\sqrt{-4}} = \frac{j\sqrt{3}}{j2} = \frac{\sqrt{3}}{2}\text{ or }\frac{1}{2}\sqrt{3}$$

Example 4: Divide 6 by j.
$$\frac{6}{j} = \frac{6}{j} \cdot \frac{j}{j} = \frac{j6}{j^2} = \frac{j6}{-1} = -j6$$

78. Complex Numbers

a. Operations With Complex Numbers. A *complex number* is a real number united to an imaginary number by a plus or minus sign; thus, $10 - j5$, $x + jy$, and $R + jx$ are complex numbers. Complex numbers are of great importance in alternating-current electricity in which many problems would be difficult to solve without their use. A complex number expressed in the form $x + jy$ may be considered a binomial; thus, the addition, subtraction, multiplication, and division of complex numbers are reduced to the corresponding operations with binomials in which one term is real and the other imaginary.

b. Addition and Subtraction of Complex Numbers. To add or subtract complex numbers, first combine the real parts, then combine the imaginary parts, and write the results as a binomial with the appropriate sign separating the real and imaginary terms.

Example 1: Add $3 + j5$ and $5 - j$.
$$(3 + j5) + (5 - j) = 3 + j5 + 5 - j$$
$$= 8 + j4$$

Example 2: Add $6 + \sqrt{-25}$ and $8\sqrt{-16}$.
$$(6 + \sqrt{-25}) + (8\sqrt{-16}) = 6 + j5 + (8 \cdot j4)$$
$$= 6 + j5 + j32$$
$$= 6 + j37$$

Example 3: Add $8 + \sqrt{-12}$ and $9 + \sqrt{-75}$.
$$(8 + \sqrt{-12}) + (9 + \sqrt{-75}) = 8 + j2\sqrt{3} + 9 + j5\sqrt{3}$$
$$= 17 + j7\sqrt{3}$$

Example 4: Subtract $7 - j6$ from $3 - j2$.
$$(3 - j2) - (7 - j6) = 3 - j2 - 7 + j6$$
$$= -4 + j4$$

Example 5: Subtract $2 - 3\sqrt{-4}$ from $10 + \sqrt{-4}$.
$$(10 + \sqrt{-4}) - (2 - 3\sqrt{-4}) = (10 + j2) - (2 - j6)$$
$$= 10 + j2 - 2 + j6$$
$$= 8 + j8 \text{ or } 8(1+j)$$

Example 6: Subtract $3 + 7\sqrt{-24}$ from $5 + 3\sqrt{-6}$.
$$(5 + 3\sqrt{-6}) - (3 + 7\sqrt{-24}) = 5 + j3\sqrt{6} - [3 + j(7 \cdot 2)\sqrt{6}]$$
$$= 5 + j3\sqrt{6} - 3 - j14\sqrt{6}$$
$$= 2 - j11\sqrt{6}$$

c. Multiplication of Complex Numbers. As in addition and subtraction, when complex numbers are multiplied they are treated as ordinary binomials. Remember, however, that $j^2 = -1$.

Example 1: Multiply $3 - j6$ by $4 + j2$.

$$\begin{array}{r} 3 - j6 \\ 4 + j2 \\ \hline 12 - j24 \\ +j6 - j^2 12 \\ \hline 12 - j18 - j^2 12 \end{array} = j12 - j18 - (-1)(12)$$
$$= 12 - j18 + 12$$
$$= 24 - j18$$

Example 2: Multiply $8 \div \sqrt{-5}$ by $-2 + \sqrt{-6}$.

$$\begin{array}{r} 8 - j\sqrt{5} \\ -2 + j\sqrt{6} \\ \hline -16 + j2\sqrt{5} + j8\sqrt{6} - j^2\sqrt{30} \end{array} = -16 + j2\sqrt{5} + j8\sqrt{6} - (-1)\sqrt{30}$$
$$= -16 + j2\sqrt{5} + j8\sqrt{6} + \sqrt{30}$$
$$= -16 + \sqrt{30} + j(2\sqrt{5} + 8\sqrt{6})$$

d. Division of Complex Numbers. When dividing complex numbers, the denominator of the expression in its fractional form must first be rationalized (par. 74). To obtain a real number as a divisor, multiply both the numerator and denominator by the complex number of the denominator with its sign changed (called the *conjugate* of the complex number). In carrying out the multiplication, the radical expression is eliminated. Since $j^2 = -1$, the sign of the coefficient of j^2 is changed; the complex number thus becomes a real number to combine with the other real number in the denominator.

Example 1: Divide $3 + j4$ by $1 + j$.
$$\frac{3 + j4}{1 + j} = \frac{3 + j4}{1 + j} \cdot \frac{1 - j}{1 - j}$$
$$= \frac{3 + j - j^2 4}{1 - j^2}$$
$$= \frac{3 + j + 4}{2}$$
$$= \frac{7}{2} + j\frac{1}{2}$$

Example 2: Divide 6 by $3 + \sqrt{-2}$.
$$\frac{6}{3 + \sqrt{-2}} = \frac{6}{3 + j\sqrt{2}} \cdot \frac{3 - j\sqrt{2}}{3 - j\sqrt{2}}$$
$$= \frac{6(3 - j\sqrt{2})}{(3 + j\sqrt{2})(3 - j\sqrt{2})}$$
$$= \frac{18 - j6\sqrt{2}}{9 - j^2 2}$$
$$= \frac{18 - j6\sqrt{2}}{11}$$

79. Review Problems—Imaginary and Complex Numbers

a. Simplify the radical, using operator j.
 (1) $\sqrt{-75}$
 (2) $\sqrt{-23}$
 (3) $-\sqrt{-64ax^2}$
 (4) $-\sqrt{-100x^4y^4}$
 (5) $\sqrt{-\frac{1}{9}}$
 (6) $\sqrt[3]{-128x^3y^3}$

b. Add.
 (1) $-47 + j17$ and $63 + j92$
 (2) $27 - j11$ and $14 - j11$
 (3) $123 - j11i$ and $-62 - j137$
 (4) $44 + j17$ and $-j7$
 (5) $6 + j10$ and $j1$
 (6) $14 + j15$ and $-16 - j62$

c. Subtract.
 (1) $-69 + j432$ from $710 + j61$
 (2) $14 - j121$ from $73 - j7$
 (3) $84 - j62$ from $62 - j47$
 (4) $-74 - j20$ from $81 - j81$
 (5) $-87 - j7$ from $82 + j16$
 (6) $-9 + j$ from $-j7$

d. Multiply.
 (1) $4 + \sqrt{-81}$ by $2 + \sqrt{-49}$
 (2) $2 + 2\sqrt{-2}$ by $8 + 3\sqrt{-3}$
 (3) $2 - j3$ by $2 + j3$
 (4) $(2 - j3)^2$
 (5) $(j^4 + j^7 2 + j^7 3 + j4)^3$
 (6) $4 - j7$ by $8 + j2$
 (7) $f + jg$ by $f + jg$
 (8) $I + jE$ by $I - jE$
 (9) $8 - j13$ by $11 - j12$
 (10) $5 + \sqrt{-16}$ by $7 - \sqrt{-81}$

e. Divide.
 (1) 1 by $3 + j2$
 (2) $6 + j$ by j
 (3) $2 + j3$ by $3 - j4$
 (4) $4 + \sqrt{-9}$ by $2 - \sqrt{-1}$
 (5) $x + jy$ by $x - jy$
 (6) 10 by $1 + j2$
 (7) 3 by $1 - j$
 (8) $3 + \sqrt{-25}$ by $4 - \sqrt{-4}$
 (9) $6 - j2$ by $4 - j7$
 (10) $I + jE$ by $I - jE$

Section VIII. EQUATIONS

80. General

An *equation* is a statement of equality between two expressions. For example, $x + y = 12$, $3x + 5 = 20$, and $3 \cdot 9 = 27$ are equations; therefore, all expressions separated by the equality sign are equations, whether the expressions are algebraic or arithmetical. The expression to the left of the equality sign is called the *left-hand member* of the equation; the expression to the right of the equality sign is called the *right-hand member*. Finding the values of the unknown quantities of an algebraic equation is known as solving the equation, and the answer is called the *solution*. If only one unknown is involved, the solution is also called the *root*.

81. Solving Simple Equations

a. Adding Same Quantity to Both Members of Equation. Equal quantities may be added to both sides of an equation without changing the equality.

Example 1: Solve the equation $x - 4 = 7$ for x.

$$x - 4 = 7$$
$$x - 4 + 4 = 7 + 4$$
$$x = 11$$

Example 2: Solve the equation $x - 7 = 14$ for x.

$$x - 7 = 14$$
$$x - 7 + 7 = 14 + 7$$
$$x = 21$$

b. Subtracting Same Quantity From Both Members of Equation. Equal quantities may be subtracted from both sides of an equation.

Example 1: Solve the equation $x + 2 = 5$ for x.

$$x + 2 = 5$$
$$x + 2 - 2 = 5 - 2$$
$$x = 3$$

Example 2: Solve the equation $x + 5 = 12$ for x.

$$x + 5 = 12$$
$$x + 5 - 5 = 12 - 5$$
$$x = 7$$

c. Multiplying Both Members of Equation by Same Quantity. Both sides of an equation can be multiplied by the same quantity.

Example 1: Solve the equation $\frac{x}{3} = 5$ for x.

$$\frac{x}{3} = 5$$
$$\frac{x}{3} \cdot \frac{3}{1} = 5 \cdot 3$$
$$x = 15$$

Example 2: Solve the equation $\frac{z}{9} + \frac{z}{9} = 4$ for x.

Multiply both sides of the equation by 9.

$$\left(\frac{z}{3} \cdot \frac{9}{1}\right) + \left(\frac{z}{9} \cdot \frac{9}{1}\right) = 4 \cdot 9$$
$$3z + z = 36$$
$$4z = 36$$
$$z = 9$$

d. Dividing Both Members of Equation by Same Quantity. Both sides of an equation may be divided by the same quantity.

Example 1: Solve the equation $3x = 12$ for x.

$$3x = 12$$
$$\frac{3x}{3} = \frac{12}{3}$$
$$x = 4$$

Example 2: Solve the equation $PV = RT$ for T.

$$PV = RT$$
$$\frac{PV}{R} = \frac{RT}{R}$$
$$T = \frac{PV}{R}$$

82. Solving More Difficult Equations

a. Transposition. The process of adding to or subtracting from both members of an equation (par. 81a and b) can be shortened by shifting a term or terms from one side of the equation to the other and changing the signs. This operation is called transposition.

Example 1: Solve the equation $6x + 4 = x - 16$ for x.

$$6x + 4 = x - 16$$
$$6x - x = -16 - 4$$
$$5x = -20$$
$$x = -4$$

Example 2: Solve the equation $5a - 7 = 2a + 2$ for a.

$$5a - 7 = 2a + 2$$
$$5a - 2a = 2 + 7$$
$$3a = 9$$
$$a = 3$$

b. Equations With Fractions. In solving a fractional equation, first find the LCD and multiply both members of the equation, term by term; then perform the operations in paragraph 81 or a above.

Example 1: Solve the equation $\frac{x}{2} + \frac{x}{3} = 10$ for x.

$$\frac{x}{2} + \frac{2x}{3} = 10$$
$$\frac{3x + 2x}{6} = 10$$
$$\frac{5x}{6} = \frac{10}{1}$$
$$5x = 60$$
$$x = 12$$

Example 2: Solve the equation $\frac{x-1}{2} = 3 + x$ for x.

$$\frac{x-1}{2} = 3 + x$$
$$\frac{x-1}{2} = \frac{3+x}{1}$$
$$1(x - 1) = 2(3 + x)$$
$$x - 1 = 6 + 2x$$
$$x - 2x = 6 + 1$$
$$-x = 7$$
$$x = -7$$

Example 3: Solve the equation $\frac{2}{x+4} = \frac{4}{x-3} = \frac{2}{x-2}+$ for x.

$$\frac{2}{x+4} = \frac{4}{x-3} = \frac{4}{x-3}$$

$$\frac{2(x+4) + 2(x-2)}{(x-2)(x+4)} = \frac{4}{x-3}$$

$$\frac{(x-2)(x+4)}{(x-2)(x+4)} = \frac{4}{x-3}$$

$$\frac{2x + 8 + 2x - 4}{(x-2)(x+4)} = \frac{4}{x-3}$$

$$\frac{4x + 4}{(x-2)(x+4)} = \frac{4}{x-3}$$

$$(4x + 4)(x - 3) = 4(x - 2)(x + 4)$$
$$4x^2 - 8x - 12 = 4(x^2 + 2x - 8)$$
$$4x^2 - 8x - 12 = 4x^2 + 8x - 32$$
$$-4x^2 - 8x - 8x = -32 + 12$$
$$-16x = -20$$
$$16x = 20$$
$$x = \frac{20}{16} = \frac{5}{4} = 1\frac{1}{4}$$

83. Written Equations

Many practical problems are stated in words and must be translated into symbols before the rules of algebra can be applied. There are no specific rules for the translation of a written problem into an equation of numbers, signs, and symbols. The following general suggestions may be helpful in developing equations:

a. From the worded statement of the problem, select the unknown quantity (or one of the unknown quantities) and represent it by a letter, such as x. Write the expression, stating exactly what x represents and the units in which it is measured.

b. If there is more than one unknown quantity in the problem, try to represent each unknown in terms of the first unknown.

Example 1: In simple problems, an equation may be written by an almost direct translation into algebraic symbols; thus,

Seven times a certain voltage diminished by 3
$$7 \quad \times \quad E \quad - \quad 3$$

gives the same result as the voltage increased by 75,
$$= \qquad E \quad + \quad 75.$$

Solving the equation:

$$7E - 3 = E + 75$$
$$7E - E = 75 + 3$$
$$6E = 78$$
$$E = 13$$

Check: $7(13) - 3 = 13 + 75$
$91 - 3 = 13 + 75$
$88 = 88$

Example 2: A triangle has a perimeter of 30 inches. The longest side is 7 inches longer than the shortest side, and the third side is 5 inches longer than the shortest side. Find the length of the three sides.

Let $x =$ length of shortest side.
$x + 7 =$ length of longest side.
$x + 5 =$ length of third side.
$x + (x + 5) + (x + 7) = 30$

Solving the equation:
$x + x + 5 + x + 7 = 30$
$3x + 12 = 30$
$3x = 30 - 12$
$3x = 18$
$x = 6 =$ shortest side.
$6 + 5 = 11 =$ third side.
$6 + 7 = 13 =$ longest side.

84. Simultaneous Equations

a. Definition. Simultaneous equations are two or more equations satisfied by the same sets of values of the unknown quantities. They are used to solve a problem with two or more unknown quantities.

b. Example. Assume that the sum of two numbers is 17, and that three times the first number less two times the second number is equal to 6. What are the numbers? In setting up equations for this problem, let x equal the first number and y equal the second number. The first equation is $x + y = 17$, and the second equation is $3x - 2y = 6$. This problem can be solved in three ways: by substitution, by addition, or by subtraction. All three methods are explained below.

(1) *Substitution.*
$x + y = 17$ or $x = 17 - y$

Substitute $x = 17 - y$ in the second equation:
$3x - 2y = 6$
$3(17 - y) - 2y = 6$

Remove the parentheses:
$51 - 3y - 2y = 6$

Transpose:
$-5y = 6 - 51$
$-5y = -45$
$5y = 45$
$y = 9$

$3x + 3y = 51$
$-3x + 2y = -6$
$5y = 45$
$y = 9$

Substitute $y = 9$ in the first equation and solve for x: Refer to (1) and (2) above.

c. Additional Examples. If the coefficients of the unknowns differ (for example, $3x$ and x and $2y$ and $4y$), multiply one or both equations to establish equal coefficients for one of the unknowns (x or y).

Example 1: Solve for x and y if $3x + 2y = 7$ and $x + 4y = 9$.
$3x + 2y = 7$
$x + 4y = 9$

Multiply the first equation by 2 so that $2y$ will become $4y$:
$6x + 4y = 14$
$x + 4y = 9$

Subtract the second equation from the first equation:
$6x + 4y = 14$
$-x - 4y = -9$
$5x = 5$
$x = 1$

Solve for y by substituting $x = 1$ in either equation.

Example 2: Solve for x and y if $2x + 3y = 24$ and $3x - 4y = 2$.
$2x + 3y = 24$
$3x - 4y = 2$

Multiply the first equation by 4 to change $3y$ to $12y$; multiply the second equation by 3 to change $4y$ to $12y$; then add the two equations:
$8x + 12y = 96$
$9x - 12y = 6$
$17x = 102$
$x = 6$

Solve for y by substituting $x = 6$ in either equation.

85. Solving Formulas

a. The Formula. A formula is a rule or law that states a scientific relationship. It can be expressed in an equation by using letters, symbols, and constant terms. For example, a formula in electricity states that the voltage across any part of a circuit is equal to the product of the current and resistance of that part of the circuit. In formula form, this is expressed as $E = IR$, where E is the *voltage or difference in potential* expressed in *volts*, I is the *current* expressed in *amperes*, and R is the *resistance* expressed in *ohms*.

b. Solving the Formula. To solve a formula, perform the same operations on both members of an equation until the desired unknown can be isolated in one member of the equation. If the numerical values for some variables are given, substitute in the formula and solve for the unknown as in any other equation.

Example 1: Solve the formula $T = \dfrac{12(D - d)}{l}$ for D.

$T = \dfrac{12(D - d)}{l}$

Multiply both sides by l:
$Tl = 12D - 12d$

Transpose and change signs:
$12D = Tl + 12d$

Divide both sides by 12:
$\dfrac{12D}{12} = \dfrac{Tl}{12} + \dfrac{12d}{12}$

$D = \dfrac{Tl}{12} + d$

Example 2: Given the formula for electrical power, $P = I^2R$, find the value of P in watts when $I = 15.4$ amperes and $R = 25.7$ ohms.
$P = I^2R$

Substituting the given numerical values for I and R:
$P = (15.4)^2 \times 25.7$
$= 237.16 \times 25.7$
$= 6{,}095$ watts

Example 3: Given the formula for the total resistance of two resistors in parallel, $R_T = \dfrac{R_1 R_2}{R_1 + R_2}$, solve for R_x in ohms when

$R_1 = 40$ ohms and $R_2 = 60$ ohms.

$$R_T = \frac{R_1 R_2}{R_1 + R_2}$$

Substitute the given numerical values for R_1 and R_2:

$$R_T = \frac{40 \times 60}{40 + 60}$$
$$= \frac{2,400}{100}$$
$$= 24 \text{ ohms}$$

86. Review Problems—Equations

a. Solve for the unknown quantity in each of the following:

(1) $y + 12 = 15$
(2) $\frac{n}{8} = \frac{1}{4}$
(3) $0.63s = 53.55$
(4) $47z - 17 = 235 - 37z$
(5) $(10m + 6) - (11 - 15m) = 14m + 6m$
(6) $x + y = 3$
    $3x + 2y = 1$
(7) $a - 3b = 0$
    $5a - 4b = 11$
(8) $7x - 5y = 1$
    $5x + y = 19$
(9) $4m - 2n = 2$
    $3m + n = 14$
(10) $3r - 9s = 15$
     $6r - 7s = 41$

b. Solve the following formulas for the quantity indicated:

(1) $Fd = Wh$ for d
(2) $v^2 = v_0^2 + 2gh$ for g
(3) $F = \frac{w}{y}a$ for a
(4) $H = \frac{D^2 N}{2,534}$ for N
(5) $F = \frac{22.5\, BIl}{10^8}$ for l

c. Solve the following linear equations for the unknown quantity:

(1) $7(2x - 6) - 8 = 10x + 10$
(2) $10(x - 2) - 10(2 - x) = 4x - 40$
(3) $9.8a - 9.4 = 6.8a + .6$
(4) $2x + 3 + \frac{11x - 11}{3} = 22$
(5) $3R + 2(R - 4) = 6R - 10(R - 2)$
(6) $\frac{5Z}{4} + 2Z = \frac{3 + Z}{3} - 7Z$
(7) $-(5x + 15) = 5x + 21 - \frac{5(2-x)}{2} =$
(8) $\frac{11y - 13}{25} + \frac{17y + 4}{21} + \frac{19y}{7} + \frac{3}{7} =$
    $28\frac{1}{7} + \frac{5y - 25\frac{1}{3}}{4}$
(9) $\frac{4X_L}{5} - 6X_L + 2 = \frac{X_L}{4}$
(10) $(x - 1)(x + 1) + x(1 - x) = 4x(2x + 1) - 8x(x - 2)$

d. Solve the following sets of simultaneous linear equations:

(1) $5x - 2y = 10$
    $3x - y = 7$
(2) $6a + 15b = 69$
    $6a - 6b = 14$
(3) $x - 3y = -17$
    $2x + 6y = 50$
(4) $6x - 8y = 20$
    $3x + 2y = -14$
(5) $-4x + y = 13$
    $8x - 5y = -29$
(6) $2l + \frac{2Z - 22}{3} = 30$
    $\frac{3l - 15}{4} + 6Z = 108$
(7) $\frac{2}{x} + y = 1$
    $\frac{1}{x} + 2y = 1\frac{1}{4}$
(8) $\frac{a}{3} + \frac{b}{4} = 1$
    $\frac{a}{5} + \frac{b}{2} = -\frac{4}{5}$
(9) $\frac{5}{x} + \frac{2}{y} = -1$
    $\frac{3}{x} + \frac{1}{y} = 1\frac{1}{2}$
(10) Solve for r and s:
     $(a - b)r + (a + b)s = a^2 - b^2$
     $(a + b)r - (a - b)s = 2ab$

e. Solve the following problems:

(1) Three times a voltage (E) diminished by 2 is equal to that voltage. What is the voltage?
(2) The sum of two resistances in series is R ohms. One resistance is 20 ohms. Give the algebraic expression for the other.
(3) If a certain voltage (E) is tripled and the result is diminished by 220 volts, the remainder is equal to the original voltage. What is the voltage?
(4) When two resistors are connected in series, the total resistance (R) is the sum of the two resistances. If one resistor is 25 ohms and the total resistance is 100 ohms, what is the value of the other resistor?
(5) The current (I) from a battery is divided among three circuits. The first circuit draws 20 milliamperes more than the second circuit, and the second circuit draws 20 milliamperes more than the third circuit. If the total current drawn is 240 milliamperes, what is the current in each circuit?
(6) Solving by the formula $I = \frac{E}{R}$, how much current (I) does an electric circuit having a resistance (R) of 20 ohms take if the voltage (E) is 110 volts?

Section IX. QUADRATIC EQUATIONS

87. General

A quadratic equation is one which can be reduced to the form $ax^2 + bx + c = 0$ where a, b, and c are known and x is the unknown quantity. In other words, a quadratic equation contains the square of the unknown quantity, such as x^2, but no higher power. For example, $3x^2 + 5x - 2 = 0$ and $x^2 - 4x + 3 = 0$ are quadratic equations. The form $ax^2 + bx + c = 0$ is called the *general quadratic equation*.

88. Pure Quadratic Equations

A pure quadratic equation is obtained from the general quadratic equation when b is equal to zero and the middle term (bx) does not appear. The equation then becomes $ax^2 + c = 0$. The pure quadratic equation has two roots that are equal in absolute value but have opposite signs. As discussed in paragraph 49, all numbers have two square roots. The equation $x^2 - 36 = 0$ is a pure quadratic equation since there are two numbers which, when substituted for x, will satisfy the equation. Thus $(+6)^2 - 36 = 0$ since $36 - 36 = 0$; also, $(-6)^2 - 36 = 0$ since $36 - 36 = 0$. Therefore, $x = \pm 6$.

Example: Solve the equation $x^2 - 5 = 20$ for x.

$$x^2 - 5 = 20$$
$$x^2 = 25$$
$$x = \pm 5$$

Check:
$$(\pm 5)^2 - 5 = 20$$
$$25 - 5 = 20$$
$$20 = 20$$

89. Solution by Factoring

a. Quadratic equations are found in many applications of even the simplest nature. For example, suppose that a sheet of metal is to be cut so that it has an area of 30 square inches, and that the length of the piece will be 1 inch longer than the width. With x representing the unknown width and $x + 1$ the unknown length, $x(x + 1)$ equals the area; therefore, the equation that must be satisfied is $x(x + 1) = 30$. By performing the indicated multiplication and subtracting 30 from each side, the equation now can be written in the form of a quadratic equation, as $x^2 + x - 30 = 0$.

b. To solve this equation, factor the left-hand side into the equivalent equation: $(x - 5)(x + 6) = 0$. The product of two factors is zero if either of the factors is zero (par. 53). Thus, each factor is set equal to zero and solved for the unknown. The equation is satisfied if $x - 5 = 0$ or $x = 5$. Also, $(-6)^2 - 36 = 0$. Note that the equation also is satisfied if $x + 6 = 0$. This illustrates an important fact concerning quadratic equations: *Every quadratic equation has two solutions.* Only one solution, however, may be appropriate when quadratic equations are used to solve actual problems. The quadratic equation only gives two *possible* solutions—the *actual* solution must be determined by referring to the facts in the original problem.

Example 1: Solve the equation $x^2 - 2x = 0$ for x.

$$x^2 - 2x = 0$$

Factoring:
$$x(x-2) = 0$$
so $\quad x = 0$
or $\quad x - 2 = 0$
$\quad x = 2$

Thus, 0 or 2 are the roots of the equation $x^2 - 2x = 0$.

Example 2: Solve the equation $2x^2 - 3x - 5 = 0$ for x.

$$2x^2 - 3x - 5 = 0$$

Factoring:
$$(2x - 5)(x + 1) = 0$$
so $\quad x + 1 = 0$
$\quad x = -1$
and $\quad 2x - 5 = 0$
or $\quad 2x = 5$
and $\quad x = \frac{5}{2} \text{ or } 2\frac{1}{2}$

Thus, -1 and $2\frac{1}{2}$ are the roots of the equation $2x^2 - 3x - 5 = 0$.

90. Solution by Completing the Square

In solving quadratic equations, the method of factoring described in paragraph 89 usually is best if the factors are immediately apparent by inspection. When the values of the unknown are not whole numbers or rational fractions, a quadratic equation can be solved more easily by the method of *completing the square*. This method also is used to derive the quadratic formula (par. 91). For example, to solve the equation $2x^2 - x - 2 = 0$ by completing the square, proceed as follows:

a. Transpose all terms involving x to the left-hand side of the equation and all other terms to the right-hand side. The equation is now in the form $2x^2 - x = 2$, or $x^2 - \frac{1}{2}x = 1$. When using this method, the coefficient of the squared term must be unity (one).

b. Add a number to both sides of the equation so that the left-hand side will be a perfect trinomial square. To determine this number, divide the coefficient of the middle term ($-\frac{1}{2}$) by 2 and square the resulting number.

$$x^2 - \frac{1}{2}x = 1$$

$$x^2 - \frac{1}{2}x + \frac{1}{16} = 1 + \frac{1}{16}$$

c. Replace the trinomial square on the left-hand side of the equation with the square of a binomial.

$$(x - \frac{1}{4})^2 = \frac{17}{16}$$

d. Extract the square root of both sides of the equation.

$$x - \frac{1}{4} = \pm \frac{\sqrt{17}}{4}$$

Thus, $\quad x = \frac{1 \pm \sqrt{17}}{4}$

91. The General Quadratic Equation

a. General. Another method of solving quadratic equations consists of substitution in a formula derived from the general quadratic equation (*b* below). The general quadratic equation is in the form $ax^2 + bx + c = 0$, and any quadratic equation can be written in this form (par. 87). Thus, in the equation $2x^2 + 5x - 3 = 0$, $a = 2$, $b = 5$, and $c = -3$. Similarly, in the equation $9x^2 - 25 = 0$, $a = 9$, $b = 0$, and $c = -25$.

b. Deriving Formula for Solving any Quadratic Equation. Since the general quadratic equation, $ax^2 + bx + c = 0$, represents any quadratic equation, the roots of this equation will represent the roots of any quadratic equation; then, if the general quadratic equation is solved for the unknown values, the roots obtained will serve as a formula for finding the roots of any quadratic equation. The formula is derived from the general form by the method of completing the square; thus, given the general equation $ax^2 + bx + c = 0$, proceed as follows:

(1) Divide through by the coefficient a.

$$x^2 + \frac{bx}{a} + \frac{c}{a} = 0$$

(2) Subtract the term $\frac{c}{a}$ from both sides of the equation.

$$x^2 + \frac{bx}{a} = -\frac{c}{a}$$

This operation prepares the equation for the addition of a quantity to both sides of the equation that will make the left-hand side a perfect square. This quantity is obtained by dividing the coefficient of the x term by 2, and squaring the quotient. Since the coefficient of the x term is $\frac{b}{a}$, the quantity to be added to both sides of the equation is $(\frac{b}{2a})^2$, or $\frac{b^2}{4a^2}$.

(3) Add $\frac{b^2}{4a^2}$ to both sides of the equation.

$$x^2 + \frac{bx}{a} + \frac{b^2}{4a^2} = \frac{b^2}{4a^2} - \frac{c}{a}$$

(4) Factor the left-hand side of the equation, and add the fraction on the right-hand side.

$$(x + \frac{b}{2a})^2 = \frac{b^2 - 4ac}{4a^2}$$

(5) Take the square root of both sides of the equation.

$$x + \frac{b}{2a} = \pm \frac{\sqrt{b^2 - 4ac}}{2a}$$

(6) Subtract $\frac{b}{2a}$ from both sides of the equation.

$$x = -\frac{b}{2a} \pm \frac{\sqrt{b^2 - 4ac}}{2a}$$

(7) Collect the terms on the right-hand side of the equation.

$$x = \frac{-b \pm \sqrt{b^2 - 4ac}}{2a}$$

This equation is known as the *quadratic formula*. The two roots of any quadratic equation can be obtained by substituting in the formula the particular values of a, b, and c.

92. Solution by the Quadratic Formula

In practical problems, pure quadratic equations (par. 88) are seldom found, and solution by factoring (par. 89) can be used only occasionally. However, any quadratic equation can be solved by the method of completing the square (par. 90)—the method used to derive the quadratic formula (par. 91). This method is unnecessary, however, when the values for a, b, and c for any quadratic equation can be substituted in the formula $x = \frac{-b \pm \sqrt{b^2 - 4ac}}{2a}$.

Example 1: Solve the equation $2x^2 - 6x + 8 = 0$ by using the quadratic formula.

$$2x^2 - 6x + 3 = 0$$
$$a = 2; b = -6; c = 3$$

Substituting in the formula:

$$x = \frac{-b \pm \sqrt{b^2 - 4ac}}{2a}$$

$$x = \frac{-(-6) \pm \sqrt{36 - (4)(2)(3)}}{4}$$

$$= \frac{6 \pm \sqrt{12}}{4}$$

$$= \frac{3 \pm \sqrt{3}}{2}$$

Thus, $x = \frac{3 + \sqrt{3}}{2}$ or $x = \frac{3 - \sqrt{3}}{2}$.

Check: $x = \frac{3 + \sqrt{3}}{2}$

$$x = \frac{3 + 1.732}{2} = 2.366$$

Substituting in the equation:
$$2(2.366)^2 - 6(2.366) + 3 = 0$$
$$11.20 - 14.20 + 3 = 0$$
$$14.20 - 14.20 = 0$$

$$x = \frac{3 - \sqrt{3}}{2}$$

$$x = \frac{3 - 1.732}{2} = .634$$

Substituting in the equation:
$$2(.634)^2 - 6(.634) + 3 = 0$$
$$2(.40) - 3.80 + 3 = 0$$
$$3.80 - 3.80 = 0$$

= 0 by using the quadratic formula.

$$3x^2 + 5x - 2 = 0$$
$$a = 3; b = 5; c = -2$$

Substituting in the formula:

$$x = \frac{-b \pm \sqrt{b^2 - 4ac}}{2a}$$

$$x = \frac{-5 \pm \sqrt{25 - (4)(3)(-2)}}{(2)(3)}$$

$$= \frac{-5 \pm 7}{6}$$

Thus, $x = \frac{1}{3}$ or $x = -2$.

Check: $x = \frac{1}{3}$

Substituting in the equation:

$$3\left(\frac{1}{3}\right)^2 + 5\left(\frac{1}{3}\right) - 2 = 0$$

$$\frac{3}{9} + \frac{5}{3} - 2 = 0$$

$$\frac{1}{3} + \frac{5}{3} - \frac{6}{3} = 0$$

$$\frac{6}{3} - \frac{6}{3} = 0$$

$$x = -2$$

Substituting in the equation:

$$3(-2)^2 + 5(-2) - 2 = 0$$
$$12 - 10 - 2 = 0$$
$$12 - 12 = 0$$

93. Character of the Roots

a. The values for unknowns that are not *irrational roots*. A *rational* number is a number which can be expressed as the ratio of two integers. For example, 9, $\frac{7}{3}$, $\frac{1}{8}$, and $\sqrt{16}$ are rational numbers. Any whole number is rational since it is the quotient of itself and unity; thus, $9 = \frac{9}{1}$. Numbers such as $\frac{7}{3}$ and $\frac{1}{8}$ are often referred to as rational fractions. A radical is rational if it can be expressed as the quotient of two whole numbers. Thus $\sqrt{16}$ is rational since $\sqrt{16} = 4 = \frac{4}{1}$. A number such as $\sqrt{3}$ which cannot be written as the ratio of two whole numbers is called irrational. Rational and irrational numbers, taken together, make up the system of real numbers. Any number, such as $3 + \sqrt{3}$, which contains a radical sign that cannot be removed also is considered irrational. Roots of quadratic equations are real if a minus sign does not occur under a radical. For example, $x = 5$ is a real root—roots such as $x = \frac{3 + \sqrt{3}}{2}$ or $x = \frac{-\sqrt{3}}{2}$ are real, but irrational.

b. One important fact to be remembered when using the quadratic formula is that the expression under the radical sign, $b^2 - 4ac$, must be regarded as a whole before the square root can be taken. The quantity $b^2 - 4ac$ is called the *discriminant* of the quadratic equation. Many things can be learned about a quadratic equation merely by inspecting the discriminant. If the value of the discriminant is positive, real roots will be obtained when the equation is solved. These roots are either rational or irrational—rational when the discriminant is a perfect square, irrational when it is not. The roots are equal only when the value of $b^2 - 4ac$ is zero. When $b^2 - 4ac$ is negative, the square root will be that of a negative number and the roots will be imaginary.

c. In summary, a *quadratic equation always has two solutions*. The solutions will be:

Real and equal _____ if $b^2 - 4ac$ equals 0.
Unequal but real ____ if $b^2 - 4ac$ is positive.
Real and rational ____ if $b^2 - 4ac$ is a perfect square.
Imaginary _____ if $b^2 - 4ac$ is negative.

94. Review Problems—Quadratic Equations

a. Solve by factoring.

(1) $2x^2 + 3x = 0$
(2) $(x - 4)x = 0$
(3) $(x + 3)\frac{x}{3} = 0$
(4) $\frac{1}{4}x^2 + \frac{1}{4}x = 0$
(5) $2x^4 - 128 = 0$
(6) $\frac{1}{4}x^2 - 2 = 1$
(7) $3x^2 - 25 = 2$
(8) $3x(x - 2) + 2x(3 - x) = 16$
(9) $x^2 - x - 42 = 0$
(10) $x^2 - 13x + 12 = 0$

b. Solve by completing the square.

(1) $x^2 + 3x - 1 = 0$
(2) $y^2 + 6y - 10 = 0$
(3) $E^2 - 4E + 1 = 0$
(4) $2E^2 + 8E - 3 = 0$
(5) $8H^2 - 8H = 5$
(6) $5L^2 - 5 = 2L^2 - 10L$
(7) $14r^2 - 28r - 42 = 0$
(8) $\frac{1}{v^2} - \frac{4}{v} = 2$
(9) $y^2 - 5 = 2y$
(10) $8z^2 - 8z = 8$

c. Solve by using the quadratic formula.

(1) $a^2 + 2a + 1 = 0$
(2) $12y^2 - 6y + y = 0$
(3) $0 = 1 + 5E + 3E^2$
(4) $6I^2 + I - 12 = 0$
(5) $2z^2 + 4z - 6 = 0$
(6) $15R^2 = 22R + 5$
(7) $\frac{Z - 2}{Z} = 1 - Z$
(8) $\frac{3}{r - 2} = 1 + \frac{2}{r + 3}$
(9) $\frac{3x + 2}{2x + 4} = \frac{x + 2}{2x}$
(10) $0 = 6 - \frac{b - 2}{b + 2} + \frac{b - 1}{b + 1}$

CHAPTER 6
GRAPHS

Section I. BASIC CHARACTERISTICS OF GRAPHS

95. General

A *graph* is a pictorial representation of the relation between two or more quantities. In many instances, problems are more clearly understood when solved graphically than when solved by other methods. Numerical data taken from an experiment or calculations derived from a formula require interpretation, and a curve on a graph depicting such data will provide a picture that shows at a glance how one factor or function depends on another.

96. The Number Line

a. In figure 15, on a straight line of indeterminate length, a point 0 has been chosen from which to measure distances. The point 0 is called the origin. A unit of measurement also has been chosen, and positive and negative integers have been marked off and labeled. The usual choice for a positive direction is shown by the arrow. On the number line, Z_1 corresponds to -4, Z_2 corresponds to $3\frac{1}{2}$, and Z_3 corresponds to 5.2.

b. Consider a number z as corresponding to a point a distance of z units from 0. If z is positive, the point will be in the direction of the arrow from 0; if z is negative, the point will be in the opposite direction from 0. The relative size of two numbers is indicated graphically by the relative positions on the number line of points corresponding to the two numbers. For example, if z is greater than w, the point corresponding to z will be to the right of the point corresponding to w; if z is less than w, the point corresponding to z will be to the left of the point corresponding to w. The number of units from the origin to the point representing a certain number, regardless of direction, is the absolute value (par. 35) of the number.

Figure 15. The number line.

97. Rectangular Coordinates

a. In the preceding paragraph, a relationship was given between numbers and points on a straight line. A similar relationship can be established between a pair of numbers and a point on a plane. In figure 16, two number lines are drawn perpendicular to each other at their origins to form a set of axes. The horizontal axis is commonly called the x *axis*;

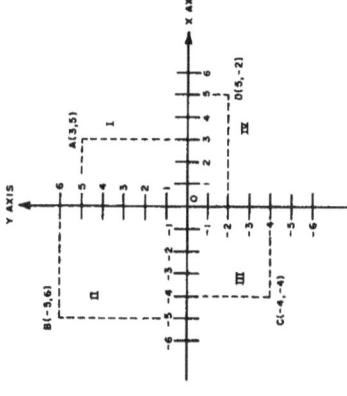

Figure 16. Rectangular coordinates.

the vertical axis is commonly called the *y axis*. Any point on the plane can be located with reference to the two axes: It must lie a certain number of units to the left (negative) or to the right (positive) of the *y* axis; and it must lie a certain number of units above (positive) or below (negative) the *x*-axis. To locate a point with reference to the set of axes, it is necessary only to know the *x* value and the *y* value of the point. These two values are known as the *coordinates* of the point. The *x* value, called the *abscissa*, is written first; the *y* value, called the *ordinate*, follows. The two numbers are separated by a comma and are usually inclosed in parentheses. Thus, in figure 16, the correct notation for the coordinates at point A is (3,5), because the *x* value is 3 and the *y* value 5.

b. The axes divide the graph into four sections, or *quadrants*, identified by the Roman numerals I, II, III, and IV in figure 16. The signs of the abscissa and the ordinate in each of the quadrants are given in the chart below.

Quadrant	Abscissa	Ordinate
I	+	+
II	−	+
III	−	−
IV	+	−

98. Plotting Points

The procedure for locating points by their coordinates is called *plotting* the points. To plot the point D (5,−2) in figure 16, for example, erect a perpendicular on the *x* axis five units to the right of the *y* axis; then erect a perpendicular to the *y* axis two units below the *x* axis; the point of intersection of these two perpendiculars is the point D (5,−2).

99. Review Problems—Plotting Points

a. Plot each of the following points and state the quadrant, if any, in which each lies:

(1) (4,2)
(2) (4,−2)
(3) (−1,3)
(4) (6,−1)
(5) (3,0)
(6) (0,−3)
(7) (−15,−27)
(8) (3¼,4½)
(9) (5.6,−6.5)

b. Plot the points in the following chart and connect them by straight segments in the order of increasing values of *x*:

x	−3	−2	−1	0	1	2	3	4
y	18	8	2	0	2	8	18	32

c. Plot the points in the following chart and sketch a smooth curve passing through them in the order of increasing values of *x*:

x	−3	−2	−1	0	1	2	3
y	−37	−8	5	2	7	7	17

d. If $y = 2x − 3$, plot the points for which $x = 4, 2, 1, 0, −1, −2,$ and $−4$ after finding the corresponding values of *y*.

e. Draw the triangle of which the vertices are (−2,6), (3,2), and (0,−3).

f. Draw the quadrilateral of which the vertices, connected in the order given, are (1,3), (−3,4), (−2,−5), and (3,−2).

Section II. GRAPHING EQUATIONS

100. Graphing Linear Equations

a. General. An equation in the first degree in two unknowns is called a *linear equation* since its graph is a straight line. For example, $x + y = 5, 2x + y = 12,$ and $x − 6y = 6$ are linear equations. An equation is said to be of the first degree in two unknowns if only the first power of either unknown is involved and

if neither of the unknowns appears in a denominator.

b. Plotting Graphs of Linear Equations.

(1) The first step in plotting the graph of a linear equation (or of any other equation or formula) is to set up a table of values for both unknowns that will satisfy the equation. In the equation $x + y = 5$, for example, it is apparent that there are a number of values for *x* and *y* that will satisfy the equation. For any number assigned to *x*, there is a corresponding number for *y* which will satisfy the equation. Consider that 4 and −4 will be the maximum plus and minus values for *x*. Using the values 4, 3, 2, 1, 0, −1, −2, −3, and −4 for *x*, the equation is solved for *y* at each value of *x*. These are arranged in tabular form as shown on figure 17.

(2) Each of these pairs of values gives a point on a graph. Consider each of the corresponding points as coordinates—the value of *x* the abscissa and the value of *y* the ordinate. The line joining these points (fig. 17) is the graph of the equation $x + y = 5$. Note that the coordinates for any two points are sufficient to determine its graph. Therefore, plotting the coordinates for any two points is sufficient to determine the graph of a first degree equation. Plotting a third point, however, will serve as a check, for if the three points are not on the same straight line, one of them is in error.

101. Graphical Solution of Simultaneous Linear Equations

a. When two *independent* linear equations contain the same two related unknowns, there will be an unlimited number of solutions for each equation. However, *there can be only one set of values that will satisfy both equations.* Determining the one set of values is known as the simultaneous solution of the two independent equations.

b. Graphically, the two equations can be solved simultaneously by plotting them on the same graph and locating their point of intersection (if there is one). For example, consider the graphical solution of the equations $3x − 2y = 0$ and $3x + 2y = 6$. Selecting 6 and −6 as the maximum plus and minus values for *x* and using $x = 4$ as a checkpoint, the coordinates for both equations are determined. For the equation $3x − 2y = 0$, these coordinates are (6,9), (4,6), and (−6,−9); for the equation $3x + 2y = 6$, (6,−6), (4,−3), and (−6,12). These coordinates are plotted on an axis and a line is drawn joining the plotted points of each equation (fig. 18). The graphs of the two independent linear equation cross at point P, where $x = 1$ and $y = 1.5$. To check the graphical solution of the equations, substitute these values for *x* and *y* in the original equations. Since they satisfy both equation, the graphical solution is correct.

c. If two *dependent* equations are plotted on a graph, their lines will coincide. For example, the equations $x + y = 4$ and $2x + 2y = 8$

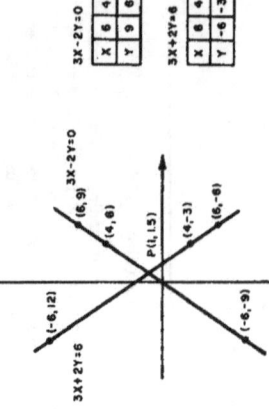

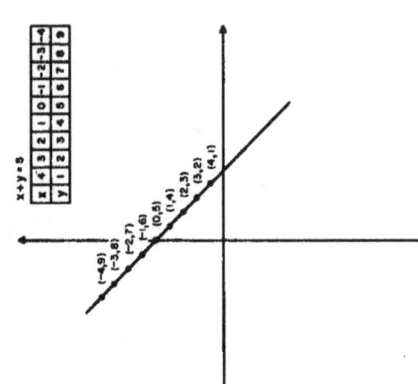

Figure 18. Graphical solution of simultaneous linear equations.

are dependent, since they can be reduced to identical forms. Selecting the same plus and minus values for x and the same checkpoint as in b above, the coordinates for both equations are found to be $(6,-2)$, $(4,0)$, and $(-6,10)$. Plotted on a graph, both equations form a single line (fig. 19).

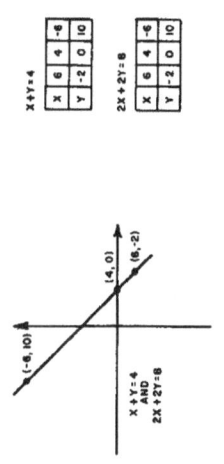

Figure 19. Graph of dependent simultaneous linear equations.

d. *Simultaneous equations that have no common solution are called inconsistent.* No solution is possible for the equations $x + y = 3$ and $x + y = 5$, because there are no values for x and y which, when added together to make 3, will also equal 5. Using 6 and -6 as maximum plus and minus values for x, and using $x = 4$ as a checkpoint, the coordinates for equation $x + y = 3$ are found to be $(6,-3)$, $(4,-1)$, and $(-6,9)$; the coordinates for $x + y = 5$ are $(6,-1)$, $(4,1)$, and $(-6,11)$. Plotted on a graph, these equations form parallel lines (fig. 20).

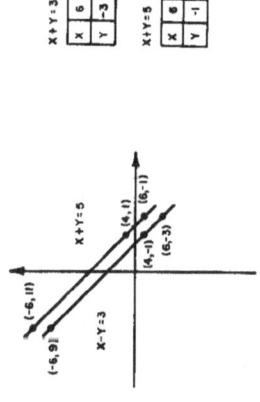

Figure 20. Graph of inconsistent simultaneous linear equations.

102. Graphing Quadratic Equations

a. *The Dependent Variable.* In graphing a quadratic equation, only two values, or points, for plotting the equation can be obtained by finding the roots of the equation (par. 88). These values do not give a complete picture of the equation. To get a continuous graph, a *dependent variable* is introduced. This variable, usually identified by the letter y, gets its name from the fact that it depends on another quantity for its value. For example, in the equation $y = x^2 - 6x + 5$, the value of y depends on the value of x; therefore, y is a dependent variable. The quantity on which y depends is called the *independent variable*. A more accurate designation for the dependent variable is $f(x)$, meaning *function of* x. Using

this designation, the equation given above would be written $f(x) = x^2 - 6x + 5$. If the independent variable in the equation were z, the equation would be written $f(z) = z^2 - 6z + 5$.

b. *Graphical Solution of Quadratic Equations.* In the original equation $f(x) = x^2 - 6x + 5$, different values are substituted for the unknown to find the corresponding values of the function; thus if x equals -1, the equation becomes $f(-1) = (-1)^2 - 6(-1) + 5 = 12$; if x equals zero, the equation becomes $f(0) = 0 - 0 + 5 = 5$; if x equals 1, the equations becomes $f(1) = (1)^2 - 6(1) + 5 = 0$, etc. Compile a table of enough values to make it possible to plot the equation, as shown in figure 21. The graph of the function crosses the x-axis at two points, 1 and 5, which give a graphical solution of the equation $x^2 - 6x + 5 = 0$. The equation also may be solved by factoring, as follows:

$$(x - 1)(x - 5) = 0$$
$$x - 1 = 0 \text{ and } x - 5 = 0$$
$$x = 1 \text{ and } x = 5$$

Thus, the solutions or the roots of the equation are obtained when $f(x) = 0$. These roots represent the points where the graph of $f(x) = x^2 - 6x + 5$ crosses the x-axis.

c. *Properties of Functions.* In addition to the original equation, $f(x) = x^2 - 6x + 5$, consider three equations that differ in one respect—their constant terms are not the same. For example:

$$f(x) = x^2 - 6x + 8$$
$$f(x) = x^2 - 6x + 9$$
$$f(x) = x^2 - 6x + 12$$

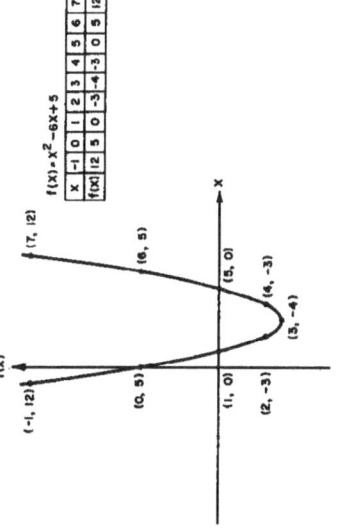

Figure 21. Graph of function of quadratic equation.

The graphs of the four corresponding functions have interesting properties and can be studied more advantageously when plotted on the same graph, as shown in figure 22.

(1) The function of $x^2 - 6x + 5$ crosses the horizontal or x-axis at two points, 1 and 5. These points indicate that the roots of the equation are $x = 1$ and $x = 5$. To compare this information with the discussion on quadratic equations in chapter 5, the discriminant of the equation must be investigated. The discriminant of $x^2 - 6x + 5$ is $(b^2 - 4ac) = (36 - 4 \cdot 1 \cdot 5) = 36 - 20 = 16$. Referring to the summary of the character of roots in paragraph 93, the roots are real and rational. To prove this, substitute the value of the discriminant in the quadratic formula.

$$x = \frac{-b \pm \sqrt{b^2 - 4ac}}{2a}$$

$$x = \frac{-(-6) \pm \sqrt{16}}{2}$$

$$x = \frac{6 + 4}{2} = 5 \text{ or } \frac{6 - 4}{2} = 1$$

Thus, the discriminant is a perfect square and the roots are real and rational.

(2) The function of $x^2 - 6x + 8$ crosses the horizontal axis at 2 and 4, indicating that the roots are $x = 2$ and $x = 4$. Calculating the discriminant,

$(b^2 - 4ac) = (36 - 4 \cdot 2 \cdot 2) = 36 - 32 = 4$. Thus, the discriminant is a perfect square and will give real and rational roots.

(3) The function of $x^2 - 6x + 9$ touches the x-axis at only one point, 3. Thus, both roots of the equation are $x = 3$. Calculating the discriminant, $(b^2 - 4ac) = (36 - 4 \cdot 9) = 0$, which indicates that the roots are real and equal. Check the graph of this equation (fig. 22); it will be seen that the curve just touches the x-axis at one point. Thus, the root $x = 3$ must be counted twice and may be called a double root.

(4) The equation $f(x) = x^2 - 6x + 12$ has a discriminant equal to $(36 - 4 \cdot 12)$ or -12. Solving for the roots of this equation,

$$x = \frac{6 \pm \sqrt{-12}}{2} = 3 \pm \sqrt{-3}.$$

This is imaginary, but the meaning becomes apparent when the graph of the function of the equation is inspected. The plot does not cross the x-axis and, therefore, both roots must be imaginary.

d. *Minimum Value of a Quadratic.*

(1) The minimum value of a quadratic function will occur at $x = \dfrac{-b}{2a}$ when

the general quadratic equation $ax^2 + bx + c = y$ (par. 91) defines the coefficients a and b. This relation can be checked by calculating the minimum value of x at which the minimum value of the function $x^2 - 6x + 5$ occurs and comparing this calculated value with the plot of the equation (fig. 21 or 22). Thus,

$$x = -\frac{b}{2a} = -\frac{(-6)}{2(1)} = \frac{6}{2} = 3,$$

and the minimum value of the function $x^2 - 6x + 5$ occurs at $x = 3$. Checking the graph verifies this statement. The minimum value of the functions $x^2 - 6x + 8$, $x^2 - 6x + 9$, and $x^2 - 6x + 12$ also occurs at $x = 3$.

(2) To find the value of the function at the minimum point, substitute for

x. The minimum occurs at $x = -\frac{b}{2a}$; therefore, substitute $-\frac{b}{2a}$ for x in the function of the general quadratic equation.

$$f(x) = ax^2 + bx + c$$
$$= a\left(\frac{-b}{2a}\right)^2 + b\left(\frac{-b}{2a}\right) + c$$
$$= \frac{b^2}{4a} + c = \frac{b^2}{4a} - \frac{2b^2}{4a} + c$$
$$= -\frac{b^2}{4a} + c$$

Thus, to find the value of the function $f(x) = x^2 - 6x + 5$ at the minimum point:

$$f(x) = -\frac{b^2}{4a} + c = \frac{-36}{4} + 5 =$$
$$-9 + 5 = -4$$

This method can be used to find the minimum value of the function if the value of x at which the minimum occurs is *not* known. However if it is known that the minimum value occurs at $x = 3$, merely substitute this value for x in the original equation.

$$f(x) = x^2 - 6x + 5$$
$$= 9 - 6 \cdot 3 + 5$$
$$= 14 - 18$$
$$f(x)\min = -4$$

(3) Note that in all cases where the word *minimum* is used, the word *maximum* is applicable if the equation $y = f(x)$ is such that its graph has a maximum instead of a minimum. It may be used, for example, to find the load resistance of a circuit in terms of the circuit components necessary to obtain maximum power transfer.

e. Practical Application. The methods of analysis presented in *c* and *d* above can be used for some very important relationships in applied electricity and electronics. It may be used, for example, to find the load resistance of a circuit in terms of the circuit components necessary to obtain maximum power transfer.

103. Review Problems—Graphs

a. Plot the graphs of the following linear equations:

(1) $2x - 5 = y$
(2) $5 - 2x = y$
(3) $y = 5x$
(4) $3x + 2y = 18$
(5) $5x - 5y = 20$
(6) $3x + y + 14 = 0$

b. Plot the graphs of the following sets of simultaneous equations:

(1) $2x + 3y = 12$
    $3y - y = 7$
(2) $x + y = 9$
    $5x + y = 17$
(3) $x + 5y = 22$
    $3x - 2y = -2$
(4) $3x - 2y = 0$
    $x - 5y = 13$
(5) $6x + 2y = 12$
    $4y + 2y = 10$
(6) $x - 2y = 0$
    $y = 1 + x$

c. Find the roots of the following quadratic equations to the nearest tenth by plotting their graphs:

(1) $y^2 - 2y - 2 = 0$
(2) $x^2 - 1 + x = 0$
(3) $9 - t^2$
(4) $x^2 - 2x + 2 = 0$
(5) $x^2 - 5x + 3 = 0$
(6) $10 - 3x - x^2 = 0$

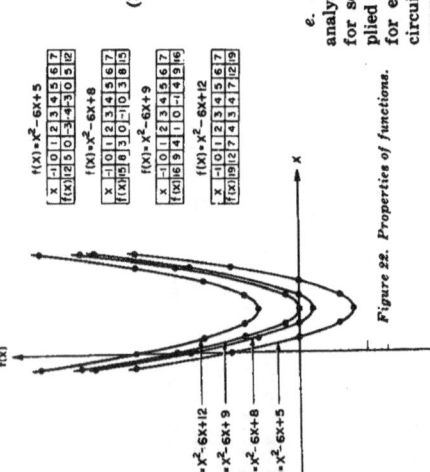

Figure 22. Properties of functions.

CHAPTER 7
POWERS OF 10

104. General

The technique of using powers of 10 can greatly simplify mathematical calculations. A number containing many zeros to the right or to the left of the decimal point can be dealt with much more readily when put in the form of powers of 10. For example, .0000037 × .000021 can be handled more easily when put in the form $3.7 \times 10^{-6} \times 2.1 \times 10^{-5}$.

105. Table of Powers of 10

The table below gives some of the values of the powers of 10. In a whole number, the exponent is positive and equals the number of zeros following the 1; in decimals, the exponent is negative and equals one more than the number of zeros immediately following the decimal point.

Number	Power of 10	Number	Power of 10
.000001	10^{-6}	1	10^0
.00001	10^{-5}	10	10^1
.0001	10^{-4}	100	10^2
.001	10^{-3}	1,000	10^3
.01	10^{-2}	10,000	10^4
.1	10^{-1}	100,000	10^5
		1,000,000	10^6

106. Expressing Numbers in Scientific Notation

Any number written as the product of an integral power of 10 and a number between 1 and 10 is said to be expressed in *scientific notation*.

Example 1: $81,000,000 = 8.1 \times 10,000,000 = 8.1 \times 10^7$

Example 2: $600,000,000 = 6 \times 100,000,000 = 6 \times 10^8$

Example 3: $.000,000,000,9 = 9 \times .000,000,000,1 = 9 \times 10^{-10}$

107. Addition and Subtraction of Numbers in Scientific Notation

Numbers expressed in scientific notation can only be added or subtracted if the powers of 10 are the same. For example, 3×10^4 can be added to 2×10^5 to get 5×10^5; however, 3×10^4 cannot be added to 2×10^5 because the powers of 10 are not the same. The number 3×10^4 can be changed to 30×10^5, however, and it can then be added to 2×10^5 to obtain 32×10^5. The answers to problems solved by using scientific notation can be left in the exponential form. In the examples below, however, the answers are converted to the decimal form to aid in understanding this technique.

Example 1: Add 450,000 and 763,000.
$$450,000 + 763,000 = 45 \times 10^4 + 76.3 \times 10^4$$
$$= 121.3 \times 10^4$$
$$= 1,213,000$$

Example 2: Add .000,068,25 and .000,007,54.
$$.000,068,25 + .000,007,54 = 6825 \times 10^{-8} + 754 \times 10^{-8}$$
$$= 7579 \times 10^{-8}$$
$$= .000,075,79$$

Example 3: Subtract .000,004,33 from .000,05.
$$.000,05 - .000,004,33 = 5000 \times 10^{-8} - 433 \times 10^{-8}$$
$$= 4567 \times 10^{-8}$$
$$= .000,045,67$$

108. Multiplication of Numbers in Scientific Notation

The general rules covering the multiplication of radicals (par. 74) also apply in the multiplication of numbers that are expressed in scientific notation.

Example 1: Multiply 100,000 by 1,000.
$$100,000 \times 1,000 = 10^5 \times 10^3 = 10^{5+3} = 10^8 = 100,000,000$$

Example 2: Multiply 25,000 by 5,000.
$$25,000 \times 5,000 = 2.5 \times 10^4 \times 5 \times 10^3 = 2.5 \times 5 \times 10^{4+3}$$
$$= 12.5 \times 10^7$$
$$= 125,000,000$$

Example 3: Multiply 1,800, .000015, 300, and .0048.
$$1,800 \times .000015 \times 300 \times .0048$$
$$= 1.8 \times 10^3 \times 1.5 \times 10^{-5} \times 3 \times 10^2 \times 4.8 \times 10^{-3}$$
$$= 1.8 \times 1.5 \times 3 \times 4.8 \times 10^{3-5+2-3}$$
$$= 38.88 \times 10^{-3}$$
$$= .03888$$

109. Division of Numbers in Scientific Notation

The general rules covering the division of radicals (par. 75) also apply in the division of numbers that are expressed in scientific notation.

Example 1: Divide 75,000 by .0005.
$$\frac{75,000}{.0005} = \frac{75 \times 10^3}{5 \times 10^{-4}} = \frac{75}{5} \times 10^{3+4} = 15 \times 10^7 = 150,000,000$$

Example 2: Divide 14,400,000 by 1,200,000.
$$\frac{14,400,000}{1,200,000} = \frac{144 \times 10^5}{12 \times 10^5} = \frac{144}{12} = 12$$

Example 3: Divide 98,100 by .0025, 180, and 1,090,000.
$$\frac{98,100}{.0025 \times 180 \times 1,090,000}$$
$$= \frac{9.81 \times 10^4}{2.5 \times 10^{-3} \times 1.8 \times 10^2 \times 1.09 \times 10^6}$$
$$= \frac{9.81 \times 10^4}{2.5 \times 1.8 \times 1.09 \times 10^{-3+2+6}}$$
$$= \frac{9.81 \times 10^4}{4.905 \times 10^5}$$
$$= 2 \times 10^{-1}$$
$$= .2$$

110. Finding the Power or Root of a Number in Scientific Notation

The general rules covering powers and roots (pars. 71 and 72) also apply to numbers expressed in scientific notation.

Example 1: Find the square root of 144,000,000.
$$\sqrt{144,000,000} = \sqrt{144 \times 10^6}$$
$$= 12 \times 10^3$$
$$= 12,000$$

Example 2: Find the cube root of .000,008.
$$\sqrt[3]{.000,008} = \sqrt[3]{8 \times 10^{-6}}$$
$$= 2 \times 10^{-2}$$
$$= .02$$

Example 3: Square 15,000.
$$(15,000)^2 = (15 \times 10^3)^2$$
$$= 225 \times 10^6$$
$$= 225,000,000$$

Example 4: Find the square root of $(160,000)^3$.
$$\sqrt{160,000^3} = (160,000)^{3/2}$$
$$= (16 \times 10^4)^{3/2}$$
$$= 64 \times 10^6$$
$$= 64,000,000$$

Example 5: Find the square root of $\frac{86,900}{3,560,000}$.
$$\sqrt{\frac{86,900}{3,560,000}} = \sqrt{\frac{8.69 \times 10^4}{3.56 \times 10^6}}$$
$$= \sqrt{2.44 \times 10^{-2}}$$
$$= 1.56 \times 10^{-1}$$
$$= .156$$

111. Review Problems—Powers of 10

In the following problems, leave the answer in powers of ten:

a. Convert the following numbers to powers of 10 and add:
(1) 1,245,000 + 368,000
(2) 79,000 + 421,000
(3) .000,007,66 + .000,054

b. Convert the following numbers to powers of 10 and subtract:
(1) 333,400 — 22,500
(2) .000,068 — .000,049
(3) .000,004,89 — .000,000,398

c. Convert the following numbers to powers of 10 and multiply:
(1) 446,000 × 200
(2) 7,700 × .008,2
(3) .000,096 × .000,33
(4) .003,66 × 4,000,000

d. Convert the following numbers to powers of 10 and divide:
(1) 668,000 ÷ 4,000
(2) 88,445,000 ÷ .000,55
(3) .000,963 ÷ .000,009
(4) .006,93 ÷ 21

e. Convert the following numbers to powers of 10 and perform the indicated operations:
(1) $\sqrt[3]{64,000,000}$
(2) $\sqrt{.000,169}$
(3) $.003^3$
(4) $27,000^{2/3}$

CHAPTER 8
LOGARITHMS

112. General

Many lengthy mathematical operations may be accomplished more easily through the use of logarithms. With logarithms (also called logs), multiplication of numbers is reduced to a simple process of addition, division becomes a process of subtraction, raising a number to a power becomes simple multiplication, and extraction of roots is done by simple division.

113. Definition

The logarithm of a given number is the power (x) to which another number (called the base) must be raised to equal the given number. The word "logarithm" has the same meaning as the word "exponent."

Example: Find the logarithm of 1,000 to the base 10.

From the definition, the logarithm of a number (1,000) is the power (x) to which another number called the base (10) must be raised to equal the given number (1,000).

Thus, $10^x = 1,000$. Since $10^3 = 1,000$, then:

$$10^x = 10^3$$ and by inspection:

$$x = 3$$

Therefore, the logarithm of 1,000 to the base 10 equals 3 or $\log_{10} 1,000 = 3$.

114. Types of Logarithms

a. Common Logarithms. Common logarithms use the number 10 as a base. They are so universally used that the 10 usually is omitted; the answer in paragraph 113 could be $\log 1,000 = 3$. Some values of common logarithms are included in the table below. The common logarithm of any number between these values consists of the logarithm of the smaller number plus a decimal. For example, the log of a number between 100 and 1,000, such as 157, consists of the log of the smaller number (10) plus a decimal. The log of 157 is 2.1959.

$\log 1 = 0$	$\log .1 = -1$
$\log 10 = 1$	$\log .01 = -2$
$\log 100 = 2$	$\log .001 = -3$
$\log 1,000 = 3$	$\log .0001 = -4$
$\log 10,000 = 4$	

b. Natural Logarithms. Natural logarithms are based upon the irrational number e, and are written both as log$_e$ and ln. Natural logarithms are used in special applications and as such are not explained further in this text.

115. Parts of Logarithms

a. Logarithms are divided into two parts, the integral and the decimal. The integral part is known as the *characteristic*, and the decimal part is called the *mantissa*.

(1) *The characteristic of any number is one less than the number of digits to the left of the decimal point.* Thus, the characteristic for the number 3 is $1 - 1$ or zero, since there is one number to the left of the decimal point. The characteristic for 30, with two numbers to the left of the decimal point, is $2 - 1$ or 1. Similarly, the characteristic for 300 is 2, and the characteristic for 3,000 is 3. The characteristic of the log of a decimal is negative and is based upon the position of the first rational number to the right of the decimal point. *If there are no numbers to the left of the decimal point, the characteristic is negative.* In the number .327, for example, the first rational number is in the first decimal place and the characteristic is -1; in the number .03, the first rational number is in the second decimal place and the characteristic is -2. Similarly, the characteristic for .003 is -3, and the characteristic for .0003 is -4.

(2) The mantissa is always the same for a given sequence of integers, regardless of where the decimal point appears among them. Thus, the *mantissa* is the same for 1570, 157, 15.7, 1.57, .157, and .0157, and the logs of these numbers differ only in respect to their characteristics. Their logarithms, respectively, are 3.1959, 2.1959, 1.1959, 0.1959, -1.1959 and -2.1959.

b. The mantissa is always positive—even when the characteristic is negative. This fact poses a problem of notation, and also complicates the addition and subtraction of logarithms.

(1) In the notation of logarithms, to say that log .157 is -1.1959 is not strictly true, for what we mean to say is -1 plus .1959. To overcome this problem, the minus sign is generally written above the characteristic, and is made long enough to cover the entire negative portion of the logarithm. More properly, therefore, log .157 is written $\bar{1}$.1959.

(2) In the addition and subtraction of logarithms, the complication can be removed by expressing the negative characteristic in a positive manner; more precisely, by adding a large enough number to the characteristic and by subtracting the same number from the entire logarithm. Thus, the log of .157 is written 9.1959-10, and the log of .0157 is written 8.1959-10.

116. Finding a Logarithm

The characteristic must be obtained, in each instance, by following the rules given in paragraph 115a(1).

Example 1: Find the logarithm of 333.

Determine the characteristic of 333. The characteristic is $3 - 1$, or 2.

Determine the mantissa of 333. In the table of common logarithms, look down the N column for the number 33. The mantissa for 333 is in this horizontal row in the column headed by the number 3. The mantissa is .5224.

Log 333 = 2.5224.

Example 2: Find the logarithm of .127.

Determine the characteristic of .127. The characteristic is -1 or 9.———10.

Determine the mantissa of .127. In the table of common logarithms, look down the N column for 12. The mantissa for 127 is in this horizontal row in the column headed by the number 7. The mantissa is .1038.

Log .127 = 9.1038—10.

117. Logarithmic Interpolation

The table of common logarithms given in appendix is adequate if the given number has three or less integers. If it has four or more integers, however, it is necessary to interpolate—that is, to find the proportional part of the difference between the logarithms shown in the table.

Example 1: Find the logarithm of 2.369.

Step 1. The characteristic of 2.369 is 0. Since the mantissa for this number cannot be found in the table, it is necessary to interpolate. Look for the mantissas of the numbers next lower and higher than 2369. The mantissa of the number 2360 is .3729 and the mantissa of the number 2370 is .3747. Since 2369 lies between 2360 and 2370, the mantissa of

2369 must lie between .3729 and .3747. This may be written:

log 2360 = .3729
log 2369 = .3729 + x
log 2370 = .3747

Step 2. Set up the proportions. The difference between 2369 and 2360 is 9. The difference between 2370 and 2360 is 10. Therefore, the desired mantissa is $\frac{9}{10}$ of the difference between these two. Let the difference between the mantissa of 2369 and 2360 equal x. The difference between .3747 and .3729 is .0018. The proportion is $\frac{x}{.0018}$.

Step 3. Solve the problem.

$$\frac{9}{10} = \frac{x}{.0018}$$
$$10x = .0162$$
$$x = .0016$$

Step 4. Since the value of x is .0016, the mantissa of 2369 is .3729 + .0016 or .3745. Therefore, log 2.369 = 0.3745.

Example 2: Find the logarithm of .017234.

Step 1. The characteristic of .017234 is −2 or 8. − − − − −10. The numbers in the table lower and higher than 17234 are 17200 and 17300. The mantissa of 17200 is .2355; the mantissa of 17300 is .2380. The difference between 17234 and 17200 is 34; the difference between 17200 and 17300 is 100; the difference between .2380 and .2355 is .0025. This may be written:

log 17200 = .2355
log 17234 = .2355 + x
log 17300 = .2380

Step 2. Let the difference between the mantissas of 17234 and 17200 equal x. The equation is as follows:

$$\frac{34}{100} = \frac{x}{.0025}$$
$$100x = .0850$$
$$x = .00085 = .0009$$

Step 3. Since the value of x is .0009, the mantissa of 17234 is .2355 + .0009 or .2364. Therefore, log .017234 = 8.2364−10.

118. Reading Antilogarithms

The process of finding the antilogarithm (also called antilog), consists of determining the number from which the logarithm was derived. This process is essentially the reverse of finding the logarithm (par. 116). Consequently, the location of the decimal point is determined from the characteristic, and the numerical value of the number is determined from the mantissa.

Example 1: Find the antilog of 1.8954.

Step 1. Since the characteristic of the logarithm is 1, there will be two digits to the left of the decimal point in the number.

Step 2. Look in the table for the mantissa, .8954. The number given for .8954 is 786.

Step 3. Count off two digits from the left and insert the decimal point. The antilog of 1.8954 is 78.6.

Example 2: Find the antilog of 7.0828−10.

Step 1. Since the characteristic of the logarithm is −3, the first significant figure will be in the third decimal place.

Step 2. Look for the mantissa .0828 in the table. The number given for .0828 is 121.

Step 3. Add two zeros to the right of the decimal point and before the first significant figure. Thus, the antilog of 7.0828−10 is .0021.

119. Antilogarithmic Interpolation

If the mantissa of a logarithm does not appear in the table, it is necessary to interpolate.

Example 1: Find the antilog of 2.7654.

Step 1. Since the characteristic of the logarithm is 2, there will be three digits to the left of the decimal point in the number.

Step 2. The mantissa lower than .7654 is .7649. The number with .7649 as a mantissa is 582.

Step 3. The mantissa higher than .7654 is .7657. The number with .7657 as a mantissa is 583.

Step 4. Set up the proportions. The difference between .7654 and .7649 is .0005; the difference between .7657 and .7649 is .0008. The proportional difference is $\frac{.0005}{.0008}$ or $\frac{5}{8}$. The difference between 583 and 582 is 1. This can be written:

antilog .7649 = 582
antilog .7654 = 582 + x
antilog .7657 = 583

Step 5. Let x equal the difference between the number represented by the mantissa .7654 and the number 582. The equation is as follows:

$$\frac{5}{8} = \frac{x}{1}$$
$$8x = 5$$
$$x = .625$$

Step 6. The number is 582 + .625. Since there are three digits to the left of the decimal point, the antilog of 2.7654 is 582.625.

Example 2: Find the antilog of 6.7166−10.

Step 1. Since the characteristic of the logarithm is −4, the first rational number will be in the fourth decimal place.

Step 2. The mantissa in the table lower than .8166 is .8162; the number with .8162 as a mnatissa is 655.

Step 3. The mantissa in the table higher than .8166 is .8169; the number with .8169 as a mantissa is 656.

Step 4. The difference between .8162 and .8166 is .0004; the difference between .8169 and .8162 is .0007. The proportional difference is $\frac{.0004}{.0007}$ or $\frac{4}{7}$. The difference between 656 and 655 is 1. This may be written:

antilog .8162 = 655
antilog .8166 = 655 + x
antilog .8169 = 656

Step 5. Let x equal the difference between the number represented by the mantissa .8166 and the number 655. The equation is as follows:

$$\frac{4}{7} = \frac{x}{1}$$
$$7x = 4$$
$$x = .57$$

Step 6. The number is 655 + .57. Since the first rational figure is in the fourth decimal place, the antilog of 6.7166−10 is .00065557.

120. Addition and Subtraction of Logarithms

Logarithms are added and subtracted arithmetically. Since every mantissa is positive (par. 115b), however, every negative characteristic should be expressed as a posiitve (par. 115b).

Example 1: Add the logarithms 3.7493 and 2.4036.

```
  3.7493
+ 2.4036
  6.1529
```

Example 2: Add the logarithms 3.4287 and 6.3982.

```
  3.4287
+ 4.3982−10
  7.8269−10
```

Example 3: Add the logarithms 8.9324−10, 7.2812−10, 5.4138−10, and 9.9918−10.

```
  8.9324−10
  7.2812−10
  5.4138−10
+ 9.9918−10
 31.6192−40
 (−30)(−30)
  1.6192−10
```

Example 4: Subtract the logarithm 9.1245 from the logarithm 6.3058.

To subtract a larger logarithm from a smaller logarithm, add 10 or a multiple of 10 to the smaller logarithm, and subtract the same number from the logarithm by writing that number with a minus sign to the right of the logarithm. The number chosen for this purpose should be the least that will cause the smaller logarithm to exceed the larger.

$$16.3058-10$$
$$-9.1245$$
$$\overline{7.1813-10}$$

Example 5: Subtract the logarithm 3.7980—10 from 2.8686. When subtracting a negative logarithm from a positive logarithm, where that part of the characteristic of the negative logarithm to the left of the mantissa is larger than the characteristic of the positive logarithm, add 10 or a multiple of 10 to the characteristic of the positive logarithm, and subtract that same amount from the right of the positive logarithm.

$$12.8686-10$$
$$-3.7980-10$$
$$\overline{9.0706}$$

121. Multiplication by Use of Logarithms

The logarithm of the product of two numbers is equal to the sum of the logarithms of the numbers. Thus, $\log (2 \times 6) = \log 2 + \log 6$; and $\log (12 \times 8) = \log 12 + \log 8$.

Example 1: Multiply 68.2 by 40.8 by using logarithms.

$\log (68.2 \times 40.8) = \log 68.2 + \log 40.8$.

$\log 68.2 = 1.8338$
$\log 40.8 = 1.6107$
$\overline{\log (68.2 \times 40.8) = 3.4445}$
antilog .4440 = 278
antilog .4445 = 278 + x
antilog .4455 = 279

$\dfrac{5}{15} = \dfrac{x}{1}$

$15x = 5$

$x = .33$

antilog .4445 = 2783

$68.2 \times 40.8 = 2,783$

Example 2: Find the product of 2.11 and 41.3 by using logarithms.

$\log (2.11 \times 41.3) = \log 2.11 + \log 41.3$.

$\log 2.11 = 0.3243$
$\log 41.3 = 1.6160$
$\overline{\log (2.11 \times 41.3) = 1.9403}$
antilog .9400 = 871
antilog .9403 = 871 + x
antilog .9405 = 872

$\dfrac{3}{5} = \dfrac{x}{1}$

$5x = 3$

$x = .6$

antilog 1.9403 = 87.16

$2.11 \times 41.3 = 87.16$

122. Division by Use of Logarithms

The logarithm of the quotient of two numbers is equal to the difference between the logarithms of the numbers. Thus, $\log (75 \div 83) = \log 75 - \log 83$, and $\log (8 \div 2) = \log 8 - \log 2$.

Example 1: Divide 785 by 329 by using logarithms.

$\log (785 \div 329) = \log 785 - \log 329$.

$\log 785 = 2.8949$
$\log 329 = 2.5172$
$\overline{\log (785 \div 329) = 0.3777}$
antilog .3766 = 238
antilog .3777 = 238 + x
antilog .3784 = 239

$\dfrac{11}{18} = \dfrac{x}{1}$

$18x = 11$

$x = .611$

antilog 0.3777 = 2.386

$785 \div 329 = 2.386$

Example 2: Find the value of $\dfrac{3}{7}$ by using logarithms.

$\log \dfrac{3}{7} = \log 3 - \log 7$.

$\log 3 = 0.4771$
$\log 7 = 0.8451$

Since the logarithm of 7 is greater than the logarithm of 3, it is necessary to add 10.———10 to the logarithm of 3 before subtracting the logarithm of 7.

$\log 3 = 10.4771-10$
$\log 7 = 0.8451$
$\overline{\log (3 \div 7) = 9.6320-10}$
antilog .6314 = 428
antilog .6320 = 428 + x
antilog .6325 = 429

$\dfrac{6}{11} = \dfrac{x}{1}$

$11x = 6$

$x = .55$

antilog 9.6320—10 = .42855

$3 \div 7 = .42855$

123. Finding the Power of a Number by Logarithms

The logarithm of a number raised to a power is equal to the logarithm of the number multiplied by the power.

Example 1: Evaluate $(18.7)^3$.

$\log (18.7)^3 = 3 \log 18.7$
$= 3 \times 1.2718$
$= 3.8154$
antilog .8149 = 653
antilog .8154 = 653 + x
antilog .8156 = 654

$\dfrac{5}{7} = \dfrac{x}{1}$

$7x = 5$

$x = .7$

antilog 3.8154 = 6537

$(18.7)^3 = 6,537$

Example 2: Evaluate $(.03625)^4$.

$\log (.03625)^4 = 4 \log .03625$

$\log 3620 = .5587$
$\log 3625 = .5587 + x$
$\log 3630 = .5599$

$\dfrac{5}{10} = \dfrac{x}{.0012}$

$x = .0006$

$\log (.03625)^4 = 4 (8.5593-10)$
$= 34.2372-40$
(Subtract) $30.0000-30$
$\overline{4.2372-10}$
antilog .2355 = 172
antilog .2372 = 172 + x
antilog .2380 = 173

$\dfrac{17}{25} = \dfrac{x}{1}$

$25x = 17$

$x = .68 = .7$

antilog 4.2372—10 = .000001727

$(.03625)^4 = .000001727$

Example 3: Evaluate $(2.13)^{\frac{1}{3}}$.

$\log (2.13)^{\frac{1}{3}} = \frac{1}{3} \log 2.13$
$= \frac{1}{3} \times 0.3284$
$= 0.2189$
antilog .2175 = 165
antilog .2189 = 165 + x
antilog .2201 = 166

$\dfrac{14}{26} = \dfrac{x}{1}$

$26x = 14$

$x = .5$

antilog 0.2189 = 1.655

$(2.13)^{\frac{1}{3}} = 1.655$

124. Finding the Root of a Number by Logarithms

The logarithm of the root of a number is equal to the logarithm of the number divided by the root.

Example 1: Evaluate $\sqrt[4]{34987}$.

$\log \sqrt[4]{34987} = \dfrac{\log 34987}{4}$

$\log 34900 = .5428$
$\log 34987 = .5428 + x$
$\log 35000 = .5441$

$\dfrac{87}{100} = \dfrac{x}{.0013}$

$100x = .1131$

$x = .0011$

$= \dfrac{4.5439}{4}$

$= 1.135975 = 1.1360$

antilog .1335 = 136
antilog .1360 = 136 + x
antilog .1367 = 137

$\dfrac{25}{32} = \dfrac{x}{1}$

$32x = 25$

$x = .78$

antilog 1.1360 = 13.678

$\sqrt[4]{34987} = 13.678$

Example 2: Evaluate $\sqrt[3]{76.24}$.

$\log \sqrt[3]{76.24} = \dfrac{\log 76.24}{3}$

$\log 7620 = .8820$
$\log 7624 = .8820 + x$
$\log 7630 = .8825$

$\dfrac{4}{10} = \dfrac{x}{.0005}$

$$10x = .0020$$
$$x = .0002$$
$$\frac{1.8822}{3} = 0.6274$$
$$\text{antilog } 0.6274 = 4.24$$
$$\sqrt[3]{76.24} = 4.24$$

Example 3: Evaluate $\sqrt[3]{.0073573}$.

$$\log \sqrt[3]{.0073573} = \frac{\log .0073573}{3}$$

$$\log 73500 = .8663$$
$$\log 73573 = .8663 + x$$
$$\log 73600 = .8669$$

$$\frac{73}{100} = \frac{x}{.0006}$$
$$100x = .0438$$
$$x = .0004$$

$$\frac{7.8667 - 10}{3}$$

The quotient of $7.8667-10$ divided by 3 is $2.6222-3\frac{1}{3}$. By adding $20.0000-20$ to $7.8667-10$, the sum, $27.8667-30$, can be divided by 3 and the quotient will be a workable logarithm.

$$\log .0073573 = 7.8667 - 10$$
$$\text{add } \frac{20.0000 - 20}{27.8667 - 30}$$

$$\frac{27.8667 - 30}{3} = 9.2889 - 10$$

$$\text{antilog } .2878 = 194$$
$$\text{antilog } .2889 = 194 + x$$
$$\text{antilog } .2900 = 195$$

$$\frac{11}{22} = \frac{x}{1}$$
$$22x = 11$$
$$x = .5$$

$$\text{antilog } 9.2889 - 10 = .1945$$
$$\sqrt[3]{.0073573} = .1945$$

126. Computation by Logarithms

In performing logarithmic computations, follow the principles given in paragraphs 117 through 125. When negative quantities are involved (in multiplication and division), disregard the minus sign when making logarithmic calculations. After calculating the antilog, the sign is determined in accordance with the algebraic law of signs for multiplication and division.

Example 1: Evaluate $\sqrt[3]{\dfrac{(94.7)^2 \cdot (.00789)}{(3.71)^3 \cdot (.345)}}$.

$$\log (94.7)^2 = 2 \log 94.7$$
$$= 2 \times 1.9763$$
$$= 3.9526$$

$$\log (94.7)^2 + \log (.00789) = \frac{7.8971 - 10}{3}$$
$$\log (.00789) = 11.8497 - 10 = 1.8497$$

$$\log (3.71)^3 = 3 \log 3.71$$
$$= 3 \times 0.5694$$
$$= 1.7082$$

$$\log (3.71)^3 + \log (.345) = \frac{9.5378 - 10}{3} = 11.2460 - 10 = 1.2460$$
$$\log (94.7)^2 \cdot (.00789) = 1.8497$$
$$\log (3.71)^3 \cdot (.345) = 1.2460$$
$$\overline{0.6037}$$

$$\log \sqrt[3]{\dfrac{(94.7)^2 (.00789)}{(3.71)^3 (.345)}} = \frac{0.6037}{3}$$
$$= .2012$$
$$\text{antilog } .2012 = 1.5892$$

Example 2: Evaluate $\sqrt[4]{\dfrac{(6.484)^2 \cdot \sqrt[3]{7.667}}{(12.35)^2 \cdot \sqrt[3]{3007}}}$.

$$\log (6.484)^2 = 2 \log 6.484$$
$$= 2 \times 0.8118$$
$$= 1.6236$$

$$\log \sqrt[3]{7.667} = \frac{\log 7.667}{3}$$
$$= \frac{0.8846}{3}$$
$$= 0.2949$$

$$\log (6.484)^2 + \log \sqrt[3]{7.667} = 1.6236 + .2949$$
$$= 1.9185$$

$$\log (12.35)^2 = 2 \log 12.35$$
$$= 2 \times 1.0917$$
$$= 2.1834$$

$$\log \sqrt[3]{3007} = \frac{\log 3007}{3}$$
$$= \frac{3.4782}{3}$$
$$= 1.1594$$

$$\log (12.35)^2 + \log \sqrt[3]{3007} = 2.1834 + 1.1594$$
$$= 3.3428$$

$$\log (6.484)^2 \cdot \sqrt[3]{7.667} = 11.9185 - 10$$
$$\log (12.35)^2 \cdot \sqrt[3]{3007} = \frac{3.3428}{8.5757 - 10}$$

125. Cologarithms

The *cologarithm* of a number is the logarithm of the reciprocal of the number. For example, $\operatorname{colog} N = \log \dfrac{1}{N}$. However,

$$\log \frac{1}{N} = \log 1 - \log N$$
$$= 0 - \log N$$
$$\log \frac{1}{N} = -\log N$$

Therefore, $\operatorname{colog} N = \log \dfrac{1}{N} = -\log N$. Thus the cologarithm of a number is the logarithm of the number subtracted from the logarithm of 1 (0.0000 or, to avoid a negative mantissa, $10.0000-10$).

Example 1: Evaluate the cologarithm of 373.

$$\operatorname{colog} 373 = \log \frac{1}{373}$$
$$\log 1 = 10.0000 - 10$$
$$\log 373 = 2.5717$$
$$\operatorname{colog} 373 = 7.4283 - 10$$

Example 2: Evaluate $\dfrac{2.37}{3.61}$.

$$\log \frac{2.37}{3.61} = \log 2.37 - \log 3.61$$
$$= \log 2.37 + \operatorname{colog} 3.61$$
$$\log 1 = 10.0000 - 10$$
$$\log 3.61 = 0.5575$$
$$\operatorname{colog} 3.61 = 9.4425 - 10$$
$$\log 2.37 = 0.3747$$
$$\overline{9.8172 - 10}$$
$$\text{antilog } 9.8172 - 10 = .65643$$

$$\log \sqrt[4]{\frac{(6.484)^2 \sqrt[3]{7.667}}{(12.35)^2 \sqrt[5]{3007}}} = \frac{38.57157-40}{4} = 9.6439-10$$

antilog $9.6439-10 = .4405$

127. Review Problems—Logarithms

a. Find the logarithms of the following numbers to the base 10:

(1) 785
(2) 3.57
(3) .0345
(4) .000476
(5) 49.6
(6) 273.5
(7) 760.1
(8) 7.234
(9) .009875
(10) .00005254

b. Find the antilogs of the following logarithms:

(1) 4.8457
(2) 2.4330
(3) 9.5453—10
(4) 6.8299—10
(5) 0.6010
(6) 2.5690
(7) 5.4343—10
(8) 5.6994
(9) 0.2018
(10) 4.5872—10

c. Using logarithms, find the products of the following to four significant figures:

(1) 6.93×23.7
(2) 186×215
(3) 64.3×21.4
(4) $.089 \times .076$
(5) 135×42.3

d. Using logarithms, find the quotients of the following to four significant figures:

(1) $148 \div 297$
(2) $\dfrac{251}{648}$

(3) $14.9 \div 37.4$
(4) $47.38 \div 63.29$
(5) $\dfrac{1.06}{4.35}$

e. Using logarithms, evaluate the following:

(1) $(.0293)^4$
(2) $(1.756)^7$
(3) $(7.953)^3$
(4) $(69.37)^{.7}$
(5) $(27.98)^2$
(6) $\sqrt[3]{.01325}$
(7) $\sqrt[4]{815}$
(8) $\sqrt[3]{7698}$
(9) $\sqrt[5]{8.942}$
(10) $\sqrt[4]{.000079911}$

f. Using logarithms, compute the following:

(1) $\dfrac{3.8 \times 2.6}{4.3}$
(2) $\sqrt[3]{\dfrac{541 \times 47.3}{.0157}}$
(3) $\dfrac{44.1 \times 1.82}{10.27 \times .32}$
(4) $\dfrac{85.21 \times \sqrt[3]{4651}}{\sqrt{46.82} \times 6.230}$
(5) $\dfrac{(31.21)^3}{40.70}$
(6) $\sqrt[3]{\dfrac{(57.20)^2}{(31.42)^3}}$
(7) $\dfrac{.08152 \times 1.963}{95.27}$
(8) $\sqrt{\dfrac{.8531}{9.327}} \times \sqrt{\dfrac{518.2}{61.52}}$
(9) $\dfrac{48.19 \times \sqrt{56.02}}{431.5 \times \sqrt[3]{46.25} \times \sqrt{16.34}}$
(10) $\sqrt{\dfrac{.008150 \times .08532}{.01234 \times \sqrt[3]{.09156}}}$

CHAPTER 9
PLANE GEOMETRY

128. Introduction

Plane geometry is that part of geometry which deals with plane figures. In electronics, as in many other fields, it is necessary to know how to deal with areas of common plane figures. This chapter presents the formulas for finding the areas of triangles, quadrilaterals (plane figures having four sides and four angles), and circles. No effort has been made to cover the entire field of geometry. Only those principles and proofs are presented that are of value in practical work.

129. Definitions

a. Lines. A line has length, but no width or thickness. What is drawn on paper and called a line has thickness and breadth because of the material used to draw it—however, this mark only *represents* the actual line.

b. Angles. An angle, such as *ABC* in *A*, figure 23, is formed by the intersection of two lines. An angle, therefore, is the measure of the difference in direction of two straight lines that meet. The lines which form the angle, *AB* or *BC*, are called the *sides* of the angle, and the point of meeting, *B*, the vertex. The symbol ∠ is used to indicate angles. Angles usually are measured in *degrees*. A complete circle or rotation consists of 360 degrees. The symbol ° is used to indicate degrees; it is written to the right and slightly above the number. For example, 30 degrees is written 30°. Each degree consists of 60 *minutes*, and each minute is further broken down into 60 *seconds*. The symbol ′ is used to indicate minutes; the symbol ″ indicates seconds. For example, 20 minutes is written 20′; 15 seconds is written 15″.

(1) When one straight line is *perpendicular* to another straight line, the angle formed is a right angle (90°) (B, fig. 23).

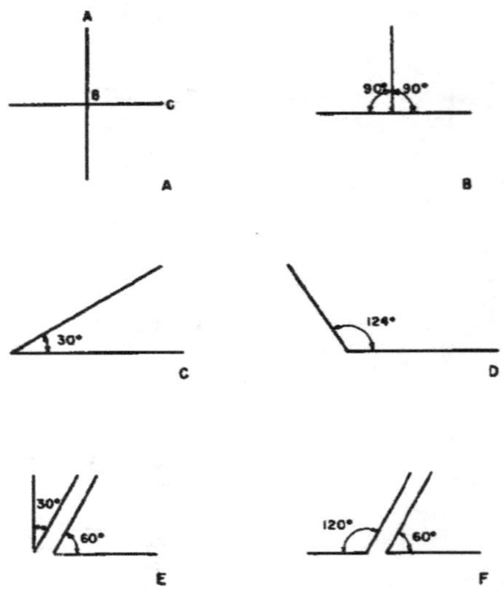

Figure 23. Angles.

(2) Two right angles, added together, form a *straight angle*. A straight angle, therefore, is an angle of 180°.
(3) Any angle less than a right angle is an *acute angle* (C, fig. 23).
(4) Any angle greater than a right angle and less than 180° is an *obtuse angle* (D, fig. 23).
(5) Two angles whose sum is one right angle are called *complementary angles* (E, fig. 23).
(6) Two angles whose sum is a straight angle are called *supplementary angles* (F, fig. 23).

130. Basic Principles of Geometric Construction

a. Reproducing Angles. To draw an angle equal to a given angle BAC (fig. 24)—

(1) Draw a line, A'C'.

(2) With A as the center, use a compass to strike an arc that cuts the sides of the given angle at X and Y. Using the same radius, strike a similar arc, X'Y', on the line, A'C'.

(3) Measure the opening of the given angle by setting one point of the compass at Y and the other at X. With the compass at this distance and with Y' as the center, strike an arc as shown in figure 24. This will cut the first arc at point X'.

(4) Draw a line, A'B', through X'. The new angle, B'A'C', is the same size as angle BAC.

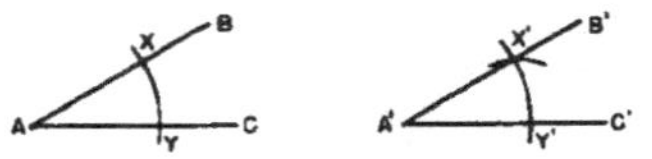

Figure 24. Reproducing an angle.

b. Finding the Midpoint of a Straight Line Segment. To find the midpoint of any straight line segment, such as AB in figure 25—

(1) Use a radius greater than half the length of AB. Using point A as the center, draw arcs CD and C'D'. With point B as the center, and using the same radius, draw arcs EF and E'F'.

(2) Draw a straight line to connect the points where the arcs intersect. Point X, where this line intersects AB, is the midpoint of straight line segment AB.

c. Constructing a Perpendicular. To construct a perpendicular to a straight line at a given point—

(1) On the straight line, such as AB in figure 26, mark point P at which the perpendicular is to be constructed.

(2) Set a compass for a radius less than the shorter of the two segments, AP

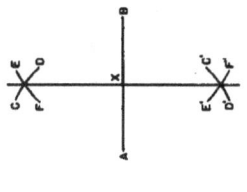

Figure 25. Bisecting a straight line segment.

or PB. With P as a center, draw arcs, cutting line AB at points X and Y.

(3) Set the compass for a radius greater than PX. With X as a center, draw an arc above point P (fig. 26). Keep the compass at the same setting and, with Y as a center, draw another arc intersecting the one drawn with X as a center. (The two arcs may be drawn to intersect below point P instead of above.)

(4) Draw a straight line from the point where the two arcs intersect to point P. The line is perpendicular to AB.

(5) To construct the perpendicular bisector of a straight line segment, first find the midpoint of the line segment (b above), and construct the perpendicular at that point.

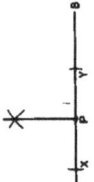

Figure 26. Constructing a perpendicular to a straight line at a point on the line.

d. Constructing a Perpendicular to a Straight Line from a Point Not on the Line. To draw a perpendicular to a straight line from a point outside the line, such as point P in figure 27—

(1) With point P as the center, draw an arc cutting line AB at points X and Y.

(2) Using a radius greater than one-half the distance between X and Y and, with points X and Y as centers, draw arcs that intersect.

(3) Draw a straight line from point P, through the point where the two arcs intersect, to line AB. The line is perpendicular to AB.

e. Finding the Center of a Circle.

(1) Draw any two chords, such as AB and AC in figure 28.

(2) Construct the perpendicular bisector of each chord (c above). Point X, where the two perpendicular bisectors meet, is the center of the circle.

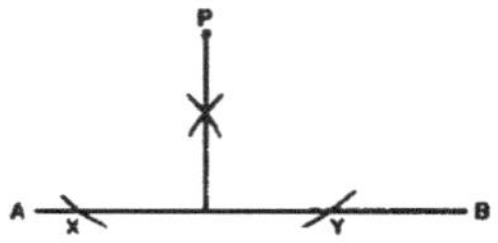

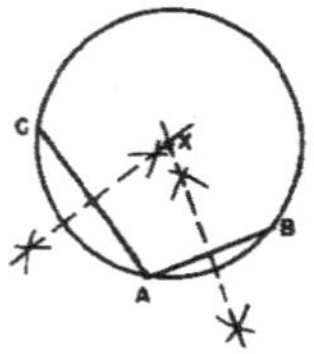

Figure 27. Constructing a perpendicular to a straight line from a point not on the line.

Figure 28. Finding the center of a circle.

f. Bisecting an Angle. Any angle, such as angle CAB in figure 29, can be divided into two equal angles. An angle, thus divided, is said to be bisected. To bisect an angle—

(1) Using A as a center, draw an arc cutting the sides of angle CAB at X and Y.

(2) With X and Y as centers, draw intersecting arcs.

(3) Draw a straight line from A through the point where the arcs intersect. The line divides angles CAB into two

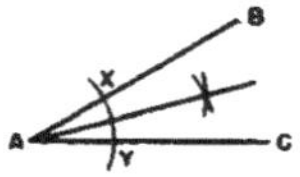

Figure 29. Bisecting an angle.

equal angles and is called the bisector of angle CAB.

131. Triangles

a. General. A triangle is a plane figure bounded by three straight lines. There are several different kinds of triangles.

(1) An *equilateral triangle* (A, fig. 30) has three equal sides and three equal angles; each angle equals 60°.

(2) An *isosceles triangle* has two equal

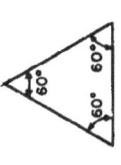 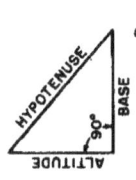 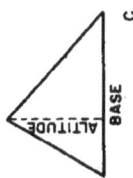 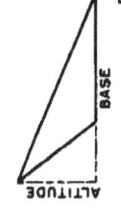

Figure 30. Triangles.

sides and two equal angles. The equal sides are opposite the equal angles.

(3) A *right triangle* (B, fig. 30) has one right angle.

(4) An *oblique triangle* (C and D, fig. 30) is one that does not contain a right angle. Thus, all except right triangles are oblique triangles.

b. *Base.* The base of a triangle is the side on which the triangle is supposed to stand. However, any side of a triangle may be used as the base.

c. *Altitude.* The altitude is the perpendicular line distance from the vertex of the triangle to the base or the base extended. In B, figure 30, the altitude of a right triangle is shown, in C, figure 30, the altitude of an acute triangle, and in D, figure 30, the altitude of an obtuse triangle. Note that in an obtuse triangle, it is necessary to extend the base of the triangle to find the altitude.

d. *Area.* The area of a triangle is the entire surface within the perimeter.

e. *Hypotenuse.* The side opposite the right angle of any right triangle is the hypotenuse (B, fig. 30).

132. Law of Angles of Any Triangle

The sum of the angles of any triangle is equal to 180°. When given any two of three angles of a triangle, the third angle can be found by subtracting the sum of the given angles from 180°.

Example 1:

If two angles of a triangle are 90° and 45°, what is the size of the third angle?

$90° + 45° = 135°$
$180° - 135° = 45°$

Therefore, the third angle is 45°.

Example 2:

Angle A of triangle ABC is 100°; angle B is 30°. What is the size of angle C?

$\angle A + \angle B + \angle C = 180°$
$\angle A = 100°$
$\angle B = 30°$
$\angle A + \angle B = 130°$
$\angle C = 180° - 130°$
$\angle C = 50°$

133. Law of Right Triangles

a. *The Pythagorean Theorem.* This theorem, which applies to any right triangle, states that *the square of the hypotenuse is equal to the sum of the squares of the other two sides.* The Pythagorean theorem is of prime importance in trigonometry (ch. 10) since the value of one side of a right triangle can be found if the other two sides are known. Thus, in figure 31:

$c^2 = a^2 + b^2$ or $25 = 16 + 9$
$a^2 = c^2 - b^2$ or $16 = 25 - 9$
$b^2 = c^2 - a^2$ or $9 = 25 - 16$

Example 1: Find the hypotenuse of a right triangle if the sides are 3 and 4 inches long, respectively.

$c^2 = a^2 + b^2$
$c^2 = 9 + 16$
$c^2 = 25$
$c = \sqrt{25}$
$c = 5 \text{ inches}$

Example 2: The hypotenuse of a right triangle is 13 inches long and one side is 5 inches long. Find the length of the other side.

$c^2 = a^2 + b^2$
$13^2 = 5^2 + b^2$
$b^2 = 169 - 25$
$b^2 = 144$
$b = \sqrt{144}$
$b = 12 \text{ inches}$

Example 3: Given the right triangle ABC (fig. 31), find c if $a = 7$ and $b = 6$.

$c^2 = a^2 + b^2$
$c^2 = 49 + 36$
$c^2 = 85$
$c = \sqrt{85}$
$c = 9.22-$

```
    9. 2 2
 √85.00 00
  81
  ---
  182  400
       364
       ---
  1842 3600
       3684
```

Example 4: Given the right triangle ABC (fig. 31), find b if $a = 9$ and $c = 12$.

$b^2 = c^2 - a^2$
$b^2 = 144 - 81$
$b^2 = 63$
$b = \sqrt{63}$
$b = 7.93+$

```
     7. 9 3
 √63.00 00
  49
  ---
  149  1400
       1341
       ---
  1583 5900
       4749
```

Example 5: Given the right triangle ABC (fig. 31), find a if $b = 6$ and $c = 13$.

$a^2 = c^2 - b^2$
$a^2 = 169 - 36$
$a^2 = 133$
$a = \sqrt{133}$
$a = 11.53+$

```
    1 1. 5 3
 √1 33.00 00
  1
  ---
  21  33
      21
      ---
  225 1200
      1125
      ---
  2303 7500
       6909
```

b. *Special Right Triangles.* The two right triangles in examples 1 and 2 of a above are special right triangles with sides that have whole numbers. These triangles are called the 3-4-5 right triangle and the 5-12-13 right triangle, although their sides may also be multiples of these numbers. For example, a triangle having sides of 6, 8, and 10 inches is also a 3-4-5 right triangle, because its sides are multiples of 3, 4, and 5. When determining the unknown side of a right triangle, the process is greatly simplified if the triangle is a 3-4-5 or 5-12-13 right triangle. In these cases, the unknown side can often be determined by inspection.

Example 1: The hypotenuse of a right triangle is 15 inches long, and one side is 12 inches long. Find the other side.

Since 15 and 12 can be divided by 3 to give 5 and 4, the triangle is a 3-4-5 right triangle. The third side, therefore, is equal to 3 times 3, or

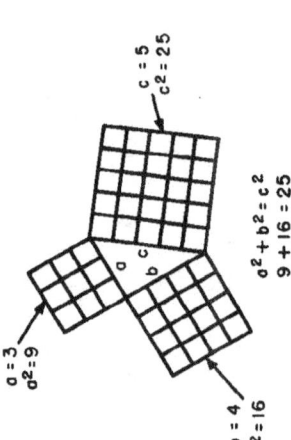

Figure 31. The Pythagorean theorem.

9 inches. The answer can be checked by the Pythagorean theorem.

Example 2: The two sides of a triangle are 10 and 24 feet long. Find the length of the hypotenuse.

Dividing 10 and 24 by 2 gives 5 and 12, the two sides of a 5–12–13 right triangle. Therefore, the hypotenuse is 2 times 13, or 26 inches.

134. Area of Any Triangle

The area of any triangle is equal to one-half the product of its base and altitude. The formula for finding the area is $A = \frac{bh}{2}$ where b is the base of the triangle and h is the altitude.

Example 1:

What is the area of a triangle with a base of 15 inches and an altitude of 10 inches?

$$A = \frac{bh}{2}$$
$$= \frac{15 \times 10}{2}$$
$$= \frac{150}{2}$$
$$= 75 \text{ square inches}$$

Example 2:

Find the area of a right triangle if the base measures 7 feet and the hypotenuse 25 feet.

$c^2 - b^2 = a^2$
$a^2 = 25^2 - 7^2 = 625 - 49$
$a^2 = 576$
$a = \sqrt{576} = 24$ feet altitude

$$A = \frac{bh}{2}$$
$$= \frac{7 \times 24}{2} = \frac{168}{2}$$
$$= 84 \text{ square feet}$$

135. Quadrilaterals

A quadrilateral is a plane figure bounded by four straight lines.

a. A *parallelogram* (A, fig. 32) is a quadrilateral having both pairs of opposite sides parallel.

b. A *rectangle* (B, fig. 32) is a parallelogram that has four right angles.

c. A *square* (C, fig. 32) is a rectangle, all four sides of which are equal.

d. A *trapezoid* (D, fig. 32) is a quadrilateral with two sides (called bases) parallel and unequal.

136. Area of Any Parallelogram

The area of any parallelogram is equal to the product of the base by the altitude. The formula for finding the area is $A = bh$ where b is the base and h is the height or altitude.

Example 1: Find the area of a square, each side of which is 15 inches.

$$A = bh$$
$$= 15 \times 15$$
$$= 225 \text{ square inches}$$

Example 2: What is the area of a rectangle with a base of 12 inches and an altitude of 7 inches?

$$A = bh$$
$$= 12 \times 7$$
$$= 84 \text{ square inches}$$

137. Area of Trapezoid

The area of a trapezoid is determined by multiplying one-half the sum of the bases by the altitude of the trapezoid.

Thus, $A = \left(\frac{B+b}{2}\right)h$.

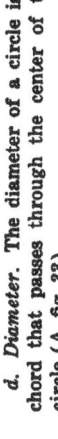

Figure 32. Quadrilaterals.

Example: Find the area of a trapezoid the bases of which are 16 and 10 inches long and the altitude is 8 inches.

$$A = \left(\frac{B+b}{2}\right)h$$
$$= \left(\frac{16+10}{2}\right)8$$
$$= \frac{26}{2} \times \overset{4}{\cancel{8}}$$
$$= 104 \text{ square inches}$$

138. Circles

a. General. A circle is a plane figure bounded by a closed curve, every point of which is equidistant from the center.

b. Circumference. The circumference is the curved line that bounds a circle (A, fig. 33).

c. Chord. A chord is a straight line drawn through a circle and terminated at its intersections with the circumference (B, fig. 33).

d. Diameter. The diameter of a circle is a chord that passes through the center of the circle (A, fig. 33).

e. Radius. The radius of a circle is a straight line from the center to a point on the circumference (A, fig. 33). All radii of the same circle are of equal length, one-half of the diameter.

f. Arc. An arc is any part of the circumference of a circle.

g. Segment. A segment is that area of a circle bounded by a chord and the arc subtended by that chord (C, fig. 33).

h. Sector. A sector is the area between an arc and two radii drawn to the ends of the arc (C, fig. 33).

i. Tangent. A tangent is a straight line that touches the circumference of a circle at only one point and is perpendicular to the radius drawn to the point of contact (B, fig. 33). This

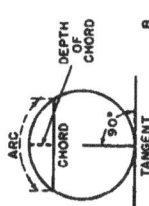

Figure 33. Circles.

point is called the *point of tangency* or the *point of contact*.

j. Concentric Circles. Concentric circles are circles having a common center (D, fig. 33).

k. Pi(π). The Greek letter π is used to represent the relationship of the circumference of any circle to its diameter. Roughly, it equals $\frac{22}{7}$. More approximately, it equals 3.1416. In many applications, it is rounded off to 3.14.

139. Circumference of Any Circle

The circumference of any circle is π times the diameter; therefore, $C = \pi D$.

Example 1: Find the circumference of a circle if the diameter is 6½ inches.

$C = \pi D$
$= 3.14 \times 6.5$
$= 20.42$ inches

Example 2: Find the diameter of a circular tank having a circumference of 31½ inches.

When the circumference of a circle is given, the diameter is calculated by dividing the circumference by $\pi - D = \frac{C}{\pi}$.

$D = \frac{C}{\pi}$
$= \frac{31.5}{3.1416}$
$= 10.03$ inches

140. Area of Any Circle

a. The area of any circle is equal to π multiplied by the radius squared; therefore, $a = \pi r^2$.

Example 1: Find the area of a circle having a diameter of 5 feet 6 inches.

$A = \pi r^2$
$= \pi \left(\frac{5.5}{2}\right)^2$
$= \pi (2.75)^2$
$= 3.14 \times 7.56$
$= 23.76$ square feet

Example 2: What is the diameter of a circle the area of which is 78.54 square rods?

$A = \pi r^2$ and $r = \frac{D}{2}$
$A = \pi \left(\frac{D}{2}\right)^2$
$A = \frac{\pi D^2}{4}$

Transposing:

$D^2 = \frac{4A}{\pi}$
$D = \sqrt{\frac{4A}{\pi}}$
$D = 2\sqrt{\frac{A}{\pi}}$

Substituting and solving for D:

$D = 2\sqrt{\frac{78.54}{3.1416}}$
$D = 2\sqrt{25}$
$D = 2 \times 5$
$D = 10$ rods

b. The area of any circle also is equal to one-half the product of the circumference and the radius.

Example: If the diameter of a circle is 10 inches, and the circumference of the circle is 31.416 inches, what is the area of the circle?

$A = \frac{1}{2}Cr$
$r = \frac{1}{2}D$ or $r = 5$
$A = \frac{1}{2}(31.416 \times 5)$
$= \frac{157.08}{2}$
$= 78.54$ square inches

141. Area of Ring

A ring is the area between the circumferences of two concentric circles. The area of a ring may be found by subtracting the area of the small circle from the area of the large circle. If R is the radius of the large circle and r is the radius of the small circle, a simplified formula for the area of the ring can be developed as follows:

Area of ring = area of large circle − area of small circle
$= \pi R^2 - \pi r^2$
$= \pi (R^2 - r^2)$

By factoring $(R^2 - r^2)$ into $(R + r)(R - r)$, the formula also can be written:

$A = \pi (R + r)(R - r)$

Example: Find the area of a ring having an inside diameter of 8 inches and an outside diameter of 12 inches.

$A = \pi (R + r)(R - r)$
$= 3.14(6 + 4)(6 - 4)$
$= 3.14 \times 10 \times 2$
$= 62.8$ square inches

142. Review Problems—Plane Geometry

a. Find the area of a rectangle having a base of 12 inches and an altitude of 8 inches.

b. What is the area of a square, each side of which is 6 inches?

c. Find the area of a triangle of which the altitude is 5 inches and the base is 10 inches.

d. Find the area of a triangle having an altitude of 15 inches and a base of 2 inches.

e. What is the hypotenuse of a right triangle the sides of which are 12 and 8 inches?

f. Find the third side of a right triangle if one side is 7 inches and the hypotenuse is 9 inches.

g. Identify the following figures, give the formulas, and solve for the required quantity.

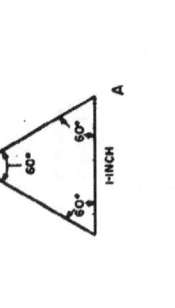

A

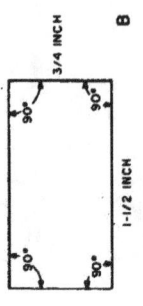

B

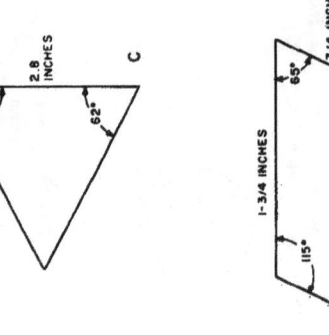

C

D

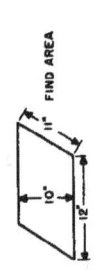

(1) FIND AREA

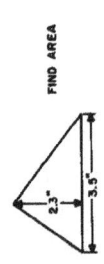

(2) FIND AREA

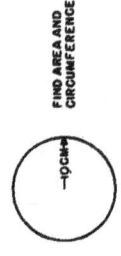

(3) FIND AREA AND CIRCUMFERENCE

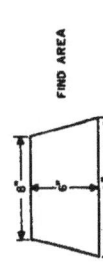

(4) FIND AREA

h. What are the perimeters of the following figures?

i. Find the area of the largest circle that can be cut from a square piece of sheet metal with sides of 10 inches.

j. If the height of an antenna is 80 feet, how far from its top is an object on the ground 60 feet from the base of the pole?

k. How many square feet of lumber are needed to build 10 boxes 18 inches by 16 inches by 9 inches?

l. A metal plate is in the shape of an equilateral triangle. If the altitude is 14 inches, what is the perimeter,

CHAPTER 10
TRIGONOMETRY

Section I. BASIC TRIGONOMETRIC THEORY

143. Introduction

a. Definition. Trigonometry deals with the relationships between the sides and angles of triangles. It uses the theories of basic mathematics—the numbers of arithmetic, the equations of algebra, and the theorems of geometry —to aid in the measurement of the sides and angles of triangles.

b. Application. The ability to use angles and their trigonometric relationships in electrical calculations is especially important in the study of alternating current (ac). Most effects of ac circuit components can be studied or described only in terms of the part of a cycle by which a current lags behind a corresponding voltage, or vice versa. A large percentage of the problems relating to the analysis of ac circuits and communication networks involves the solution of the right triangle in some form. Certain facts about right triangles are familiar (ch 9) —namely, that the square of the hypotenuse is equal to the sum of the squares of the other two sides ($c^2 = a^2 + b^2$), that the sum of the acute angles of a right triangle is 90°, and that the sum of the interior angles of any triangle is 180°. However, it would be impossible to solve certain problems with only this information. After learning other relationships between the sides and angles of triangles, it will be found that trigonometry is an easy and accurate method of solving many problems in ac electricity.

144. Trigonometric Functions

a. General. Trigonometry is based on the six trigonometric functions involved in the study of the right angle. If the value of one quantity depends on the value of a second quantity, the first quantity is said to be a function of the second. The six trigonometric functions —sine (sin), cosine (cos), tangent (tan), co-tangent (cot), secant (sec), and cosecant (csc) —are derived from the ratios of the sides of a right triangle to each other.

b. The Right Triangle. Figure 34 shows a right triangle, with the angles labeled A, B, and C; C is the right angle. The sides of the triangle are labeled a, b, and c, with the side opposite each angle given the same letter as the angle. The following are the trigonometric ratios of the sides of a triangle:

$$\sin = \frac{\text{opposite side}}{\text{hypotenuse}}$$

$$\cos = \frac{\text{adjacent side}}{\text{hypotenuse}}$$

$$\tan = \frac{\text{opposite side}}{\text{adjacent side}}$$

$$\cot = \frac{\text{adjacent side}}{\text{opposite side}}$$

$$\sec = \frac{\text{hypotenuse}}{\text{adjacent side}}$$

$$\csc = \frac{\text{hypotenuse}}{\text{opposite side}}$$

c. Angle A. Refer again to figure 34. Using the acute angle A, a is the opposite side, b is the adjacent side, and c, which is the side opposite the right angle, is the hypotenuse. Therefore,

$$\sin A = \frac{a}{c}$$

$$\cos A = \frac{b}{c}$$

$$\tan A = \frac{a}{b}$$

$$\cot A = \frac{b}{a}$$

$$\sec A = \frac{c}{b}$$

$$\csc A = \frac{c}{a}$$

d. Angle B. Using the acute angle B in figure 34, b is the opposite side, a is the adjacent side, and c is the hypotenuse. Therefore,

$$\sin B = \frac{b}{c}$$

$$\cos B = \frac{a}{c}$$

$$\tan B = \frac{b}{a}$$

$$\cot B = \frac{a}{b}$$

$$\sec B = \frac{c}{a}$$

$$\csc B = \frac{c}{b}$$

e. Angle C. Right angle C is the angle which establishes the relationship between the other sides and other angles and thus may be called a constant. Although it is possible to obtain functions for angle C, they are not covered here because they are not needed in solving problems of this type.

Example:

Determine the values of the trigonometric functions of a right triangle with sides as follows: $a = 3$, $b = 4$, $c = 5$ (fig. 35).

Functions of angle A:

$$\sin A = \frac{a}{c} = \frac{3}{5}$$

$$\cos A = \frac{b}{c} = \frac{4}{5}$$

$$\tan A = \frac{a}{b} = \frac{3}{4}$$

$$\cot A = \frac{b}{a} = \frac{4}{3}$$

$$\sec A = \frac{c}{b} = \frac{5}{4}$$

$$\csc A = \frac{c}{a} = \frac{5}{3}$$

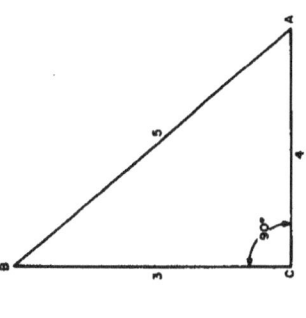

Figure 34. Trigonometric functions of the right triangle.

Functions of angle B:

$$\sin B = \frac{b}{c} = \frac{4}{5}$$

$$\cos B = \frac{a}{c} = \frac{3}{5}$$

$$\tan B = \frac{b}{a} = \frac{4}{3}$$

$$\cot B = \frac{a}{b} = \frac{3}{4}$$

$$\sec B = \frac{c}{a} = \frac{5}{3}$$

$$\csc B = \frac{c}{b} = \frac{5}{4}$$

Figure 35. Right triangle with sides known.

145. Reciprocal Relations of Trigonometric Functions

From the definitions of the six trigonometric functions (par. 144), the reciprocal relations (listed below) can be determined. The cosecant, secant, and cotangent should always be thought of as the reciprocals of the sine, cosine, and tangent, respectively.

$$\sin A = \frac{a}{c} = \frac{1}{\frac{c}{a}} = \frac{1}{\csc A}$$

$$\cos A = \frac{b}{c} = \frac{1}{\frac{c}{b}} = \frac{1}{\sec A}$$

$$\tan A = \frac{a}{b} = \frac{1}{\frac{b}{a}} = \frac{1}{\cot A}$$

$$\csc A = \frac{c}{a} = \frac{1}{\frac{a}{c}} = \frac{1}{\sin A}$$

$$\sec A = \frac{c}{b} = \frac{1}{\frac{b}{c}} = \frac{1}{\cos A}$$

$$\cot A = \frac{b}{a} = \frac{1}{\frac{a}{b}} = \frac{1}{\tan A}$$

146. Functions of Complementary Angles

a. The function of an acute angle is equal to the cofunction of its complementary angle. Apply the definitions of the trigonometric functions (par. 144) to angles A and B to obtain the following relations:

$$\sin B = \frac{b}{c} = \cos A$$
$$\tan B = \frac{b}{a} = \cot A$$
$$\sec B = \frac{c}{a} = \csc A$$
$$\cos B = \frac{a}{c} = \sin A$$
$$\cot B = \frac{a}{b} = \tan A$$
$$\csc B = \frac{c}{b} = \sec A$$

b. With angle B equal to $90° - A$, these relations may be written:

$$\sin (90° - A) = \cos A$$
$$\tan (90° - A) = \cot A$$
$$\sec (90° - A) = \csc A$$
$$\cos (90° - A) = \sin A$$
$$\cot (90° - A) = \tan A$$
$$\csc (90° - A) = \sec A$$

147. Solving for Unknown Functions

If one trigonometric function of a right triangle is known, the other trigonometric functions can be determined. This is done by using the Pythagorean theorem (par. 133).

Example 1: Given the right triangle ABC (fig. 23): side a is 4; side C is 9. Since $\sin A = \frac{4}{9}$, find the other trigonometric functions of angle A.

$$\sin A = \frac{a}{c}; \text{ also, } \sin A = \frac{4}{9}$$

Therefore, $a = 4, c = 9$

$$b^2 = c^2 - a^2$$
$$b^2 = 81 - 16$$
$$b^2 = 65$$
$$b = \sqrt{65}$$
$$b = 8.06$$

```
         8. 0 6
   √65.00 00
        64
   1606  10000
          9636
```

$$\sin A = \frac{4}{9}$$
$$\cos A = \frac{8.06}{9}$$
$$\tan A = \frac{4}{8.06}$$
$$\cot A = \frac{8.06}{4}$$
$$\sec A = \frac{9}{8.06}$$
$$\csc A = \frac{9}{4}$$

Example 2: Given the right triangle ABC (fig. 23): side A is $\sqrt{3}$; side b is 7. Since $\tan A = \frac{\sqrt{3}}{7}$ or $\frac{1}{7}\sqrt{3}$, find the other trigonometric functions of angle A.

$\tan A = \frac{a}{b}$; also, $\tan A = \frac{1}{7}\sqrt{3} = \frac{\sqrt{3}}{7}$.

Therefore,
$$a = \sqrt{3}, b = 7$$
$$c^2 = a^2 + b^2$$
$$c^2 = 3 + 49$$
$$c^2 = 52$$
$$c = \sqrt{52}$$
$$c = \sqrt{4} \cdot \sqrt{13}$$
$$c = 2\sqrt{13}$$

$$\sin A = \frac{\sqrt{3}}{2\sqrt{13}}$$
$$\cos A = \frac{7}{2\sqrt{13}}$$
$$\tan A = \frac{\sqrt{3}}{7}$$
$$\cot A = \frac{7}{\sqrt{3}}$$
$$\sec A = \frac{2\sqrt{13}}{7}$$
$$\csc A = \frac{2\sqrt{13}}{\sqrt{3}}$$

148. Solving for Sides and Trigonometric Functions When One Side and One Function Are Given

When one side and one function of an angle of a right triangle are given, the two other sides and the remaining trigonometric functions of the given angle can be found. These are determined by use of the Pythagorean theorem.

Example 1: Given the right triangle ABC (fig. 34): if the hypotenuse is 30 inches and sec $A = 5$, solve for sides a and b and the trigonometric functions of angle A.

Sec $A = \frac{c}{b}$; also, sec $A = \frac{30}{b}$; but sec $A = 5$ or $\frac{5}{1}$.

Therefore, $\frac{30}{b} = \frac{5}{1}$

$$5b = 30$$
$$b = 6 \text{ inches}$$

$$a^2 = c^2 - b^2$$
$$a^2 = 900 - 36$$
$$a^2 = 864$$
$$a = \sqrt{864}$$
$$a = \sqrt{144}\sqrt{6}$$
$$a = 12\sqrt{6} \text{ inches}, b = 6 \text{ inches}, c = 30 \text{ inches}$$

sin A = $\frac{12\sqrt{6}}{30} = \frac{12}{30}\sqrt{6} = \frac{2}{5}\sqrt{6}$

cos A = $\frac{\sqrt{6}}{30} = \frac{1}{5}$

tan A = $\frac{12\sqrt{6}}{6} = 2\sqrt{6}$

cot A = $\frac{6}{12\sqrt{6}} = \frac{1}{2\sqrt{6}} \cdot \frac{\sqrt{6}}{\sqrt{6}} = \frac{\sqrt{6}}{(2)(6)} = \frac{\sqrt{6}}{12} = \frac{1}{12}\sqrt{6}$

sec A = $\frac{30}{6} = 5$

csc A = $\frac{30}{12\sqrt{6}} = \frac{5}{2\sqrt{6}} \cdot \frac{\sqrt{6}}{\sqrt{6}} = \frac{5\sqrt{6}}{(2)(6)} = \frac{5\sqrt{6}}{12} = \frac{5}{12}\sqrt{6}$

Example 2: Given the right triangle *ABC* (fig. 34): solve for sides *b* and *c* and the trigonometric functions of angle *A* when side *a* is 21.2 inches and sin $A = \frac{4}{7}$.

Sin $A = \frac{a}{c}$; also, sin $a = \frac{21.2}{c}$, but sin $A = \frac{4}{7}$.

Therefore, $\frac{21.2}{c} = \frac{4}{7}$

$4c = 148.4$
$c = 37.1$ inches

$b^2 = c^2 - a^2$
$b^2 = 1376.41 - 449.44$
$b^2 = 926.97$
$b = \sqrt{926.97}$
$b = 30.4$ inches, $a = 21.2$ inches, $c = 37.1$ inches

sin $A = \frac{21.2}{37.1} = \frac{4}{7}$ cot $A = \frac{30.4}{21.2} = \frac{7.6}{5.3}$

cos $A = \frac{30.4}{37.1}$ sec $A = \frac{37.1}{30.4}$

tan $A = \frac{21.2}{30.4} = \frac{5.3}{7.6}$ csc $A = \frac{37.1}{21.2} = \frac{7}{4}$

149. Constructing an Acute Angle of Right Triangle When One Trigonometric Function Is Known

When the trigonometric function of an acute angle is given, the angle may be constructed geometrically. Use the definition given for the given function.

Example: Construct the acute angle *A* of right triangle *ABC* if tan $A = \frac{1}{4}$.

Step 1. Let $a = 1$ unit and $b = 4$ units.

Step 2. Erect perpendicular lines *AC* and *BC*. Use cross-sectional paper if available.

Step 3. Measure off 1 unit along *BC* and 4 units along *AC* (A, fig. 36).

Step 4. Join *A* and *B*, thus forming the right triangle *ABC* (B, fig. 36).

Step 5. Tan $A = \frac{1}{4}$; therefore, *A* is the required angle. Measuring angle *A* with a protractor shows it to

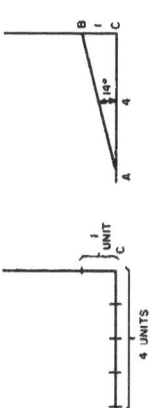

Figure 36. Constructing an angle when one function is known.

be an angle of approximately 14°.

150. Common Trigonometric Functions

a. General. There are two special-case right triangles that are commonly used in solving mathematical problems. These are the right isosceles triangle (par. 131a) with equal acute angles of 45° (fig. 37) and the right triangle with equal acute angles of 30° and 60°. The functions of these angles are tabulated in appendix III.

b. Trigonometric Functions of 45°. Draw the right triangle *ABC* (fig. 37) with angle *A* equal to 45°. Because the acute angles of a right triangle are complementary, angle *A* plus angle *B* equals 90°. Thus, angle *B* is also 45°. Since sides opposite equal angles are equal, side *a* is equal to side *b*.

Let $a = 1$ and $b = 1$.

$c^2 = a^2 + b^2$
$c^2 = 1 + 1$
$c^2 = 2$
$c = \sqrt{2}$

sin 45° = $\frac{1}{\sqrt{2}} \cdot \frac{\sqrt{2}}{\sqrt{2}} = \frac{\sqrt{2}}{2} = \frac{1}{2}\sqrt{2}$

cos 45° = $\frac{1}{\sqrt{2}} \cdot \frac{\sqrt{2}}{\sqrt{2}} = \frac{\sqrt{2}}{2} = \frac{1}{2}\sqrt{2}$

tan 45° = $\frac{1}{1} = 1$

cot 45° = $\frac{1}{1} = 1$

sec 45° = $\frac{\sqrt{2}}{1} = \sqrt{2}$

csc 45° = $\frac{\sqrt{2}}{1} = \sqrt{2}$

c. Trigonometric Functions of 30° and 60°. Draw the equilateral triangle *ABX* (fig. 38). The angles of any equilateral triangle are 60° and the sides are equal (par. 131a). Drop a perpendicular *BC* to the center of the base *AX*. Right angles *ACB* and *BCX* are formed by the perpendicular and the base. The angles *ABC* and *XBC* are 30° angles. Since the sides of the equilateral triangle are equal, the perpendicular bisecting the base makes the base *AC* of the right triangle *ABC* one-half the length of the base *AX* of the equilateral triangle. Thus, the side opposite the right angle in a right triangle

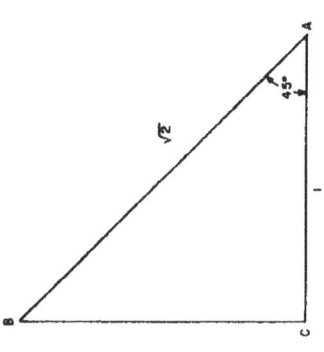

Figure 37. Right isosceles triangle—trigonometric functions of 45°.

is twice the length of the side opposite the 30° angle.

Let $b = 1$ and $c = 2$.

$a^2 = c^2 - b^2$
$a^2 = 4 - 1$
$a^2 = 3$
$a = \sqrt{3}$

sin 60° = $\frac{\sqrt{3}}{2} = \frac{1}{2}\sqrt{3}$

cos 60° = $\frac{1}{2}$

tan 60° = $\frac{\sqrt{3}}{1} = \sqrt{3}$

cot 60° = $\frac{1}{\sqrt{3}} \cdot \frac{\sqrt{3}}{\sqrt{3}} = \frac{\sqrt{3}}{3} = \frac{1}{3}\sqrt{3}$

sec 60° = $\frac{2}{1} = 2$

csc 60° = $\frac{2}{\sqrt{3}} \cdot \frac{\sqrt{3}}{\sqrt{3}} = \frac{2\sqrt{3}}{3} = \frac{2}{3}\sqrt{3}$

sin 30° = $\frac{1}{2}$

cos 30° = $\frac{\sqrt{3}}{2} = \frac{1}{2}\sqrt{3}$

tan 30° = $\frac{1}{\sqrt{3}} \cdot \frac{\sqrt{3}}{\sqrt{3}} = \frac{\sqrt{3}}{3} = \frac{1}{3}\sqrt{3}$

cot 30° = $\frac{\sqrt{3}}{1} = \sqrt{3}$

sec 30° = $\frac{2}{\sqrt{3}} \cdot \frac{\sqrt{3}}{\sqrt{3}} = \frac{2\sqrt{3}}{3} = \frac{2}{3}\sqrt{3}$

csc 30° = $\frac{2}{1} = 2$

152. Calculations Involving Angles

a. Addition. To add angles, arrange the degrees, minutes, and seconds in separate columns and add each column separately. If the sum of the seconds column is 60 or more, subtract 60 or a multiple of 60 from that column, and add 1 minute or the same multiple of 1 minute to the minutes column. If the sum of the minutes column is 60 or more, subtract 60 from that column and add 1° to the degree column.

Example 1: Add 20° 40′ 25″, 8° 35′ 5″, and 30° 58′ 51″.

```
 20°  40′  25″
  8°  35′   5″
 30°  58′  51″
 58° 133′  81″
```

Subtract 60″ from 81″ and add 1′ to 133′.

```
58° 133′  81″
     +1′ −60″
58° 134′  21″
```

Subtract 120′ from 134′ and add 2° to 58°.

```
 58° 134′  21″
 +2° −120′
 60°  14′  21″
```

Example 2: Add 15° 44′ 36″ and 12° 38′ 35″.

```
15° 44′ 36″
12° 38′ 35″
27° 82′ 71″ = 27° 83′ 11″ = 28° 23′ 11″
```

b. Subtraction. To subtract angles, arrange the degrees, minutes, and seconds in separate columns with the larger angle on top. Then, subtract the individual columns. If the upper number in a column is too small to allow subtraction, one unit must be taken away from the preceding column and 60 units added to the insufficient number to make subtraction possible.

Example 1: Subtract 14° 51′ 30″ from 86° 45′ 10″.

```
 86° 45′ 10″
−14° 51′ 30″
```

Subtraction cannot be performed in either the seconds or minutes columns. Subtract 1′ from 45′ leaving 44′, and add 60″ to 10″ for a total of 70″.

```
 86° 44′ 70″
−14° 51′ 30″
```

Subtraction still cannot be performed in the minutes column. Subtract 1° from 86°, leaving 85°, and add 60′ to 44′ for a total of 104′.

```
 85° 104′ 70″
−14°  51′ 30″
 71°  53′ 40″
```

Example 2: Subtract 10° 35′ 42″ from 19° 20′ 20″.

```
 19° 20′ 20″
−10° 35′ 42″
```

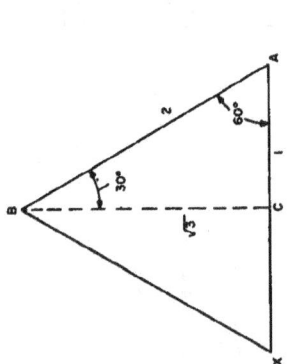

Figure 38. Equilateral right triangle—trigonometric functions of a right triangle with angles of 30° and 60°

151. Solving for Sides of 45°–45°–90° or 30°–60°–90° Triangles When One Side Is Given

In special cases, right triangles can be solved when only one side is given. These are the 45°–45°–90° isosceles triangle and the 30°–60°–90° triangle.

Example 1: Solve for the unknown sides of right triangle ABC if angle $A = 60°$ and $b = 4$ inches.

$\tan 60° = \dfrac{a}{b} = \dfrac{a}{4}$; however, $\tan 60° = \sqrt{3}$.

Therefore,

$\dfrac{a}{4} = \dfrac{\sqrt{3}}{1}$

$a = 4\sqrt{3}$ inches

$\cos 60° = \dfrac{b}{c} = \dfrac{4}{c}$; however, $\cos 60° = \dfrac{1}{2}$.

Therefore,

$\dfrac{4}{c} = \dfrac{1}{2}$

$c = 8$ inches

Thus, $a = 4\sqrt{3}$ inches, $b = 4$ inches, $c = 8$ inches.

Example 2: Solve for the unknown sides of right triangle ABC if angle $A = 45°$ and $c = 6$ inches.

$\sin 45° = \dfrac{a}{c} = \dfrac{a}{6}$; however, $\sin 45° = \dfrac{\sqrt{2}}{2}$.

Therefore;

$\dfrac{a}{6} = \dfrac{\sqrt{2}}{2}$

$2a = 6\sqrt{2}$

$a = 3\sqrt{2}$

$\cos 45° = \dfrac{b}{c} = \dfrac{b}{6}$; however, $\cos 45° = \dfrac{\sqrt{2}}{2}$.

Therefore,

$\dfrac{b}{6} = \dfrac{\sqrt{2}}{2}$

$2b = 6\sqrt{2}$

$b = 3\sqrt{2}$ inches

Thus, $a = 3\sqrt{2}$ inches, $b = 3\sqrt{2}$ inches, $c = 6$ inches.

Subtraction cannot be performed in either the minutes or seconds columns. Therefore, change 19° 20′ 20″ to 18° 79′ 80″ and subtract.

18° 79′ 80″
−10° 35′ 42″
─────────────
 8° 44′ 38″

c. *Multiplication.* To multiply an angle by a given number, multiply each column by the number. If the answer in the seconds or minutes column is greater than 60, reduce as in the addition of angles (*a* above).

Example 1: Multiply 15° 21′ 40″ by 3:

15° 21′ 40″
       3
─────────────
45° 63′ 120″ = 45° 65′ 0″ = 46° 5′

Example 2: Multiply 12° 14′ 36″ by 5.

12° 14′ 36″
       5
─────────────
60° 70′ 180″ = 60° 73′ 0″ = 61° 13′

d. *Division.* To divide an angle by a given number, divide each column by the number (beginning with the degrees column). Change the remainder in degrees, if any, into minutes and add it to the minutes column; then, perform division on the numbers in the minutes column. Change the remainder in minutes, if any, to seconds and add it to the seconds column; then, perform division on the numbers in the seconds column.

Example 1: Divide 71° 22′ 21″ by 3.

```
        23°  47′  27″
      3)71°  22′  21″
         69   22″
         ──   120
          2°  142′
              141′
               1′ = 60″
                   81″
                   81″
```

Example 2: Divide 166° 17′ 36″ by 6.

```
        27°  42′  56″
      6)166° 17′  36″
        162   17″
        ───   300
          4° = 240′
               257′
               252′
                 5′ = 300″
                      336″
                      336″
```

153. Review Problems—Basic Trigonometry

Note. In the following problems, angle C is the right angle and equals 90°.

a. Find the third side of each of the following right triangles ABC, if two sides are:

(1) $a = 5, b = 7$
(2) $b = 18, c = 19$
(3) $a = 17, c = 43$
(4) $a = 3b$
(5) $a = 2m, c = m^2 + 1$

b. Given the right triangle ABC, solve for the trigonometric functions of angle A in each of the following cases:

(1) $\sin A = \dfrac{4}{7}$
(2) $\tan A = \dfrac{2}{3}$
(3) $\cos A = \dfrac{\sqrt{3}}{2}$
(4) $\csc A = 2.4$
(5) $\cot A = \dfrac{1}{y}$
(6) $\sec A = 2\dfrac{2}{3}$

c. Solve each of the right triangles (ABC) for the two unknown sides:

(1) $\sin A = \dfrac{1}{2}, a = 17$
(2) $\tan A = \dfrac{3}{4}, b = 12$
(3) $\cos A = \dfrac{4}{5}, c = 20$
(4) $\csc A = \dfrac{15}{7}, c = 37.5$
(5) $\cot A = \dfrac{3}{5}, a = 10$
(6) $\sec A = \dfrac{9}{4}, b = 18.4$

Section II. NATURAL TRIGONOMETRIC FUNCTIONS

154. Tables and Their Uses

For convenience in computing, trigonometric functions are arranged in tables similar to the tables of logarithms. The ratios themselves are called *natural* sines, cosines, tangents, cotangents, etc. The tables give the sines and cosines, the tangents and cotangents, and the secants and cosecants of the angles from 0° to 90°. Angles less than 45° are read down the page; the degrees are at the top of the page and the minutes are on the left. Angles greater than 45° are read up the page; the degrees are at the bottom of the page and the minutes are on the right. As with logarithms, it is necessary to interpolate to find the function of an angle which does not reduce to an integral number of minutes. When working with the sine and tangent, which are increasing in size from 0° to 90°, it is necessary to add in interpolation. When working with the cosine and cotangent, which are decreasing in size from 0° to 90°, it is necessary to subtract.

155. Finding the Function of an Angle From the Table

To find the function of an angle from the table, proceed much the same as with the table of logarithms. This is illustrated by the following examples:

a. *When an Angle Is Given in the Table.*

Example 1: Find the cosine of 44° 27′.

Step 1. Turn to the table of sines and cosines.
Step 2. Locate the 44° column at the top of the page.
Step 3. Locate the 27′ at the left of the page.
Step 4. Read .71386 in the column headed Cosin.
Step 5. Cos 44° 27′ = .71386.

Example 2: Fine the tangent of 86° 18′.

Step 1. Turn to the table of tangents and cotangents.
Step 2. Locate the 86° column at the bottom of the page.
Step 3. Locate the 18′ at the right of the page.
Step 4. Read 15.4638 in the column headed Tang.
Step 5. Tan 86° 18′ = 15.4638.

b. *When an Angle Is Not Given in the Table.*

Example 1: Find the sine of 32° 46′ 36″.

sin 32° 46′   = .54122
sin 32° 46′ 36″ = .54122 + x
sin 32° 47′   = .54146

47

$$\sin 32° 46' 36''$$
$$-32° 46'$$
$$\overline{36''}$$

$$32° 47'$$
$$-32° 46'$$
$$\overline{1'} = 60''$$

$$\text{ratio} = \frac{36}{60} = \frac{6}{10} = \frac{3}{5}$$

$$.54146 - .54122 = .00024$$

$$\text{ratio} = \frac{x}{.00024}$$

$$\frac{3}{5} = \frac{x}{.00024}$$

$$5x = .00072$$

$$x = .000144$$

$$\sin 32° 46' 36'' = .54122 + .000144 = .54136$$

Example 2: Find the tangent of 56° 43′ 27″.

$$\tan 56° 43' = 1.52332$$
$$\tan 56° 43' 27'' = 1.52332 + x$$
$$\tan 56° 44' = 1.52429$$

$$\frac{x}{.00097}$$

$$\frac{27}{60} \text{ or } \frac{9}{20} = \frac{x}{.00097}$$

$$20x = .00873$$
$$x = .000436 \text{ or } .00044$$

$$\tan 56° 43' 27'' = 1.52332 + .00044 = 1.52376$$

156. Finding an Angle When the Trigonometric Function Is Given

The procedure for using the table to find an angle corresponding to a function is similar to that of logarithms. This is illustrated in the examples in a and b below.

a. When the Function Is Given in the Table.

Example: Find the value of angle A if sine A = .27284.

Step 1. Find .27284 in the Sine column of the Sines and Cosines table.

Step 2. Reading 15° at the top of the column and 50′ in the minutes column on the left, angle A = 15° 50′.

b. When the Function Is Not Given in the Table.

Example 1: Find the value of angle A when sine A = .78112.

$$.78098 = \sin 51° 21'$$
$$.78112 = \sin 51° 21' + x$$
$$.78116 = \sin 51° 22'$$

$$\begin{array}{r}.78112\\-.78098\\\hline .00014\end{array}$$

$$\begin{array}{r}.78116\\-.78098\\\hline .00018\end{array}$$

$$\text{ratio} = \frac{.00014}{.00018} = \frac{14}{18} = \frac{7}{9}$$

$$51° 22' - 51° 21' = 1' = 60''$$

$$\text{ratio} = \frac{x}{60}$$

$$\frac{7}{9} = \frac{x}{60}$$

$$9x = 420$$
$$x = 47$$

$$\text{angle } A = 51° 21' 47''$$

Example 2: Find the value of angle A when cot A = .33820.

$$.33848 = \cot 71° 18'$$
$$.33820 = \cot 71° 18' + x$$
$$.33816 = \cot 71° 19'$$

$$\frac{28}{32} \text{ or } \frac{7}{8} = \frac{x}{60}$$

$$8x = 420$$
$$x = 53$$

$$\text{angle } A = 71° 18' 53''$$

157. Solving a Right Triangle When an Acute Angle and the Hypotenuse Are Given

To solve for the unknowns in a right triangle when an acute angle and the hypotenuse are given, proceed as in a and b below. In both examples, angle C is the right angle; therefore, angle C = 90°.

Example 1: Find the unknown sides a and b, and the value of angle B in right triangle ABC (fig. 39) if angle A is 33° 15′ and the hypotenuse, c is 9 inches.

$$\angle A + \angle B + \angle C = 180°$$
$$\angle B = 180° - \angle A - \angle C$$
$$\angle B = 180° - 33° 15' - 90°$$
$$\angle B = 56° 45'$$

$$\sin A = \frac{a}{c}$$

$$\sin 33° 15' = \frac{a}{9}$$

$$a = 9 \sin 33° 15'$$
$$a = 9 \times .54829 = 4.93461$$
$$a = 4.93461$$

$$\cos A = \frac{b}{c}$$

$$\cos 33° 15' = \frac{b}{9}$$

$$b = 9 \cos 33° 15'$$
$$b = 9 \times .83629$$
$$b = 7.52661$$

Therefore, $\angle A = 33° 15'$ $a = 4.93461$ inches
$\angle B = 56° 45'$ $b = 7.52661$ inches
$\angle C = 90°$ $c = 9$ inches

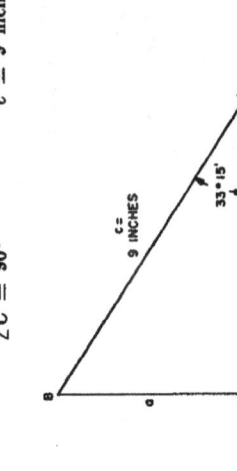

Figure 39. Solving a right triangle when an acute angle (33° 15′) and the hypotenuse are given.

158. Solving a Right Triangle When an Acute Angle and the Adjacent Side Are Given

To solve a right triangle when an acute angle and the adjacent side are given, proceed as shown in the example below. Angle C is the right angle.

Example: Find the unknown sides a and c and the value of angle B in the right triangle ABC (fig. 41) if angle A is $37° \ 42' \ 42''$ and the side adjacent to angle A is 8 inches.

$$\angle B = 180° - 90° - 37° \ 42' \ 42''$$
$$\angle B = 52° \ 17' \ 18''$$

$$\cos A = \frac{b}{c}$$

$$\cos 37° \ 42' \ 42'' = \frac{8}{c}$$

$$c \ (\cos 37° \ 42' \ 42'') = 8$$

$$\cos 37° \ 42' \quad = .79122$$
$$\cos 37° \ 42' \ 42'' = .79122 - x$$
$$\cos 37° \ 43' \quad = .79105$$

$$\frac{42}{60} \text{ or } \frac{7}{10} \quad \frac{x}{.00017}$$
$$10x = .00119$$
$$x = .00012$$

$$\cos 37° \ 42' \ 42'' = .79122 - .00012 = .79110$$

$$.79110c = 8$$
$$c = \frac{8}{.79110}$$
$$c = 10.11$$

$$\tan A = \frac{a}{b}$$

$$\tan 37° \ 42' \ 42'' = \frac{a}{8}$$

$$a = 8 \tan 37° \ 42' \ 42''$$

$$\tan 37° \ 42' \quad = .77289$$
$$\tan 37° \ 42' \ 42'' = .77289 + x$$
$$\tan 37° \ 43' \quad = .77335$$

$$\frac{42}{60} \text{ or } \frac{7}{10} \quad \frac{x}{.00046}$$
$$10x = .00322$$
$$x = .00032$$

$$\tan 37° \ 42' \ 42'' = .77289 + .00032 = .77321$$

$$a = 8 \times .77321$$
$$a = 6.18568$$

Therefore, $\angle A = 37° \ 42' \ 42''$ $a = 6.18568$ inches
$\angle B = 52° \ 17' \ 18''$ $b = 8$ inches
$\angle C = 90°$ $c = 10.11$ inches

Example 2: Solve for the unknown sides a and b, and the value of angle B in right triangle ABC (fig. 40) if angle A is $24° \ 35' \ 36''$ and the hypotenuse, c, is 12 inches.

$$\angle B = 180° - \angle A - \angle C$$
$$\angle B = 180° - 24° \ 35' \ 36'' - 90°$$
$$\angle B = 65° \ 24' \ 24''$$

$$\sin A = \frac{a}{c}$$

$$\sin 24° \ 35' \ 36'' = \frac{a}{12}$$

$$a = 12 \sin 24° \ 35' \ 36''$$

$$\sin 24° \ 35' \quad = .41602$$
$$\sin 24° \ 35' \ 36'' = .41602 + x$$
$$\sin 24° \ 36' \quad = .41628$$

$$\frac{36}{60} \text{ or } \frac{3}{5} \quad \frac{x}{.00026}$$
$$5x = .00078$$
$$x = .00016$$

$$\sin 24° \ 35' \ 36'' = .41602 + .00016 = .41618$$

$$a = 12 \times .41618$$
$$a = 4.99416$$

$$\cos A = \frac{b}{c}$$

$$\cos 24° \ 35' \ 36'' = \frac{b}{12}$$

$$b = 12 \cos 24° \ 35' \ 36''$$

$$\cos 24° \ 35' \quad = .90936$$
$$\cos 24° \ 35' \ 36'' = .90936 - x$$
$$\cos 24° \ 36' \quad = .90924$$

$$\frac{36}{60} \text{ or } \frac{3}{5} \quad \frac{x}{.00012}$$
$$5x = .00036$$
$$x = .00007$$

$$\cos 24° \ 35' \ 36'' = .90936 - .00007 = .90929$$

$$b = 12 \times .90929$$
$$b = 10.91148$$

Therefore, $\angle A = 24° \ 35' \ 36''$ $a = 4.99416$ inches
$\angle B = 65° \ 24' \ 24''$ $b = 10.91148$ inches
$\angle C = 90°$ $c = 12$ inches

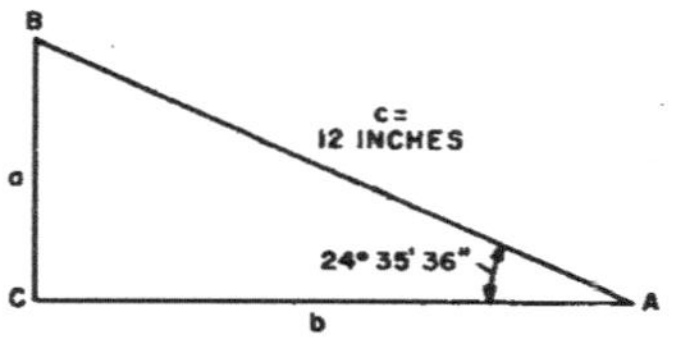

Figure 40. Solving a right triangle when an acute angle ($24°35'36''$) and the hypotenuse are given.

159. Solving a Right Triangle When Hypotenuse and One Side Are Given

Given the hypotenuse and one other side of a right triangle, solve for the unknown angles and side as illustrated in the example below.

Example: Find the unknown angles A and B, and side c of right triangle ABC (fig. 42) if the hypotenuse is 12 inches and the side opposite angle A is 8 inches.

$$b^2 = c^2 - a^2$$
$$b^2 = 12^2 - 8^2$$
$$b^2 = 144 - 64$$
$$b^2 = 80$$
$$b = \sqrt{80}$$
$$b = 8.94$$

$$\sin A = \frac{a}{c}$$
$$\sin A = \frac{8}{12} = \frac{2}{3}$$
$$\sin A = .66667$$

$$.66653 = \sin 41°\ 48'$$
$$.66667 = \sin 41°\ 48' + x$$
$$.66675 = \sin 41°\ 49'$$

$$\frac{14}{22} = \frac{x}{60}$$
$$22x = 840$$
$$x = \frac{840}{22} = 38$$

$$.66667 = \sin 41°\ 48'\ 38''$$

angle $A = 41°\ 48'\ 38''$
$\angle B = 180° - \angle C - \angle A$
$\angle B = 180° - 90° - 41°\ 48'\ 38''$
$\angle B = 48°\ 11'\ 22''$

Therefore, $\angle A = 41°\ 48'\ 38''$ $a = 8$ inches
$\angle B = 48°\ 11'\ 22''$ $b = 8.94$ inches
$\angle C = 90°$ $c = 12$ inches

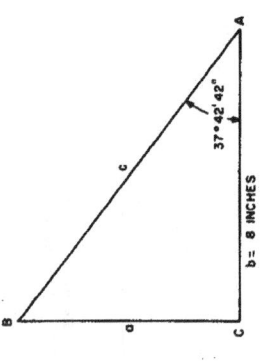

Figure 41. Solving a right triangle when an acute angle and the adjacent side are given.

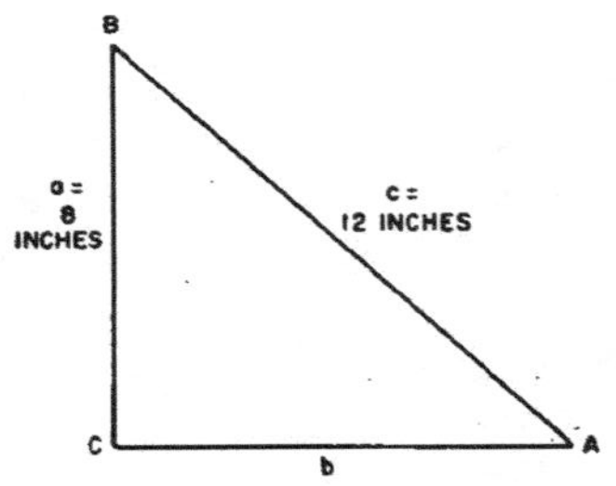

160. Solving a Right Triangle When Two Sides Are Given

When two sides of a right triangle are given, solve for the unknown angles and the hypotenuse as shown in the example below.

Example: Find the unknown angles A and B and side c in right triangle ABC (fig. 43) if side a is 8 inches and side b is 10 inches.

$$c^2 = a^2 + b^2$$
$$c^2 = 64 + 100$$
$$c^2 = 164$$
$$c = \sqrt{164}$$
$$c = 12.8$$

$$\tan A = \frac{a}{b}$$
$$\tan A = \frac{8}{10}$$
$$\tan A = .80000$$

$$.79972 = \tan 38°\ 39'$$
$$.80000 = \tan 38°\ 39' + x$$
$$.80020 = \tan 38°\ 40'$$

$$\frac{28}{48} \text{ or } \frac{7}{12} = \frac{x}{60}$$
$$12x = 420$$
$$x = 35$$

$$.80000 = \tan 38°\ 39'\ 35''$$

angle $A = 38°\ 39'\ 35''$
$\angle B = 180° - \angle C - \angle A$
$\angle B = 180° - 90° - 38°\ 39'\ 35''$
$\angle B = 51°\ 20'\ 25''$

Therefore, $\angle A = 38°\ 39'\ 35''$ $a = 8$ inches
$\angle B = 51°\ 20'\ 25''$ $b = 10$ inches
$\angle C = 90°$ $c = 12.8$ inches

Figure 42. Solving a right triangle, when the hypotenuse and one side are given.

161. Solving a 30°–60°–90° Triangle When One Side Is Given

In a 30°–60°–90° triangle, the side opposite the 30° angle is equal to one-half the hypotenuse. Refer to paragraph 150c for the derivation of the trigonometric functions. Solve for the unknown sides as shown in the example below.

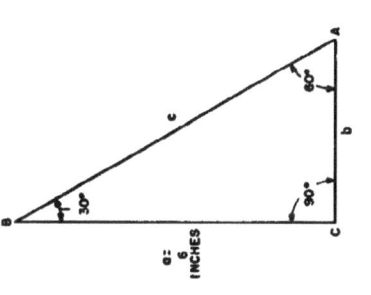

Figure 44. Solving a 30°–60°–90° triangle when one side is given.

Example: Find the unknown sides b and c of 30°–60°–90° triangle ABC (fig. 44) if the side opposite the 60° angle is 6 inches.

$$\sin 60° = \frac{\sqrt{3}}{2}; \text{ also, } \sin 60° = \frac{a}{c} = \frac{6}{c}$$

$$\frac{\sqrt{3}}{2} = \frac{6}{c}$$

$$\sqrt{3}\,c = 12$$

$$c = \frac{12}{\sqrt{3}}$$

Eliminate $\sqrt{3}$ in the denominator by multiplying $\frac{12}{\sqrt{3}}$ by $\frac{\sqrt{3}}{\sqrt{3}}$:

$$c = \frac{12}{\sqrt{3}} \cdot \frac{\sqrt{3}}{\sqrt{3}} = \frac{12\sqrt{3}}{\sqrt{9}} = \frac{12\sqrt{3}}{3} = 4\sqrt{3}$$

$$c = 4\sqrt{3} = 4 \times 1.7321 = 6.9284$$

$$\tan 60° = \frac{\sqrt{3}}{1}; \text{ also, } \tan A = \frac{a}{b} = \frac{6}{b}$$

$$\frac{\sqrt{3}}{1} = \frac{6}{b}$$

$$\sqrt{3}\,b = 6$$

$$b = \frac{6}{\sqrt{3}} \cdot \frac{\sqrt{3}}{\sqrt{3}} = \frac{6\sqrt{3}}{\sqrt{9}} = \frac{6\sqrt{3}}{3} = 2\sqrt{3}$$

$$b = 2\sqrt{3} = 2 \times 1.7321 = 3.4642$$

Therefore, $a = 6$ inches
$b = 3.4642$ inches
$c = 6.9284$ inches

162. Solving a 45°–45°–90° Triangle When One Side Is Given

In a 45°–45°–90° triangle, the sides opposite the equal angles are equal. Refer to paragraph 150b for the derivation of the trigonometric functions. Solve for the unknown sides as shown in the example below.

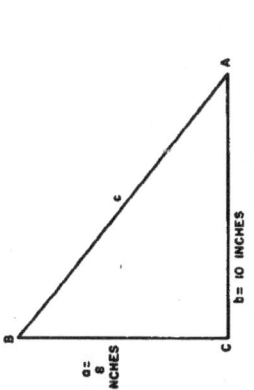

Figure 45. Solving a right triangle when two sides are given.

Example: Find the unknown sides a, b, and c of 45°–45°–90° triangle ABC (fig. 45) if the side opposite acute angle A is 5 inches.

$$\sin 45° = \frac{1}{\sqrt{2}}; \text{ also, } \sin A = \frac{a}{c} = \frac{5}{c}$$

$$\frac{1}{\sqrt{2}} = \frac{5}{c}$$

$$c = 5\sqrt{2}$$

$$c = 5 \times 1.4142 = 7.0710$$

$$\tan 45° = \frac{1}{1}; \text{ also, } \tan A = \frac{a}{b} = \frac{5}{b}$$

$$\frac{1}{1} = \frac{5}{b}$$

$$[b = 5]$$

Therefore, $a = 5$ inches
$b = 5$ inches
$c = 7.071$ inches

(5) Side c in right triangle ABC when $A = 14° 35'$ and $b = 12$.
(6) Angle A in right triangle ABC when $b = 7$ and $c = 12$.
(7) Side a in right triangle ABC when $A = 47° 22' 52''$ and $b = 31$.
(8) Side b in right triangle ABC when $A = 56° 31' 25''$ and $b = 25$.
(9) Angle A in right triangle ABC when $a = 17$ and $b = 23$.
(10) Side b in right triangle ABC when $A = 7° 32' 54''$ and $a = 17$.
(11) Side c in right triangle ABC when $a = 15$ and $b = 27$.
(12) Angle A in right triangle ABC when $a = 15$ and $b = 27$.

d. Solve the following problems:

(1) Over a distance of 300 feet, the angle of elevation of a road is 8° 24′ 30″. What is the rise in feet?

(2) The angle of elevation to the top of an antenna mast is 34° 17′ 50″. If the distance from the transit to the center of the mast is 110 feet, how high is the mast? The transit is 5 feet high.

(3) If a ladder 15 feet long just touches the top of a wall and subtends an angle of 35° 24′ 16″ with the ground, how far is the lower end of the ladder from the wall and how high is the wall?

(4) A captive balloon is anchored by 950 feet of cable. A man observes that the angle of elevation from his point of observation to the bottom of the balloon is 16° 47′ 12″. How far is he from the balloon anchor?

(5) An excavation is 33 feet wide. The angle of depression from the top of one side to the bottom of the other side is 19° 34′ 24″. How deep is the excavation?

(6) The angle of elevation from a given

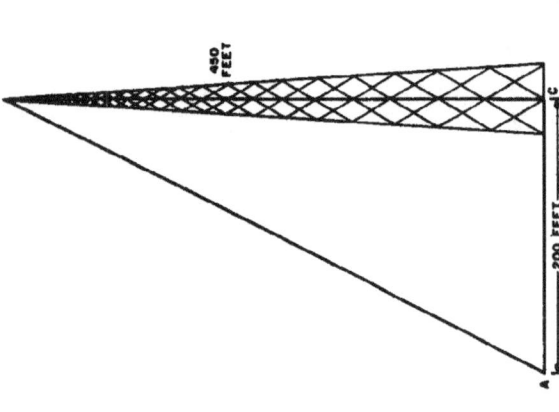

Figure 47. Finding the angle of elevation to top of an antenna mast.

(3) cos $A = .94000$
(4) tan $A = .47237$
(5) cot $A = 1.17529$
(6) cos $A = .36243$
(7) sin $A = .37778$
(8) tan $A = .67676$
(9) tan $A = 1.29000$
(10) cot $A = .79653$

c. Solve for the following (angle $C = 90°$):

(1) Angle A in right triangle ABC when $a = 19$ and $c = 27$.
(2) Side a in right triangle ABC when $A = 37° 15'$ and $c = 17$.
(3) Side c in right triangle ABC when $A = 42° 37' 15''$ and $a = 22$.
(4) Side B in right triangle ABC when $A = 37° 45' 42''$ and $c = 25$.

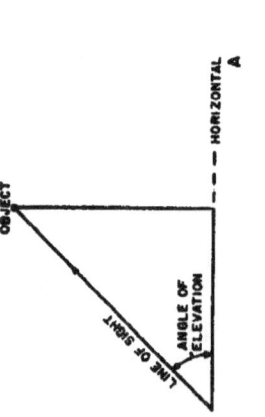

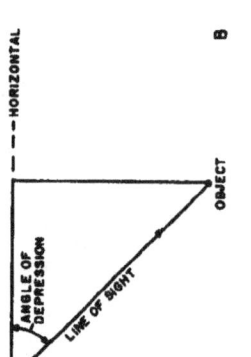

Figure 46. Angles of elevation and depression.

164. Review Problems—Natural Trigonometric Functions

a. Find the sine, cosine, tangent, and cotangent of the following angles:

(1) 1° 30′
(2) 15° 25′
(3) 32° 10′
(4) 36° 39′
(5) 44° 59′
(6) 44° 59′ 45″
(7) 35° 12′ 15″
(8) 54° 27′ 32″
(9) 48° 25′ 37″
(10) 67° 33′ 42″

b. Solve for the values of the following angles in degrees, minutes and seconds:

(1) sin $A = .25737$
(2) cot $A = .43279$

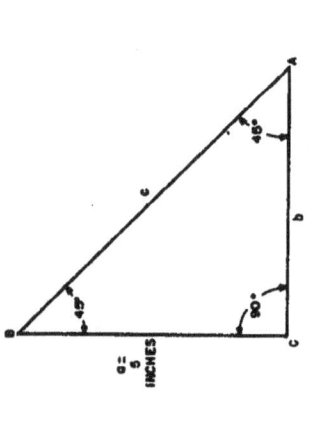

Figure 45. Solving a 45°–45°–90° triangle when one side is given.

163. Angles of Elevation and Depression

When an object is higher than the observer's eye, the angle between the horizontal and the line of sight to the object is called the *angle of elevation* (A, fig. 46). When an object is lower than the observer's eye, the angle between the line of sight to the object and the horizontal is called the *angle of depression* (B, fig. 46).

Example:

A television antenna mast is 450 feet high (fig. 47). Find to the nearest second the angle of elevation to its top at a point 200 feet from the base of the mast.

$$\tan A = \frac{a}{b}$$

$$\tan A = \frac{450}{200}$$

$$\tan A = 2.2500$$

$2.2496 = \tan 66° 2'$
$2.2500 = \tan 66° 2' + x$
$2.2513 = \tan 66° 3'$

$$\frac{4}{17} = \frac{x}{60}$$

$17x = 240$
$x = 14$
$2.2500 = \tan 66° 2' 14''$
$A = 66° 2' 14''$

point to the top of a tower is 17° 37′ 15″. Moving back 40 feet in a direct line, the angle of elevation from this point to the top of the tower is 15° 35′ 20″. Find the height of the tower.

(7) To determine the height of a tower, two sights are taken on a straight line perpendicular to the tower. If the distance between the points of observation is 60 feet and the angles of elevation are 32° 30′ 15″ and 28° 15′ 30″, respectively, what is the height of the tower?

(8) From a point in an open field a man sights on two mileposts along the side of a highway. The angles formed by an imaginary line perpendicular to the highway and the sights on the mileposts are 33° 20′ and 39° 17′ 30″. How far is the man from the closest point on the highway?

(9) An airplane is flying between two towns at an altitude of 5,000 feet. The angle of depression to the outskirts of one town is 50° 26′ 14″, while the angle to the outskirts of the other town is 64° 44′ 12″. How far apart, in a direct line, are the two towns?

(10) A radio antenna on top of a building is 10 feet high. The angle of elevation to the base of the pole is 37° 17′ 20″; the angle of elevation to the top of the antenna is 40° 30′ 15″. How high is the building?

(11) In a 45°–45°–90° right triangle the hypotenuse is 2 inches long. Find the length of the other two sides.

(12) In a 30°–60°–90° right triangle the hypotenuse is 6 inches long. Find the length of the other two sides.

Section III. TRIGONOMETRIC LAWS

165. Solving Oblique Triangles

An oblique triangle is one in which one of the angles is a right angle. The formulas in this section are used primarily to solve oblique triangles, but may also be used to solve right triangles. In the solution of triangles by trigonometric laws, the four following cases arise:

a. When any side and any two angles are given.

b. When any two sides and the angle opposite one of them are given.

c. When any two sides and the angle included between them are given.

d. When the three sides are given.

166. Law of Sines

In any triangle, the sides are proportional to the sines of the opposite angles.

Thus, $\dfrac{a}{\sin A} = \dfrac{b}{\sin B} = \dfrac{c}{\sin C}$.

a. *Two Angles and One Side Given.*

Example: Solve for the unknowns in oblique triangle ABC (fig. 48) when angle $A = 35°\ 47′\ 36″$, angle $B = 68°\ 42′\ 27″$, and the side opposite angle A is 15 inches.

$\angle C = 180° - \angle A - \angle B$
$\angle C = 180° - 35°\ 47′\ 36″ - 68°\ 42′\ 27″$
$\angle C = 75°\ 29′\ 57″$

$\dfrac{a}{\sin A} = \dfrac{b}{\sin B}$
$b \sin A = a \sin B$
$b = \dfrac{a \sin B}{\sin A}$
$b = \dfrac{15 \sin 68°\ 42′\ 27″}{\sin 35°\ 47′\ 36″}$

sin 68° 42′ = .93169
sin 68° 42′ 27″ = .93169 + x
sin 68° 43′ = .93180

$\dfrac{27}{60}$ or $\dfrac{9}{20} = \dfrac{x}{.00011}$

$20x = .00099$
$x = .000049 = .00005$

sin 68° 42′ 27″ = .93169 + .00005 = .93174
sin 35° 47′ = .58472
sin 35° 47′ 36″ = .58472 + x
sin 35° 48′ = .58496

$\dfrac{36}{60}$ or $\dfrac{3}{5} = \dfrac{x}{.00024}$

$5x = .00072$
$x = .00014$

sin 35° 47′ 36″ = .58472 + .00014 = .58486

$b = \dfrac{15 \times .93174}{.58486}$

$b = \dfrac{13.97610}{.58486}$

$b = 23.89$

$\dfrac{a}{\sin A} = \dfrac{c}{\sin C}$
$c \sin A = a \sin C$
$c = \dfrac{a \sin C}{\sin A}$
$c = \dfrac{15 \sin 75°\ 29′\ 57″}{\sin 35°\ 47′\ 36″}$

sin 75° 29′ = .96807
sin 75° 29′ 57″ = .96807 + x
sin 75° 30′ = .96815

$\dfrac{57}{60}$ or $\dfrac{19}{20} = \dfrac{x}{.00008}$

$20x = .00152$
$x = .000076 = .00008$

sin 75° 29′ 57″ = .96807 + .00008 = .96815

$c = \dfrac{15 \times .96815}{.58486}$

$c = \dfrac{14.52225}{.58486}$

$c = 24.83$

Therefore,
$\angle A = 35°\ 47′\ 36″$ $a = 15$ inches
$\angle B = 68°\ 42′\ 27″$ $b = 23.89$ inches
$\angle C = 75°\ 29′\ 57″$ $c = 24.83$ inches

b. Two Sides and One Angle Given.

Example: Find the unknowns in oblique triangle ABC (fig. 49) when angle $A = 53° 35' 40''$, the side opposite angle A is 10 inches, and the side opposite angle B is 12 inches.

$$\frac{a}{\sin A} = \frac{b}{\sin B}$$

$$a \sin B = b \sin A$$

$$\sin B = \frac{b \sin A}{a}$$

$$\sin B = \frac{12 \sin 53° 35' 40''}{10}$$

$$\sin 53° 35' = .80472$$
$$\sin 53° 35' 40'' = .80472 + x$$
$$\sin 53° 36' = .80489$$

$$\frac{40}{60} \text{ or } \frac{2}{3} = \frac{x}{.00017}$$

$$3x = .00034$$
$$x = .00011$$

$$\sin 53° 35' 40'' = .80472 + .00011 = .80483$$

$$\sin B = \frac{12 \times .80483}{5}$$

$$\sin B = \frac{4.82898}{5}$$

$$\sin B = .965796 = .96580$$

$$.96578 = \sin 74° 58'$$
$$.96580 = \sin 74° 58' + x$$
$$.96585 = \sin 74° 59'$$

$$\frac{2}{7} = \frac{x}{60}$$

$$7x = 120$$
$$x = 17$$

$$.96580 = \sin 74° 58' 17''$$

$$\angle B = 74° 58' 17''$$
$$\angle C = 180° - \angle A - \angle B$$

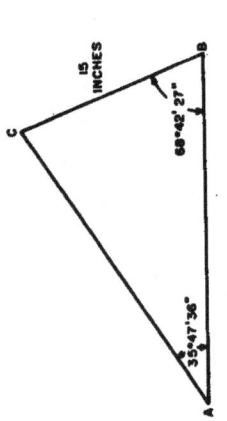

Figure 48. Solving an oblique triangle by the law of sines when two angles and a side are given.

$$\angle C = 180° - 53° 35' 40'' - 74° 58' 17''$$
$$\angle C = 51° 26' 3''$$

$$\frac{a}{\sin A} = \frac{c}{\sin C}$$

$$c \sin A = a \sin C$$

$$c = \frac{a \sin C}{\sin A}$$

$$c = \frac{10 \sin 51° 26' 3''}{\sin 53° 35' 40''}$$

$$\sin 51° 26' = .78188$$
$$\sin 51° 26' 3'' = .78188 + x$$
$$\sin 51° 27' = .78206$$

$$\frac{3}{60} \text{ or } \frac{1}{20} = \frac{x}{.00018}$$

$$20x = .00018$$
$$x = .000009 = .00001$$

$$\sin 51° 26' 3'' = .78188 + .00001 = .78189$$

$$c = \frac{10 \times .78189}{.80483}$$

$$c = \frac{7.8189}{.80483}$$

$$c = 9.71$$

Therefore, $\angle A = 53° 35' 40''$
$\angle B = 74° 58' 17''$
$\angle C = 51° 26' 3''$
$a = 10$ inches
$b = 12$ inches
$c = 9.71$ inches

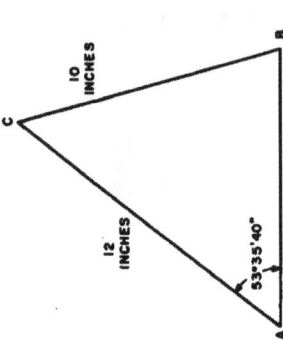

Figure 49. Solving an oblique triangle by the law of sines when two sides and an angle are given.

167. Law of Cosines

In any triangle, the square of any side equals the sum of the squares of the other two sides minus twice the product of these two sides times the cosine of the angle between them.

Thus, $a^2 = b^2 + c^2 - 2bc \cos A$
$b^2 = a^2 + c^2 - 2ac \cos B$
$c^2 = a^2 + b^2 - 2ab \cos C$

Example: Find the unknowns in oblique triangle ABC (fig. 50) when angle $C = 56° \ 45' \ 24''$, the side opposite angle A is 6 inches, and the side opposite angle B is 8 inches.

$$
\begin{aligned}
c^2 &= a^2 + b^2 - 2ab \cos C \\
c^2 &= 6^2 + 8^2 - 2(6)(8) \cos 56° \ 45' \ 24'' \\
c^2 &= 36 + 64 - 96 \cos 56° \ 45' \ 24'' \\
c^2 &= 100 - 96 \cos 56° \ 45' \ 24''
\end{aligned}
$$

$$
\begin{aligned}
\cos 56° \ 45' &= .54829 \\
\cos 56° \ 45' \ 24'' &= .54829 - x \\
\cos 56° \ 46' &= .54805 \\
\frac{24}{60} \text{ or } \frac{2}{5} &= \frac{x}{.00024} \\
5x &= .00048 \\
x &= .000096 \text{ or } .00010 \\
\cos 56° \ 45' \ 24'' &= .54829 - .00010 = .54819
\end{aligned}
$$

$$
\begin{aligned}
c^2 &= 100 - 96(.54819) \\
c^2 &= 100 - 52.62624 \\
c^2 &= 47.37376 \\
c &= \sqrt{47.37376} \\
c &= 6.882
\end{aligned}
$$

$$
\begin{aligned}
\frac{a}{\sin A} &= \frac{c}{\sin C} \\
c \sin A &= a \sin C \\
\sin A &= \frac{a \sin C}{c} \\
\sin A &= \frac{6 \sin 56° \ 45' \ 24''}{6.882}
\end{aligned}
$$

$$
\begin{aligned}
\sin 56° \ 45' &= .83629 \\
\sin 56° \ 45' \ 24'' &= .83629 + x \\
\sin 56° \ 46' &= .83645 \\
\frac{24}{60} \text{ or } \frac{2}{5} &= \frac{x}{.00016} \\
5x &= .00032 \\
x &= .000064 = .00006 \\
\sin 56° \ 45' \ 24'' &= .83629 + .00006 = .83635
\end{aligned}
$$

$$
\begin{aligned}
\sin A &= \frac{6(.83635)}{6.882} \\
\sin A &= \frac{5.01810}{6.882} \\
\sin A &= .72916
\end{aligned}
$$

$$
\begin{aligned}
.72897 &= \sin 46° \ 48' \\
.72916 &= \sin 46° \ 48' + x \\
.72917 &= \sin 46° \ 49' \\
\frac{19}{20} &= \frac{x}{60} \\
20x &= 1140 \\
x &= 57 \\
.72917 &= \sin 46° \ 48' \ 57''
\end{aligned}
$$

$$
\begin{aligned}
\angle A &= 46° \ 48' \ 57'' \\
\angle B &= 180° - \angle C - \angle A \\
\angle B &= 180° - 56° \ 45' \ 24'' - 46° \ 48' \ 57'' \\
\angle B &= 76° \ 25' \ 39''
\end{aligned}
$$

Therefore,

$$
\begin{aligned}
\angle A &= 46° \ 48' \ 57'' & a &= 6 \text{ inches} \\
\angle B &= 76° \ 25' \ 39'' & b &= 8 \text{ inches} \\
\angle C &= 56° \ 45' \ 24'' & c &= 6.882 \text{ inches}
\end{aligned}
$$

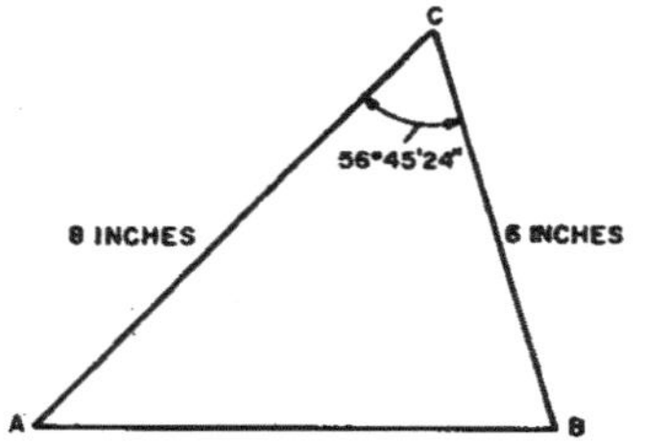

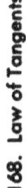

Figure 50. Solving an oblique triangle by the law of cosines when an angle and two sides are given.

168. Law of Tangents

The law of tangents is expressed by the formula $\frac{a - b}{a + b} = \frac{\tan \frac{1}{2}(A - B)}{\tan \frac{1}{2}(A + B)}$ where a and b are any two sides and A and B are the angles opposite these sides.

Example: Find the unknowns in oblique triangle ABC (fig. 51) when two sides of the triangle are 9 and 11 inches, respectively, and angle C, the angle included between these two sides, is $40° \ 40' \ 40''$.

$$
\begin{aligned}
\angle A + \angle B + \angle C &= 180° \\
\angle A + \angle B + 40° \ 40' \ 40'' &= 180° \\
\angle A + \angle B &= 180° - 40° \ 40' \ 40'' \\
\angle A + \angle B &= 139° \ 19' \ 20'' \\
\tfrac{1}{2}(A + B) &= \frac{139° \ 19' \ 20''}{2} \\
\tfrac{1}{2}(A + B) &= 69° \ 39' \ 40'' \\
\frac{a - b}{a + b} &= \frac{\tan \frac{1}{2}(A - B)}{\tan \frac{1}{2}(A + B)} \\
\frac{11 - 9}{11 + 9} \text{ or } \frac{2}{20} &= \frac{\tan \frac{1}{2}(A - B)}{\tan 69° \ 39' \ 40''} \\
20 \tan \tfrac{1}{2}(A - B) &= 2 \tan 69° \ 39' \ 40'' \\
10 \tan \tfrac{1}{2}(A - B) &= \tan 69° \ 39' \ 40'' \\
\tan \tfrac{1}{2}(A - B) &= \frac{\tan 69° \ 39' \ 40''}{10}
\end{aligned}
$$

$$
\begin{aligned}
\tan 69° \ 39' &= 2.69612 \\
\tan 69° \ 39' \ 40'' &= 2.69612 + x \\
\tan 69° \ 40' &= 2.69853 \\
\frac{40}{60} \text{ or } \frac{2}{3} &= \frac{x}{.00241} \\
3x &= .00482 \\
x &= .00161 \\
\tan 69° \ 39' \ 40'' &= 2.69612 + .00161 = 2.69773
\end{aligned}
$$

$\tan \frac{1}{2}(A - B) = \frac{2.69773}{10}$
$\tan \frac{1}{2}(A - B) = .26977$

.26951 = tan 15° 5'
.26977 = tan 15° 5' + x
.26982 = tan 15° 6'

$\frac{26}{31} = \frac{x}{60}$
$31x = 1560$
$x = 50$

.26977 = tan 15° 5' 50"
$\frac{1}{2}(A - B) = 15° 5' 50"$

$\frac{1}{2}(A + B) = \frac{1}{2}A + \frac{1}{2}B = 69° 39' 40"$
$\frac{1}{2}(A - B) = \frac{1}{2}A - \frac{1}{2}B = 15° 5' 50"$
(add)
$A = 84° 45' 30"$

$\angle A = 84° 45' 30"$
$\frac{1}{2}(A + B) = \frac{1}{2}A + \frac{1}{2}B = 69° 38' 100"$
$\frac{1}{2}(A - B) = \frac{1}{2}A - \frac{1}{2}B = 15° 5' 50"$
(subtract)
$B = 54° 33' 50"$

$\angle B = 54° 33' 50"$

$\frac{a}{\sin A} = \frac{c}{\sin C}$

$c \sin A = a \sin C$

$c = \frac{a \sin C}{\sin A}$

$c = \frac{11 \sin 40° 40' 40"}{\sin 84° 45' 30"}$

sin 40° 40' 40" = .65166
sin 40° 40' 40" = .65166 + x
sin 40° 41' = .65188

$\frac{40}{60}$ or $\frac{2}{3} = \frac{x}{.00022}$
$3x = .00044$
$x = .000146 = .00015$
sin 40° 40' 40" = .65166 + .00015 = .65181

sin 84° 45' = .99580
sin 84° 45' 30" = .99580 + x
sin 84° 46' = .99583

$\frac{30}{60}$ or $\frac{1}{2} = \frac{x}{.00003}$
$2x = .00003$
$x = .000015 = .00002$
sin 84° 45' 30" = .99580 + .00002 = .99582

$c = \frac{11 \sin 40° 40' 40"}{\sin 84° 45' 30"}$
$c = \frac{11 \times .65181}{.99582}$
$c = \frac{7.16991}{.99582}$
$c = 7.2$

Therefore, $\angle A = 84° 45' 30"$ $\quad a = 11$ inches
$\angle B = 54° 33' 50"$ $\quad b = 9$ inches
$\angle C = 40° 40' 40"$ $\quad c = 7.2$ inches

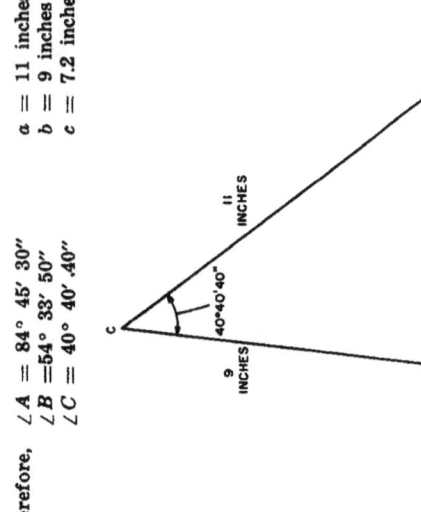

Figure 51. Solving an oblique triangle by the law of tangents when an angle and two sides are given.

169. Finding an Angle When Three Sides Are Given

The following formulas are used to find the angles of a triangle when three sides of the triangle are given:

$$\sin \tfrac{1}{2}A = \sqrt{\frac{(s-b)(s-c)}{bc}}$$

$$\sin \tfrac{1}{2}B = \sqrt{\frac{(s-a)(s-c)}{ac}}$$

$$\sin \tfrac{1}{2}C = \sqrt{\frac{(s-a)(s-b)}{ab}}$$

In these formulas, a, b, and c are the sides of the triangle, and $s = \tfrac{1}{2}(a + b + c)$.

Example: Find the angles of an oblique triangle if $a = 5$ inches, $b = 8$ inches, and $c = 11$ inches.

$s = \tfrac{1}{2}(a + b + c)$
$s = \tfrac{1}{2}(5 + 8 + 11)$
$s = \tfrac{1}{2}(24)$
$s = 12$

$\sin \tfrac{1}{2}A = \sqrt{\frac{(s-b)(s-c)}{bc}}$

$\sin \tfrac{1}{2}A = \sqrt{\frac{(12-8)(12-11)}{(8)(11)}}$

$\sin \tfrac{1}{2}A = \sqrt{\frac{(4)(1)}{88}}$

$\sin \tfrac{1}{2}A = \sqrt{\frac{4}{88}} = \sqrt{\frac{1}{22}}$

$\sin \tfrac{1}{2}A = \sqrt{.045454\overline{5}}$

$\sin \frac{1}{2}A = .21319$

$.21303 = \sin 12° 18'$
$.21319 = \sin 12° 18' + x$
$.21331 = \sin 12° 19'$
$\frac{16}{28}$ or $\frac{4}{7} = \frac{x}{60}$
$7x = 240$
$x = 34$
$.21319 = \sin 12° 18' 34''$
$\frac{1}{2}A = 12° 18' 34''$
$\angle A = 24° 36' 68''$ or $24° 37' 8''$

$\sin \frac{1}{2}B = \sqrt{\frac{(s-a)(s-c)}{ac}}$
$\sin \frac{1}{2}B = \sqrt{\frac{(12-5)(12-11)}{(5)(11)}}$
$\sin \frac{1}{2}B = \sqrt{\frac{(7)(1)}{55}}$
$\sin \frac{1}{2}B = \sqrt{\frac{7}{55}}$
$\sin \frac{1}{2}B = \sqrt{.12727272}$
$\sin \frac{1}{2}B = .35675$

$.35674 = \sin 20° 54'$
$.35675 = \sin 20° 54' + x$
$.35701 = \sin 20° 55'$
$\frac{1}{27} = \frac{x}{60}$
$27x = 60$
$x = 2$

$.35675 = \sin 20° 54' 2''$
$\frac{1}{2}B = 20° 54' 2''$
$\angle B = 40° 108' 4''$ or $41° 48' 4''$
$\angle C = 180° - \angle A - \angle B$
$\angle C = 180° - 24° 37' 8'' - 41° 48' 4''$
$\angle C = 180° - 66° 25' 12''$
$\angle C = 113° 34' 48''$

Therefore, $\angle A = 24° 37' 8''$
$\angle B = 41° 48' 4''$
$\angle C = 113° 34' 48''$

170. Finding the Area of a Triangle When Two Sides and the Included Angle Are Given

The formula for finding the area of a triangle when two sides and the included angle are given is $S = \frac{1}{2}ab \sin C$ where S is the area of the triangle, a and b are the given sides, and C is the included angle.

Example: Find the area of oblique triangle ABC (fig. 52) when two sides are 7 and 8 inches, respectively, and the included angle is 50° 50' 50''.

$S = \frac{1}{2}ab \sin C$
$S = \frac{1}{2} \times 7 \times 8 \times \sin 50° 50' 50''$
$\sin 50° 50' = .77531$
$\sin 50° 50' 50'' = .77531 + x$

$\sin 50° 51' = .77550$
$\sin 50° 50' 50'' = \frac{x}{.00019}$
$\frac{50}{60}$ or $\frac{5}{6} = \frac{x}{.00019}$
$6x = .00095$
$x = .00016$

$\sin 50° 50' 50'' = .77531 + .00016 = .77547$
$S = \frac{1}{2} \times 7 \times 8 \times .77547 = 21.71316$
$S = 21.71316$ square inches

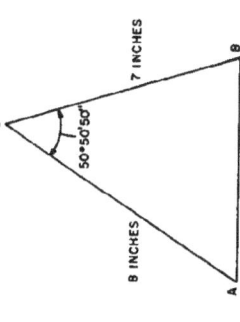

Figure 52. Solving for the area of an oblique triangle when two sides and the included angle are given.

171. Finding the Area of a Triangle When Two Angles and a Side Are Given

The formula for finding the area of a triangle when two angles and a side are given is $S = \frac{a^2 \sin B \sin C}{2 \sin A}$ where S is the area of the triangle, B and C are the given angles, and a is the given side.

Example: Find the area of oblique triangle ABC (fig. 53) when the two angles are 38° 42' 48'' and 68° 52' 42'' and the side is 10 inches.

$\angle A = 180° - \angle B - \angle C$
$\angle A = 180° - 38° 42' 48'' - 68° 52' 42''$
$\angle A = 180° - 107° 35' 30''$
$\angle A = 72° 24' 30''$

$S = \frac{a^2 \sin B \sin C}{2 \sin A}$
$S = \frac{10^2 \sin 38° 42' 48'' \sin 68° 52' 42''}{2 \sin 72° 24' 30''}$

$\sin 38° 42' = .62524$
$\sin 38° 42' 48'' = .62524 + x$
$\sin 38° 43' = .62547$
$\frac{48}{60}$ or $\frac{4}{5} = \frac{x}{.00023}$
$5x = .00092$
$x = .00018$

$\sin 38° 42' 48'' = .62524 + .00018 = .62542$
$\sin 68° 52' = .93274$
$\sin 68° 52' 42'' = .93274 + x$

$\sin 68° 53' = .93285$
$\frac{42}{60}$ or $\frac{7}{10} = \frac{x}{.00011}$
$10x = .00077$
$x = .000077$ or $.00008 = .93282$
$\sin 68° 53' 42'' = .93274 + .00008 = .93282$
$\sin 72° 24' = .95319$
$\sin 72° 24' 30'' = .95319 + x$
$\sin 72° 25' = .95328$
$\frac{30}{60}$ or $\frac{1}{2} = \frac{x}{.00009}$
$2x = .00009$
$x = .000045$ or $.00005 = .95319 + .00005 = .95324$
$\sin 72° 24' 30'' = .95319 + .00005 = .95324$

$S = \frac{100 \times .62542 \times .93282}{2 \times .95324}$

$S = \frac{50 \times .62542 \times .93282}{.95324}$

$S = \log 50 + \log .62542 + \log .93282 - \log .95324$
$\log 50 = 1.6990$
$\log .62500 = 9.7959-10$
$\log .62542 = 9.7959-10 + x$
$\log .62600 = 9.7966-10$
$\frac{42}{100} = \frac{x}{.0007}$
$100x = .0294$
$x = .000294$ or $.0003 = 9.7962-10$
$\log .62542 = 9.7959-10 + .0003 = 9.7962-10$
$\log .93200 = 9.9694-10$
$\log .93282 = 9.9694-10 + x$
$\log .93300 = 9.9699-10$
$\frac{82}{100} = \frac{x}{.0005}$
$100x = .0410$
$x = .00041$ or $.0004 = 9.9698-10$
$\log .93282 = 9.9694-10 + .0004 = 9.9698-10$
$\log .95300 = 9.9791-10$
$\log .95324 = 9.9791-10 + x$
$\log .95400 = 9.9795-10$
$\frac{24}{100} = \frac{x}{.0004}$
$100x = .0096$
$x = .000096$ or $.0001 = 9.9792-10$
$\log .95324 = 9.9791-10 + .0001 = 9.9792-10$

$S = 1.6990 + 9.7962-10 + 9.9698-10 - 9.9792-10$

$\begin{array}{r} 1.6990 \\ + 9.7962-10 \\ + 9.9698-10 \\ \hline 21.4650-20 \\ - 9.9792-10 \\ \hline 11.4858-10 \text{ or } 1.4858 \end{array}$

antilog $1.4857 = 30.6$
antilog $1.4858 = 30.6 + x$
antilog $1.4871 = 30.7$
$\frac{1}{14} = \frac{x}{.1}$
$14x = .1$
$x = .007$
antilog $1.4858 = 30.6 + .007 = 30.607$
$S = 30.607$ square inches

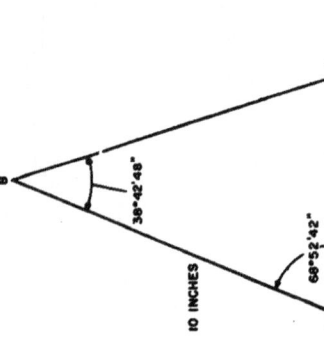

Figure 58. Solving for the area of an oblique triangle when two angles and a side are given.

172. Finding the Area of Triangle When Three Sides Are Given

To find the area of triangle when three sides are given, use the formula

$$S = \sqrt{s(s-a)(s-b)(s-c)}$$

where a, b, and c are the sides of the triangle and $s = \frac{1}{2}(a + b + c)$.

Example: Find the area of an oblique triangle when the sides are 8, 11, and 15 inches, respectively.

$s = \frac{1}{2}(a + b + c)$
$s = \frac{1}{2}(8 + 11 + 15)$
$s = \frac{1}{2}(34)$
$s = 17$
$S = \sqrt{s(s-a)(s-b)(s-c)}$
$S = \sqrt{17(17-8)(17-11)(17-15)}$
$S = \sqrt{17(9)(6)(2)}$
$S = \sqrt{1836}$
$S = 42.84$ square inches

173. Review Problems—Trigonometric Laws

a. In an oblique triangle ABC, angle $A = 42°\ 15'\ 12''$, angle $B = 75°\ 28'\ 10''$, and side b measures 21 inches. Solve the triangle for angle C and side a.

b. In an oblique triangle ABC, angle $C = 52°\ 30'$, side $b = 45$ inches, and side $c = 38$ inches. Solve for angle B.

c. In an oblique triangle ABC, sides a, b, and c opposite angles A, B, and C have lengths of 9, 16, and 21 inches, respectively. Find the three angles of the triangle.

d. In an oblique triangle where a and b are any two sides and A and B are the angles opposite these sides, angle $C = 57°\ 20'\ 45''$, $a = 9.73$ inches, and $b = 6.47$ inches. Find angles A and B.

e. The three sides of a triangle are 40, 37, and 13 inches, respectively. Find the area of the triangle.

f. Two sides of an oblique triangle measure 12 and 18 feet, respectively. The angle between the two sides is 115°. Find the area of the triangle.

g. In a triangle ABC, angle $A = 30°$ and angle $B = 60°$. The side opposite angle $C = 16$ inches. Find the area of the triangle.

h. In an oblique triangle ABC, angle $C = 62°\ 50'$. The side opposite angle A measures 9.65 inches, and the side opposite angle B measures 17.85 inches. Find angles A and B and the length of the side opposite angle C.

CHAPTER 11

RADIANS

174. Angular Measurement Using Radians

a. Definition. A radian is a unit of angular measurement equal to that angle which, when its vertex is upon the center of a circle, intercepts an arc that is equal in length to the radius of the circle. Thus, in figure 54, central angle AOB is equal to 1 radian because arc AB is equal to radius OA.

(1) The system that makes use of the radian is called the *natural system* of angular measurement because it has no arbitrary unit, such as the degree, but is founded upon the observation that the absolute size of any angle is the ratio of its arc to the radius of that arc. Where the arc and radius are equal, the ratio is 1, and this unit is the radian.

(2) The natural system of angular measurement—also called the circular system and the radian system—is used extensively in electrical formulas (part II).

b. Finding Any Angle. To find any angle, such as angle AOC in figure 54, when the length of arc AB is known, determine the number of times that radius r will go into arc length ABC, thus determining the number of radians in the angle.

Thus,

$$\text{Angle} = \frac{\text{arc}}{\text{radius}}$$

or, if angle AOC is denoted by the Greek letter θ (Theta) and arc ABC by s,

$$\theta = \frac{s}{r} \text{ radians}$$

Example: A circle has a radius of 6 inches. Find the angle subtended at the center of the circle by an arc 9 inches in length.

$$\theta = \frac{s}{r}$$
$$= \frac{9}{6}$$
$$= 1.5 \text{ radians}$$

c. Finding Length of Arc. To find the length of an arc intercepted by a central angle when the radius of the circle and the number of radians in the angle are known, use the formula in *b* above in the form—

$$s = r\theta$$

Example: A circle has a radius of 5 feet. How long is the arc intercepted by a central angle of 1.5 radians?

$$s = r\theta$$
$$= 5 \times 1.5$$
$$= 7.5 \text{ feet}$$

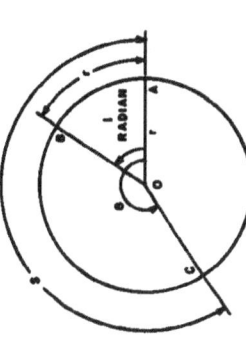

Figure 54. The radian or circular system of measurement.

175. The Relation Between Degrees and Radians

a. General. It is often necessary to convert an angle from degrees to radians or from radians to degrees. If the angle is one complete revolution, the arc is one complete circumference of a circle; thus, it is 2π times the radius. Therefore, the angle is equal to $2\pi r$ divided by r—that is, 2π radians ($\pi = 3.1416$).

Therefore,

$$1 \text{ revolution} = 2\pi \text{ radians}$$

also

$$1 \text{ revolution} = 360°$$

Thus,

$$2\pi \text{ radians} = 360°$$

$$1 \text{ radian} = \frac{360°}{2\pi} = \frac{180°}{\pi} = 57.29578°$$

and since

$$360° = 2\pi \text{ radians}$$

$$1° = \frac{2\pi}{360} = \frac{\pi}{180} = 0.017453 \text{ radians}$$

To change radians to degrees, accurate to seconds, use figures accurate to at least five decimal places.

b. Changing Degrees to Radians and Radians to Degrees.

Example 1: Change 2.74 radians to degrees, minutes, and seconds.

$$1 \text{ radian} = 57.29578°$$
$$2.74 \text{ radians} = 2.74(57.29578)$$
$$= 156.99044°$$
$$1° = 60'$$
$$.99044° = .99044(60)'$$
$$= 59.4264'$$
$$.4264' = .4264(60)''$$
$$= 25.5''$$
$$2.74 \text{ radians} = 156° \ 59' \ 25.5''$$

Example 2: Change 57° 15′ 18″ to radians.

Step 1. Change the minutes and seconds to decimals of a degree:

$$1' = 60''$$
$$18'' = \frac{18}{60}$$
$$= .3'$$
$$15.3' = \frac{15.3}{60}$$
$$= .255°$$
$$57° \ 15' \ 18'' = 57.255°$$

Step 2. Change to radians:

$$1° = .017453 \text{ radian}$$
$$57.255° = 57.255(.017453)$$
$$= .99927 \text{ radian}$$

c. Expressing Angles in Radians as Multiples of π. It is often convenient to express angles in radians as multiples of π. Since $360° = 2\pi$ radians, $90° = \frac{1}{2}\pi$ radians, $40° = \frac{1}{9}\pi$ radians, etc. It is necessary only to multiply the degrees by $\frac{\pi}{180}$ to change to radians.

Example: Express 135° in radians as a multiple of π.

$$135° = 135\left(\frac{\pi}{180}\right)$$
$$= \frac{3}{4}\pi \text{ radians}$$

176. Review Problems—Radians

a. Find the angle θ for the following arc lengths and radii:

(1) $r = 5$ inches, $s = 2$ inches.
(2) $r = 3$ feet, $s = 12$ feet.
(3) $r = .8$ miles, $s = 6.4$ miles.
(4) $r = 27$ meters, $s = 75$ meters

b. Find the arc lengths for the following angles and radii:

(1) $\theta = 5$ radians, $r = 7$ inches
(2) $\theta = 8$ radians, $r = 2.2$ feet
(3) $\theta = 2.1$ radians, $r = 9$ miles
(4) $\theta = .03$ radians, $r = .066$ inch

c. Express the following angles in radians:

(1) 30°
(2) 263° 12′
(3) 158° 33′
(4) 336° 24′ 22″

d. Express the following angles in degrees:

(1) .8 radians
(2) 25 radians
(3) 3.45 radians
(4) 3π radians

e. Express the following angles as multiples of π:

(1) 30°
(2) 60°
(3) 225°
(4) 720°

CHAPTER 12
VECTORS

177. Plane Vectors

a. A line segment used to represent a quantity that has direction as well as magnitude is called a vector. The length of a vector is proportionate to the magnitude, and the arrow, or head, of the vector indicates the direction of the quantity represented.

b. The quantity represented by a vector is called a vector quantity. This is the directed magnitude itself. Electrical quantities, such as current and voltage, are vector quantities in ac circuits.

Example: An airplane is flying northeast at 120 miles per hour. Its speed is represented on figure 55 by line *OA*. The direction in which the airplane is traveling is represented by the direction of the line.

178. Vector Notation

Because a vector quantity has direction as well as magnitude, the methods of denoting a vector are different from the methods of denoting a scalar quantity. A vector may be denoted by two letters, the first indicating the origin, or initial point, and the other indicating the head or terminal point. For example, a vector may be represented by the letters *AB*, indicating that the quantity went from *A* to *B*. A small arrow sometimes is placed over the letters for emphasis; for example, $\overrightarrow{AB}$. Another method of notation is $A\underline{/\theta}$, where *A* represents the magnitude of the quantity, and $\underline{/\theta}$ represents the angle the vector makes with some reference line. For example, if line *OE* in figure 55 were used as the reference line, vector *OA* could be represented by the notation $120\underline{/45°}$, where 120 represents the magnitude of the quantity, and $\underline{/45°}$ represents the direction with respect to line *OE*. With respect to line *ON*, vector *OA*, would be represented by the notation $120\underline{/-45°}$.

179. Addition of Vectors, Parallelogram Method

The addition of vectors by the parallelogram method is shown in figure 56. To add vector *OA* to *OC*, draw a vector *OC* with its initial point located at the initial point of vector *OA*, and complete the parallelogram with these vectors forming two sides. The diagonal vector *OB*, with its initial point at the same initial point of *OA* and *OC* and its terminal point at the opposite vertex of the parallelogram, is the sum of *OA* and *OC*. Thus, two vectors (*OA* and *OC*) acting simultaneously on a point or object may be replaced by a single vector called the resultant (*OB*). The resultant vector will produce the same effect on the object as the joint action of the two vectors.

180. Addition of More Than Two Vectors

a. In determining the resultant (par. 179) of vectors when more than two quantities are represented, proceed as follows:

(1) Find the resultant of two of the vector quantities.

(2) Determine the final resultant between the third quantity and the resultant obtained from (1), above.

b. Assume three forces U, V, and W are acting on point O as shown in A, figure 57. Force U exerts 100 pounds at an angle of 60°, V exerts 150 pounds at an angle of 135°, and W exerts 150 pounds at an angle of 260°. Find the resultant of forces on point O.

(1) The resultant of any two vectors, such as U and W, are determined graphically by the line R_1 (B, fig. 57). To solve this problem first draw the vectors to scale at the designated angles; then construct the parallelogram OUTW with adjacent sides WT and UT. The resultant R_1 of OW and OU will be the diagonal OT.

(2) Combine the resultant R_1 with force V, then construct another parallelogram to scale as in (1), above. The final resultant R_2 is similarly determined by the line SO (C, fig. 57).

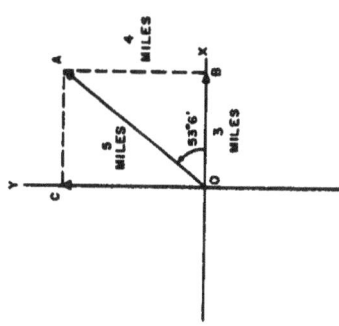

Figure 55. The velocity of an airplane described by a vector.

Figure 56. Adding vectors, parallelogram method.

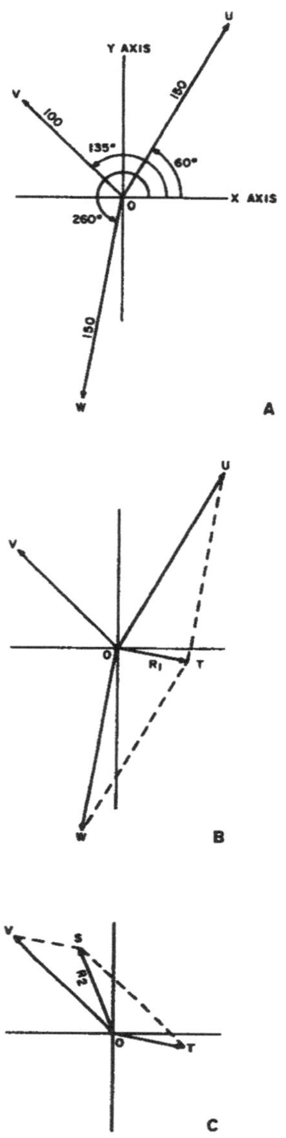

Figure 57. Resolution of three vectors.

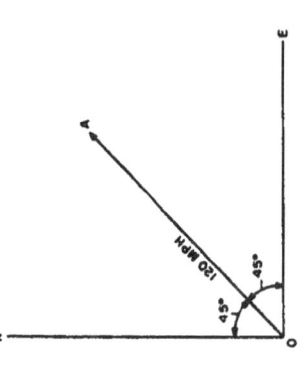

Figure 58. Horizontal and vertical components of vector.

This, then, is the resolution of all three forces U, V, and W acting on point O.

181. Components of a Vector

a. A vector may be resolved into components along any two specified directions. If the directions of the components are chosen so that they are at right angles to each other, the components are called *rectangular components*.

b. By placing the initial point of a vector at the origin of the X and Y axes, the rectangular components are readily obtained either graphically or by computation. In figure 58, a vector with a magnitude of 5 and a direction of 53° 6′ is shown broken down into a horizontal compo-

nent of 3 and a vertical component of 4. This is done by using the sine and cosine function as follows:

$$\sin 53° 6' = \frac{BA}{5}$$

$$.79968 = \frac{BA}{5}$$

$$BA = 5 \times .79968$$
$$= 4 \text{ (approx)}$$

$$\cos 53° 6' = \frac{OB}{5}$$

$$.60042 = \frac{OB}{5}$$

$$OB = 5 \times .60042$$
$$= 3 \text{ (approx)}$$

ANSWERS TO PROBLEMS

Paragraph 12.

a(1) $\frac{3}{5}$; .6; 60%. (2) $\frac{1}{2}$; .5; 50%. (3) $\frac{3}{8}$; .375; $37\frac{1}{2}$%. (4) $\frac{1}{4}$; .25; 25%. (5) $\frac{5}{8}$; .625; $62\frac{1}{2}$%. (6) $\frac{3}{5}$; .6; 60%. (7) $\frac{3}{10}$; .3; 30%. (8) $\frac{7}{10}$; .7; 70%. (9) $2\frac{1}{4}$; 2.25; 225%. (10) $8\frac{7}{8}$; 1.875; $187\frac{1}{2}$%. (11) $\frac{2}{25}$; .08; 8%. (12) $\frac{3}{50}$; .06; 6%. (13) $\frac{9}{50}$; .18; 18%. (14) $\frac{1}{400}$; .0025. .25%. (15) $\frac{1}{40}$; .025; $2\frac{1}{2}$%. (16) $\frac{1}{20}$; .05; 5%. (17) $\frac{1}{12}$; .08$\frac{1}{3}$ (See note below; $8\frac{1}{3}$%. (18) $\frac{3}{8}$; .375; $37\frac{1}{2}$%. (19) $1\frac{1}{20}$; 1.05; 105%. (20) $\frac{1}{25}$; .04; 4%.

Note. This mixed decimal and fractional form is often used when an unending decimal would result.

b(1) 150; (2) 50; (3) 4; (4) 900.

c(1) 150%; (2) 275%; (3) 150%; (4) 550%.

d(1) 1.64; (2) 2,496; (3) .34; (4) 4.42.

e(1) .207%; (2) .028%.

f(1) $433\frac{1}{3}$; (2) 2,500; (3) 520; (4) 200; (5) 200.

Paragraph 21.

a 336.6 pounds. b $3\frac{3}{7}$ days. c $5.00. d $1400.00. e .372 ohm. .298 ohm; .459 ohm; .893 ohm. f 2.820 pounds; 3.776 pounds; 4.119 pounds; 2,567 pounds. g 300 rpm. h 157.5 rpm.

Paragraph 25.

a(1) 21; (2) 33; (3) 50; (4) 2.90; (5) 50.1; (6) 70.01; (7) 86.5; (8) 75.89.
b(1) 2.236; (2) 2.646; (3) 3.317; 3.606; (5) 3.873; (6) 4.123.
c(1) .158 ampere; (2) .085 ampere; (3) .283 ampere; (4) 1.118 amperes.

Paragraph 42.

a(1) 17; (2) 58; (3) −21; (4) −139°; (5) −252 volts.
b(1) 251 amperes; (2) −8 volts; (3) −.6375cy. (4) −31.99ax^2; (5) 1.810x^2y.
c(1) −17.92; (2) −72; (3) $\frac{-8}{35}$; (4) .075852; (5) .0028125; (6) 120.
d(1) 9; (2) $-\frac{20}{21}$; (3) 700; (4) 250; (5) $+\frac{2}{3}$ ampere; (6) −.0025.
e(1) −4; (2) 14; (3) −25; (4) 19; (5) 11; (6) 16; (7) 44; (8) 66; (9) +2; (10) 18.

Paragraph 50.

a(1) $6a^4 - 4a^2b^2 + 4b^4$. (2) $E + 3RI + 20ZI$. (3) $w + x + 9y + 8z$.
b(1) $19ax + 17by - 9cz$. (2) $-25w - 3z + 8y + 2z$. (3) $4a^2 - 34ab + 6b^2$.
c(1) 7. (2) 1. (3) 1.
d(1) f^{10}. (2) y^{r+b}. (3) y^{2m}. (4) r^5. (5) R^{3n}. (6) r^{m+1}.
e(1) $\frac{4}{x^4}$. (2) $\frac{1}{r^3}x^7$. (3) $\frac{1}{36a^{3b}}$. (4) $\frac{1}{PR}$. (5) $\frac{a^2}{8b^2}$. (6) $\frac{3E}{4PR}$.
f(1) $10a^2b - 15a^2b^3 + 35ab^3$. (2) $4a^3 + 12a^3 + 4a$. (3) $x^3 - 27$. (4) $2x^4 + 5x^2y + 4x^2y^2 + 2xy^3 - y^4$. (5) $9x^4 - 34x^2y^2$

$+ 25y^4$. (6) $\frac{a-c}{ca}$. (7) $\frac{3L-R^2}{R}$.

(8) $1 - 2a^2b + 3a^4b^3$. (9) $2z^2 + z - 1 + \frac{3z+4}{z^2-z+3}$. (10) $4b^2 - b$.

Paragraph 61.

a(1) $5(5+1-6)$; (2) $4(2+1-8)$; (3) $3(3-6+7)$; (4) $7r(1-3+5)$; (5) $2(5x+4y+3z)$.

b(1) $49z^2y^6$; (2) $4u^{10}$; (3) $64a^4b^8$; (4) $729a^9b^3$; (5) $-27b^3z^{12}$.

c(1) 5; (2) $+8$; (3) $\pm ab^3$; (4) $\pm 6yz^2$; (5) $\pm 10ab^5$; (6) $\pm 20a$; (7) -3; (8) $-x^3$; (9) 4; (10) $5x^4y^5z^2$.

d(1) $3(x+2)$; (2) $5a(a+3)$; (3) $2x(5x^2 - 7z - 1)$; (4) $3z(2ay+3bz-4c)$; (5) $m(m^2+m-5x)$; (6) $3a^3(a^2-2ab-b^2)$; (7) $7ry^3(1-2+3)$ or 14^3ry; (8) $2xam(6x+7a+8m)$; (9) $\pi(r_1^2+r_2^2)$; (10) $\frac{1}{16}cd(4c^2-2cd+d^2)$.

Paragraph 69.

a(1) $x = 5\frac{2}{5}$; (2) $x = 4$; (3) $r = 2$; (4) $x = \frac{-13}{16}$; (5) $t = 1$; (6) $x = 7\frac{3}{4}$; (7) $r = 4$; (8) $x = 1$.

b(1) 8; (2) z; (3) $3(r+s)$; (4) $3(a-8)$; (5) $(I-6)(I-9)$; (6) $\frac{8EI^2}{2I^2R}$; (7) $\frac{2f}{6\pi f^2 c}$.

c(1) $\frac{rR}{rR^2}$, $\frac{r}{rR^2}$, $\frac{R^2}{rR^2}$; (2) $\frac{a-1}{a^2-1}$,

$\frac{x(a+1)}{a^2-1}$; (3) $\frac{3b}{6x}$, $\frac{2c}{6x}$; (4) $\frac{y(y+3)}{2(y+3)}$, $\frac{3c}{c(c+1)}$; (5) $\frac{2(c+1)}{c(c+1)}$, $\frac{i}{c(c+1)}$; (7) $\frac{y}{C^2-d^2}$,

$\frac{z(c+d)}{C^2-d^2}$.

d(1) $\frac{12}{a}$; (2) $\frac{7s+11}{4t}$;

(3) $\frac{9y^2a + 10xb}{12x^2y^3}$; (4) $\frac{6(z^2-2)}{z^4-5z^2+4}$;

(5) $\frac{9c^2+2cd-12d^2}{12c^2d^2}$; (6) $\frac{2r^2+r-13}{r^2+2r-15}$.

(7) $\frac{12y-1}{4}$; (8) $\frac{4ab}{a^2-b^2}$;

(9) $\frac{16(2-5q)}{25q^2}$; (10) $\frac{3t+4v}{12tv^2}$.

e(1) $\frac{3y^2}{8}$; (2) $\frac{a^9}{b^6}$; (3) $\frac{xz}{21my}$; (4) $\frac{(s-r)^2}{s^2}$; (5) $\frac{3}{5x}$; (6) $\frac{1}{a^3}$.

(7) $15z$; (8) $\frac{a^3}{6cd}$; (9) $\frac{4su}{5}$;

(10) $\frac{e+3}{e+2}$.

Paragraph 76.

a(1) 2; (2) 16; (3) $5\sqrt{2}$; (4) $\frac{\sqrt[3]{4}}{4}$;

(5) $3\sqrt{2x}-1$; (6) $\frac{x^{\frac{1}{2}}\sqrt[3]{6}}{y}$; (7) x^2y;

(8) $\sqrt[9]{d^2e^{\frac{5}{2}}}$; (9) $\frac{4r^2}{s}$; (10) a^2b.

b(1) $\sqrt[3]{4}$; (2) $\sqrt[6]{a^3b^4}$; (3) $\sqrt[6]{6^5}$; (4) $2 \cdot \sqrt{2f}$; (5) $5\sqrt{x}$; (6) $\sqrt[6]{c\sqrt{a^3c^2}}$ (7) $6\sqrt[3]{r}$; (8) $2b \cdot \sqrt[3]{a^2}$; (9) $\sqrt{2r_1} + 3\sqrt{r_2}$; (10) $3y^3\sqrt{x}$.

c(1) $a^{\frac{1}{4}}$; (2) $(5x)^{\frac{1}{4}}$; (3) $6xd^{\frac{1}{4}}$; (4) $z^{\frac{1}{3}}$; (5) $(3a^3b^5)^{\frac{1}{4}}$; (6) $y^3a^{\frac{1}{2}}$; (7) $8(3e)^{\frac{1}{4}}$; (8) $9g^{\frac{1}{4}}$; (9) $3bcdd^{\frac{1}{2}}$; (10) $(x-y)^{\frac{1}{3}}$.

d(1) $2\sqrt{3}$; (2) $2\sqrt{5}$; (3) $3\sqrt{7}$; (4) $12ab^2\sqrt{2}$; (5) $2bd\sqrt{15}$; (6) $2I\sqrt{2R}$; (7) $9px\sqrt{7p}$; (8) $12d^4s\sqrt{3ds}$; (9) $45a^2\sqrt{b}$; (10) $112w^4x^2y\sqrt{2xx}$.

e(1) $\frac{\sqrt{2}}{10}$; (2) $\frac{\sqrt{z}}{2x}$; (3) $\frac{\sqrt[3]{3a}}{3}$; (4) $\frac{\sqrt[3]{x^2}}{x}$;

(5) $\frac{\sqrt[4]{27a^2x^4}}{3ax}$; (6) $\frac{\sqrt[3]{(3-2x)^2}}{3-2x}$;

(7) $\frac{\sqrt[3]{a}(a+b)}{a}$; (8) $\frac{\sqrt[3]{ab^2c}}{bc}$;

(9) $\frac{\sqrt[5]{s+1}}{s+1}$; (10) $\sqrt[5]{(t+3)^3}$.

f(1) 10; (2) $14\sqrt{5}$; (3) $x - \frac{x\sqrt{3}}{2}$; (4) $\frac{3a\sqrt{2}+a}{2}$; (5) $(r+1)\sqrt{rst}$; (6) $\frac{2y\sqrt{x^2-y^2}}{x^2-y^2}$; (7) $\sqrt[3]{5} + 8\sqrt{x}$; (8) $7\sqrt{a} - 6\sqrt{5}$; (9) $3\sqrt{x+y} - 4\sqrt{x-y}$; (10) $7ab\sqrt{5a}$.

g(1) $12\sqrt{10}$; (2) 18; (3) $8ab^2$; (4) $2z\sqrt{3z}$; (5) $2xy^5\sqrt{xy}$; (6) $\frac{24pq}{q^2}\sqrt[3]{q^2}$; (7) $a+b+c+2(\sqrt{ab}+\sqrt{ac}+\sqrt{bc})$; (8) $ax\sqrt{a}(a+x+1)$; (9) 8; (10) $2axy^{\frac{1}{2}}\sqrt[3]{3}\sqrt{a}$.

h(1) 2; (2) 5; (3) $2\sqrt[3]{x}$; (4) $3\sqrt{zy}$; (5) $\sqrt{6}+2$; (6) $12a^{\frac{1}{2}}\sqrt[12]{2^3 \cdot 3^5 \cdot 5^4 \cdot a^7}$; (7) $\frac{c-\sqrt{2c}-4}{c-8}$; (8) $\sqrt{15}$; (9) $\frac{e^2+f^2+2f\sqrt{e^2+f^2}}{e^2}$; (10) $\frac{4b\sqrt{1-4b^2}+1}{8b^2-1}$.

Paragraph 79.

a(1) $j5\sqrt{3}$; (2) $i\sqrt{23}$; (3) $\frac{j}{3}$;

(4) $-j10z^2y^2\sqrt{x}$; (5) $\frac{j^2y}{4}$;

(6) $-4xy\sqrt[3]{2x^2y^2}$.

b(1) $16 + j109$; (2) $41 - j22$; (3) $61 - j251$; (4) $44 + j10$; (5) $6 + j11$; (6) $-2 - j47$.

c(1) $779 - j371$; (2) $59 + j114$; (3) $-22 + j15$; (4) $155 - j61$; (5) $169 + j23$; (6) $9 - j8$.

d(1) $-55 + j46$; (2) $6 - 6\sqrt{6} + j(6\sqrt{2}+6\sqrt{3})$; (3) 13; (4) $-5 - j12$; (5) $-j8$; (6) $46 - j48$; (7) $f^2 + j2fg - g^2$; (8) $I^2 + E^2$; (9) $-68 - j239$; (10) $71 - j17$.

e(1) $\frac{3}{13} - j\frac{2}{13}$; (2) $1 - j6$; (3) $-\frac{6}{25}$

$+j\frac{17}{25}$; (4) $1 + j2$; (5) $\frac{(x^2+j2xy-y^2)}{(x^2+y^2)}$;

(6) $2(1-j2)$; (7) $\frac{3(1+j)}{2}$; (8) $\frac{1+j13}{10}$;

(9) $\frac{38+j34}{65}$; (10) $\frac{I^2+j2IE-E^2}{I^2+E^2}$.

Paragraph 86.

a(1) 3; (2) 2; (3) 85; (4) 3; (5) 1; (6) $x = -5, y = 8$; (7) $a = 3, b = 1$; (8) $x = 3, y = 4$; (9) $m = 3, n = 5$; (10) $r = 8, s = 1$.

b(1) $d = \frac{Wh}{F}$. (2) $g = \frac{v^2-v_o^2}{2h}$.

(3) $a = \frac{Fg}{w}$. (4) $N = \frac{2.534H}{D^2}$. (5) $l = \frac{10^8F}{22.5BI}$.

c(1) 15; (2) 0; (3) $\frac{10}{3}$; (4) 4; (5) $\frac{28}{9}$;

(6) $\frac{12}{119}$; (7) $-\frac{12}{25}$; (8) 8; (9) $\frac{40}{109}$;

(10) $-\frac{1}{19}$.

d(1) $x = 4, y = 5$; (2) $a = 4.95, b = 2.62$; (3) $x = 4, y = 7$; (4) $x = -2, y = -4$; (5) $x = -3, y = 1$; (6) $I = 13, Z = 17$;

(7) $x = 4, y = \frac{1}{2}$; (8) $a = 6, b = -4$;

(9) $x = 5, y = -1$; (10) $r = \frac{(a+b)}{2}$

$s = \frac{(a-b)}{2}$.

e(1) 1 volt; (2) $R - 20$ ohms; (3) 110 volts; (4) 75 ohms; (5) 100 milliamperes, 80 milliamperes, 60 milliamperes; (6) 5.5 amperes.

Paragraph 94.

a(1) $0, -\frac{3}{2}$; (2) $0, 4$; (3) $0, -3$; (4) $0, -2$; (5) ± 8; (6) ± 3; (7) ± 3; (8) ± 4; (9) $7, -6$; (10) $1, 12$.

b(1) $\frac{-3 \pm \sqrt{13}}{2}$; (2) $-3 \pm \frac{\sqrt{22}}{2}$; (5) $\frac{1}{2} \pm$

$\frac{\sqrt{14}}{4}$; (6) $-\frac{5}{3} \pm \frac{2\sqrt{10}}{3}$; (7) $-1, 3$;

(8) $-1 \pm \sqrt{6}$; (9) $1 \pm \sqrt{6}$; (10) $\frac{1}{2} \pm \frac{\sqrt{5}}{2}$

$c(1) -1; (2) -\frac{3}{4}, \frac{2}{3}; (3) \frac{-5 \pm \sqrt{13}}{6};$
$(4) -\frac{3}{2}, \frac{4}{3}; (5) -3, 1; (6) -\frac{1}{5}, \frac{5}{3};$
$(7) \pm \sqrt{2}; (8) \pm \sqrt{19}; (9) -1, 2;$
$(10) \frac{-5 \pm \sqrt{7}}{3}.$

Paragraph 111.

$a(1)$ 1,613 × 10³; (2) 500 × 10³, or 5 × 10⁵; (3) 6,166 × 10⁻⁸.
$b(1)$ 3,109 × 10²; (2) 19 × 10⁻⁶; (3) 4,492 × 10⁻⁹.
$c(1)$ 892 × 10⁴; (2) 2,464 × 10⁻⁸, or 24.64; (3) 3,168 × 10⁻¹¹; (4) 14,640.
$d(1)$ 167; (2) 1,608 × 10⁸ (3) 10⁷; (4) 33 × 10⁻³.
$e(1)$ 4 × 10²; or 400; (2) 13 × 10⁻³; (3) 27 × 10⁻⁷; (4) 9 × 10², or 900.

Paragraph 127.

$a(1)$ 2.8949; (2) 0.5527; (3) 8.5378−10; (4) 6.6776−10; (5) 1.6955; (6) 2.4370; (7) 2.8809; (8) 0.8593; (9) 7.9946−10; (10) 5.7205−10.
$b(1)$ 70,097 (2) 271; (3) .351; (4) .000676; (5) 3.99; (6) 370.67; (7) .00002718; (8) 500,500; (9) 1.5915; (10) .000003445.
$c(1)$ 164.2; (2) 39,990 (3) 1,376; (4) .006764; (5) 5,710.
$d(1)$ .4983; (2) .3874; (3) .3984; (4) .7487; (5) .2437.
$e(1)$ .00000007372; (2) 51.46; (3) 3.47; (4) 19.43; (5) 783; (6) .2367; (7) 5.343; (8) 87.74; (9) 1.55; (10) .09456.
$f(1)$ 2.298; (2) 11.77; (3) 24.43; (4) 33.37 (5) .4509; (6) .4725; (7) .04088; (8) .6153; (9) .0576; (10) .35367.

Paragraph 142.

a 96 square inches. b 36 square inches. c 25 square inches. d 15 square inches. e 14.422 square inches. f 5.657 square inches. $g(1)$ Parallelogram, $A = bh$, 120 square inches; (2) Triangle, $A = \frac{bh}{2}$ 4.025 square inches; (3) Circle, $A = \pi r^2$, 314 square centimeters; $C = \pi D$, 62.8 centimeters; (4) Trapezoid, $A = \frac{B+b}{2} h$, $A = 60$ square inches. $h(1)$ 3 inches; (2) $4\frac{1}{2}$ inches; (3) 8.8 inches; (4) 5 inches. i 78.5 square inches. j 100 feet. k 82.5 square feet. l 48.496 inches.

Paragraph 153.

$a(1)$ $c = 8.603$. (2) $a = 6.08$. (3) $b = 39.5$. (4) $c = b\sqrt{10}$. (5) $b = m^2 - 1$.
$b(1)$ $\sin A = \frac{4}{7}$, $\cos A = \frac{\sqrt{33}}{7}$, $\tan A = \frac{4}{\sqrt{33}}$, $\cot A = \frac{\sqrt{33}}{4}$, $\sec A = \frac{7}{\sqrt{33}}$, $\csc A = \frac{7}{4}$.
(2) $\sin A = \frac{2}{13}\sqrt{13}$, $\cos A = \frac{3}{13}\sqrt{13}$, $\tan A = \frac{2}{3}$, $\cot A = \frac{3}{2}$, $\sec A = \frac{\sqrt{13}}{3}$, $\csc A = \frac{\sqrt{13}}{2}$.
(3) $\sin A = \frac{1}{2}$, $\cos A = \frac{\sqrt{3}}{2}$, $\tan A = \frac{\sqrt{3}}{3}$, $\cot A = \sqrt{3}$, $\sec A = \frac{2}{3}\sqrt{3}$, $\csc A = 2$.
(4) $\sin A = \frac{1}{2.4}$, $\cos A = \frac{1.09}{1.2}$, $\tan A = \frac{1}{2.18}$, $\cot A = 2.18$, $\sec A = \frac{1.2}{1.09}$, $\csc A = 2.4$.
(5) $\sin A = \frac{\sqrt{y^2+1}}{y^2+1}$, $\cos A = \frac{\sqrt{y^2+1}}{y^2+1}$, $\tan A = y$, $\cot A = \frac{1}{y}$, $\sec A = \sqrt{y^2+1}$, $\csc A = \frac{\sqrt{y^2+1}}{y}$.
(6) $\sin A = \frac{\sqrt{55}}{8}$, $\cos A = \frac{3}{8}$, $\tan A = \frac{\sqrt{55}}{3}$, $\cot A = \frac{3\sqrt{55}}{55}$, $\sec A = 2\frac{2}{3}$, $\csc A = \frac{8\sqrt{55}}{55}$.
$c(1)$ $a = 17$, $b = 29.4$, $c = 34$. (2) $a = 9$, $b = 12$, $c = 15$. (3) $a = 12$, $b = 16$, $c = 20$. (4) $a = 17.5$, $b = 10\sqrt{11}$, $c = 37.5$. (5) $a = 10$, $b = 6$, $c = 2\sqrt{34}$. (6) $a = 37.08$, $b = 18.4$, $c = 41.4$.
$d(1)$ $b = 10\sqrt{3}$, $c = 20$. (2) $a = 7$, $c = 7\sqrt{2}$. (3) $a = 4\sqrt{3}$, $b = 4$. (4) $b = 3\sqrt{3}$, $c = 6\sqrt{3}$. (5) $a = 12.5$, $b = 12.5\sqrt{3}$.

Paragraph 164.

$a(1)$ .02618, .99966, .02619, 38.1885. (2) .26584, .96402, .27576, 3.622636. (3) .53238, .84650, .62892, 1.59002. (4) .59693, .80230, .74402, 1.34405. (5) .70690, .70731, .99942, 1.00058. (6) .70706, .70716, .99986, 1.00014. (7) .57649, .81710, .70553, 1.41737. (8) .81370, .58129, 1.39982, .71438. (9) .74811, .66357, 1.12740, .88700. (10) .92429, .38169, 2.42158, .41295.
$b(1)$ 14° 54′ 51″; (2) 66° 35′ 51″; (3) 19° 56′ 54″; (4) 25° 17′ 5″; (5) 40° 23′ 35″; (6) 68° 45′ 2″; (7) 22° 11′ 47″; (8) 34° 5′ 19″; (9) 52° 13′ 2″; (10) 51° 29′ 49″
$c(1)$ 44° 43′ 29″; (2) 10.29; (3) 32.5 (4) 19.76; (5) 12.4; (6) 54° 18′ 52.5″; (7) 33.69; (8) 16.5; (9) 36° 28′ 9″; (10) 128.3; (11) 30.9 (12) 29° 3′ 15″
$d(1)$ 52.28 feet; (2) 80.027 feet; (3) 47.63 feet, 8.69 feet high; (4) 3,149 feet; (5) 11.734 feet; (6) 91.77 feet; (7) 206 feet; (8) 3,578 feet; (9) 16,647 feet (3.153 miles); (10) 82.12 feet; (11) 1.414 inches each; (12) side opposite 60° ∠ 5.196 inches, side opposite 30° ∠ 3 inches.

Paragraph 173.

a $C = 62° 16′ 38″$, $a = 14.59$. b $B = 69° 58′$. c $A = 23° 33′ 22″$, $B = 45° 16′ 31″$, $C = 111° 10′ 7″$. d $A = 81° 31′ 41″$, $B = 41° 7′ 29″$. e 240 square inches. f 97.880 square feet. g 55.424 square inches. h $A = 32° 33′ 45″$, $B = 84° 36′ 15″$, $c = 15.95$ inches.

Paragraph 176.

$a(1)$ .4 radian; (2) 4 radians; (3) 8 radians; (4) 2.78 radians.
$b(1)$ 35 inches; (2) 17.6 feet; (3) 18.9 miles; (4) .00198 inch.
$c(1)$ .52 radian; (2) 4.6 radians; (3) 2.77 radians; (4) 5.89 radians.
$d(1)$ 45° 50′ 11.8″; (2) 1432′ 23′ 40.2″; (3) 197° 40′ 13.44″; (4) 540°.
$e(1)$ $\pi/6$; (2) $\pi/3$; (3) $5\pi/4$; (4) 4π.

GLOSSARY OF MATHEMATICAL TERMS

CONTENTS

	Page
Abacus……….Basic Combinations	1
Cancellation……….Cube Root	2
Decade……….Formula	3
Fraction……….Least Common Denominator	4
Least Common Multiple……….Obtuse Angle	5
Partition vs. Quotition……….Scale Drawing	6
Short Cuts – Shortened Algorism……….Unitary Analysis vs. Ratio Analysis of a Problem	7
Vulgar Fractions	8

GLOSSARY OF MATHEMATICAL TERMS

A

ABACUS: A calculating instrument used in ancient and medieval Europe and still used in various Asian countries for performing calculations by sliding counters on rods or in grooves.

ABSTRACT NUMBERS: Abstract numbers are numbers that are not applied to any particular thing, such as 22, 4, 3½.

ACUTE ANGLE: Less than 90°.

ADDEND: A number or quantity to be added to another.

ADDITIVE SUBTRACTION: According to this method, subtraction can be reduced to addition and, therefore, should be taught not as a new process but as an application of the older one. For example, John has 8¢ and Frank 10¢. How much does John need to have as much as Frank? The answer is obtained by saying: John's money plus how much will equal Frank's? 8 + ? = 10.

ADJACENT ANGLE: Two angles having a common vertex and a common side.

ALGEBRA COMPARED WITH ARITHMETIC: Arithmetic deals with concrete quantities. Algebra deals with symbols whose values may be any out of a given number field.

ALGORISM: A term that refers to the arrangement of an arithmetic solution.

$$\frac{3}{4} \text{ of } \overset{17}{\cancel{68}} = 51 \qquad \begin{array}{r} 68 \\ \times\ 24\tfrac{3}{4} \\ \hline 51 \\ 272 \\ \underline{136\ \ \ } \\ 1683 \end{array}$$

ALIQUANT PART: Designating a part of a number or quantity that does not divide the number or quantity without leaving a remainder. (Example: 5 is an aliquant part of 16.)

ALIQUOT PART: Designating a divisor which divides without a remainder a number greater than the divisor. (Example: 5 is a aliquot part of 15.)

APOTHECARIES' WEIGHT: Used in weighing medicines. Terms include grains, scruples, drams, ounce, pound.

AVERAGE: A useful measure of the central tendency of a group of marks or scores.

AVOIRDUPOIS WEIGHT: The system in common use in English-speaking countries for weighing all commodities except precious stones, precious metals, and drugs.

B

BASIC COMBINATIONS: In addition, the sums, never greater than 18, obtained by adding any two digits. There are 45 basic combinations in addition. There are 81 combinations if we consider 5 + 4 separate from 4 + 5. There are 100 combinations if we include the 19 zero combinations (0 + 1, 0 + 0, 2 + 0, 0 + 2, etc.). There are basic combinations in subtraction, multiplication, and division as well.

C

CANCELLATION: A short-cut method in multiplying fractions with whole numbers, and mixed numbers, enabling us to obtain a product that does not have to be reduced to lower terms because the reduction has already been done, and giving us a smaller dividend and a smaller divisor to work with in changing an improper fraction to a mixed number.

CARDINAL VS. ORDINAL NUMBER: Cardinal numbers ae those used in counting: 1, 2, 100, etc. Ordinal numbers are those indicating order and succession, as first, second, etc.

CASTING OUT NINES: Dividing a number by 9 and finding the remainder, called the *excess*. The excess in 16 is 7, in 27 is 0. It is known that a number is divisible by 9 if the sum of its digits is divisible by 9. To find the excess of a large number, 2,202,443, add the digits and you get 17. Now add 1 and 7, and the answer is 8, the remainder that will be gotten if the number given is divided by 9. The process of casting out nines may be used to check multiplication.

```
    4327      Casting out nines excess = 7   7 × 2 = 14
   ×569       Casting out nines excess = 2   Excess = 5
   38943
   25962
   21635
 2462063      Casting out nines excess = 5
```

CENTIGRADE: Centigrade thermometer, named for Anders Celsius, a Swedish astronomer, who invented it in 1742. On the present scale, zero (0°) is the freezing point; 100° is the boiling point.

COMMON FRACTIONS: Ordinary as distinguished from decimal fractions. Historically, common fractions came before decimal fractions. Common fractions may also denote those of frequent occurrence, as against those that are of infrequent or uncommon occurrence.

COMPLEMENTARY ANGLES: Two adjacent angles the sum of which is 90°, or a right angle.

COMPLEX FRACTIONS: Fractions having a fraction or a mixed number in the numerator or denominator or in each. Examples: $\dfrac{\frac{3}{4}+\frac{5}{6}}{\frac{1}{9}}$, $\dfrac{\frac{6}{7}}{\frac{3}{2}}$

Complex fractions are also called compound fractions.

COMPOSITE NUMBERS: A composite number is a number which is divisible without a remainder by one or more whole numbers in addition to itself and 1, as 4, 6, 8, 10, etc.

COMPOUND FRACTIONS: Compound fractions are complex fractions. Example: 2/3 of 6/7.

COMPOUND NUMBER: Compound number involving different denominations, or more than one unit. Example: 2 yards, 4 feet, 3 inches.

CONCRETE NUMBER: Concrete numbers ae numbers that are attached to specific objects or quantities, as 7 baskets, $32, 10 gallons, 340 pages.

CONCRETE TEACHING: Utilization of objective aids. Not the age of pupils but the newness of experience determines degree of objective teaching.

CONGRUENT FIGURES: Congruent figures are figures that have the same shape and the same size.

CRUTCHES: Crutches are auxiliary figures and markings used in teaching children when new topics or operations are introduced.

CUBE ROOT: A number of quantity whose cube is the given number or quantity. Example: 4 is the cube root of 64.

D

DECADE: A group or division of ten.

DECIMAL: A number expressed in the scale of tens; especially a decimal fraction. A mixed decimal is a number expressed as an integer plus a decimal fraction. Example: 47.74.

DECIMAL FRACTION: A proper fraction in which the denominator is some power of 10, usually not expressed, but signified by a point placed at the left of the numerator, as $.5 = \frac{5}{10}$, $.50 = \frac{50}{100}$.

DENOMINATE NUMBER: Deals with units of measure.

DENOMINATOR: The divisor, the number below the line in a fraction that indicates into how many equal parts the unit is supposed to be divided.

DIGITS: The numbers from 1 to 9 (some include 0) so called because of the use of the fingers in counting and computing—whereby all numbers may be expressed.

DIVIDEND: The number of quantity to be divided.

DIVISOR: The number by which the dividend is divided.

DRY MEASURE: A system of measures of volume for dry commodities, as grains, fruits, etc., pints, quarts, pecks, bushels.

DUO DECIMAL SYSTEM: A system of numbers whose denominations rise in a scale of twelves.

E

EQUATION: An expression of equality between two magnitudes, the sign = being placed between them.

EXAMPLE VS. PROBLEM: An example is an exercises clothed in words so that the task seems more social and becomes, therefore, more interesting. A problem is a challenging situation that calls for a solution.

EXERCISE: An exercise is a direction to perform an operation. *Find 4/5 of 20* is an exercise, an indicated arithmetical procedure. Turned into an example, this becomes: *A store bought 20 picture books, 4/5 to be returned. How many books were returned?*

F

FACTORS: Factors can divide a larger number without a remainder. Factors are any of the numbers which when multiplied together form a product.

FAHRENHEIT VS. CENTIGRADE: Fahrenheit invented the mercury thermometer in 1714. On the Fahrenheit scale, commonly used in England and the United States, under standard atmospheric pressure, the boiling point of water is at 212°, and the freezing point at 32° above the zero scale. Centigrade thermometer, named after Anders Celsius, a Swedish astronomer, who invented it in 1742. On the present scale, zero (0°) is the freezing point; 100° is the boiling point. To change to degrees Fahrenheit, multiply degrees centigrade by nine-fifths and add 32.

FIGURE VS. NUMBER: Figure is the symbol in which number is expressed. According to Pestalozzi, *Number comes before figure*.

FORMULA: Any general fact, rule, or principle expressed in algebraic symbols. Example: The volume of a cylinder is expressed by the formula $V = Bh$. The area of the base of a cylinder is expressed by the formula $B = \pi r^2$.

FRACTION: One or more aliquot (equal) parts of a unit or integer. A fraction is one of the equal parts of a number of units. ¾ may mean ¼ of 3 as well as ¾ of 1.

FRACTIONS AS DIVISION: A fraction is an indicated division. To obtain ¼ of 3, we divide 3 into 4 equal parts. ¾ = ¼ of 3; that is, 3 is divided into 4 equal parts = 3 ÷ 4.

FRACTION AS RATIO: Each part is a fraction of the whole. Example: *A boy has 2 marbles. If he loses 1 marble, he has ½ of the marbles left.*

FRUSTRUM: The part or segment of a solid formed by two planes.

FORMAL VS. FUNCTIONAL DRILL: Formal drill is to drill on arithmetic facts in isolation. Example: 8 + 4 = ? 4 + ? = 12. Functional drill involves practice in solving a large number of problems.

FUNDAMENTAL OPERATIONS: Addition, subtraction, multiplication, and division.

G

GEOMETRY: The branch of mathematics which investigates the relations, properties, and measurement of solids, surfaces, lines, and angles.

GRADATION: In all situations concerned primarily with the development of skill, proper gradation is of great importance in facilitating the learning process.

GRAPHS: Present in graphic form quantitative relationships. Circle graphs, pictographs, bar graphs, map graphs, line graphs, rectangle graphs, histograms, or column diagrams.

GREATEST COMMON DIVISOR: In arithmetic, the greatest common divisor corresponds to the highest common factor in algebra, the factor of highest degree common to two or more numbers. Example: $\frac{14}{42} = \frac{2 \times 7}{2 \times 7 \times 3}$. The greatest common divisor or highest common factor is 2×7 or 14.

H

HINDU-ARABIC NUMERALS: Hindu-arabic numerals are the numerals now in common use.

HYPOTENUSE LAW: In a right angle triangle, the square of the hypotenuse is equal to the sum of the squares of the other two sides. (The Theorem of Pythagoras)

I

INCOMPLETE PROBLEMS: In incomplete problems and problems without numbers, the concern is with the comprehension of the conditions of the problem and with the development of sequential thinking, not the fundamental operations. Example: If a room is twice as long as it is wide and you knew its length, how would you find the area of the floor?

INTEGER: A whole number.

INTEREST: Simple interest is that paid only on capital lent. Compound interest is that paid on capital plus interest paid or unpaid added to the amount.

L

LEAST COMMON DENOMINATOR: The lowest common multiple of the various denominators of several fractions.

LEAST COMMON MULTIPLE: The multiple that is exactly divisible by each of several integers. It is the product obtained by multiplying all of the prime factors of two or more numbers.
LIKE VS. UNLIKE FRACTIONS: Like fractions: $3^1/_8$, $2^7/_8$. Unlike fractions: $4¼$, $5½$.
LINEAR MEASURE: Linear measure is a measurement of length.
LIQUID MEASURE: Liquid measure is a unit or system for the measurement of liquids.
LITERAL NUMBERS: Literal numbers refer to letters which are sometimes used to represent numbers. Examples: $(a+b)^2$; $a^2 + 2ab + b^2$; $V = Bh$

M

MEASURES: Measures deal with units of measure. Examples: pints, bushels, pecks.
MENSURATION MEASUREMENTS: Mensuration is the branch of applied geometry concerned with finding the length of lines, areas of surfaces, and volumes of solids from certain simple data of lines and angles.
METRIC SYSTEM: A decimal system of measures and weights with meter and gram as base.
MINUEND: Minuend is the number from which another number is to be subtracted.
MIXED NUMBERS: Mixed numbers is the sum of an integer and a fraction.
MULTIPLE: Multiple is the product of a quantity by an integer. It is a number that can contain or can be divided by smaller numbers (factors) without a remainder.
MULTIPLICAND MULTIPLIER: Multiplicand multiplier is the number to be multiplied by a multiplier.

N

NORM VS. STANDARD IN ACHIEVEMENT: A norm represents the achievement of the average pupil or the average performance of a group of pupils. A standard is higher than a norm and refers to a level of achievement beyond which it is usually uneconomical to continue to practice.
NUMERATOR: The term in a fraction which indicates the number of fractional units taken. In a common fraction, the numerator is written above a line. In a decimal fraction, it is the number that follows the decimal point.

O

OBJECTIVE TEACHING: This does not refer merely to the things that can be sensed. It refers to things that are familiar. With the aid of four toothpicks, a child can learn all the ratios of 4. He can arrange them to make a box.

	4 × 1
2 Indian tents	2 × 2
4 Indians	1 + 1 + 1 + 1
A weather flag	3 + 1
A chair	1 + 3

But diagrammatic representations like dots, rectangles, and circles are not what is altogether comprehended by the term. For illustrative material, we may draw on familiar occupations, games, measurement of material in manual work, and on record keeping in home, classroom, and recreational experiences.
OBTUSE ANGLE: An obtuse angle is an angle greater than 990°, and less than 180°.

P

PARTITION VS. QUOTITION: Partition takes place in the process of division when the dividend and quotient refer to the same things. Example: If 48 pencils are to be divided among 12 pupils, how many pencils will there be for each pupil? Answer: 4 pencils. Quotition takes place in the process of division when the divisor and the dividend refer to the same thing. Example: If we have 48 pencils and 4 pencils are given to a pupil, among how many pupils may the pencils be distributed? Answer: 12 pupils.

PLURALITY VS. MAJORITY: Plurality is the difference between the highest number of votes and the next highest number. Majority is more than one-half of the votes cast.

PRIME NUMBER: A number divisible by no number except itself and unity. Example: 1, 2, 3,, 5, 7, 11, 13, etc.

PRODUCT: Product is the result of any kind of multiplication.

PROPER FRACTION: Proper fraction is the one in which the numerator is less than the denominator.

Q

QUOTIENT: Quotient is the number resulting from the division of one number by another.

R

RATIONALIZATION: Rationalization bases the learning of number facts and processes in reason. Rationalization leads to an understanding of the reasons for the steps taken in solving a problem or in performing a process.

REDUCTION OF FRACTIONS: Reduction of fractions refers to changing the form without altering the value of a fraction.
   (1)   Reduction may be to lower terms: $2/4 = 1/2$;
   (2)   or to higher denominators: $1/2 = 4/8$;
   (3)   to common denominators: $2/3$ and $5/6 = 4/6$ and $5/6$;
   (4)   to improper fractions: $1\frac{1}{4} = 5/4$;
   (5)   to mixed numbers: $21/8 = 2\frac{5}{8}$;
   (6)   to decimal fractions: $1/4 = .25$.

RIGHT ANGLE: A right angle is equal to 90°.

ROMAN NUMERALS: Of the Roman system of notation using the following symbols, chiefly: I = 1, V = 5, X = 10, L = 50, C = 100, D = 500, M = 1000

S

SCALE DRAWING: Scale drawing is a representation of large units or objects on a reduced proportion or fixed scale.

SHORT CUTS – SHORTENED ALGORISM: 254 1¼

Do This	Rather Than
256	254
63½	1¼
317½	254
	63½
	317½

SOLUTION OF PROBLEMS BY FORMULA OR RULE:
    $d = rt$ for finding the distance traveled in t hours at r miles per hour.
    $I = prt$, to find the interest on a sum of money
    $C = \frac{5}{9}(f-32)$ for changing degrees Fahrenheit to degrees Centigrade
    Circumference of a circle = $2\pi r$
    Area of a circle = πr^2

SPIRAL COURSE OF STUDY IN ARITHMETIC: Under the more modern plan of organization, the various branches of arithmetic are taught simultaneously, and spiral fashion are repeated in successive grades, but in ever-winding circles.

SQUARE ROOT: A number which multiplied by itself gives another number.

SUBMULTIPLE: (Aliquot part) is a number that divides another number exactly.

SUBTRAHEND: The quantity to be subtracted.

T

TRAPEZIUM: A plane figure formed by four right lines, of which no two are parallel.

TRAPEZOID: A plane four-sided figure with two parallel sides.

TRAVEL ARITHMETIC: Travel arithmetic deals with timetables, cost of travel and distances, use of road maps, estimating distance according to scale, etc.

TRIAL QUOTIENTS: Graded practice is needed in finding trial quotients digits.

TRIGONOMETRY: Trigonometry is the branch of mathematics that deals with the relations holding among the sides and angles of triangles and among closely related magnitudes such as exist between arcs and angles.

TROY WEIGHTS: A system used in England and the United States for gold, silver, etc.

U

UNIT FRACTION: Unit fraction is a fraction whose numerator is 1.

UNITARY ANALYSIS VS. RATIO ANALYSIS OF A PROBLEM:
    Problem: A druggist paid $2.31 for $\frac{7}{8}$ of a pound of a drug. What will $6\frac{1}{8}$ pounds of this drug cost him?

Unitary Analysis
$\frac{7}{8}$ lb. cost $2.31
$\frac{1}{8}$ lb. cost $\frac{1}{7}$ of $2.31 or $.33
$\frac{8}{8}$ lb. cost 8 × $.33 = $2.64
6½ lb. or $\frac{49}{8}$ cost $2.64 × $\frac{48}{8}$ = $16.17

Ratio Analysis
$6\frac{1}{8}$ lbs. = $\frac{49}{8}$ lb.
$\frac{49}{8}$ lb. = 7 × $\frac{7}{8}$ lb.
$6\frac{1}{8}$ lb. cost 7 × $2.31 or $16.17

V

VULGAR FRACTIONS: Ordinary as distinguished from decimal fractions. Historically, common fractions came before decimal fractions. Common fractions may also denote those of frequent occurrence as against those that are of infrequent or uncommon occurrence.